HIDDEN®

Los Angeles

HIDDEN®

Los Angeles

Including Hollywood, Beverly Hills,
Pasadena, Venice, Santa Monica, Malibu,
and Santa Catalina Island

Ellen Clark & Ray Riegert

Ulysses Press®
BERKELEY, CALIFORNIA

Published by:
ULYSSES PRESS
P.O. Box 3440
Berkeley, CA 94703
www.ulyssespress.com

ISSN 1545-5610
ISBN 1-56975-396-2

Printed in Canada by Transcontinental Printing

10 9 8 7 6 5 4 3 2 1

EDITORIAL DIRECTOR: Leslie Henriques
MANAGING EDITOR: Claire Chun
EDITOR: Lynette Ubois
COPY EDITOR: Lily Chou
EDITORIAL ASSOCIATES: Kate Allen, Laura Brancella
TYPESETTING: Steven Schwartz, Lisa Kester, James Meetze
CARTOGRAPHY: Pease Press
COVER DESIGN: Sarah Levin, Leslie Henriques
INDEXER: Sayre Van Young
COVER PHOTOGRAPHY: Mike Perry (Venice mural)

Distributed in the United States by Publishers Group West and in Canada by Raincoast Books

Write to us!

If in your travels you discover a spot that captures the spirit of the Los Angeles area, or if you live in the region and have a favorite place to share, or if you just feel like expressing your views, write to us and we'll pass your note along to the author.

We can't guarantee that the author will add your personal find to the next edition, but if the writer does use the suggestion, we'll acknowledge you in the credits and send you a free copy of the new edition.

Ulysses Press
P.O. Box 3440
Berkeley, CA 94703
E-mail: readermail@ulyssespress.com

What's Hidden?

At different points throughout this book, you'll find special listings marked with a hidden symbol:

◄ HIDDEN

This means that you have come upon a place off the beaten tourist track, a spot that will carry you a step closer to the local people and natural environment of the Los Angeles area.

The goal of this guide is to lead you beyond the realm of everyday tourist facilities. While we include traditional sightseeing listings and popular attractions, we also offer alternative sights and adventure activities. Instead of filling this guide with reviews of standard hotels and chain restaurants, we concentrate on one-of-a-kind places and locally owned establishments.

Our authors seek out locales that are popular with residents but usually overlooked by visitors. Some are more hidden than others (and are marked accordingly), but all the listings in this book are intended to help you discover the true nature of the Los Angeles area and put you on the path of adventure.

Contents

Maps

OUTDOOR ADVENTURE SYMBOLS

The following symbols accompany national, state and regional park listings, as well as beach descriptions throughout the text.

Camping

Hiking

Biking

Swimming

Snorkeling or Scuba Diving

Surfing

Horseback Riding

Waterskiing

Windsurfing

Kayaking/Canoeing

Boating

Boat ramps

Fishing

Downhill Skiing

Cross-Country Skiing

ONE

Los Angeles

Land of dreams, fulfiller of promises—from its conception, Los Angeles, with its rich soil and mild temperatures, called to immigrants looking for the good life. Since its founding as a pueblo in 1781, the city has recast itself as a promised land, health haven, agricultural paradise, movie capital, and international trade center.

The second-largest city and largest county in the country, Los Angeles rests in a bowl surrounded by five mountain ranges and an ocean, holding within its ambit sandy beaches, tawny hills, and wind-ruffled deserts. At night from the air, Los Angeles is a massive gridwork, an illuminated checkerboard extending from the ink-colored Pacific to the dark fringe of the mountains.

Greater metropolitan L.A. leads the nation in tourism, boasts one of the country's largest concentrations of high-tech industries, and possesses the fastest growing major port in the country. Disparagingly referred to as the "cow counties" by Northern Californians in the 19th century, today the formerly rough-and-tumble town is a megalopolis unified by a convoluted freeway system—a congeries of cloverleafs, overpasses, and eight-lane speedways that lies snarled with traffic much of the day. A distinctly Western city, L.A. has grown out toward the open range, not up within tightly defined perimeters. In fact, there are 88 incorporated cities in Los Angeles County, as well as 1500 miles of freeways and 19,000 miles of surface streets.

While the statistics are impressive, if not overwhelming, what really defines Los Angeles is its residents. This is a town where a far from young, though still voluptuous, screen star wannabe can finally become a celebrity just by buying billboard space. Banners on Sunset Boulevard lampposts urge gay men to inform their partners of their sexual history. And weightlifters of all ages pump iron at a full-scale, open-air weight-training center on a public beach. No, Dorothy, this is definitely not Kansas—this is a larger-than-life slice of the country that breaks the rules and sets the trends.

Life along coastal L.A. reflects the culture of the beach, a freewheeling, hedonist philosophy that combines pleasure-seeking with healthfulness. Perfectly fitted to this philosophy is the weather. The coastal climatic zone, called a maritime fringe, is characterized by cooler summers, warmer winters, and higher humidity than elsewhere is California. Sea breezes and salt air keep the beaches relatively free from smog. During summer months the thermometer hovers around 75 or 80 degrees and water temperatures average 67 degrees. Winter carries intermittent rain and brings the ocean temperature down to a chilly 55.

Add a broadly ranging coastal topography and Los Angeles has an urban escape valve less than an hour from downtown. The shoreline lies along the lip of the Los Angeles basin, a flat expanse interrupted by the sharp cliffs of the Palos Verdes Peninsula and the rocky heights of the Santa Monica Mountains. There are broad strands lapped by gentle waves and pocket beaches exploding with surf. Though most of the coast is built up, some sections remain raw and undeveloped.

The earthquakes responsible for creating the coastline still rattle the region with disturbing frequency. The last colossal quake was back in the 1850s when almost every building in Los Angeles collapsed. More recently, major earthquakes rocked the San Fernando Valley in 1971 and 1994. Though property damage was high, the loss of life—fortunately—was not.

Perhaps with an eye to earthquakes, not to mention Southern California's flaky reputation, architect Frank Lloyd Wright developed a theory of "continental tilt" by which all the loose nuts slid into Hollywood. Its penchant for health, fitness, and glamour has always rendered L.A.'s hold on reality a bit shaky, but it is the city's appeal to religious sects that has particularly added to its aura of unreality. Televangelism is big business throughout the area, and Hollywood serves as headquarters for Scientology.

Los Angeles, with its casual lifestyle and sun-baked climate, is the perfect target for snipes and sarcasm from the rest of the country. Such derogatory monikers as La-La-Land, Hollyweird, and Land of Fruits and Nuts are followed by snickers and disparaging remarks. Angelinos are constantly accused of being shallow and self-absorbed, with brains turned to mush by continual sunshine and warm temperatures. Detractors herald L.A. as just one big movie set, a fake and hedonistic place where everything comes too easily and the residents lack depth and substance. Truth or jealousy? It's probably a little of both, but Los Angeles, regardless of its bad press, remains a presence.

Love it or loath it, Los Angeles is never boring. It's a city that grabs you and demands attention. A hotbed of creativity, L.A. exudes a free and easy, live-and-let-live attitude that encourages acceptance of even the most outrageous and bizarre. The radical, the conservative, the aristocratic, and the blue collar manage to co-exist in this sun-drenched land full of promise and dreams. And every

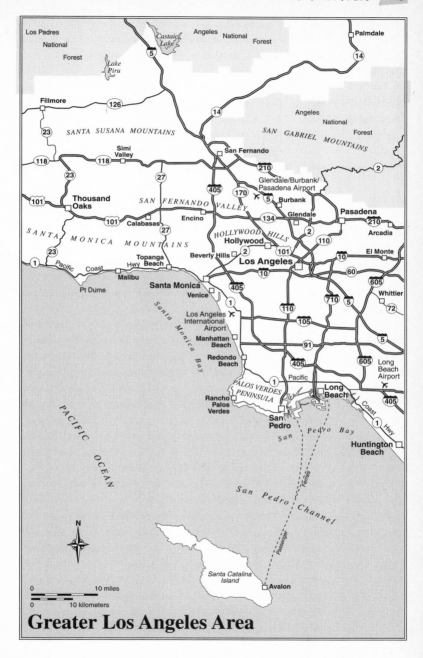

Greater Los Angeles Area

News Year's Day, millions of Americans buried knee deep in snow watch as elaborate flower-festooned floats sail down Pasadena's Colorado Boulevard under sunny skies and more about-to-be-Angelinos vow to move west.

The Story of Los Angeles

The first "foreigners" to see Los Angeles' potential were Padre Junípero Serra, Gaspar de Portolá, and Father Juan Crespi; they spent the night in what is now downtown Los Angeles on August 2, 1769, on their way to establish California's missions. Before leaving the area, Portolá named the river *El Río de Nuestra Señora la Reina de los Angeles de Porciuncula* (The River of Our Lady the Queen of the Angels of Porciuncula). Despite being jolted by three earthquakes during his brief stay, Father Crespi wrote in his journal of the possibilities for a mission and settlement in this "delightful place among the trees on the river."

On September 4, 1781, the first settlers, a mixed bag of Spaniards, Indians, mestizos, mulattos, and blacks, arrived at this riverside site. Felip de Neve, the new governor of California, gave a speech, the mission fathers provided prayers and a blessing, and *El Pueblo de Nuestra Señora la Reina del los Angeles de Porciuncula* (The Town of Our Lady the Queen of the Angels of Porciuncula) came into existence. Over the next 50 years the settlers planted vines, olives, and grains, and their population expanded to 700. As the town continued to grow, Spain doled out land grants to retired soldiers who used large plots for grazing their cattle. After Mexico declared independence from Spain, Mexican governors continued to give additional grants to other settlers, including those from Europe and America's East Coast, who became ranchers, merchants, and winemakers.

One group that never became part of this sun-baked melting pot were the Indians. For American Indians, Padre Serra's dream of a New World was a nightmare. Before the advent of Westerners, the Tongva, or, as the Spanish called them, the Gabrieleños, held sway around Los Angeles. Like other groups west of the Sierra Nevada they were hunter-gatherers, exploiting the boundless resources of the ocean, picking wild plants, and stalking local prey. Less materially developed than the agricultural tribes of the American Southwest, the Tongva fashioned dome-shaped dwellings from wooden poles and woven grasses.

The conquistadors eventually overcame American Indian resistance, forcibly converting these native spiritualists to Catholicism and pressing them into slavery. Eventually American Indians built a chain of missions that formed the backbone of the Spanish empire, which broke the back of the tribal nations. While their slaves were dying in terrible numbers, the Spanish, dangerously overextended, fell plague to problems throughout their empire. Finally, in 1821 Mexico declared its independence and seized California from Spain.

Then in 1846, American settlers, with assistance from the United States government, fomented the Bear Flag Revolt. That summer Captain John C. Fremont pursued Governor Pío Pico from Los Angeles south to San Juan Capistrano, forcing the Mexican official to flee across the border. In February 1848, at a home in the San Fernando Valley, a treaty was signed and the Stars and Stripes flew over California.

As the 19th century progressed, Los Angeles developed into a tough Western town. The population totaled less than 3000 but L.A. still managed to average a murder a day. By the time the transcontinental railroad connected California with the rest of the country in 1869, Southern California's economy trailed far behind its northern counterpart.

During the 1870s things began to improve. The Southern Pacific railroad linked San Pedro and Santa Monica with interior valleys where citrus cultivation was flourishing. Southern California's rich agriculture and salubrious climate led to a "health rush." Magazines and newspapers romanticized the region's history and beauty; one writer proclaimed that "if the Pilgrim fathers had landed on the Pacific Coast instead of the Atlantic, little old New York wouldn't be on the map."

WATERWORKS

Los Angeles, with its back to the desert, solved its water problem back in 1913 when the Los Angeles Aqueduct was completed. This engineering marvel stretched almost 250 miles from the Sierra Nevada. By bleeding water from the distant Owens Valley, the controversial pipeline supplied enough water to enable Los Angeles to annex the entire San Fernando Valley.

In the latter part of the 19th century, Santa Monica became a fashionable resort town and the port of San Pedro expanded exponentially, making Los Angeles a major shipping point. As the century drew to a close, Henry Huntington, nephew of railroad baron Collis P. Huntington, established the Pacific Electric Railway Company and created a series of land booms by extending his red trolley lines in all directions.

When oil was discovered early in the 20th century, Southern California also became a prime drilling region. Oil wells sprang up along Huntington Beach, Long Beach, and San Pedro, adding to coastal coffers while destroying the aesthetics of the shore. The Signal Hill field in Long Beach, tapped by Shell Oil in the 1920s, turned out to be the richest oil deposit in the world and Los Angeles became the largest oil pot.

Little wonder that by 1925, flush with petroleum just as the age of the automobile was shifting into high gear, Los Angeles became the most motor-conscious city in the world. The Pacific Coast Highway was completed during the 1930s, and "auto camps" and "tourist cabins" mushroomed. The first piece of the Arroyo Seco Parkway (Pasadena Freeway) opened in 1940, becoming the first freeway in the western United States, and cars began filling Los Angeles' streets, lanes, and highways.

The rise in automobile traffic wasn't the only thing that was important to the history of L.A. during the 1920s and '30s. The Jazz Age saw the population hit the 1 million mark, the first Mickey Mouse cartoon made, and the first Academy Awards presented. Los Angeles City Hall, Central Library, and the UCLA campus opened. And yet L.A., city of broken dreams, was found to have the highest suicide rate in the nation. The 1930s brought the Tenth Olympic Games, the opening of Santa Anita Racetrack, the first drive-in movie theater, and the Long Beach Earthquake.

CITY OF GODS

The first book printed in Los Angeles was a religious tract by a heretical Scotsman. Aimee Semple McPherson preached her Four Square Gospel here in the 1920s and other groups have included everything from the Theosophists and Krishnamurtis to the Mankind United and Mighty I Am movements.

The 1940s was a bleak decade for a city that seemed to have all the makings of paradise. The Los Angeles River overflowed and caused floods three years in a row, President Roosevelt decreed that 10,000 Los Angeles–based Japanese Americans be banished to interment camps, Latino neighborhoods suffered riots as police and Mexican-American youths tangled, and Los Angeles experienced its first smog attack. Smog became one of the city's biggest issues in the 1950s as the air became increasingly polluted. It was also the decade for sports, with Brooklyn losing its beloved Dodgers to L.A., the Lakers moving west from Minneapolis, and the Los Angeles Memorial Sports Arena opening. In the ensuing decades, despite earthquakes, floods, riots, crime, and smog, people of all ethnic backgrounds would continue to pour into Los Angeles, looking for the good life in this temperate and pleasant place.

Today, with a census numbering almost four million urban dwellers and nearly ten million throughout Los Angeles County, L.A. is a multicultural city. Here, minorities have become the majority. Latinos, who were once driven from Los Angeles, now make up more than 40 percent of the population and represent the largest concentration of Mexicans outside Mexico. Over 80 different languages are spoken in the schools and on the streets. Neighborhoods are given over to Latinos, blacks, Chinese, Japanese, Koreans, Jews, Laotians, Filipinos, Vietnamese, Russians, and Armenians. There are gay communities and nouveau riche neighborhoods, not to mention subcultures such as low riders, Valley girls, beach bums and bunnies, punks, and aging hippies.

This fantastic mix of ethnic cultures and varying lifestyles has produced an immigrant-built metropolis that cannot be categorized nor contained. Never static, thanks to those that came before and those that arrive daily, Los Angeles continues to develop its unique character.

When to Go

SEASONS

In Los Angeles the average temperature is 75° during the warm period and about 50° in mid-winter. Along the Pacific, the weather corresponds to a Mediterranean climate with mild temperatures year-round. Because the coastal fog creates a natural form of air conditioning and insulation, the mercury rarely drops below 40° or rises above 80°. Both in the

Text continued on page 10.

One-week Getaway

Discovering the Many Faces of L.A.

The greater Los Angeles area has such an abundance of attractions that not even most locals have seen them all. You can find virtually anything you want here, and we urge you to browse thoroughly through Chapters Two, Three, and Four of *Hidden Los Angeles* to customize a tour that will fit your interests. For an introductory look at some classic highlights of L.A., try the following.

DAY 1
- Start your visit with a look at old-time Hollywood. Check out the hand-, foot-, and nose-prints in the sidewalk in front of **Mann's Chinese Theatre** (page 98) and stargaze your way along at least a part of the **Walk of Fame** (page 96). Then head for the **Hollywood Entertainment Museum** (page 99) for an interactive look at filmmaking's first century.

- Visit the **Hollywood Wax Museum** (page 97) and check out your favorite stars in the flesh—wax flesh that is. Next, drive down Santa Monica Boulevard to **Beverly Hills** to see old-time movie stars' mansions (see the Scenic Drive on pages 148–49) and window-shop on Rodeo Drive. In the evening, attend a film screening at the **Egyptian Theatre** (page 97).

DAY 2
- Sample the Los Angeles art scene. While there are several outstanding art museums, none can really rival the exquisite collections at the hilltop **Getty Center** (page 158) or the **Norton Simon Museum** (page 254) in Pasadena. If you prefer your art a little folksier, drive to Watts to see the **Watts Towers** (page 76), the neighboring arts center, and **Farmer John's Pig Mural** (page 76).

DAY 3
- Search out L.A.'s ethnic diversity, starting as the city did—at **Olvera Street** (pages 42–47) and the nearby **Grand Central Public Market** (page 61).

- Head over to **Chinatown** (pages 47–49), stroll along North Spring Street, and visit the **Kong Chow Temple**.

- Drive to **Exposition Park** (pages 72–75) to visit the **California African American Museum**.

- Dine on Japanese delights in **Little Tokyo** (pages 65–69), then consider seeing a show at the **Japan America Theatre** (page 66).

DAY 4 • Take advantage of the legendary Los Angeles weather in the city's largest urban park. After hobnobbing with the animals at the **Los Angeles Zoo** (page 88), walk across the street to the **Autry Museum of Western Heritage** (page 88) for a dose of the Old West. Drink in the spectacular city views from the **Griffith Observatory and Planetarium** (page 87). During the summer months, stop by **Louise's Trattoria** (page 89) in nearby Los Feliz for dinner to go and enjoy a picnic before watching a live concert under the stars at the **Greek Theater** (page 90).

DAY 5 • A day at the beach starts by watching early morning surfers silhouetted against a rosy sunrise at the **Malibu Pier** (page 174). Stop for breakfast at **Coogie's Beach Cafe** (page 175) and then head for Santa Monica's **Third Street Promenade** (page 189). Rent skates or a bike or just hoof it along the sand to Venice. Pick up a hot dog and a cold drink and watch the action at the paddle tennis courts, then return to Santa Monica for a ride on the vintage carousel at **Santa Monica Pier** (page 184).

DAY 6 • Take a drive down to Long Beach to get up close and personal with Pacific marine life. After a hearty breakfast at Long Beach's **Porch Cafe** (page 246), stop at the **Aquarium of the Pacific**, where sea creatures that inhabit the Pacific Ocean from Baja to Micronesia are on display. In the afternoon, hit the **Redondo Beach Pier** (page 230) seafood markets for a freshly cooked crab outdoor picnic, followed by a visit to Manhattan Beach's **Roundhouse Marine Studies Lab and Aquarium** (page 224) to check out local marine life.

DAY 7 • For an island getaway, take the early morning ferry from San Pedro to Santa Catalina Island. Rent a golf cart and drive around the winding streets of Avalon past the **Wrigley Mansion** (page 216), **Wrigley Memorial and Botanical Garden** (page 208), and **Avalon Casino** (page 208). After an oceanside lunch at **The Beachcomber Café** (page 212), check out the island marine life from **Santa Catalina Island Company**'s (page 208) semi-submersible vessel. Enjoy a frosty margarita on the waterside patio at **Armstrong's Seafood Restaurant and Fish Market** (page 212) before heading back to L.A.

city and along the coast, September and October are the hottest months, and December and January the coolest.

Spring and particularly autumn are ideal times to visit. Winter is the rainy season, which extends from November to March, with the heaviest showers from December to February. During the rest of the year there is almost no rain. Summer is the peak tourist season, when large crowds can present problems. Like spring, it's also a period of frequent fog; during the morning and evening, fog banks from offshore blanket the coast, burning off around midday.

Most winter storms sweep in from the north, and Los Angeles averages about 15 inches of rain a year. The ocean air also creates significant moisture, keeping the average humidity around 65 percent and making some areas seem colder than the thermometer would indicate.

Smog is heaviest during August and September. Then in the autumn, the Santa Ana winds kick up out of the desert. Hot, dry winds from the northeast, they sometimes reach velocities of 35 to 50 miles per hour, blowing sand, fanning forest fires, and making people edgy.

CALENDAR OF EVENTS

JANUARY   **Los Angeles**   The **Tournament of Roses Parade** kicks off the **Rose Bowl** game in Pasadena on New Year's Day. The **Greater Los Angeles Auto Show** at the Convention Center boasts more than 1000 new and concept cars.

FEBRUARY   **Los Angeles**   **Chinese New Year** celebrations snake through L.A.'s Chinatown. The **Firecracker 5K/10 Run** also takes place in Chinatown.

MARCH   **Los Angeles**   Herald in the arrival of spring with Japanese and Polynesian dancers, food, and fun at the **Cherry Blossom Festival** in West L.A. Thousands of runners and bicyclists compete for a chance to win the **City of Los Angeles Marathon**.
Los Angeles Coast   Join thousands of revelers at Hermosa Beach's **Saint Patrick's Day Parade and Festival**, where there's food, crafts, and family entertainment.

APRIL   **Los Angeles**   **Easter Sunrise Services** are marked at the famed Hollywood Bowl. In Little Tokyo **Buddha's Birthday** is celebrated; along nearby Olvera Street the **Blessing of the Animals**, a Mexican tradition, is re-enacted. In Palmdale the **Lilac Festival** signals the advent of spring. The **City of Lights, City of Angels** film festival screens the latest French movies at the Directors Guild of America Theatre on Sunset Boulevard.

Los Angeles Coast   Race car buffs train their binoculars on the **Toyota Grand Prix** in Long Beach.

Los Angeles   Dancers, revelers, and mariachi bands around   **MAY**
Olvera Street and East Los Angeles mark **Cinco de Mayo**, the festival celebrating the Battle of Puebla in the French-Mexican War. The UCLA **Mardi Gras** offers games, entertainment, and food. In the San Fernando Valley, the **Memorial Day Parade** honors the armed forces with a parade of exotic cars, floats, circus performers, and stars.

Los Angeles Coast   Long Beach hosts an AIDS **Walk** and a **Lesbian and Gay Pride Parade and Festival**, complete with decorated floats, pop and country music, dancing, food, and international booths.

Los Angeles   Gay Pride Week is celebrated by a parade through   **JUNE**
West Hollywood. The **Playboy Jazz Festival** hosts both famous and up-and-coming musicians at the Hollywood Bowl.

Los Angeles Coast   Ocean breezes complement the Bard's immortal words during free outdoor performances of **Shakespeare by the Sea** at Point Fermin Park in San Pedro. The **Long Beach Chili Cook-Off** features unusual races and contests.

Los Angeles   The **Hollywood Bowl Summer Festival** explodes   **JULY**
with a Fourth of July concert.

Los Angeles Coast   Every Thursday evening from July through August the **Santa Monica Pier Twilight Dance Series** features a variety of live music from reggae to Western swing. Surfers hang ten at the **International Surf and Health Festival** on Hermosa, Manhattan, Torrance, and Redondo beaches.

Los Angeles   The **Nisei Week Japanese Festival** in Little Tokyo   **AUGUST**
is L.A.'s oldest ethnic festival, celebrating Japanese American cultural heritage with folk dancing, bands, exhibits, carnivals, and parades. The **Watts Summer Festival** features concerts, film, sports and children's villages, a carnival, and a parade.

Los Angeles Coast The three-day **Long Beach Jazz Festival** brings together some of the world's best jazz performers.

SEPTEMBER **Los Angeles** **Los Angeles County Fair**, the nation's largest county fair, offers music, food, carnival rides, livestock competitions, and just about everything else you can imagine. The **City of Los Angeles Birthday Celebration** takes place at Olvera Street, where you'll find historic re-enactments, artisan demonstrations, and a variety of entertainment and food.

Los Angeles Coast The **Manhattan Beach Arts Festival** promotes local artists with music, dancing, workshops, and all forms of art. At the **Festival of Philippine Arts & Culture** in San Pedro, Philippine independence is heralded with music, dance, Filipino films, food, arts, crafts, and children's games.

OCTOBER **Los Angeles** More than 150 free events are featured in the **Los Angeles County–Wide Arts Open House**, including jazz, classical, and rock concerts. The Pasadena area remembers the Wild West with the **San Dimas Western Days Rodeo**, a community event with a parade, a carnival, a pageant contest, a car show, arts and crafts, food, and, of course, a rodeo. Hollywood hosts its own **Day of the Dead** with music, performance art, artisans, and decorated altars at the Hollywood Forever Cemetery.

Los Angeles Coast The **Catalina Island Jazz Trax Festival**, held in the historic Avalon Casino ballroom, features great contemporary jazz music. In Long Beach, the *Queen Mary* oceanliner is transformed into a most gruesome collection of terrifying mazes for the annual **Queen Mary Halloween Terrorfest**.

NOVEMBER **Los Angeles** Shake your maracas at the **Los Angeles Mariachi Festival**, a celebration of Mexico's contribution to California's cultural and musical heritage with mariachi music, ballet folklorico, and authentic Mexican food. From mid-November through Christmas, Crystal Springs Road in Griffith Park sparkles at night during the **Griffith Park Light Festival**, which features spectacularly lighted re-creations of L.A. landmarks. Santa arrives early at the **Hollywood Christmas Parade** and is joined by television and movie stars. In Pasadena, the rollicking **Doo Dah Parade** parodies the city's staid Rose Parade.

Los Angeles Coast The **Catalina Island Triathalon** sends athletes scurrying over the island's outback, running on unpaved roads, biking over hills, and swimming in the bay. **Long Beach Veteran's Day Parade** salutes U.S. military veterans of all ages.

Los Angeles **Las Posadas**, a traditional Mexican festival and procession down Olvera Street, re-enacts the nine day journey of Mary and Joseph's journey to Bethlehem, with singing and a candlelight procession. In the Pasadena area, **Christmas Tree Lane** in Altadena dresses up Main Street with majestic cedars decorated with thousands of lights.

DECEMBER

Los Angeles Coast During the **Naples Island Christmas Parade** a spectacular display of decorated boats sails through the charming canals of Naples Island in Long Beach. The **Marina Del Rey Boat Parade** is another seaside holiday processional.

Several agencies provide free information to travelers. The **California Office of Tourism** will help guide you to areas throughout the state. ~ 801 K Street, Suite 1600, Sacramento, CA 95814; 800-862-2543; www.visitcalifornia.com. You'll find information at the **Los Angeles Visitors and Convention Bureau**. ~ 333 South Hope Street, 18th Floor, Los Angeles, CA 90071; 213-624-7300; www.visitlanow.com.

▼▼▼▼▼▼▼▼▼▼
Before You Go

VISITORS CENTERS

There are two important guidelines when deciding what to take on a trip. The first is as true for Los Angeles as anywhere in the world—pack light. Dress styles here are relatively informal unless you're planning to spend all of your time in Beverly Hills (in which case you should pack an Armani suit and a Dior dress!). Otherwise, try to keep it casual. The airlines allow two suitcases and a carry-on bag.

PACKING

The second rule is to prepare for temperature variations. While day-time temperatures often hover in the mid-70s, evenings can bring on temperatures in the mid-50s. A warm sweater and jacket are absolute necessities year-round, in addition to shorts and T-shirts. Pack a raincoat if you're planning to visit from December to February.

Overnight accommodations in Los Angeles are as varied as the city itself. They range from highrise hotels and neon motels to hostels and bed-and-breakfast inns. Check through the various chapters and you're bound to find something to fit your budget and taste.

LODGING

The neon motels offer bland facilities at low prices and are excellent if you're economizing or don't plan to spend much time in the room. Larger hotels often lack intimacy, but provide such conveniences as restaurants and shops in the lobby. My personal preference is for historic hotels, those slightly faded classics that offer charm and tradition at moderate cost. Bed-and-breakfast inns present an opportunity to stay in a homelike setting. Like hostels, they are an excellent way to meet fellow travelers.

To help you decide on a place to stay, I've organized the accommodations not only by area but also according to price (prices listed are for double occupancy during the high season; prices may decrease in low season). *Budget* hotels generally are less than $60 per night for two people; the rooms are clean and comfortable, but not luxurious. The *moderately* priced hotels run $60 to $120 and provide larger rooms, plusher furniture, and more attractive surroundings. At a *deluxe* hotel you can expect to spend between $120 and $175 double. You'll check into a spacious, well-appointed room with all modern facilities; downstairs the lobby will be a fashionable affair, usually with a restaurant, lounge, and cluster of shops. If you want to spend your time (and money) in the city's very finest hotels, try an *ultra-deluxe* facility, which will include all the amenities and cost more than $175.

DINING   It seems as if Los Angeles has more restaurants than people. To establish a pattern for this parade of dining places, I've organized them according to location and cost. Restaurants listed in this book offer lunch and dinner unless otherwise noted.

Within a particular chapter, the restaurants are listed geographically, with each restaurant entry describing the establishment as budget, moderate, deluxe, or ultra-deluxe in price. Dinner entrées at *budget* restaurants usually cost $9 or less. The ambience is informal café-style and the crowd is often a local one. *Moderately* priced restaurants range between $9 and $18 at dinner and offer pleasant surroundings, a more varied menu, and a slower pace. *Deluxe* establishments tab their entrées above $18, featuring sophisticated cuisines, plush decor, and more personalized service. *Ultra-deluxe* dining rooms, where $25 will only get you started, are gourmet gathering places in which cooking (one hopes) is a fine art form and service is a way of life.

Breakfast and lunch menus vary less in price from restaurant to restaurant. Even deluxe kitchens usually offer light breakfasts and lunch sandwiches, which place them within a few dollars of their budget-minded competitors. These early meals can be a good time to test expensive restaurants.

TRAVELING WITH CHILDREN

Visiting Los Angeles with kids can be a real adventure, and if properly planned, a truly enjoyable one. To ensure that your trip will feature the joy, rather than the strain, of parenthood, remember a few important guidelines.

Use a travel agent to help with arrangements; they can reserve spacious bulkhead seats on airlines and determine which flights are least crowded. Also plan to bring everything you need on board—diapers, food, toys, and extra clothes for kids and parents alike. If the trip to L.A. involves a long journey, plan to relax and do very little during the first few days.

Always allow extra time for getting places. Book reservations well in advance and make sure the hotel has the extra crib, cot, or bed you require. It's smart to ask for a room at the end of the hall to cut down on noise.

Finding activities to interest children in Los Angeles couldn't be easier. Especially helpful in deciding on the day's outing is the "Calendar" section of the Sunday *Los Angeles Times*.

Hotels often provide access to babysitters, or check the Yellow Pages for state licensed and bonded babysitting agencies. A first-aid kit is always a good idea. Consult with your pediatrician for special medicines and dosages for colds and diarrhea.

WOMEN TRAVELING ALONE

Traveling solo grants an independence and freedom different from that of traveling with a partner, but single travelers are more vulnerable to crime and should take additional precautions.

It is better not to let strangers know you are traveling alone or where you are staying or planning to travel. It's unwise to hitchhike and probably best to avoid inexpensive accommodations on the outskirts of town; the money saved does not outweigh the risk. Bed and breakfasts, youth hostels, and YWCAs are generally your safest bet for lodging, and they also foster an environment ideal for bonding with fellow travelers.

It's best to avoid accommodations at motels in industrial areas or other places where there is no real neighborhood after dark. When requesting reservations at hotels and motels, ask for

Text continued on page 18.

United Nations of Food

Like one big ethnic smorgasbord, Los Angeles consists of an ecclectic mix of people from all over the world, making it one of the most diverse cities in the country. According to the last census, nearly half of L.A.'s residents are foreign-born, hailing from 140 countries and speaking 224 different languages. For gastronomes, this means it's possible to go around the world in 80 restaurants (give or take a few) while staying within a few square miles of urban L.A. Food defines Los Angeles' multicultural population, helps to give the city its character, and gently encourages cross-cultural understanding. Though some dishes, like *huitlacoche* and *bulgogi*, may require the services of an interpreter, eating in one of the city's ethnic restaurants can be a first-class adventure.

With Hispanics comprising almost half of Los Angeles' population, it's no wonder that Mexican restaurants can be found in almost every corner of the city. While the uninitiated often write off Mexican food as being nothing more than ersatz tacos and enchiladas, authentic Mexican food is far more varied and tasty.

Regional Mexican cuisine can run the gamut from the dark, chocolaty *mole* sauces of central Mexico to the chili-laced stews of the south. Besides basic ingredients such as corn, chilies, beans, and tomatoes, dishes may contain *flor de calabaza* (squash blossoms), *huitlacoche* (a fungus that grows on a corn stalk), and *pepitas* (pumpkin seeds). **La Casita Mexicana** in the East L.A. area is a hidden gem of a place. Specialties here include quesadillas stuffed with cheese and pumpkin flower petals, and *pozole* (pork stew) with purple hominy, which is made from scratch. ~ 4030 East Gage Avenue, East Los Angeles; 323-733-1898; www.lacasitamexicanala.com. BUDGET.

Koreatown, a 16-square-mile ethnic ghetto near Downtown, is home to the largest Korean population outside of Seoul. Koreans here speak their native language, and follow the customs of their ancestors. The traditional foods are spicy and use seasonings such as red pepper and garlic to give dishes zip. Korea's best-known food, *kimchi*, a sidedish of vegetables marinated with peppers and garlic, can also be its hottest. *Bulgogi*, known to Westerners as Korean barbecue, is another traditional dish and amounts to marinated meat cooked over a tableside fire. For a typical Korean barbecue, Koreatown's **Soot Bull Jeep** is smoky, noisy, and thoroughly authentic. Short ribs and pork loin are cooked on charcoal grills in the middle of the table, and the waitstaff speak very little English. ~ 3136 West 8th Street, Koreatown; 213-387-3865. MODERATE.

Chinese immigrants started pouring into Los Angeles in the mid-19th century, bringing with them their native cuisine. The style of cooking is defined by the province it comes from, and the best-known to Westerners is perhaps Cantonese, famous for dishes such as beef in oyster sauce and sweet-and-sour pork. Lovers of hot and spicy gravitate to dishes such as *kung pao* chicken and twice-cooked pork from the Szechwan province.

Though Cantonese and Szechwan dominate L.A.'s Chinese restaurant scene, tucked away in San Gabriel Valley is **Shiang Garden**, a restaurant featuring Hunan specialties such as savory house bean curd in casserole and a noodle dish with peanuts and ground pork floating in a hot herb sauce. ~ 111 North Atlantic Boulevard #351, Monterey Park; 626-458-4508. BUDGET.

African Americans that migrated from the Southern states to Los Angeles introduced "soul food" to the city. Developed by dirt-poor slaves and sharecroppers, recipes had to make do with meager ingredients and still be hearty and tasty. Seafood gumbo, black-eyed peas, cornbread, and collard greens are all Southern favorites that can be found in Los Angeles' African-American neighborhoods.

To try some down-home Southern food in an upscale setting, nothing beats **Harold & Belle's** in the Crenshaw district near Exposition Park. Serving the affluent black community for over 30 years, the lighting is low, the tablecloths crisply starched, and the food, such as peppery Southern fried chicken and file gumbo, heart-stoppingly delicious. ~ 2920 West Jefferson Boulevard; 323-735-9023. MODERATE.

Over the years, Jews in Los Angeles have become assimilated into the general population and Jewish food is available citywide. The Fairfax district and West Pico Boulevard in West Los Angeles, however, boast the largest concentration of Kosher eateries and markets.

Jewish food reflects the places that Jews have lived throughout the centuries, as well as being influenced by the constraints of Jewish food laws, such as not eating meat at the same meal as dairy. To many, Jewish food consists primarily of deli dishes like lox and bagels, blintzes, and matzoh ball soup, but Jewish restaurants, where the food is certified Kosher by a rabbi, specialize in all kinds of food, including pizza and egg rolls.

For a Kosher meal that transcends the usual deli fare, elegant **Nessim's**, owned by a Moroccan Jew, serves Middle Eastern dishes such as lamb couscous and Moroccan lemon chicken with olives. For a cross-cultural experience, order the sushi. ~ 8939 West Pico Boulevard, Beverly Hills; 310-859-9429. MODERATE.

rooms near the elevator or facing a central courtyard rather than find yourself in a remote location. For more hints, get a copy of *Safety and Security for Women Who Travel* (Travelers Tales).

Keep all valuables well-hidden and clutch cameras and purses tightly. Avoid late-night treks or strolls through undesirable parts of town, but if you find yourself in this situation, continue walking with a confident air until you reach a safe haven. A fierce scowl never hurts.

These hints should by no means deter you from seeking out adventure. Wherever you go, stay alert, use your common sense and trust your instincts. If you are hassled or threatened in some way, never be afraid to call for assistance. It's also a good idea to carry change for a phone call and to know a number to call in case of emergency. A helpful resource is the **Women's Yellow Pages**. ~ 818-995-6646; www.referral-guide.com.

GAY & LESBIAN TRAVELERS

L.A.'s largest gay area is centered in and around the city of West Hollywood. It is estimated that about one-third of the city's population of 35,000 is gay and lesbian, a fact that makes West Hollywood one of the most gay-friendly municipalities in the country. The city's first mayor was lesbian; other gays have since filled that rotating position, and many councilmembers have also been gay. On and near Santa Monica Boulevard, the main drag through the city's gay commercial district, you'll find hotels, shops, restaurants, and nightclubs catering to gay and lesbian travelers. (See "West Hollywood Gay Scene" in Chapter Four.)

One of the best places to get plugged into L.A.'s LGBT scene is **A Different Light Bookstore**. Besides stocking hundreds of titles appealing to gay and lesbian readers, A Different Light hosts readings and other community events. It's also the place to pick up copies of local publications, most of which are free (see below). ~ 8853 Santa Monica Boulevard, West Hollywood; 310-854-6601; www.adlbooks.com. Pick up a copy of *iN* magazine, which comes out twice a month—almost as often as the average Sunset Strip pedestrian—and covers the goings-on for men in L.A. County. ~ 8235 Santa Monica Boulevard, Suite 306, West Hollywood; 323-848-2200; www.inmagla.com. Also look for the biweekly *Frontiers Magazine*; it's full of movie, theater, and club reviews that cover the area between San Fran-

West Hollywood was the first city in the nation to boast a gay city government.

cisco and San Diego. ~ 5657 Wilshire Boulevard, Los Angeles, CA 90036; 323-848-2222; www.frontiersnewsmagazine.com. Women may consult *Lesbian News*, a monthly publication based in L.A. that covers the Southern California entertainment scene. Along with reviews, interviews, health, and travel, the magazine has a comprehensive club guide and calendar of events. ~ P.O. Box 55, Torrance, CA 90507; 800-458-9888; www.lesbiannews.com.

SENIOR TRAVELERS Los Angeles is ideal for older vacationers. The mild climate makes touring in the off-season possible, helping to cut down on expenses. Many museums, theaters, restaurants, and hotels have senior discounts (with a driver's license, Medicare card, or other age-identifying card). Ask your travel agent when booking reservations.

The **AARP** offers members travel discounts and provides referrals for escorted tours. ~ 3200 East Carson Street, Lakewood, CA 90712; 562-496-2277, 800-424-3410; www.aarp.org. For those 55 or over, **Elderhostel** provides educational programs in California. ~ 11 Avenue de Lafayette, Boston, MA 02111; 877-426-8056; www.elderhostel.org.

Be extra careful about health matters. Bring along any medications you ordinarily use, together with the prescriptions for obtaining more. Consider carrying a medical record with you— including your medical history and current medical status as well as your doctor's name, phone number, and address. Also be sure to confirm that your insurance covers you away from home.

DISABLED TRAVELERS California stands at the forefront of social reform for travelers with disabilities. During the past decade, the state has responded with a series of progressive legislative measures to the needs of the blind, wheelchair-bound, and others.

There are also agencies in Los Angeles assisting persons with disabilities. For tips and information, contact the **Westside Center for Independent Living**. ~ 12901 Venice Boulevard, Los Angeles; 310-390-3611; www.wcil.org.

There are numerous national organizations offering general information. Among these are:

The **Society for Accessible Travel & Hospitality** (SATH). ~ 347 5th Avenue #610, New York, NY 10016; 212-447-7284; www.sath.org.

Flying Wheels Travel. ~ 143 West Bridge Street, P.O. Box 382, Owatonna, MN 55060; 507-451-5005; www.flyingwheels travel.com.

Travelin' Talk, a network of people and organizations, also provides assistance. ~ P.O. Box 1796, Wheat Ridge, CO 80034; 303-232-2979; www.travelintalk.net.

Be sure to check in advance when making room reservations. Many hotels and motels have facilities for travelers in wheelchairs.

Access-Able Travel Source has worldwide information online. ~ 303-232-2979; www.access-able. com.

Or consult the comprehensive guidebook, *Access to the World—A Travel Guide for the Handicapped*, by Louise Weiss (Henry Holt & Company, Inc.).

The Department of Motor Vehicles provides special parking permits for the disabled (check the phone book for the nearest location). Many local bus lines and other public transit facilities are wheelchair accessible.

FOREIGN TRAVELERS

Passports and Visas   Most foreign visitors need a passport and tourist visa to enter the United States. Contact your nearest U.S. Embassy or Consulate well in advance to obtain a visa and to check on any other entry requirements.

Customs Requirements   Foreign travelers are allowed to carry in the following: 200 cigarettes (1 carton), 50 cigars, or 2 kilograms (4.4 pounds) of smoking tobacco; one liter of alcohol for personal use only (you must be 21 years of age to bring in alcohol); and US$100 worth of duty-free gifts that can include an additional quantity of 100 cigars (except Cuban cigars). You may bring in any amount of currency, but must fill out a form if you bring in over US$10,000. Carry any 90-day supply of prescription drugs in clearly marked containers. (You may have to produce a written prescription or doctor's statement for the custom's officer.) Meat or meat products, seeds, plants, fruits, and narcotics are not allowed to be brought into the United States. Contact the **United States Customs and Border Protection** for further information. ~ 1300 Pennsylvania Avenue NW, Washington, DC 20229; 202-927-1770; www.cbp.gov.

Driving   If you plan to rent a car, an international driver's license should be obtained before arriving in the United States. Some car rental agencies require both a foreign license and an international driver's license. Many also require a lessee to be at least 25 years of age; all require a major credit card. Remember: Seat belts are mandatory for the driver and all passengers. Children under age 5 or 40 pounds should be in the back seat in approved child safety restraints.

Currency United States money is based on the dollar. Bills generally come in denominations of $1, $5, $10, $20, $50, and $100. Every dollar is divided into 100 cents. Coins are the penny (1 cent), nickel (5 cents), dime (10 cents), and quarter (25 cents). Half-dollar and dollar coins are rarely used, as are $2 bills. You may not use foreign currency to purchase goods and services in the United States. Consider buying traveler's checks in dollar amounts. You may also use credit cards affiliated with an American company such as Interbank, Barclay Card, Visa, and American Express.

Electricity and Electronics Electric outlets use currents of 110 volts, 60 cycles. For appliances made for other electrical systems, you need a transformer or other adapter. Travelers who use laptop computers for telecommunication should be aware that modem configurations for U.S. telephone systems may be different from their European counterparts. Similarly, the U.S. format for videotapes is different from that in Europe; National Park Service visitors centers and other stores that sell souvenir videos often have them available in European format on request.

Weights and Measurements The United States uses the English system of weights and measures. American units and their metric equivalents are: 1 inch = 2.5 centimeters; 1 foot (12 inches) = 0.3 meter; 1 yard (3 feet) = 0.9 meter; 1 mile (5280 feet) = 1.6 kilometers; 1 ounce = 28 grams; 1 pound (16 ounces) = 0.45 kilogram; 1 quart (liquid) = 0.9 liter.

Outdoor Adventures

SPORTFISHING

Fish the waters around Los Angeles and you can try your hand at landing a barracuda, calico bass, halibut, white sea bass, white croaker, or maybe even a relative of Jaws.

WESTSIDE BEACHES For half- and three-quarter-day trips seeking yellowtail and white sea bass, contact **Marina del Rey Sportfishing**. ~ 13759 Fiji Way, Marina del Rey; 310-822-3625.

SANTA CATALINA ISLAND In Catalina you can contact the **Santa Catalina Island Visitors Bureau and Chamber of Commerce** for listings of private boat owners who outfit sportfishing expeditions. ~ 310-510-1520; www.catalina.com.

SOUTH BAY BEACHES   **Redondo Sportfishing** offers half- and three-quarter-day trips in and around the Santa Monica Bay on three 65-foot boats. ~ 233 North Harbor Drive, Redondo Beach; 310-372-2111; www.redondosportfishing.com. **L.A. Harbor Sportfishing** offers scheduled and chartered trips for yellowtail, bass, tuna, barracuda, and bonito. ~ 1150 Nagoya Way, Berth 79, San Pedro; 310-547-9916; www.laharborsportfishing.com. **Pierpoint Landing** has seven charter boats offering half-day to overnight fishing charters. ~ 200 Aquarium Way, Long Beach; 562-983-9300; www.pierpoint.net.

DIVING   If you'd rather search for starfish than stars along L.A.'s coastline, you'll find an active diving scene.

WESTSIDE BEACHES   **Malibu Divers** rents and sells gear and periodically runs full-day trips to Catalina. Private lessons are available. ~ 21231 Pacific Coast Highway, Malibu; 310-456-2396; www.malibudivers.com. **Blue Cheer Ocean Water Sports** runs trips from Ventura to Anacapa and Santa Cruz islands. ~ 1112 Wilshire Boulevard, Santa Monica; 310-828-1217; www.divers4hire.com. For NAUI certification classes and dive trips near the islands contact **Scuba Haus**. ~ 2501 Wilshire Boulevard, Santa Monica; 310-828-2916.

SANTA CATALINA ISLAND   Without doubt Santa Catalina offers some of the finest scuba diving anywhere in the world. Perfectly positioned to attract fish from both the northern and southern Pacific, it teems with sea life. Large fish ascend from the deep waters surrounding the island while small colorful species inhabit rich kelp forests along the coast. There are caves and caverns to explore as well as the wrecks of rusting ships.

Several outfits rent skindiving and scuba equipment and sponsor dive trips, including **Catalina Divers Supply**. ~ 310-510-0330. **Island Charters, Inc.** offers similar services. ~ 310-510-2616. For guided or unguided full-day chartered trips try **Argo Diving Service**. ~ 310-510-2208.

SOUTH BAY BEACHES   Lessons at **Dive 'n Surf** are also PADI-certified; dive trips to Catalina and Santa Barbara are available. ~ 504 North Broadway, Redondo Beach; 310-372-8423; www.divensurf.com. For full-day trips around local islands call **Sea D Sea**. ~ 1911 South Catalina Avenue, Redondo Beach; 310-373-

6355. **Pacific Wilderness** is a PADI training center that sells and rents equipment. ~ 1719 South Pacific Avenue, San Pedro; 310-833-2422. To explore L.A.'s submerged depths, contact **Pacific Sporting Goods**, which provides lessons and equipment and organizes boat trips. ~ 11 39th Place, Long Beach; 562-434-1604.

During the annual migration (January through March) several outfits offer local whale-watching trips. This is a fun thing to do on a clear day, whether you see any whales or not. **WHALE WATCHING**

SOUTH BAY BEACHES **Spirit Cruises** gives you a guarantee with your trip. You see a whale or you get a gift certificate for a later trip. ~ Berth 77, San Pedro; 310-548-8080; www.spiritmarine.com. **L.A. Harbor Sportfishing** offers two-hour trips. ~ Berth 79, San Pedro; 310-547-9916; www.laharbor sportfishing.com. **Pierpoint Landing** will take you out on the briny deep for a three-hour cruise. ~ 200 Aquarium Way, Long Beach; 562-495-6250. **Harbor Breeze Corporation** takes two-and-a-half-hour trips along the coast. ~ Dock #2, 100 Aquarium Way, Long Beach; 310-831-0996; www.longbeachcruises.com.

Camping in L.A.? Sure, at the beaches or in the San Gabriel Mountains. Contact the CA Department of Parks and Recreation (916-653-6995) or the National Park Service (415-556-0561) for more information.

Redondo Sports Fishing offers whale-watching cruises during the winter when the whales are migrating south to Mexico. And if the trip is whale-less, passengers are given a rain check good for another try. ~ 233 North Harbor Drive; 310-372-2111; www. redondosportfishing.com.

"Surfing is the only life," so when in the Southland, sample a bit of Los Angeles' seminal subculture. Redondo, Hermosa, and Manhattan beaches have come to represent the L.A. scene. Other popular spots include Royal Palms State Beach and Torrance County Beach's Malaga Cove. If you're in Malibu, check out the waves at Topanga Beach, Malibu Surfrider Beach, and Leo Carrillo State Beach. Santa Catalina also has its share of waves: Ben Weston Beach for surfing and Shark Harbor for bodysurfing. Remember, it's more fun to hang ten than just hang out. **SURFING & WINDSURFING**

WESTSIDE BEACHES You'll find surfboard, boogieboard, and wetsuit rentals in Malibu at **Zuma Jay Surfboards**. ~ 22775 Pacific Coast Highway, Malibu; 310-456-8044.

SOUTH BAY BEACHES   Rent a surfboard, bodyboard, or wet-suit from **Manhattan Beach Bike and Skate Rentals**. Closed Tuesday in winter. ~ 1116 Manhattan Avenue, Manhattan Beach; 310-372-8500. **Jeffers** offers surfboards and boogieboards. ~ 39 14th Street, Hermosa Beach; 310-372-9492.

WATER SPORTS

Though the beach isn't far away, Los Angeles also contains several lakes that provide ample opportunity for water sports.

SAN FERNANDO VALLEY   If you'd like to waterski or windsurf, try **Frank G. Bonelli Park**, but bring your own equipment. Vehicle fee. ~ 120 Via Verde, San Dimas; 909-599-8411. Anglers can rent motorized fishing boats at **Castaic Lake Recreation Area**. ~ 32132 Castaic Lake Drive, Castaic; 661-775-6232.

For those who are happier lolling about in a boat, there are rowboat rentals at **Santa Fe Dam**. Vehicle fee. ~ 15501 East Arrow Highway, Irwindale; 626-334-1065

KAYAKING

WESTSIDE BEACHES   For half-day ocean kayak tours along the Malibu coast, kayaking lessons, and kayak rentals, contact **Malibu Ocean Sports**. The tours last about two and a half hours and include some basic instruction. Tours are offered only on weekends between April and October. ~ 22935 Pacific Coast Highway; 310-456-6302, fax 310-456-6302; www.malibuoceansports.com.

SANTA CATALINA ISLAND   On Santa Catalina Island, **Descanso Beach Ocean Sports** offers rentals and several different guided expeditions in the waters around Catalina, among them a short 90-minute paddle to a cove near Avalon and a full-day excursion that includes hiking and picnicking. ~ Descanso Beach, Avalon; 310-510-1226, fax 310-510-3577; www.kayakcatalina island.com.

SKATING & SKATE-BOARDING

Los Angeles may well be the skating capital of California, and skateboarding, of course, is the closest thing to surfing without waves. Between the two of them, you can't get much more L.A., so find a way to put yourself on wheels.

WESTSIDE BEACHES   **Manhattan Beach Bike and Skate Rentals** rents skates. ~ 1116 Manhattan Avenue, Manhattan Beach; 310-372-8500. **Rollerskates of America** has inline skates and gear. ~ 1312 Hermosa Avenue, Hermosa Beach; 310-372-8812. **Rentals on the Beach** offers inline skates, bikes, tandems, and other gear at three beach locations. ~ Near the parking lots at Washington Boulevard, Venice Boulevard, and Rose Avenue. **Spokes 'n Stuff** has two convenient locations and rents both in-line skates and rollerskates. ~ At the parking lot on Admiralty Way at Jamaica Bay Inn Hotel, Marina del Rey, 310-306-3332; and near the Santa Monica Pier in Loews Santa Monica, 310-395-4748. Along the Santa Monica Pier, **Sea Mist Skate Rentals** has inline skates, rollerskates, mountain bikes, and everything else needed for a day on the South Bay Trail. ~ 1619 Ocean Front Walk, Santa Monica; 310-395-7076.

Though driving seems almost an addiction in the city, many Angelenos still manage to exercise. Filling your lungs with smoggy air might not be the healthiest thing to do, but if you're interested in jogging anyway, join the troopers at **Elysian Park**, located just north of downtown L.A. near the intersection of Routes 110 and 5. Visit **San Vicente Boulevard** in the Brentwood area or **Lacy Park** at 1485 Virginia Road in San Marino. Another popular area is the **arroyo** near the Rose Bowl in Pasadena, or **Griffith Park** at 4730 Crystal Springs Drive in Los Angeles.

JOGGING

What better way to let yourself go than by coasting or floating on high? The adventurous can try hang gliding at **Windsports Soaring Center,** which offers lessons and trips off the San Gabriel Mountains. ~ 12623 Gridley Street, Sylmar; 818-367-2430.

HANG GLIDING

HOLLYWOOD/WILSHIRE   Sunset Ranch offers trail rides on specific park trails, and one that takes you to a Mexican restaurant. Trips usually last from one to two hours. ~ 3400 North Beachwood Drive, Hollywood; 323-464-9612; www.sunsetranchholly wood.com.

RIDING STABLES

ONE MILLION YEARS YOUNG

Ironically, the semi-arid Los Angeles Basin was once underwater. Built by volcanic activity, the geologic area is so young that the Palos Verdes Peninsula was a chain of offshore is lands just one million years ago. Today, Los Angeles' oceanfront property stretches for 74 miles, from Malibu south to Long Beach, and attracts visitors in the tens of millions every year.

PASADENA AREA   In Burbank consider **Circle K Stables** for smaller group rides. Trail rides can be as short as one hour or as long as five. ~ 914 South Mariposa Street; 818-843-9890. Another Burbank offering is **Griffith Park Horse Rentals,** which takes you on one- to two-hour rides into the hills of Griffith Park. Maximum group of 20. ~ 480 Riverside Drive; 818-840-8401.

Rent horses from **Bar S Stables** and lead yourself through the Glendale portion of the park. Guides can be arranged beforehand. You must be at least seven years old to ride. ~ 1850 Riverside Drive, Glendale; 818-242-8443.

GOLF

In Los Angeles it's as easy to tee off at a golf course as it is to get teed off in a traffic jam. If you left your cart (or clubs) at home, you're in luck; most courses rent both.

GREATER DOWNTOWN   One of the many challenging or interesting courses is the **Montebello Country Club,** a regulation 18-hole public course. They rent carts only. ~ 901 Via San Clemente, Montebello; 323-887-4565.

In Los Angeles, **Wilson and Harding Golf Courses** are both 18-hole, par-72 public greens. ~ Griffith Park; 323-664-2555; www.griffithparkgolfshop.com.

THE WESTSIDE   Westchester Golf Course is a privately owned, public 15-hole course. You can also get in some driving practice. ~ 6900 West Manchester Avenue; 310-670-5110; www.americangolf.com.

With its curving hills and flowering meadows, Griffith Park is a favorite spot among urban equestrians. Several places on the edge of the park provide facilities.

WESTSIDE BEACHES   If you can take a break from the action in Venice, head to the nine-hole **Penmar Golf Course.** ~ 1233 Rose Avenue, Venice; 310-396-6228.

SANTA CATALINA ISLAND   Catalina Visitors Golf Club is a par-32 nine-hole course with plenty of sand traps. ~ 1 Country Club Drive, Avalon; 310-510-0530; www.scico.com.

SOUTH BAY BEACHES   The coastal **Los Verdes Golf Course** is one of the finest public facilities in Southern California; along with spectacular views you'll find a driving range and two putting greens. ~ 7000 West Los Verdes Drive, Rancho Palos Verdes; 310-377-7370; www.americangolf.com.

The beautiful **El Dorado Park Municipal Golf Course,** home of the Long Beach Open, has two putting greens and a driving range. ~ 2400 Studebaker Road, Long Beach; 562-430-5411. The 18-hole **Skylink Golf Course** is a duffer's delight with club and cart rentals, a driving range, night lighting, and a sports bar on the premises. ~ 4800 East Wardlow Road, Long Beach; 562-421-3388. The hilly Recreation Park offers both an 18-hole and a 9-hole course. ~ 5001 Deukmeijian Drive, Long Beach; 562-494-5000.

PASADENA AREA If you are in Pasadena, stop by the two 18-hole courses at the public **Brookside Golf Course**. Located right next to the Rose Bowl, this green features many lakes and trees. ~ 1133 North Rosemont Avenue; 626-796-0177. In the eastern end of the county part of the public, 18-hole **Marshall Canyon Golf Course** runs over a canyon. There's also a driving range. ~ 6100 North Stephens Ranch Road, La Verne; 909-593-8211; www.marshallcanyon.com. The public 18-hole **San Dimas Canyon Golf Course**, designed by Dan Murray, is the premier facility in the Foothill area. ~ 2100 Terrebonne Avenue, San Dimas; 909-599-2313. Duffers in Pomona head to the 18-hole **Mountain Meadows Golf Course**, a public course with three water holes, rolling hills, and tiered greens. ~ 1875 Fairplex Drive, Pomona; 909-623-3704; www.americangolf.com. Rosemead's **Whittier Narrows**, an Arnold Palmer–managed golf course, is also a good choice, with three public nine-hole, courses. ~ 8640 East Rush Street, Rosemead; 626-280-8225.

SAN FERNANDO VALLEY In the San Fernando Valley consider **Knollwood Golf Course**, an 18-hole, public course with a driving range. ~ 12040 Balboa Boulevard, Granada Hills; 818-363-8161, 800-345-4259. Another option is the public **Sepulveda Golf Complex**, which features two 18-hole courses. ~ 16821 Burbank Boulevard, Encino; 818-986-4560.

GREATER DOWNTOWN Most public parks have at least one tennis court; the city's largest facility, **Griffith Park**, has many outdoor lighted courts. ~ 4730 Crystal Springs Drive, Los Angeles; 323-662-7772. Or try **Elysian Park**, which has two unlighted courts. ~ Near the intersection of Route 5 and Route 110, Los Angeles.

TENNIS

WESTSIDE BEACHES In Santa Monica, it's a good idea to call for reservations at public tennis courts during the summer. **Reed**

Park has six lighted courts. ~ 1133 7th Street; 310-394-6011. **Memorial Park** offers four lighted courts. ~ Olympic Boulevard at 14th Street, Santa Monica; 310-394-6011. Also try one of the six courts at **Ocean View Park**. ~ Barnard Way south of Ocean Park Boulevard, Santa Monica; 310-394-6011.

SOUTH BAY BEACHES   The **Alta Vista Tennis Courts** have eight lighted courts as well. Membership is required. ~ 715 Julia Avenue, Redondo Beach; 310-318-0670. Two lighted courts are available at **The Sport Center at King Harbor**. ~ 819 North Harbor Drive, Redondo Beach; 310-372-8868. There are 15 lighted courts available at **El Dorado Park**. ~ 2800 Studebaker Road, Long Beach; 562-425-0553. The **Billie Jean King Tennis Center** offers eight lighted courts. ~ 1040 Park Avenue, Long Beach; 562-438-8509.

PASADENA AREA   Tennis clubs dot Los Angeles County; one such club is the **Racquet Center**. The Pasadena location has nine lighted courts and seven racquetball courts. They also rent racquets and have lessons. ~ 920 Lohman Lane, South Pasadena; 323-258-4178.

For further information about clubs and tournaments, contact the **Southern California Tennis Association**. ~ P.O. Box 240015, Los Angeles, CA 90024; 310-208-3838; www.usta.com/scta.

BIKING

Bikeways in Los Angeles are almost as plentiful as freeways. Unlike the freeways, few of them are normally congested. Many run parallel to parks, rivers, aqueducts, and lakes, offering a different view of this diverse area.

There are scores of shoreline bike trails and routes for scenic excursions. Whether you're up for a leisurely and level beachfront loop, or a more strenuous trek through coastal cliffside communities, the weather and scenery make this area a beautiful place for a bike ride.

For maps, brochures, and additional information on bike routes in Los Angeles contact the **Department of Transportation**. ~ 205 South Broadway, Suite 400; 213-485-9957.

GREATER DOWNTOWN   Over 14 miles of bike routes wind through Griffith Park. Two notable excursions skirt many of the park attractions: **Crystal Springs Loop**, which follows Crystal Springs Drive and Zoo Drive along the park's eastern edge, passes the merry-go-round and Travel Town; **Mineral Wells Loop**, an arduous uphill climb, passes Harding Golf Course, then coasts downhill to Zoo Drive, taking in Travel Town and the zoo.

In the Mt. Washington area, the **Arroyo Seco Trail** includes a loop past Heritage Square, the Lummis House, and Casa de Adobe. The trail begins at the Montecito Heights Recreation Center on Homer Street and runs along an arroyo.

In the Whittier–El Monte area, bikers can choose a long jaunt along the 15-mile **Rio Hondo River Trail** or a leisurely go-round on the **Legg Lake Loop** in Whittier Narrows Recreation Area.

WESTSIDE BEACHES   The **Santa Monica Loop** is an easy ride starting at San Vicente Boulevard and going up Ocean Avenue, past Palisades Park and the Santa Monica Pier. Most of the trail is on bike lanes and paths; five miles roundtrip.

A strenuous but worthwhile excursion is a bike ride along **Mulholland Drive**. Not recommended during commuter hours, this route traverses the spine of the Santa Monica Mountains and offers fabulous views of the city and ocean.

> The Venice Boardwalk is a casual, two-mile bike ride where a host of kooky characters and performers line the promenade, vying for your attention.

SANTA CATALINA ISLAND   In Catalina, free use of bikes is allowed only in Avalon. Elsewhere permits are required: they may be obtained from the **Santa Catalina Island Conservancy**. ~ 125 Claressa Avenue, Avalon; 310-510-2595; www.catalinaconservancy.org. Cross-channel carriers have special requirements for transporting bicycles and must be contacted in advance for complete details.

SOUTH BAY BEACHES   Foremost is the **South Bay Bike Trail**, with over 22 miles of coastal vistas. The trail, an easy ride and extremely popular, runs from RAT Beach in Torrance to Will Rogers State Beach in Pacific Palisades. The path intersects the Ballona Creek Bikeway in Marina Del Rey, which extends seven miles east and passes the Venice Boardwalk, as well as piers and marinas along the way.

Naples, a Venice-like neighborhood in Long Beach, provides a charming area for freeform bike rides. There are no designated paths but you can cycle with ease past beautiful homes, parks, and canals.

Of moderate difficulty is the **Palos Verdes Peninsula** coastline trail. Offering wonderful scenery, the 14-mile roundtrip ride goes from Malaga Cove Plaza in Palos Verdes Estates to the Wayfarers Chapel. (Part of the trail is a bike path, the rest follows city streets.)

PASADENA AREA   The **Kenneth Newell Bikeway** begins on Arroyo Boulevard in Pasadena, then dips down to Arroyo Seco and the famed Rose Bowl. The bikeway follows a flood basin, climbs a steep hill into Linda Vista, and continues to Devil's Gate Dam and the world-renowned Jet Propulsion Laboratory.

Greg LeMond, the first American to win the Tour de France, was born in L.A. in 1961.

For a look at the good life, check out the route from **San Gabriel Mission to the Huntington Library**, which winds from San Gabriel through the exclusive town of San Marino.

The most scenic bike path in the L.A. area is the **West Fork Trail** in the San Gabriel Mountains—6.7 miles of gentle, paved path that parallels the west fork of the San Gabriel River. Take Route 210 to Azusa, then Route 39 ten miles north to a parking lot a little past the Rincon Ranger Station.

SAN FERNANDO VALLEY   The flat, nine-mile **Sepulveda Basin Bikeway** circumnavigates the Sepulveda Dam Recreation Area in the heart of the San Fernando Valley.

Bike Rentals   **Hollywood Pro Bicycles** rents mountain and road bikes by the day and by the week. Helmet and lock are included in the rental. ~ 6731 Hollywood Boulevard; 323-466-5890, 888-775-2453; www.hollywoodprobicycles.com.

To rent mountain bikes, cruisers, or tandems, try **Manhattan Beach Bike and Skate Rentals**. ~ 1116 Manhattan Avenue, Manhattan Beach; 310-372-8500. In Hermosa Beach, **Jeffers** rents beach cruisers. ~ 39 14th Street, Hermosa Beach; 310-372-9492. **Spokes 'n Stuff** offers mountain bikes, tandems, and cruisers. ~ Near the pier in Loews Santa Monica; 310-395-4748. Also in Santa Monica, **Sea Mist Skate Rentals** has mountain bikes and helmets. ~ 1619 Ocean Front Walk, Santa Monica; 310-395-7076. In Catalina try **Brown's Bikes**. ~ 107 Pebbly Beach Road, Avalon; 310-510-0986.

HIKING   The idea of natural areas in Los Angeles seems to be a contradiction in terms. But the city is so vast—sprawling from the Pacific Ocean to the mountains—that even ambitious developers have been unable to pave it all. For backpackers and daytrippers alike, miles of hiking trails still lace the hills and canyons that lie just beyond the housing tracts and shopping malls.

For more information and maps, call **Los Angeles County Riding and Hiking Trails.** ~ 626-575-5756, fax 626-652-0748. All distances listed for hiking trails are one way unless otherwise noted.

GREATER DOWNTOWN Los Angeles' outback is found a few miles from the center of Downtown amid the forested hills of **Griffith Park**. With more than 55 miles of trails to explore, the park rests along the Hollywood Hills at the edge of the Santa Monica Mountains. For information and maps contact the local ranger station. ~ 323-913-7390, fax 213-485-8775.

Among the best hikes here is the **Mt. Hollywood Loop Trail** (6 miles). Beginning near the merry-go-round, the path follows a stream, passes deer and coyote habitats, then leads up out of the canyon onto the chaparral-covered slopes of Mt. Hollywood.

For a combination sightseeing-hiking venture take the **Mineral Wells Trail** (4.3 miles). The hike begins on a level bridle trail, then wends its way down toward the zoo, and back to Mineral Wells.

The **Pacific Electric Quarry–Bronson Cave Trail** (2.3 miles) snakes through Brush Canyon to an abandoned rock quarry and the Bronson Caves, an area ripe for exploring. If it seems like you've been here before, that's because this was the location for such shows as *Bonanza*, *Mod Squad*, and *Star Trek*.

Near Roland Heights, in Schabarum Regional County Park, the **Skyline Trail: Schabarum Park to Hacienda Boulevard** (3 miles) traverses the Puente Hills. The hike leads through wild mustard fields to an overlook with views of the San Gabriel Valley.

WESTSIDE BEACHES It's difficult to imagine, but Los Angeles does have undeveloped mountain wilderness areas prime for hiking. The Santa Monica Mountains offer chaparral-covered landscapes, grassy knolls, mountain streams, and dark canyons.

When visiting Will Rogers State Historic Park, take a moderate hike down **Inspiration Point Trail** (2-mile loop) for a view overlooking the Westside.

Topanga State Park has over 36 miles of trails. The **Musch Ranch Loop Trail** (5 mile loop) passes through five different types of plant communities. Or try the moderate **Santa Ynez Fire Road Trail** (7 miles), which guides you along the Palisades Highlands with views of the ocean and Santa Ynez Canyon. In spring wild-flowers add to the already spectacular scenery.

Several trails trace the "backbone" of the Santa Monica Mountains. In fact, the **Backbone Trail** roughly follows the crest of these mountains, from Will Rogers State Historic Park to Point Mugu State Park—a 70-mile stretch. If you're not up for the long haul, you can pick up pieces of the trail at several points along the way, including the Circle X Ranch, Malibu Creek State Park, and Topanga State Park.

The moderate **Eagle Rock to Eagle Springs Loop Trail** (6 miles), for instance, begins in Topanga State Park and traverses oak and chaparral countryside on its way to Eagle Spring. Another section of the "Backbone Trail," **Malibu Creek State Park Loop** (15.5 miles roundtrip) begins near the crossroads of Piuma Road and Malibu Canyon Road. The difficult trail follows fire roads and offers choice views of the ocean and Channel Islands before it climbs up to Kanan-Dume Road. **Charmlee Park** is a little-visited wildflower paradise in the hills overlooking the ocean. A 1.75-mile trail offers great coastal views. Take Encinal Canyon Road four miles into the mountains from Pacific Coast Highway. **Solstice Canyon Park** is another hidden beauty with trails offering hikes of up to six miles. The moderate three-mile roundtrip to the Roberts Ranch House ruins follows a perennial stream and ends at the burned-out remains of a terraced dream house that retains a palm-shaded charm. Take Corral Canyon Road a quarter-mile north from Pacific Coast Highway.

HIDDEN ►

HIDDEN ►

An easy (though in spots difficult) climb up **Zuma Ridge Trail** (6 miles) brings you to the center of the Santa Monica Mountains and affords otherworldly views of the Pacific. The trail begins off

AUTHOR FAVORITE

A canopy of mature sycamores and oaks shade hikers as they start on the Westside's **Temescal Loop Trail** (4.4 miles) at the corner of Temescal Canyon and Sunset Boulevard. Hiking through Temescal Canyon, it's hard to believe the city is only minutes away until a heart-pounding climb to one of the overlooks provides stunning ocean and city views. During the rainy season the trail follows a babbling brook to a waterfall. ~ 15601 Sunset Boulevard; smmc.ca.gov/temtrail.html.

Encinal Canyon Road, one and a half miles from Mulholland Highway. **Zuma-Dume Trail** (3 miles) in Malibu takes you on an easy walk from Zuma Beach County Park, along Pirate's Cove (which used to be a nude beach) to the Point Dume headlands and Paradise Cove, a popular diving spot.

For a pleasant, easy hike along part of the Malibu coast dotted with coves and caves and providing terrific swimming, surfing, and skindiving, head out the **Leo Carrillo Trail** (1.5 miles), located at Leo Carrillo State Beach. Or to hike up a gently sloping hill for a view of the coastline, take the easy, nearby **Yellow Hill Trail** (2 miles).

SANTA CATALINA ISLAND   For a true adventure in hiking, gather your gear and head for Santa Catalina. A network of spectacular trails crisscrosses this largely undeveloped island. Bring plenty of water and beware of rattlesnakes and poison oak. You'll also need a hiking permit, free from the Santa Catalina Island Conservancy. ~ 125 Claressa Avenue, Avalon; 310-510-1421.

Empire Landing Road Trail (11.5 miles) begins at BlackJack Junction and ends up at Two Harbors. The path passes a lot of interesting terrain and provides glimpses of island wildlife, especially buffalo. (You can arrange with the ferry service to ride back to the mainland from Two Harbors.)

Other routes to consider are **Sheep Chute Trail** (3.3 miles), a moderate hike between Little Harbor and Empire Landing; and **Parson's Landing to Starlight Trail** (4 miles), a strenuous trek between Silver Peak Trail and Parsons Landing.

SOUTH BAY BEACHES   Set beneath wave-carved bluffs, the moderate **Palos Verdes Peninsula Trail** (5 miles) takes you along a rocky beachside past coves and teeming tidepools. The trail begins at Malaga Cove and ends at Point Vicente Lighthouse.

If you're interested in exploring a shipwreck, head to Palos Verdes Estate Shoreline Preserve, near Malaga Cove, and hike the **Seashore–Shipwreck Trail** (2.25 miles). The moderate-to-difficult trail hugs the shoreline (and requires an ability to jump boulders), skirting tidepools and coves, until it arrives at what is left of an old Greek ship, the *Dominator*. Wear sturdy hiking shoes and bring water.

The Los Angeles portion of the **California Coastal Trail** begins on Naples Island in Long Beach. From here the trail is a varied journey across open bluffs, boat basins, rocky outcroppings accessible only at low tide, along beachwalks filled with rollerskaters, jugglers, and skate boarders, and up goat trails with stunning views of the Pacific Ocean.

PASADENA AREA   Several years ago the San Gabriel portion of the **Pacific Crest Trail**, which leads from Canada to Mexico, was completed. One part of that great system, the **Mill Creek Summit to Pacifico Mountain Trail** (4 miles) follows a route through spruce and oak forests to a view overlooking the Mojave Desert.

At the end of Chaney Trail Road in Altadena there's a lovely spot for a family hike through a tree-shrouded canyon. **Lower Millard Canyon Falls Trail** (.5 mile) leads to a 50-foot waterfall surrounded by huge boulders. If you're a little more adventurous, try **Upper Millard Canyon Trail** (2.5 miles).

An even more ambitious hike from the same trailhead is the **Mount Lowe Railway Trail** (3.5 miles). At the end you'll discover an abandoned rail line, the old "Railway to the Clouds," and the ruins of Ye Alpine tavern. It's a moderate trek offering spectacular views of Los Angeles.

In Altadena's Eaton Canyon, the strenuous **Altadena Crest Trail** (7 miles) explores the foothills of the San Gabriels. A side trip to **Eaton Falls** (.5 mile) follows the stream bed.

Big Santa Anita Canyon north of Sierra Madre is another popular area for hiking. **Sturtevant Falls Trail** (1.8 miles) leads upstream to a 50-foot waterfall. The trailhead is located in Chantry Flat. (Don't climb on the rocks at the waterfall; several people have been seriously hurt here.)

Not as well-known as popular Mount Wilson is a neighboring peak, 5994-foot **Mount Disappointment** (2.8 miles), which offers another opportunity to view Los Angeles from on high. You will walk through Douglas fir and Coulter pine forests and climb along chaparral-covered ridges. The trailhead is just beyond Red Box off the Mount Wilson Road.

Fourteen miles of trails abound in **Frank G. Bonelli Regional Park** in San Dimas. To get an overview of the park, hike along the southern hills above Puddingston Reservoir. Maps are available at the park headquarters.

It's all downhill to begin with when you hike **Devil's Canyon Trail** (5.5 miles). This trek through an alder-studded canyon, with a bubbling creek for company, goes from Upper Chilao Campground in the San Gabriel Wilderness.

The **Arroyo Seco Canyon Trail** (9.8 miles), beginning at Switzer's Picnic Area (off Route 2), is a challenging way to explore the serene canyons of the San Gabriels. The trail overlooks Switzer Falls, joins the **Gabrieleño Trail** (3.5 miles), then descends to the tree-laden floor of the canyon. En route is Oakwilde Trail Camp, an ideal spot for an overnight visit. The trail continues to the mouth of the canyon, which overlooks the massive Jet Propulsion Laboratory.

> The San Gabriel Mountains are crisscrossed with hiking trails ripe for exploring.

SAN FERNANDO VALLEY   Leading up a 5074-foot peak, the highest within the Los Angeles city limits, **Mount Lukens Stone Canyon Trail** (3.3 miles) is a hearty uphill trek. On a clear day the Pacific looms in the distance, beyond a jigsaw puzzle of housing tracts and rolling hills. The trailhead is located in Sunland off Doske Road; be sure to bring water.

At the northern edge of the San Fernando Valley, **Placerita Canyon to Sylmar Trail** (9 miles) offers conditioned hikers an opportunity to climb along a chaparral-covered hillside to an oak-studded canyon. The hike begins in Placerita Canyon State and County Park and goes along the Wilson Canyon Saddle. Another challenging trek is the climb up **Manzanita Mountain** (1 mile), with its picturesque views.

The old stage road that connected the San Fernando and San Joaquin valleys is now the route of **Beale's Cut Trail** (.3 mile). This short but steep hike cuts through the San Fernando Pass, with its earthquake fault and twisted rock formations.

One of Los Angeles' hidden gems is **O'Melveny Park**, a 672-acre preserve in the Santa Susana Mountains at the north end of the San Fernando Valley. **O'Melveny Park Trail** (2.5 miles) begins in Bee Canyon and follows an old fire road past a stream, then climbs through fields of wildflowers to a series of bluffs. After the steep climb, you are rewarded with a panoramic view of Los Angeles, the Santa Clarita Valley, and the San Gabriel Mountains. The trailhead is near Sesnon Boulevard in Granada Hills.

◄ HIDDEN

In Chatsworth, **Devil's Canyon Trail** (1.5 miles) offers a peaceful walk along a streambed through stands of sycamore and oak trees. Look for the caves that have been etched into the sides of the canyon. Also in Chatsworth is a honeycomb of hiking trails winding around **Stoney Point,** located at the north end of Topanga Boulevard just before it meets Route 118.

Transportation

CAR

Arriving in Los Angeles by car means entering a maze of freeways. For most Angelenos this is an every day occurrence; they know where they are going and are accustomed to spending a lot of time getting there. It's an intimate affair, a personal relationship between car and driver; they even refer to their freeways by name rather than number.

For the visitor the experience can be very intimidating. The best way to determine a path through this labyrinth is by learning the major highways to and from town.

From the north and west, **Route 101**, the Ventura Freeway, extends from Ventura to Sherman Oaks, then turns southeast to become the Hollywood Freeway.

The Santa Monica Freeway, **Route 10**, cuts through the heart of Los Angeles. It begins in Santa Monica and then becomes the San Bernardino Freeway in downtown Los Angeles.

Route 1 parallels the coast throughout Los Angeles County, undergoing several name changes during its course, is the main coastal route.

From Northern California, **Route 5**, the Golden State Freeway, runs south into the center of the city where it changes its name to the Santa Ana Freeway. **Route 405**, better known as the San Diego Freeway, cuts through the San Fernando Valley and the Westside.

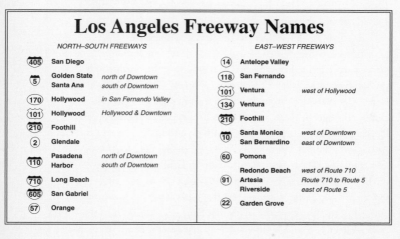

Los Angeles Freeway Names

NORTH–SOUTH FREEWAYS		EAST–WEST FREEWAYS	
405 San Diego		14 Antelope Valley	
5 Golden State	north of Downtown	118 San Fernando	
Santa Ana	south of Downtown	101 Ventura	west of Hollywood
170 Hollywood	in San Fernando Valley	134 Ventura	
101 Hollywood	Hollywood & Downtown	210 Foothill	
210 Foothill		10 Santa Monica	west of Downtown
2 Glendale		San Bernardino	east of Downtown
110 Pasadena	north of Downtown	60 Pomona	
Harbor	south of Downtown	91 Redondo Beach	west of Route 710
710 Long Beach		Artesia	Route 710 to Route 5
605 San Gabriel		Riverside	east of Route 5
57 Orange		22 Garden Grove	

Three airports bring visitors to the L.A. area: the very big, very
busy Los Angeles International Airport, the smaller Long Beach
Airport, and the less crowded Burbank-Glendale-Pasadena Airport. Los Angeles International is convenient if you are headed
for the downtown area or out to the coast. Traffic around this
major hub is generally ferocious. Those planning to stay around
Hollywood and Beverly Hills, in the San Fernando Valley, or out
around Pasadena, are better advised to fly in to the Burbank-
Glendale-Pasadena Airport.

Los Angeles International Airport, better known as LAX, is
served by many domestic and foreign carriers. Currently (and
this seems to change daily) the following airlines fly into LAX:
Alaska Airlines, America West Airlines, American Airlines, Continental Airlines, Delta Air Lines, Hawaiian Airlines, Northwest
Airlines, Southwest Airlines, and United Airlines.

International carriers are also numerous: Air Canada, Air
France, Air New Zealand, All Nippon Airways, British Airways,
Canadian Airlines International, China Airlines, Japan Airlines,
KLM, Lufthansa German Airlines, Mexicana Airlines, Philippine
Airlines, QANTAS Airways, Singapore Airlines, and TACA Inter-
national Airlines. ~ 310-646-5252; www.lawa.org/lax.

Presently, carriers into **Long Beach Airport** are America West,
Great America Airways, SunJet International, and United
Airlines.

The **Airport in the Sky,** set at 1600-foot elevation in the
mountains of Santa Catalina, may be the prettiest landing strip
anywhere. The small terminal building conveys a mountain
lodge atmosphere with a stone fireplace adorned by a trophy
bison head. ~ 310-510-0143. **National Air,** also called **Catalina
Vegas Airlines,** services the airport from the mainland. ~ 800-
339-0359.

Another means of transportation to Catalina is **Island Express,** a helicopter service from Long Beach and San Pedro. They
also offer around-the-island tours. ~ 310-510-2525; www.island
express.com.

Flights to and from **Burbank-Glendale-Pasadena Airport** are
currently provided by Alaska Airlines, America West Airlines,
American Airlines, Skywest Airlines, Southwest Airlines, United
Airlines, and United Shuttle. ~ 818-840-8847.

Taxis, limousines, and buses line up to transport passengers from LAX and Burbank. **SuperShuttle** travels between hotels, businesses, and residences to both Burbank and Los Angeles airports. ~ 818-556-6600.

BUS

Greyhound Bus Lines (800-231-2222) has service to the Los Angeles area from all around the country. The main L.A. terminal is at 1716 East 7th Street (213-629-8401). Other stations are in Hollywood at 1715 North Cahuenga Boulevard (323-466-6381); Pasadena at 645 East Walnut Street (626-792-5116); Glendale at 400 West Cerritos Avenue (818-244-7295); and North Hollywood at 11239 Magnolia Boulevard (818-761-5119). The Long Beach terminal is at 1498 Long Beach Boulevard (562-218-3011).

TRAIN

Amtrak will carry you into Los Angeles via the "Coast Starlight" from the North, the "San Diegan" from San Diego, the "Southwest Chief" from Chicago, and the "Sunset Limited" from New Orleans. The L.A. terminal, Union Station, is at 800 North Alameda Street. There are also stations in Pasadena at 150 South Los Robles Avenue and Glendale at 400 West Cerritos Avenue. ~ 800-872-7245.

BOAT

Several companies provide regular transportation to Catalina by boat. The island is just 22 miles across the sea, but it's still necessary to make advance reservations. **Catalina Express** has service to Avalon and Two Harbors from the Catalina Terminal in San Pedro; service to Avalon leaves from Long Beach next to the *Queen Mary*. ~ 310-519-1212. **Catalina Passenger Service** makes daily trips to Catalina from Orange County. ~ 400 Main Street, Newport Beach; 949-673-5245.

CAR RENTALS

Having a car in Los Angeles is practically a must. Distances are great and public transportation leaves much to be desired. As you can imagine, it's not difficult to find a car rental agency. The challenge is to find the best deal. Be sure to request a mileage-free rental, or one with at least some free mileage. One thing is certain in the Los Angeles area, you'll be racking up mileage on the odometer.

If you arrive by air, consider renting a car at the airport. These cost a little more but eliminate the hassles of getting to the rental agency.

Looking for a car at Los Angeles International Airport will bring you to **Avis Rent A Car** (800-331-1212), **Budget Rent A Car** (800-527-0700), **Hertz Rent A Car** (800-654-3131), or **National Car Rental** (800-227-7368).

Agencies providing free airport pick-up service include **Enterprise Rent A Car** (800-736-8222) and **Thrifty Car Rental** (800-367-2277).

Avis Rent A Car (800-331-1212), **Budget Rent A Car** (800-527-0700), **Enterprise Rent A Car** (800-325-8007), **Hertz Rent A Car** (800-654-3131), and **National Car Rental** (800-227-7368) are located at, or within shuttle distance of, the Long Beach Airport.

To save even more money, try agencies that rent used cars. In the Long Beach area try **Robin Hood Rent A Car.** ~ 310-518-2292, 800-743-2992. Among the used car rentals in the greater L.A. area are **Rent A Wreck** (800-535-1391) and **G & R Rent A Car** (310-478-4208).

In Catalina, golf carts are the only vehicles permitted for sightseeing in Avalon. Check with **Catalina Auto and Bike Rental.** ~ 301 Crescent Avenue; 310-510-0111. **Island Rentals** is another option. ~ 125 Pebbly Beach Road; 310-510-1456. For further information on vehicle rentals on Catalina see Chapter Seven.

> In the 1930s it took 19 hours to fly from New York to L.A., including four stops to refuel the plane.

At the Burbank airport several companies rent autos: **Avis Rent A Car** (800-331-1212), **Enterprise Rent A Car** (800-736-8222), **Hertz Rent A Car** (800-654-3131), and **National Car Rental** (800-227-7368). **American Eagle Car and Truck Rental** (818-840-8816) offers free pick-up service from the airport.

If there was ever a place to rent a limousine, Los Angeles is it. Dozens of companies specialize in "elegant service for elegant people." Check the Yellow Pages for listings.

PUBLIC TRANSIT

If you arrive in Los Angeles without a car, believe it or not you can still get around. **Los Angeles County Metropolitan Transportation Authority,** or MTA, has over 200 bus routes covering more than 2200 square miles. "Rapid" transit may be a misnomer, but buses do get you where you want to go. Seven customer service centers are located throughout Los Angeles; call for the nearest location. Disabled riders can call a hotline for information, 800-621-7828 (this number is functional only within the designated area). ~ 213-626-4455; www.mta.net.

The **Metro Red Line** runs between Downtown (from the Union Station rail passenger terminal) and the MacArthur Park area in seven minutes; it also extends along Wilshire Boulevard and into Hollywood and the San Fernando Valley. The **Metro Gold Line** runs from Union Station to Pasadena. The **Metro Blue Line** operates daily between Downtown and Long Beach. The **Metro Green Line** trains travel from Norwalk and Redondo Beach to Los Angeles International Airport.

When using the bus for an extended period of time, you can save money by purchasing an MTA Day, Weekly, Semi-Monthly, or Monthly Pass. The EZ Transit pass, good for a month, will get you on any Metro Bus or Metro Rail line. Passes are available at any ticket machine or Metro Customer Center.

For traveling around downtown Los Angeles or Westwood, the DASH shuttle service is available Monday through Saturday (except holidays). ~ 213-626-4455.

In Santa Monica, call the **Big Blue Bus**, which hits such destinations as the LAX and downtown L.A. ~ Santa Monica Municipal Bus Lines, 612 Colorado Avenue; 310-451-5444; www.big bluebus.com.

In Catalina, **Catalina Safari Bus** provides daily buses from Avalon to Two Harbors and all campgrounds. This shuttle service also takes passengers from Avalon to the Airport in the Sky. ~ 310-510-2800, 800-785-8425.

Long Beach Transit transports riders throughout the Long Beach area. Among the services is the Tour of the Art bus, which carries visitors between major points of interest. ~ 1963 East Anaheim, Long Beach; 562-591-2301; www.lbtransit.com.

TAXIS   Several cab companies serve Los Angeles International Airport, including **United Independent Taxi** (323-934-6700) and **Yellow Cab** (213-627-7000).

In Santa Monica, call **Taxi Taxi**. ~ 310-828-2233. In Catalina you'll find the **Catalina Cab Company**. ~ 310-510-0025. **Manhattan Beach Yellow Cab** provides service in the South Bay. ~ 310-545-7520. **Long Beach Yellow Cab** provides taxi service in Long Beach. ~ 562-435-6111.

From Burbank Airport, **Taxi Services** provides taxi service. ~ 818-843-8500, 818-558-3000.

TWO

Downtown

Contrary to the opinion of Los Angeles bashers, the city does indeed possess a center. Ever since the town was settled in 1781, the focus of the community has been near Olvera Street and what is now the Civic Center, along the Los Angeles River. Though today the river is usually no more than a trickle, and the Downtown area stretches for more than 60 blocks, the scene of Los Angeles' beginnings remains an integral part of the city center.

At the turn of the 20th century, the elite Bunker Hill section of Downtown was full of Victorian houses and elegant hotels. Now it is the city's cultural center. It wasn't transformed overnight, though. Over the years the formerly tony neighborhood deteriorated into a slum, until in the 1960s the area was leveled, leaving dirt, weeds, and seemingly endless parking lots. Things changed in the 1980s, when towering glass and steel high-rises started shooting up here and in the adjoining Financial District, and suddenly Los Angeles had a skyline. Today these lofty skyscrapers share space with innovative structures for the visual and performing arts, the most recent addition being the Walt Disney Concert Hall with its softly curving architecture. As the city center spreads east, architecturally important buildings and upscale restaurants are replaced by streetside pizza joints and bargain clothing stores, with Downtown becoming more rundown and shabbier as it works its way to the railroad tracks.

A veritable buzz of activity during the work week, when over 200,000 commuters flood into the area, in past years Downtown was like a ghost town after the workers and theater goers went home. Now, thanks to the introduction of luxury apartment buildings, condos, and lofts, more affluent Angelinos are moving in, adding an air of gentrification and livening up the city late at night and on the weekends.

Not surprisingly, Downtown has become a melting pot of cultures. Mexico collides with Asia in the northern section of the city center. Olvera Street, with its historic adobe, shaded square, and colorful shopping street, looks more like a Mexican village than part of an urban metropolis. Walk a bit farther and suddenly signs are written in Chinese characters instead of Spanish, and curio shops sell tea pots and mahjong tiles rather than tortilla makers and sombreros. As Chinatown tumbles into Little Tokyo, sushi replaces dim sum as the number-one food choice.

Many suburban Angelinos hardly ever visit Downtown and that's a shame, because there's plenty to recommend it. Where else can you eat a French dip sandwich at the place where they originated, buy diamond earrings wholesale, or listen to a free concert on a 6019-pipe organ?

To help you navigate around the Downtown area, I've divided the district into several sections: Olvera Street, Chinatown, the Civic Center, Central Downtown (which includes the financial district), and Little Tokyo. In exploring each neighborhood, remember that the DASH shuttle, a purple-striped minibus, serves most of Downtown for just 25 cents a ride. Downtown is also served by the Metro Red Line, Los Angeles' first subway. Starting at Union Station, the line that serves the Downtown area runs between Union Station and MacArthur Park, at the corner of Wilshire and Alvarado boulevards.

▼▼▼▼▼▼▼▼▼▼▼

Olvera Street

Olvera Street is commonly, but erroneously, called the birthplace of Los Angeles. The actual 1781 founding site was moved to its present Olvera Street location after a flood in 1815. Olvera Street is, however, the oldest surviving section of the city, featuring 27 historic buildings, some dating from the early 19th century. It's about as close to a Mexican village as you can get without actually crossing the border. Stalls sell all sorts of Mexican-made goodies, from *huaraches* (Mexican sandals) to *piñatas*. Restaurants specialize in spicy Mexican dishes, and tortillas are made by hand.

The area is not just populated by hoards of tourists, however; Latino families worship and celebrate weddings and baptisms at the Old Plaza Church and join in Hispanic festivals that take place in the central square.

SIGHTS

Start your visit to Olvera Street at the **visitors center**, which provides maps, brochures, and walking tours. It's located in one of the pueblo's vintage buildings, an 1887 brick-faced Victorian called the Sepulveda House. Walking tours are offered Tuesday through Saturday mornings; two-hour bus tours of historic Los

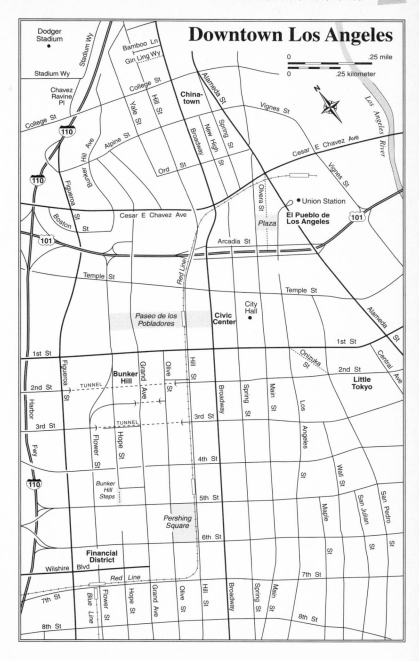

Downtown Los Angeles

Dodger Stadium

Stadium Wy

Bamboo Ln

Gin Ling Wy

Stadium Wy

Chavez Ravine Pl

College St

College St

110

Alameda St

China-town

Hill St

Yale St

Bunker Hill Ave

Alpine St

Figueroa St

Ord St

Broadway

New High St

Spring St

Ord St

Boston St

Cesar E Chavez Ave

101

Vignes St

Cesar E Chavez Ave

Vignes St

Los Angeles River

Union Station

Olvera St

El Pueblo de Los Angeles

Plaza

101

Arcadia St

Red Line

Temple St

Temple St

Paseo de los Pobladores

Civic Center

City Hall

Alameda St

1st St

1st St

1st St

Figueroa St

Harbor Fwy

2nd St

TUNNEL

Bunker Hill

Grand Ave

Olive St

Hill St

Onizuka St

2nd St

Central Ave

Little Tokyo

3rd St

TUNNEL

3rd St

Flower St

Hope St

Broadway

Spring St

Main St

Los Angeles St

Wall St

4th St

110

Bunker Hill Steps

5th St

San Julian St

San Pedro St

Pershing Square

6th St

Maple St

Financial District

Wilshire Blvd

Red Line

7th St

7th St

Blue Line

Flower St

Hope St

Grand Ave

Olive St

Hill St

Broadway

Spring St

Main St

8th St

8th St

8th St

0   .25 mile

0   .25 kilometer

N

Angeles begin here on the third Wednesday of every month. Closed Sunday. ~ 622 North Main Street; 213-628-1274, fax 213-485-8238.

Heart of hearts is the **Plaza**, a tree-shaded courtyard adorned with statues and highlighted by a wrought-iron bandstand. A colorful gathering place, it's a frequent site for fiestas and open-air concerts. ~ North Main and Los Angeles streets.

Anchoring one corner of the plaza is **Firehouse No. 1**, Los Angeles' original fire station. Built in 1884, the brick structure served the fire department for little more than a decade, after which it became a saloon, boarding house, and store. Today it's a miniature museum filled with horse-drawn fire wagons, old-time helmets, and an ample inventory of memories. ~ 134 Paseo de la Plaza.

The plaza's most prestigious building, **Pico House** was built in 1870 by Pío Pico, the last Mexican governor of California. Italianate in style, it represented the grandest hotel of its era. Today it houses art and historical exhibits celebrating Latino culture. ~ Paseo de la Plaza and North Main Street.

Old Plaza Church, first dedicated as a church in 1822, also faces the square. The city's oldest Catholic church, it is unassuming from the outside but displays an interior that is a study in wrought iron and gold leaf. Murals cover the ceiling of the diminutive chapel and a collection of religious canvases adorns the altar. ~ 535 North Main Street.

Mexicans with more worldly matters in mind gather in large crowds outside the **Biscailuz Building**, a whitewashed structure decorated with brightly hued murals by Leo Politi, El Pueblo's resident artist for over 30 years. It serves as the main office for El Pueblo de Los Angeles. ~ 125 Paseo de la Plaza, northeast corner of the plaza.

For the full flavor of Spanish California, wander down **Olvera Street**. Lined with *puestos* (stands) selling Mexican handicrafts, it provides a window into Mexican culture. The brick-paved alleyway is also one of the West's first pedestrian shopping malls.

Among the antique buildings bordering this narrow corridor is the **Ávila Adobe**, a classic mud-brick house constructed around 1818. The oldest house in Los Angeles, it has undergone numerous incarnations, serving as a private residence, boarding house, and restaurant and surviving several earthquakes. Today it's a museum, fully restored and filled with period pieces.

A nearby historical marker points out the vital water source for early Los Angeles. **La Zanja Madre,** the mother ditch, channeled the precious waters of the Los Angeles River to the fledgling community for more than a century.

Located just off the plaza is **Masonic Hall,** an 1858 building that houses a museum of Masonic Order memorabilia. With wrought-iron balcony and ornate facade it follows an Italianate design. ~ 416½ North Main Street. Even more elaborate, though of later vintage, the neighboring **Merced Theatre** was constructed in 1870 and represents the city's first theatrical center. It is currently under repair.

Union Station, just across the street from Ávila Adobe, is one of the country's great train depots, and has been a Los Angeles landmark since 1939. With a Spanish-Mexican exterior, the sta-

Olvera Street & Chinatown

tion is a cavernous structure boasting marble floors, a beam ceiling 52 feet high, arched corridors, and walls of inlaid tile. Embodying the romance and promise of travel, it is a destination with a distinct identity, a point of departure for the far fringes of the imagination. ~ 800 North Alameda Street.

DINING   Olvera Street, where the Spanish originally located the pueblo of Los Angeles, is still a prime place for Mexican food. Tiny **taco stands** line this brick-paved alley. Little more than open-air kitchens, they dispense fresh Mexican dishes at budget prices. You'll also find bakeries and candy stands, where old Mexican ladies sell *churros* (Mexican donuts) and candied squash. BUDGET.

La Golondrina provides something more formal. Set in the historic Pelanconi House, an 1850s-era home built of fired brick, it features an open-air patio and a dining room with stone fireplace and *viga* ceiling. The bill of fare includes a standard selection of tacos, tostadas, and enchiladas as well as specialties such as fajitas and crab-meat enchiladas. ~ 17 West Olvera Street; 213-628-4349, fax 213-687-0800. MODERATE.

Across from Union Station, midway between Olvera Street and Chinatown, stands one of the city's most famous cafeterias.

HIDDEN ▶ **Philippe The Original** has been around since 1908, serving pork, beef, turkey, and lamb sandwiches in a French-dip style. With sawdust on the floors and memories tacked to the walls, this antique eatery still serves ten-cent cups of coffee. Open for breakfast, lunch, and dinner. ~ 1001 North Alameda Street; 213-628-3781, fax 213-628-1812; www.philippes.com, e-mail philippe@philippes.com. BUDGET.

THE LAST OF THE BUNCH

Take a short drive up North Main Street and discover **San Antonio Winery**, the last of a disappearing breed. Years ago vineyards dotted the San Gabriel foothills, but Los Angeles' phenomenal urbanization steadily displaced them. Somehow this family-operated facility remained, situated surprisingly close to the center of the city. Today second- and third-generation members of the Riboli clan lead tasting tours through the vintage 1917 building. ~ 737 Lamar Street; 323-223-1401, fax 323-221-7261; www.sanantoniowinery.com, e-mail wineshop@sanantonio winery.com.

Historic **Olvera Street**, the site of Los Angeles' original pueblo, is the setting for a traditional Mexican marketplace. Its brick-paved walkways are lined with shops and stalls selling Mexican artworks and handicrafts. **Casa de Sousa** sells Mexican Indian folk art and Ecuadorean clothing, and also operates as a coffee house. Stroll the plaza, where restaurants serve homemade *maza* (cornmeal) tortillas, fresh tropical fruits, and tempting *nopales* (fresh diced cactus candies). ~ 19 West Olvera Street; 213-626-7076; e-mail casadesouza@hotmail.com.

SHOPPING

Mariachi music and margaritas draw Angelenos and outlanders alike to **La Golondrina**. You can sit by the fireplace or out on the patio of this historic adobe building. ~ 17 Olvera Street; 213-628-4349.

NIGHTLIFE

Chinese immigrants first arrived in Los Angeles in 1852. By about 1900, the Chinese community, located about a mile south of today's Chinatown, numbered 3000. When the original Chinatown was torn down during the 1930s to build Union Station, the community moved in increasing numbers to modern-day Chinatown, officially acknowledged in 1938 with the dedication of the central plaza.

▼ ▼ ▼ ▼ ▼ ▼ ▼ ▼ ▼ ▼ ▼
Chinatown

Despite being developed fairly recently, Chinatown has plenty of ambiance and character. Many of the buildings are built in Chinese style with curved roof lines, brightly colored accents, and traditional ornamentation. Shops are stuffed to bursting with Chinese goods and souvenirs, from pointed straw hats to fortune-telling sticks. Chinese medicines of all kinds can be had at local pharmacies and herb shops, while live poultry and fish can be purchased at local specialty shops.

Sunday morning sees scores of Angelinos lined up outside Chinatown's dim sum restaurants. Once inside (and this can take a while), diners are assailed by a cacophony of chatter and clatter as rolling carts loaded with an astounding assortment of dumplings and "teacakes" are paraded in front of hungry customers.

For an authentic view, stroll the **600 block of North Spring Street** past the herb shops and fresh fish stores. Here local residents buy goat meat and fresh produce and choose from among the racks of roast ducks that hang forlornly in store windows.

SIGHTS

HIDDEN ►   Don't miss **Kong Chow Benevolent Association and Temple**, a tiny chapel tucked away on the second floor of an unassuming building. Crowded with elderly Chinese, the place is heavy with incense and handwoven tapestries. Gilded altars and bas-relief figures add a touch of the exotic. Closed Monday. ~ 931 North Broadway; 213-626-1955.

The commercial heart of the district lies along Broadway and Hill Street, with stores lining both boulevards for several blocks. Connecting these two thoroughfares is **Central Plaza** (Gin Ling Way), a two-block-long pedestrian mall. Traditional gates with swirling outlines mark the entranceways to this enclave. Figures of animals and ceremonial fish adorn the buildings and dragons breathe fire from the rooftops.

LODGING   An 80-room establishment, the **Metro Plaza Hotel** is close to Union Station and across the street from the historic Olvera Street complex. This four-story hostelry offers rooms and suites decorated in a contemporary style. Downstairs you'll find a small lobby with two sitting rooms. ~ 711 North Main Street; 213-680-0200, 800-223-2223; www.metroplazahotel.com, e-mail res@metroplazahotel.com. MODERATE.

DINING   **Chinese Friends Restaurant** is a postage-stamp eatery with plastic chairs, Chinese-style paintings of birds and flowers. In addition to the standard selection of shrimp, pork, and vegetable dishes they offer several unusual specials such as hot-and-sour chicken. There's little else to note except one salient point: the place is inevitably crowded with Chinese. Closed Tuesday. ~ 984 North Broadway; 213-626-1837. BUDGET TO MODERATE.

One of Chinatown's dim sum dining rooms, **Ocean Seafood** is a voluminous second-floor establishment. The dim sum service, in which you choose finger foods from passing carts, is only during lunch. At dinner there's a comprehensive Cantonese menu. With its fragile lamps and molded woodwork, Ocean Seafood has established a solid reputation for good food in sumptuous surroundings. No dinner. ~ 747 North Broadway; 213-687-3088, fax 213-687-8549. MODERATE.

HIDDEN ►   It just figures that **Chow Fun** noodle house would be a step above the norm, considering that it is owned by the heirs to a nationally known noodle company. Specialties such as flaky scallion pancakes and ground pork-chive crêpes are served in a mock Chinese village setting, complete with tile roofs and rustic furniture. ~ 686 North Spring Street; 213 626-1238. BUDGET.

SHOPPING

The heart of Chinatown, where local Chinese shop at food emporiums, markets, and cookware stores, rests along **North Spring Street.**

Ornate Chinese-style roofs in reds and greens adorn **Chinatown Plaza,** the focal point of Chinatown. Along this promenade, well-stocked gift shops offer everything from imported trinkets to very fine, very ancient antiques and artworks. ~ 900 block of North Broadway.

On Thursday from 3 to 7 p.m., the Chinatown Farmer's Market sells a wide assortment of exotic Asian goods. ~ 727 North Hill Street.

Walk through the Plaza, then cross Hill Street, and you'll discover a treasure trove of antique stores dotting Chung King Road. **Fong's** carries a fine array of Chinese antique pieces. Closed Monday. ~ 943 Chung King Road; 213-626-5904. For beautiful screens and antique teapots, check out **The Jade Tree.** ~ 957 Chung King Road; 213-624-3521.

The smell alone will lure you into the **Phoenix Bakery.** A Chinatown institution since 1938, this Asian-style bakery prepares whimsical confections that seem inevitably to attract a long line to its door. ~ 969 North Broadway; 213-628-4642.

Mandarin Plaza is a "modern" pedestrian mall, that houses **Asian Craft Imports** (213-626-5386), an imaginative shop filled with a large selection of import gift items. ~ 970 North Broadway.

Civic Center

Downtown's toniest area, Civic Center is an enclave of towering highrises, stately city buildings, and impressive entertainment complexes. This is where high-powered politicians, Armani-suited business executives, and Westside theater goers rub elbows at some of the city's best restaurants and fanciest hotels. L.A.'s city center may be small by comparison, but it is as close to the big city feel of New York or Chicago as you're likely to find in what is otherwise a metropolis that has spread out, not up.

SIGHTS

The centerpiece of the area is **City Hall,** a vintage 1928 building. Rendered famous by the old *Dragnet* television show, this pyramid-topped edifice is also a frequent backdrop in many contemporary movies. The tile-and-marble rotunda on the third floor is a study in governmental architecture. But the most impressive feature is the **observation deck** on the 27th floor, from which you can enjoy a 360-degree view of Los Angeles' smog banks. ~ 200 North Spring Street; 213-978-1995; www.lacity.org.

Those who report on City Hall reside across the street at the **Los Angeles Times Building**. One of the nation's largest and finest newspapers, the *Times* sits in a classic 1935 moderne-style building to which latter day architects, in a fit of ego and insanity, added a glass box monstrosity that appears to be devouring the original. The older structure, housing the newspaper, is open to guided tours; the glass accretion contains corporate offices. Call ahead for times. Closed Saturday and Sunday. ~ 145 South Spring Street; 213-237-3178; www.latimes.com.

Completed in 2002, the controversial contemporary design of **Cathedral of Our Lady of Angels** is in striking contrast to the traditional 1876-vintage cathedral that it replaced. Built of concrete with virtually no right angles, and painted adobe yellow, only the 50-foot cross on the front gives a clue as to its use. On Wednesdays at 12:45 p.m., free recitals are offered on the 42-ton, 6019-pipe organ. ~ 555 West Temple Street; 213-680-5200; www.olacathedral.org.

The **Performing Arts Center of Los Angeles**, locally known as the Music Center, is one of the three largest performing-arts centers in the nation and welcomes more than 1.3 million people a year to its performances. Gathered into one stunningly designed complex are the **Dorothy Chandler Pavilion**, a marble-and-black-glass music hall that hosts the opera and symphony; the **Mark Taper Forum**, a world-renowned theater that presents contemporary and experimental drama; and the **Ahmanson Theatre**, a 2000-seat auditorium where touring Broadway plays are staged. Not to be outdone, the visual arts are represented by a pulsating fountain with more than 100 rhythmically timed streams. Guided tours are available. ~ 135 North Grand Avenue, between 1st and Temple streets; 213-972-7211; www.musiccenter.org, e-mail general@musiccenter.org.

Designed by architect extraordinaire Frank Gehry, the latest entertainment venue to hit the Downtown area is the much talked about **Walt Disney Concert Hall**. While the curving stainless-steel structure looks more like a piece of sculpture than the home of the Los Angeles Philharmonic, don't be fooled—the acoustics are state of the art. The 3.6-acre complex's main auditorium is a 2265-seat, wood-paneled space where the audience surrounds the orchestra platform, creating a visually intimate and musically exciting experience. Outside, stairs curl around the building's curves, which open out into secluded garden areas shadowed by neighboring high-rise office buildings, a great place for a picnic lunch on a sunny day. ~ 111 South Grand Avenue; 323-850-2000; wdch.laphil.com.

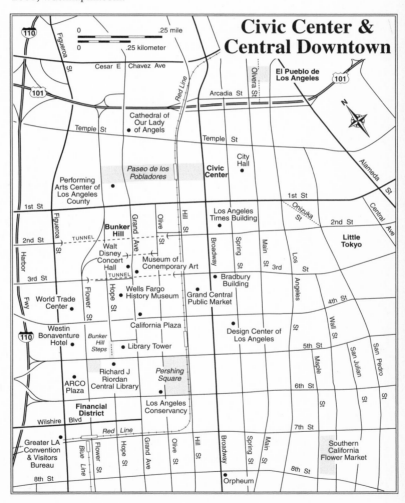

The **Museum of Contemporary Art**, affectionately dubbed "the MOCA," is an ultramodern showplace designed by Japanese architect Arata Isozaki. It's an exotic mix of red sandstone and pyramidal skylights with a sunken courtyard. The galleries consist of expansive open spaces displaying a variety of traveling exhibits and the works of Mark Rothko, Robert Rauschenberg, Jackson Pollock, and others. Closed Tuesday and Wednesday. Admission. ~ 250 South Grand Avenue; 213-626-6222, fax 213-620-8674; www.moca.org.

HIDDEN ► The **Water Court at California Plaza** is a pleasant oasis amid the towers of glass and steel. Surrounded by shops and restaurants, this space centers around the "Water Feature," an elaborate combination of water jets and cascades that converts to a performance space during the summer months. ~ 350 South Grand Avenue; 213-687-2190.

At the beginning of the 20th century, Bunker Hill was a residential neighborhood of Victorian homes and residential hotels.

HIDDEN ► A funicular, or cable, railway called **Angels Flight** connected Bunker Hill with the commercial district that lay below on 3rd and Hill streets. For a quarter, you can ride the "world's shortest railway" up or down the steep incline between Hill and Olive streets. The ride may last less than a minute, but it's a long reach back into Los Angeles history. Temporarily closed for renovations; call ahead for availability. ~ Water Court at California Plaza, and Hill Street at 4th Street; 213-626-1901.

One of the focal points of Bunker Hill is the city's tallest

HIDDEN ► building, **Library Tower** (formerly known as First Interstate World Center), which rises 74 stories. For some reason, the developers did not include an observation deck, so unless you've got business in the tower, the lobby is about as far as you'll get. But that's worth a peek. ~ 633 West 5th Street.

sights

AUTHOR FAVORITE

Grand Performances at California Plaza offers a full summer schedule (June through October) of free outdoor entertainment in the Water Court. You can see everything from solo artists in dance, music, and theater to fully staged opera, Shakespeare, and hula performances. This venue is one of L.A.'s most exciting performance spaces, featuring international artists. ~ 350 South Grand Avenue; 213-687-2190; www.grandperformances.org.

Next door to the Library Tower are the bottom of **Bunker Hill Steps**. This monumental stairway leads from 5th Street to Hope Street. Water from a fountain at the top of the stairs cascades down a narrow channel to a small pool at the foot of the steps. Terrace landings relieve the climb, as do food and beverage kiosks along the way.

At the top of the steps, walk to the corner of Hope and 4th streets to the sleek **Stuart M. Ketchum** YMCA and take a stroll ◀ HIDDEN through the sculpture courtyard wrapped around three sides of the modern building. On a clear day the view to the northeast, of the San Gabriel Mountains, is stunning. ~ 401 South Hope Street.

If you survive the Bunker Hill Steps (or even if you opt for the escalators), cross 4th Street to the **Wells Fargo History Museum**, where you can view displays re-creating more than a century of Western history. Closed weekends. ~ 333 South Grand Avenue; 213-253-7166, fax 213-680-2269; www.wellsfargohistory.com.

The **World Trade Center**, another architectural extravaganza, looms nearby. Closed weekends. ~ 350 South Figueroa Street.

At ARCO **Plaza**, a twin-tower, 52-story behemoth, you'll encounter the MTA (Metropolitan Transportation Authority, Level C), where you can obtain route maps of the city's largest transportation agency. ~ Flower Street between 5th and 6th streets; 213-626-4455; www.mta.net.

Amid all these elite and expensive office buildings, one structure stands forth like a visitor from the future. Its five mirror-glass cylinders resembling a space station with legs, the **Westin Bonaventure Hotel** is easily the city's most imaginative skyscraper. Because of its unique design, together with an interior of reflecting pools and bubble elevators, the 1976 building is a favorite backdrop for sci-fi movies. ~ 404 South Figueroa Street; 213-624-1000, fax 213-612-4800; www.westin.com.

Across the street from this symbol of tomorrow stands an emblem of the past. The **Richard J. Riordan Central Library**, built in the 1920s, incorporates Egyptian, Roman, and Byzantine elements into a beaux-arts design. The most striking feature of all is the pyramid tower inlaid with colorful tile patterns. In 1986, fire gutted the interior and the city closed the library for repairs—and expansion. Seven years later, it reopened its doors, doubling the floor space with the addition of a new wing and a one-and-a-half-acre garden atop the parking garage—an oasis of greenery replete with five fountains. It is now the third largest central library in the nation. ~ 630 West 5th Street; 213-228-7000; www.lapl.org, e-mail phoneref@lapl.org.

LODGING What can you say about a place that became a landmark as soon as it was built? To call the **Westin Bonaventure Hotel** ultramodern would belittle the structure. "Post Future" is a more appropriate tag. Its dark glass silos rise 35 stories from the street like a way station on the road to the 21st century. Within are five levels of shops, 1354 rooms, more than 15 restaurants, and a revolving cocktail lounge. The atrium lobby features reflecting pools, glass-shaft elevators, and lattice skylights. Considering all this, the guest rooms seem almost an afterthought; because of the building's configuration they are small and pie-shaped but offer good views of the surrounding financial district. ~ 404 South Figueroa Street; 213-624-1000, 800-228-3000, fax 213-612-4800; www.westin.com. ULTRA-DELUXE.

The past rests safely ensconced a few blocks distant at **The Millennium Biltmore Hotel**. Here the glamour and elegance of the Roaring '20s endure in a grand lobby replete with stately pilasters and floor-to-ceiling mirrors. A classic in the tradition of grande-dame hotels, the Biltmore conveys an Old World ambience with hand-oiled wood panels, frescoes, and ornamental molding. Its gourmet restaurants and sumptuous lounges reflect the rich Spanish–Italian Renaissance style that makes this 683-room hostelry a kind of museum for overnight guests. The bedrooms are moderately sized, adorned with contemporary artworks and provided with traditional French furniture. Among the other amenities is an elegant health club with swimming pool, jacuzzi, and sauna. ~ 506 South Grand Avenue; 213-612-1575, 800-245-8673, fax 213-612-1545; www.thebiltmore.com. ULTRA-DELUXE.

Located downtown is the European-style **Hilton Checkers Hotel**. This 188-room luxury hostelry originally opened in 1927 as the Mayflower Hotel. Its impressive modeled art stone facade of two carved ships, the *Mayflower* and the *Santa Maria*, made it one of the most strikingly beautiful buildings of its time. A massive renovation has restored it beyond its original elegance into one of the swankier hotels in town. Posh rooms come complete with original artwork, marble bathrooms, and three telephones. A gourmet restaurant, comfortable lounge, library, and rooftop spa make Checkers well worth the price tag. ~ 535 South Grand Avenue; 213-624-0000, 800-423-5798, fax 213-626-9906; www. hiltoncheckers.com. ULTRA-DELUXE.

The tasteful and contemporary 17-story **Omni Los Angeles Hotel at California Plaza,** is perched on Bunker Hill next to California Plaza's one-and-a-half-acre Water Court (check out the dancing waters). Sunlight streams through the lobby's glass walls, creating a bright, open atmosphere. The 443 guest rooms are large, comfortably furnished, and decorated in Asian and neo-classical themes. Guests can also enjoy the health club that has a sauna, hot tub, and an outdoor swimming pool. ~ 251 South Olive Street; 213-617-3300, 800-843-6664, fax 213-617-3399; www. omnihotels.com. ULTRA-DELUXE.

DINING

Completely subterranean, **Casey's Bar and Grill** is one of those marvelous old dining lounges with dark paneling, trophy cases, a 50-foot mahogany bar and graying photographs. One room displays antique song sheets, another is covered with sports photos; my personal favorite is the back room, where you can request a private booth with curtain. Lunch consists of hamburgers, sandwiches, and entrées such as Dublin broil (steak with mushrooms, spinach, and mashed potatoes). For dinner there are pasta dishes, fish and chips, barbecued ribs and crab-stuffed salmon. Bottoms up! Closed Saturday during the day and Sunday. ~ 613 South Grand Avenue; 213-629-2353, fax 213-629-5922. MODERATE.

You might recognize Casey's Bar and Grill from episodes of "Murder, She Wrote" or the movie *Mulholland Falls.*

The best of France and California meet in **Patina**—beautiful, intimate, expensive, and worth it. Housed in the Walt Disney Concert Hall, its specialties include shrimp with mashed potatoes and potato truffle chips and peppered tournedos of tuna with Chinese vegetables and ponzu sauce. Try the chocolate plate for dessert. Dinner is served daily; lunch is served on Friday only. ~ 111 South Grand Avenue; 213-972-3331; www.patinagroup.com, e-mail patina@patinagroup.com. DELUXE TO ULTRA-DELUXE.

Part of the ever-growing dynasty of California French bistros and cafés presided over by the inventive Joachim and Christine Splichal (of Patina fame) are Cafe Pinot and Patinette at MOCA. **Cafe Pinot,** set next to Macguire Gardens behind the Central Library, is a downtown oasis of fine bistro-style dining and sophistication. You can't go wrong with the rôti chicken and Pinot fries, especially sitting in the garden. No lunch on weekends. ~ 700 West 5th Street; 213-239-6500, fax 213-239-6514; www.patinagroup.com. ULTRA-DELUXE.

Tucked below street level in the courtyard of MOCA is **Patinette**, a stylish little eatery where you step up to the counter, order a green-bean salad with artichokes, tomatoes, and Black Forest ham, or smoked turkey on dark wheat bread, then take a seat outside under the umbrellas. It's a great place to stop for a cappuccino or espresso, or a glass of wine. Lunch only, but open until 8 p.m. on Thursday. Closed Monday. ~ 250 South Grand Avenue; 213-626-1178, fax 213-626-0773. BUDGET TO MODERATE.

Food Network devotees will recognize Mary Sue Milliken and Susan Feniger as the "Too Hot Tamales." Besides hosting a cooking show and writing cookbooks, they create restaurants. Their latest venture, **Ciudad**, draws its culinary inspiration from Latin countries worldwide. Dishes ranging from Argentine empanadas to Brazilian fish stew cooked in coconut-lime broth are served in a retro-1950s setting with Latin motif murals. No lunch Saturday or Sunday. ~ 445 South Figueroa Street; 213-486-5171, fax 213-486-5172 . MODERATE TO DELUXE.

Elegance 24 hours a day? In a restaurant on wheels? Somehow all-night restaurants conjure visions of truck-stop dives, but at **Pacific Dining Car** 'round-the-clock service is provided in dark wood surroundings. Modeled after an old-style railroad dining car, with plush booths and outsized plate-glass windows, this destination has been a Los Angeles landmark since 1921. The cuisine is well-heeled all-American: breakfast includes eggs Benedict and eggs Sardou, and the dinner menu features lobster and some of the best steaks in the city. The Dining Car offers a complimentary shuttle to the Performing Arts Center and the Staples Center. ~ 1310 West 6th Street; 213-483-6000, fax 213-483-4545; www.pacificdiningcar.com, e-mail pdc@pacificdiningcar.com. ULTRA-DELUXE.

SHOPPING   At the **Atlantic Richfield Shopping Center** 55 shops and restaurants create one of the largest subterranean shopping centers in the country. ~ ARCO Plaza, 5th and Flower streets.

In a space age linkup, this mall connects via glass footbridge with the **Westin Bonaventure Shopping Gallery**, where numerous

The Sporting Life

Angelenos have always been passionate about their local teams. Ironically, in keeping with L.A.'s history for luring newcomers, few of its professional sporting teams are native-born: the Dodgers, for instance, arrived in 1958 via Brooklyn, and the Lakers moved from Minneapolis in 1960. Even the Rams, who transplanted to St. Louis in the 1990s, originally hailed from Cleveland in 1946. Regardless of their adopted team's origins, the L.A. fans were supportive, and games well-attended. Beginning in the 1920s, sporting events in Los Angeles moved from local parks into stadiums specifically built for them. And though professional sports teams came and went, most only played a season or two, until 1946 when the Rams football team moved to Los Angeles where they stayed for almost 50 years.

The first great Los Angeles sports venue, the **Rose Bowl**, was built in Pasadena in 1922. Designed to host the New Year's Day football match that followed the Tournament of Roses, it was officially dedicated on January 1, 1923. ~ 1001 Rose Bowl Drive, Pasadena; 626-577-3100; www.rosebowl stadium.com.

In 1923, the **Los Angeles Memorial Coliseum** at Exposition Park opened. It was originally built as a football stadium, hosting college games as well as being the home of the Rams, Chargers, and Raiders. From 1958–61, it doubled as a baseball stadium for the Dodgers and the Lakers sunk baskets here from 1960–68. This State and Federal Historic Landmark also hosted two Olympic Games, one World Series, and two Super Bowls. ~ 3911 South Figueroa Street; www.lacoliseum.com.

In 1962, the Dodgers finally got their own stadium. Legendary players such as Don Drysdale and Sandy Koufax ran the bases at **Dodger Stadium**, winning both the 1963 and 1965 World Series. Between 1974 and 1988, the Dodgers were the team to beat, with stars like Don Sutton and Fernando Valenzuela. ~ 1000 Elysian Park Avenue; 323-224-1448; www.dodgers.com.

Needing somewhere to showcase his Los Angeles Kings hockey team, Jack Kent Cooke built **The Forum** in 1967. In 1968, the Lakers began sharing this venue with the Kings. Today The Forum is used mainly for concerts. ~ 3900 West Manchester Boulevard, Inglewood; 310-419-3100.

The newest and most lavish Los Angeles sport venue is the multimillion dollar, state-of-the-art **Staples Center**. This is where you can see Jack Nicholson cheer on his beloved Lakers and watch the Kings score goals on ice. ~ 1111 South Figueroa Street; 213-742-7340.

other stores, located on three levels, surround the Bonaventure's vaulting atrium lobby. ~ 404 South Figueroa Street.

NIGHTLIFE   Its dual role as music center of the United States and film capital of the world makes Los Angeles one very hot entertainment destination. There are nightclubs frequented by Hollywood stars, movie theaters premiering major films, and dancehalls headlining top musicians from local recording studios. With so much talent concentrated in one city, the performing arts also flourish. Attending the theater in Los Angeles often means seeing a famous movie star playing the lead in a new drama.

To find out what's happening all over town, check out the "Calendar" section in the *Los Angeles Times*, the *L.A. Weekly*, and *Los Angeles* magazine.

The most prestigious performing arts complex on the West Coast, the **Performing Arts Center of Los Angeles County** consists of four major theaters located within a massive, white marble plaza. The elegant **Dorothy Chandler Pavilion**, home to the Los Angeles Opera, is a spectacular 3200-seat facility. The concert hall also hosts performances by the Joffrey Ballet and American Ballet Theatre. The 2000-seat **Ahmanson Theatre** presents classic dramas and comedies as well as West Coast premieres like *Phantom of the Opera*. The more intimate 760-seat **Mark Taper Forum** is ideal for contemporary dramatic and musical performances. The resident Center Theater Group, associated with the Ahmanson Theatre and the Mark Taper Forum, is committed to the development of new works and artists and has produced such award-winning plays as *Zoot Suit*, *Children of a Lesser God*, and *The Shadow Box*. ~ 135 North Grand Avenue; 213-972-7211; www.music center.org, e-mail general@musiccenter.org.

> The city known more for its cars and freeways than its public transit system once possessed the finest electric trolley network in the world; the system covered 1150 miles of tracks with a peak ridership of 109 million passengers.

Tickets for performances at all three theaters are available through Ticketmaster. ~ 213-480-3232; www.ticketmaster.com.

Across the street, the Frank Gehry–designed **Walt Disney Concert Hall** hosts the Los Angeles Philharmonic and Master Chorale. ~ 111 South Grand Avenue; 323-850-2000; wdch.laphil.com.

The **Public Rush ticket program** at the Mark Taper Forum gives you a great deal on same-day performances. Two hours before curtain, canceled reservations and remaining tickets are released at $12 per ticket on a first-come, first-served basis. If spontaneity and the risk of disappointment aren't for you, then visit the theater box office or call for reservations. Public Rush purchases are cash only. Not available for Saturday evenings and Sunday matinees. ~ 213-628-2772.

A lovely place for evening cocktails, **BonaVista** offers a revolving 360° panorama of the city from the 34th floor of the Westin Bonaventure Hotel. One floor up, **L.A. Prime**, a New York–style steakhouse, also sports a tremendous although nonrevolving view. ~ 404 South Figueroa Street; 213-624-1000; www.westin.com/bonaventure.

The **Grand Avenue Bar** offers 13 TV screens broadcasting sports events in the stately Biltmore Hotel. For a more upscale scene, check the hotel's **Rendezvous Court**. ~ 506 South Grand Avenue; 213-624-1011; www.millenniumhotels.com.

Located a block away from the Biltmore, **Casey's Bar and Grill** may well be the most popular downtown bar. A comfortable Irish-style pub filled with sports memorabilia, it draws business people on weekdays until 10 p.m. ~ 613 South Grand Avenue; 213-629-2353.

Central Downtown

Just blocks from Los Angeles' center of culture and politics, a jumble of gaudily signed storefronts and sidewalk stands make up the Latino shopping district. This stretch of Broadway, not Olvera Street, is where today's Mexican population shops. A multiblock strip, it is crowded with cut-rate clothing stores, swap meets, pawn shops, and bridal boutiques whose windows display mannequin brides in wedding-cake gowns standing next to black-haired mannequin grooms in tuxedos and pink- or blue-ruffled shirts. For bargain hunters, the nearby wholesale district is Mecca. Forget that the neighborhood's a bit unsavory—the bargains to be had in toys, produce, flowers, fashion, and jewelry more than make up for the sleazy surroundings.

SIGHTS

The **Bradbury Building** across the street from Grand Central Public Market (see "Food, Flowers, and More") has undergone a massive restoration. The interior of this National Historic Landmark features an extraordinary courtyard illuminated by a skylight, as well as wrought-iron grillwork and winding stairs surrounding an open-cage elevator. Add flourishes of marble and brick to finish off this 1893 masterpiece. Access granted to ground floor only. ~ 304 South Broadway; 213-626-1893, fax 213-626-2945.

During the 1940s Broadway was the city's Great White Way, where stars mingled and Hollywood premiered its greatest films. Today the boulevard's diminished glory is evident in the old theaters between 3rd and Olympic streets. Once the pride of the studios that built them, they are now in varying stages of disrepair. **The Million Dollar Theater**, where movie mogul Sid Grauman began as a showman, is now a church. ~ 307 South Broadway.

Also of note are the magnificent **Orpheum**, at 842 South Broadway, a 2000-seat Spanish and French Gothic hybrid built in 1926, and the **United Artists Theatre**, situated on 933 South Broadway, a 1927 Spanish Gothic structure with murals depicting Charlie Chaplin and Mary Pickford, now restored for service as Dr. Gene Scott's Los Angeles University Cathedral. Many of these grande dames currently show Spanish-language films from noon 'til night, but most will allow you to glance inside.

The **Los Angeles Conservancy** seeks to recapture the city's past. This preservation group conducts Saturday tours of the theaters and other places of historic interest. Reservations required. Fee. ~ 523 West 6th Street, Suite 826; 213-623-2489, fax 213-623-3909; www.laconservancy.org, e-mail info@laconservancy.org.

A multimillion-dollar renovation of Downtown's main public park, **Pershing Square**, transformed what had become a rundown refuge for transients into a colorful urban construction of pink columns, a purple water tower, and yellow structures. Low walls and benches provide places to rest and enjoy occasional entertainment or an alfresco lunch of sandwiches from a concession stand. ~ Bounded by Olive, Hill, 5th, and 6th streets; www.la parks.org/pershingsquare/pershing.htm.

If Broadway was once the Great White Way, **Spring Street** was once the Wall Street of the West. Like its theatrical counterpart, this faded financial district is now the venue of historians and sentimentalists. ~ Between 4th and 7th streets. The former **Pacific Coast Stock Exchange**, a 1930 masterpiece of moderne architecture, has been closed. ~ 618 South Spring Street. Among the other hallowed halls of finance is the **Design Center of Los Angeles**, a

Food, Flowers, and More

Perhaps because of its long Spanish and Mexican heritage, Los Angeles has more public markets than almost any other city in the country. Here's a sampling of the best.

Grand Central Public Market is a fresh food bazaar in the tradition of Mexico's *mercados*. More than 50 fruit stalls, vegetable stands, butchers, and fresh fish shops line the aisles; juice stands dispense dozens of flavors; and vendors sell light meals. More than 30,000 people pass through every day, making it one of the city's most vital scenes. ~ 317 South Broadway; 213-624-2378, fax 213-624-9496.

The life of the barrio is evident at **El Mercado**, an indoor market crowded with shoppers and filled with the strains of Spanish songs. Clothing shops, fresh food markets, and stores sell everything from cowboy boots to Spanish-language videos. The signs are bilingual and the clientele represents a marvelous multicultural mix. ~ 3425 East 1st Street; 323-268-3451, 800-434-5273, fax 323-768-3295.

Back in 1934 local farmers created a market where they could congregate and sell their goods. Today the **Farmers Market** is an open-air labyrinth of stalls, shops, and grocery stands. Tables overflow with vegetables, fruits, meats, poultry, fish, cheeses, and baked goods—a total of over 120 outlets. Stop by for groceries, gifts, and finger foods or simply to catch Los Angeles at its relaxed and informal best. ~ 6333 West 3rd Street; 323-933-9211, fax 323-549-2145; www.farmersmarketla.com.

At the **Produce Market**, the bounty from California's interior valleys goes on the block every morning. The place is a beehive of business, a fascinating area where the farm meets the city. You can purchase produce by the lug or bushel. Even if a box of lettuce doesn't sound like the perfect souvenir from your L.A. sojourn, plan to visit these early-morning markets. Burly truckers, out-of-town farmers, and Latino workers are all part of this urban tableau. Closed Sunday. ~ Central Avenue and 7th Street; www.citymarketla.com.

For a view of blue-collar L.A., depart central downtown for the **Flower District**. Here, huge warehouses are filled with flowers and potted plants in one of the region's most amazing floral displays. There are Southern California proteas, New Zealand calla lilies, Dutch lilacs, Columbian roses, and French tulips. ~ Wall Street between 7th and 8th streets. Within the Flower District is the **Southern California Flower Market**, where wholesale flower merchants line an entire block and the air is redolent with fragrant merchandise. Closed Sunday. ~ 742 Maple Avenue; 213-627-2482.

1928 building with tile murals and zigzag facade. ~ 433 South Spring Street. Another worthy stop is the **Banco Popular**, a 1903 beaux-arts office building. ~ 354 South Spring Street.

Today the focus of finance has shifted to a highrise district between Grand Avenue, Figueroa Street, 3rd Street, and 8th Street.

HIDDEN ▶

After a stint at Universal CityWalk, the **Museum of Neon Art** (MONA) has settled once again in downtown Los Angeles. In addition to its gallery of neon and electric-media art, the museum still maintains an outdoor exhibition of historic neon signs that now decorate building exteriors at Universal CityWalk. Closed Monday and Tuesday. Admission. ~ 501 West Olympic Boulevard at Hope Street; 213-489-9918, fax 213-489-9932; www.neon mona.org, e-mail info@neonmona.org.

The Museum of Neon Art conducts guided Saturday-night bus tours of neon landmarks in the city from March through October.

The **Staples Center**, L.A.'s latest major sports and entertainment venue, takes up 900,000 square feet in Downtown's south end and cost a staggering $375 million to build. Three home teams, the Lakers, the Clippers, and the Kings, play to crowds of up to 20,000. A sweeping theater-size screen follows the action, helping to maintain at least some measure of fan intimacy. ~ 1111 South Figueroa Street; 213-742-7340; www.staplescenter.com.

The **Greater Los Angeles Convention & Visitors Bureau** is the city's main information center. There you'll find maps, leaflets, and a friendly staff to help point the way through this urban maze. Closed Sunday. ~ 685 South Figueroa Street; 213-689-8822, 800-228-2452, fax 213-624-1992; www.lacvb.com.

LODGING

Hotel Stillwell, a competitively priced hostelry, offers 250 rooms in a vintage 1920 building. The lobby is decorated with Asian wall-hangings, matching the hotel's Indian restaurant. Each guest room has been refurbished with pastel colors, trim carpeting, and modern furniture throughout. ~ 838 South Grand Avenue; 213-627-1151, 800-553-4774, fax 213-622-8940; www.hotelstill well.com, e-mail hstillwell@aol.com. MODERATE.

In the reasonable price range it's hard to top the **Figueroa Hotel**. A 1926 Spanish-style building, it offers a beautiful lobby with tile floor and hand-painted ceiling. The palm-fringed courtyard contains a swimming pool, jacuzzi, and lounge. The rooms are very large, adequately furnished, and decorated with wall-hangings. Tile baths add a touch of class to this very appealing establishment. A lobby café is located on the premises. ~ 939 South Figueroa Street; 213-627-8971, 800-421-9092, fax 213-689-0305; www.figueroahotel.com. MODERATE TO DELUXE.

DINING

To dine in the true style of Mexico the place to go is not a restaurant at all. **Grand Central Public Market**, a block-long produce market, features stands selling Mexican finger foods. Tacos, tostadas, and burritos are only part of the fare. Try the *chile rojo* (pork in red chile sauce), *machaca* (shredded beef), and *lengua* (tongue). If you're really daring there's *rellena* (blood sausage), *buche* (hog maws), and *tripas* (intestines). *¡Mucho gusto!* ~ 317 South Broadway; 213-624-2378, fax 213-624-9496; www.grandcentralsquare.com. BUDGET.

Another funky but fabulous low-priced eating place is **Clifton's Brookdale Cafeteria**, a kind of steam-tray vistarama. The second floor of this cavernous place displays illuminated photos of California's sightseeing spots. The ground floor resembles a redwood forest, with tree trunks bolted to the walls, fake rocks stacked on the floor, and a waterfall tumbling through a cement funnel. It's a scene you cannot afford to miss. Breakfast, lunch, and dinner are served. ~ 648 South Broadway; 213-627-1673, fax 213-629-1329. BUDGET.

Gill's Cuisine of India, set in the lobby of the 1920-era Hotel Stillwell, conveys an air of South Asia. Indian fabrics adorn the walls, complementing a menu of chicken masala, tandoori shrimp, lamb vindaloo, and curry dishes. There's also a buffet-style lunch (Monday through Friday). Closed Sunday. ~ 838 South Grand Avenue; 213-623-1050, 800-553-4774, fax 213-622-8940; www.gillsindiancuisine.com. BUDGET.

The Original Pantry, short on looks but long on soul, has ◄ HIDDEN been serving meals 24 hours a day since 1924 without missing a beat. When forced to relocate in 1950, they prepared lunch in the old building and served dinner at the new place. It simply consists of a counter with metal stools and a formica dining area decorated with grease-stained paintings. The cuisine is a culinary answer to heavy metal—ham hocks, navy bean soup, standing rib roast, sirloin tips with noodles, and roast pork. ~ 877 South Figueroa Street; 213-972-9279, fax 213-972-0187. BUDGET.

SHOPPING   A charming European-style center, **7 + Fig at Ernst & Young Plaza** has dozens of shops and restaurants in an open-air setting. With an emphasis on fashion, the mall is highlighted by stores such as **Ann Taylor** (213-629-2818). ~ 735 South Figueroa Street; 213-955-7150.

Macy's Plaza lies at the heart of the downtown shopping hub and features a galleria of specialty shops as well as a Macy's department store. ~ 750 West 7th Street; 213-624-2891.

The city's old jewelry district still houses a variety of shops selling goods at competitive prices. ~ Hill Street between 6th and 7th streets. Historic **St. Vincent Jewelry Center** is reputed to be the world's largest jewelry outlet, covering an entire square block. ~ 650 South Hill Street; 213-629-2124. Here and at the **International Jewelry Center**, another mammoth complex, you'll find items in every price range, from ten dollars to ten thousand. Closed Sunday. ~ 550 South Hill Street; 213-624-3201.

As in many urban areas, warehouses and industrial districts around Los Angeles have become home to young artists seeking low rents. Among the galleries that have resulted is **Cirrus Gallery**, where contemporary works by West Coast artists are displayed. Closed Sunday and Monday. ~ 542 South Alameda Street; 213-680-3473; www.cirrusgallery.com. **L.A. Artcore** is a nonprofit artists' organization where you'll find outstanding contemporary works. Closed Monday and Tuesday. ~ 120 Judge John Aiso (North San Pedro Street); 213-617-3274; www.laartcore.org.

The former Theater District, which served as Los Angeles' Great White Way during the 1930s, is now the main shopping district for the Latino community. Today, discount clothing, luggage, and electronic stores line this crowded boulevard. Latino sounds and the spicy aroma of Mexican food fills the air. ~ Broadway between 3rd and 10th streets. The **Old Globe Theater**, once a legitimate theater, has been converted into a swap meet. ~ 744 South Broadway.

You can literally shop until you drop in Los Angeles' bustling **Garment District**. Known as a major manufacturing center since the 1930s, the district today lies concentrated along Los Angeles Street between 4th and 10th streets.

Academy Award Clothes stocks thousands of quality men's suits, as well as casual and sportswear at very reasonable prices. Closed Sunday. ~ 821 South Los Angeles Street; 213-622-9125.

The Garment District does not begin and end on Los Angeles Street, but rather extends along side streets and down alleyways. A bargain hunter's delight, **The Alley** is part and parcel of this busy neighborhood. Boxes, bins, and mannequins line the two-block-long alleyway where hawkers and vendors vie for your attention. ~ Located between Santee Street and Maple Avenue.

Consider **Bell of California**, which displays a beautiful selection of silks, cottons, linens, and more for ladies and juniors. Happy hunting! ~ 220 East Pico Boulevard; 213-748-5716.

The L.A. Lakers aren't named after any bodies of water in the Southland; the name is a holdover from the NBA team's original home: Minnesota, the "Land of Ten Thousand Lakes."

Nearby, **Basket World & Supply II** is floor to ceiling with baskets (sold at wholesale, even to retail buyers). Be forewarned: They are only open from 6 a.m. to 11:30 a.m. Closed Sunday. ~ 739 Wall Street; 213-689-0111. **Nuts To You** has been selling nuts to the public in the same location since early in the 20th century. Closed Sunday. ~ 901 South San Pedro Street; 213-627-8855.

NIGHTLIFE

Brightly painted terra-cotta warrior priests welcome guests to **The Mayan Nightclub**. Here a young and fashionable crowd dances to deejay tunes and live salsa bands in a grandiose Mayan tomb on Friday and Saturday. Cover. ~ 1038 South Hill Street; 213-746-4287; www.clubmayan.com.

The 6700-seat **Shrine Auditorium and Expo Center** hosts major musical events, including classical, opera, jazz, pop, rock, and ethnic folk music presentations. ~ 665 West Jefferson Boulevard; 213-749-5123. For same-day tickets, you'll need to go to the Shrine ticket booth.

Home to the Los Angeles Lakers, the Clippers, and the Kings, the **Staples Center** is not exclusively jock-related; high-powered entertainers such as Bruce Springsteen, the Rolling Stones, and Madonna have performed here. ~ 1111 South Figueroa Street; 213-742-7340; www.staplescenter.com.

Advance tickets for the Shrine and Staples Center are available through **Ticketmaster**. ~ 213-480-3232; www.ticketmaster.com.

Little Tokyo

Little Tokyo's history began in 1886 when an ex-seaman from Japan opened a restaurant on 1st Street. Over its long history the area has ebbed and flowed due to a series of events, including the banishing of Japanese Americans to concentration camps in the 1940s, the appropriation of a sizable piece of Little Tokyo's real estate to build the Parker Center police administration building, and new construction in the 1970s and 1980s.

Though today the Little Tokyo Historic District is small— only 15 simple buildings—and most Japanese-American Angelinos live in the suburbs, one of the most authentic cultural experiences outside of Japan can be had at local restaurants. Diners in privately screened-off rooms sit on pillows on tatami-matted floors while lovely, traditionally dressed waitresses gracefully swoop and dip as they serve Japanese delicacies on beautifully simple china.

Despite its small size, undistinguished architecture, and dwindling population, Little Tokyo is still looked upon as the symbolic heart and soul of the Japanese-American community in Los Angeles.

SIGHTS   At the heart of the district is the **Japanese American Cultural and Community Center**, a stoic plate-glass-and-poured-concrete structure designed by Buckminster Fuller and Isamu Noguchi. The complex, which houses dozens of Asian organizations, faces a spacious brick-paved courtyard. The expansive Cultural Room boasts an authentic Japanese tea room, displays of calligraphy, *ikebana*, and other traditional arts, and hosts lectures and demonstrations. ~ 244 South San Pedro Street; 213-628-2725, fax 213-617-8576; www.jaccc.org, e-mail jaccc@jaccc.org.

Part of the Japanese American Cultural and Community Center, the **Japan America Theatre** is an important showcase for kabuki theater, Asian music, and other performing arts. ~ 244 South San Pedro Street; 213-680-3700, fax 213-617-8576; www.jaccc.org, e-mail info@jaccc.org.

Follow the brick paving stones from the cultural center through **Japanese Village Plaza**, a two-block shopping mall adorned with fountains and sculptures. At the end of the plaza stands Little Tokyo's tile-roofed **fire tower**, an ornamental but practical structure that has become a local landmark.

Another cultural gathering place is the lovely **Higashi Honganji Buddhist Temple**. With its traditional tile roof, the temple represents Japanese architecture adapted to a Western cityscape. Call before visiting. ~ 505 East 3rd Street; 213-626-4200, fax 213-626-6850; www.hhbt-la.org, e-mail info@hhbt-la.org.

On the day the **Japanese American National Museum** opened ◄ *HIDDEN*
in 1992, riots were breaking out across L.A. as news of the ac-
quittal of the policemen charged in Rodney King's beating became known. The violence overshadowed the opening of a museum dedicated to improving the "understanding and appreciation
for America's ethnic and cultural diversity." The JANM, housed
in a restored Buddhist temple, is a gem. Through changing exhibits, it presents the Japanese-American experience as an integral part of the nation's heritage. The National Museum houses
the largest and most thoroughly documented collection of
Japanese-American artifacts in the world. It offers a slew of history and art exhibitions, an expansive resource and research center, family programs, and video presentations. Closed Monday.
Admission. ~ 369 East 1st Street; 213-625-0414, 800-461-5266,
fax 213-625-1770; www.janm.org.

On the third floor of the New Otani Hotel & Garden is an
authentic **Japanese garden**, where you can stroll along tranquil ◄ *HIDDEN*

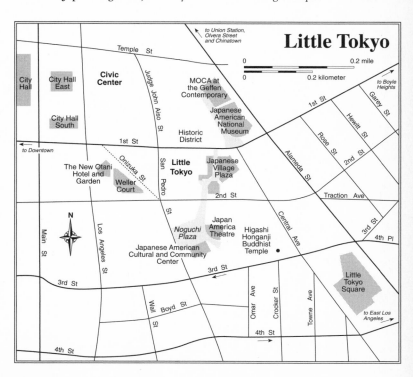

pathways, next to a stream and cascades of water. At night, the lighted towers of downtown form a magical backdrop. ~ 120 South Los Angeles Street; 213-629-1200, 800-421-8795; www. newotani.com.

LODGING   Catering largely to an international clientele, the **New Otani Hotel & Garden** is a 434-room extravaganza with restaurants, shops, lounges, spa, and a tranquil half-acre Japanese "garden in the sky." The hotel offers small rooms, many decorated in traditional Japanese style with shoji screens. Standard guest accommodations are painted in pastel hues and decorated with ultramodern furniture in curvilinear designs. Finest feature of all is the lobby, a vaulted-ceiling affair with a skylight and an eye-catching sculpture. ~ 120 South Los Angeles Street; 213-629-1200, 800-421-8795; www. newotani.com, e-mail laotani@aol.com. ULTRA-DELUXE.

DINING   **Suehiro Café** offers a Japanese menu in an American-style setting, complete with blue vinyl booths and counter service. You will find such Japanese standards as chicken teriyaki, tempura, and sukiyaki. ~ 337 East 1st Street; 213-626-9132. BUDGET TO MODERATE.

SHOPPING   **Japanese Village Plaza**, right in the heart of the neighborhood, is a commercial expression of the sights, sounds, smells, and flavors of Japan. Enter at the site of the Fire Tower, a traditional fireman's lookout facing 1st Street, and walk the Plaza's winding brick pathways while browsing its tile-roofed shops. One such store, **Mikawaya Sweet Shop** (213-613-0611), tempts you with subtle Japanese candies. ~ 333 South Alameda Street.

Little Tokyo is a busy shopping district centered along 1st Street between Main Street and Alameda Boulevard.

Just beyond the Plaza, **Bun-ka Do** offers an interesting collection of Japanese art objects, records, and books. ~ 340 East 1st Street; 213-625-1122.

Weller Court, a modern tri-level shopping arcade, boasts among its tenants **Kinokuniya Book Store of America** (213-687-4480, 800-595-2726), a branch of Japan's largest bookstore featuring a complete selection of books on Japan. ~ At Onizuka and 2nd streets.

Conveniently, Weller Court is connected via walking bridges to the **New Otani Hotel Shopping Arcade**, where a series of specialty shops showcase everything from fine jewelry to tourist trinkets. ~ 110 South Los Angeles Street.

Patterned after a Japanese department store, Little Tokyo Square is an array of small shops and restaurants on two floors clustered around a large grocery, **Mitsuwa**. The fresh fish counter is a key feature but it's overshadowed by the 40-foot-long refrigerator case of ready-to-eat sushi. You would be hard pressed to find any signs in English in either of the two Hello Kitty shops in the Square. ~ 333 South Alameda Street; 213-687-6699.

NIGHTLIFE

The **Genji Bar** at the New Otani Hotel is a Japanese karaoke bar in the heart of Little Tokyo. ~ 120 South Los Angeles Street; 213-253-9255.

Housed in the Japanese American Cultural and Community Center in Little Tokyo, the **Japan America Theatre** presents traditional and contemporary Japanese productions. Performances include Grand Kabuki, Bugaku, and Noh dramas, and Japanese-American plays. In addition, Western dance troupes and chamber orchestras are sometimes featured. ~ 244 South San Pedro Street; 213-680-3700, fax 213-617-8576; www.jaccc.org, e-mail jaccc@jaccc.org.

THREE

Greater Downtown

Like the spokes of a wheel, Greater Downtown branches off in all directions from the city center in a multicultural mix of communities that is home to an astounding diversity of ethnic and socio-economic groups. Before the automobile was a presence and freeways linked distant suburbs, the area directly adjacent to Downtown *was* the suburbs. Angelinos who wanted to escape living in the urban center ventured in all directions, building houses, planting gardens, and raising families. As time progressed, many of the families that could afford to moved away from the quickly spreading urban sprawl. The rich were replaced by those who couldn't afford to move, and today some of the swankiest early-20th-century neighborhoods are inhabited by some of the city's poorer residents.

A substantial number of the city's African-American and Latino populations live in the neighborhoods that border the Downtown area to the south and east. Both the barrio and ghetto are here, and while these areas aren't always comfortable or safe, even for the residents, Exposition Park, Watts, and East L.A. aren't, as sometimes perceived, just hot-beds of drugs, drive-by shootings, and crime. Many decent, hard-working people live in these areas, doing their best to raise their families and provide a better life for their kids. These neighborhoods are also where you can see L.A.'s most eccentric work of art, visit some impressive museums, and wolf down the best burritos in the city.

Not all of the Greater Downtown areas are rundown or struggling, however. The hills of Los Feliz, Echo Park, and Silver Lake, north of the city center, are still the domain of the affluent. Though in recent years the flats of Echo Park and Silver Lake have attracted a large low-income Latino population, the houses in the hills are mainly occupied by middle and upper-middle class artists, yuppies, and gays. There's more of an ethnic and socio-economic mix here than in the nearby Los Feliz and Griffith Park areas, where hillside houses achieve mansion proportions and are often home to some of today's richest movie stars. A planetarium, zoo, Western museum, and amphitheater are among the area's attractions, not to mention a better-than-average assortment of artsy and off-beat restaurants and cafés.

Circling the city center, in neighborhoods that run the gamut from pristine to dilapidated, is a cross section of the population that now inhabits the huge Los Angeles basin. While it isn't always peaceful, somehow this diverse group has managed to coexist as the city has sprawled beyond it.

Exposition Park Area

Like many turn-of-the-20th-century close-to-downtown residential areas, University Park has lost much of its former glory. So named because it includes the University of Southern California campus, this area was once home to tycoons and financiers. Today, the former mansions of L.A.'s founding fathers stand next to collapsing bungalows with brown lawns and peeling paint. It's ironic that USC (dubbed The University of Spoiled Children), one of the most exclusive and expensive universities in the nation, has remained in what is now a dubious area at best.

Neighboring Exposition Park is a museum lover's dream. Museum hopping is the main activity here, with the Natural History Museum, California Science Center and IMAX Theater, and the California African-American Museum all surrounding a lovely rose garden, famous for it 200-plus varieties. Best to take during the sights in the daylight hours, however: This isn't an area to be hanging out in after dark.

SIGHTS

Minutes from Los Angeles' ultramodern downtown, where real estate sells by the square foot, sits the spacious, Romanesque campus of the **University of Southern California**. Lined with sycamore and maple trees, this red-brick-and-ivy enclave boasts a park-like setting filled with historic buildings.

Among the many features of the USC campus is the **Fisher Gallery**, with an excellent collection of European and New World art from the 15th century to the present. Closed Sunday and Monday, summer, and school holidays. ~ 213-740-4561; www.usc.edu/fishergallery. Also on campus is the **Hancock Memorial Museum**, which features rooms that were removed from the Villa de Medici–

inspired 1907 Hancock Mansion and rebuilt here. In addition to the architecture, you will view the original furniture that accompanied the move. Open by appointment. ~ 213-740-5144; e-mail melindah@usc.edu.

Famous for its football team, USC has produced four Heisman trophy winners and more than 100 All-Americans. Although the school has received a lot of flack in the past for focusing on sports rather than academics, today this 28,000-student university boasts a slew of professional schools, including a well-established film program. ~ Bounded by Jefferson Boulevard, Vermont Avenue, Exposition Boulevard, and Figueroa Street; 213-740-2311.

EXPOSITION PARK   This multiblock extravaganza is long on exposition and short on park. There *is* an enchanting **sunken garden** with a fountain, gazebos, and almost 20,000 rose bushes representing nearly 200 varieties of roses. Otherwise the park blooms with museums and sports arenas. ~ Bounded by Exposition Boulevard, Vermont Avenue, Martin Luther King, Jr. Boulevard, and Figueroa Street.

The **California Science Center** is one of those hands-on, great-for-kids-of-all-ages complexes. Its halls contain over 100 exhibits devoted to health and economics and displays demonstrating everything from simple laws of science to the latest advances in high technology. ~ Exposition Park; 213-744-7400; www.cali forniasciencetheater.org, e-mail 4info@cscmail.org.

In the Science Center's **Air and Space Gallery** there are exhibits explaining the principles of aerodynamics as well as planes, jets, and space capsules suspended from the ceiling in mock flight. Climbing a catwalk-like series of staircases, you'll have a bird's-eye view of a 1920 glider, an Air Force T-38, an F-20 Tiger Shark, and a Gemini II spacecraft. ~ 700 State Drive, Exposition Park.

Also at the Science Center, an **IMAX Theater**, with a seven-story-high screen, takes viewers on film adventures of stunning, you-are-there realism. Several different films are screened daily. You might find yourself cruising with whales, sledding through Alaska, or grazing with African wildlife. Call ahead for schedule. Admission. ~ Exposition Park; 213-744-7400; www.california sciencetheater.org, e-mail 4info@cscmail.org.

The **Natural History Museum of Los Angeles County** is a world (and an afternoon) unto itself. Among the three-dozen gal-

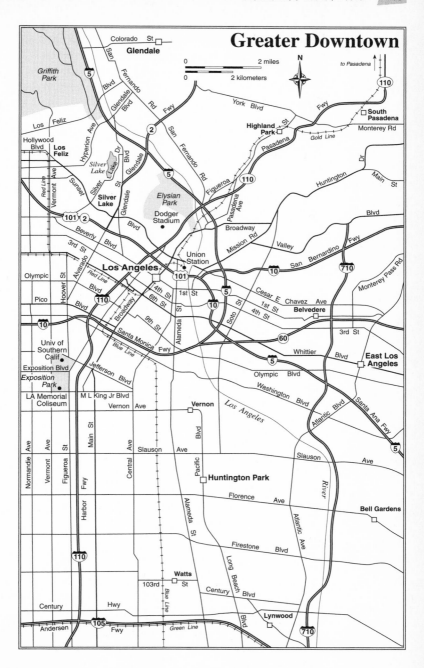

Greater Downtown

leries are rock and gem displays; dioramas of bears, wolves, and bison; set pieces from the American past, including a cut-away Conestoga wagon demonstrating life on the frontier; and, of course, the dinosaur skeletons required of every self-respecting natural history museum. If this is not enough, the museum contains bird specimens and a "discovery center" where kids can play scientist; the insect zoo features 30 live displays of critters from around the world. Admission (except on the first Tuesday of the month). ~ 900 Exposition Boulevard; 213-763-3466, fax 213-743-4843; www.nhm.org, e-mail info@nhm.org.

The movie location for everything from *The Hunchback of Notre Dame* to *The Graduate*, the University of Southern California is an ideal spot for a stroll.

Prettiest of all the buildings in this museum park is the **California African American Museum** with its glass-roofed sculpture court and bright, airy galleries. Devoted to the art, culture, and history of African Americans west of the Mississippi, the primary collection features artifacts from the 18th century to the present. Other exhibits focus on topics ranging from West African culture to Ella Fitzgerald. Closed Sunday through Tuesday. ~ 600 State Drive, Exposition Park; 213-744-7432, fax 213-744-2050; www.caam.ca.gov.

Exposition Park's most notable architectural achievement is not the museum buildings, but rather the **Los Angeles Memorial Coliseum**, a 96,000-seat arena built in 1923. One of the most beautiful stadiums in the country, site of the 1932 and 1984 Olympics, the Coliseum is a classic arena with arched entranceways and rainbow-colored seats. Today it is home to the University of Southern California football team, and hosts a variety of concerts and performances. ~ 3939 South Figueroa Street, Exposition Park; 213-748-6131.

HIDDEN ▶

Just north of the park is Fire Station 30, one of two segregated fire stations in L.A. between 1924 and 1955. This is where black firefighters worked during periods of segregation and desegregation. Today it has been proudly restored to house the **African American Firefighter Museum**. Dedicated to preserving the history and heritage of Los Angeles' African-American firemen (known today as "Old Stentorians"), the museum displays all sorts of firefighting paraphernalia from engines to historic photographs. Call for hours. ~ 1401 South Central Avenue; 213-744-1730, fax 213-744-1731; www.aaffmuseum.org, e-mail aaff museum@affmuseum.org.

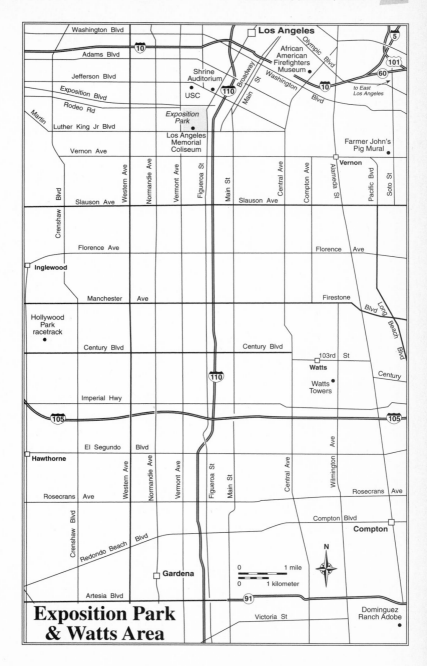

Exposition Park & Watts Area

▼▼▼▼▼▼▼▼▼▼
Watts Area

Watts, one of L.A.'s poorest neighborhoods with a reputation to match, is known for two divergent things: an
eccentric artistic creation and race riots.

A fantasy series of twisting steel towers adorned with pieces
of colored pottery, sea shells, and other cast-off items is about
the last thing you'd expect to see in this poverty-stricken area.
Still, over the years, the Watts Towers have survived not only
neglect and vandalism, but a pull-test ordered by the City of Los
Angeles that approximated the force of a 120-mile-an-hour gale
wind. Needless to say, the Towers remained standing.

In 1965, Watts became the scene of the devastating Watts
race riots, during which 43 people were killed and 4000 arrested.
Today, Watts is still one of L.A.'s poorest areas, filled with blocks
of decrepit bungalows and bisected by Southern Pacific railroad
tracks. Yet artists from local communities and visitors from
around the world come here to take inspiration from the beauty
of one immigrant's artistic achievement. And while you're in the
neighborhood, stop and explore some off-the-beaten-path sights
of L.A.'s urban industrial areas.

SIGHTS

HIDDEN ►

One of the seven wonders of Los Angeles is located northeast of
Watts in the industrial town of Vernon, where **Farmer John's Pig
Mural** covers an entire city block. Probably the biggest mural you'll
ever see, it's also one of the funniest, picturing hundreds of pigs
running through open fields. This idyllic landscape, in the midst
of miles of factories, was begun in 1957 by a movie-industry
artist named Les Grimes. For years Grimes gave everything to the
project and ultimately lost his life, falling from a scaffold while
working on the mural. His legacy is a romping, rollicking, tech-
nicolor creation. ~ 3049 East Vernon Avenue, Vernon.

After priming your eyes with this porcine art, head down to
L.A.'s legendary folk-art wonder, also the result of an individual
artist with an uncommon vision—**Watts Towers**. Fashioned by
Simon Rodia over a three-decade period, these delicate, curving
towers, inlaid with *objets trouvés*, rise nearly 100 feet. Encrusted
with tile shards, stones, and more than 70,000 sea shells, they form
a work of unsettling beauty. After five years of being untended and
vandalized, the towers were purchased by a group of volunteers,
who set up a committee to oversee their maintenance. ~ 1765
East 107th Street, in Simon Rodia State Historic Park, Watts.

The **Watts Towers Arts Center** next door features a rotating series of exhibits by artists in the black and Asian community. Tours of the towers are available through the Arts Center. Call ahead for times. Admission. Closed Monday. ~ 1727 East 107th Street, Watts; 213-847-4464, fax 323-564-7030.

Continuing farther south, Los Angeles' industrial district also contains some of California's early creations. The **Dominguez**   ◄ HIDDEN **Ranch Adobe,** in the heavy-metal town of Compton, is an 18th-century Spanish rancho and historic museum. The grounds of this sprawling hacienda are landscaped with lovely flower and cactus gardens. The museum features the original furniture and effects of the Dominguez family, the Spanish dons who first built a home here in 1826 (the land itself was the first land grant decreed by the King of Spain in 1784). Guided tours are conducted from 9 to 11 a.m. Tuesday and Thursday and 1 to 3 p.m. Wednesday. It is open on the first and last Sunday of the month from 1 to 3 p.m. ~ 18127 South Alameda Street, Compton; 310-631-5981, fax 310-631-3518; e-mail dominguezadobe@comcast.net.

After half a lifetime of work Simon Rodia finished the Watts Towers in 1954, gave the property to a neighbor, and left Los Angeles, never to visit his towers again.

When you've had your fill of history and art, head up to **Hollywood Park,** one of the Southland's great tracks, where you'll find thoroughbred racing from the end of April until the end of July, and again in November and December. Beautifully laid out, the track features a landscape complete with palm trees, lagoon, and children's play area. Closed Monday and Tuesday. Admission. ~ 1050 South Prairie Avenue, Inglewood; 310-419-1500; www.hollywoodpark.com.

East Los Angeles

The sprawling Latino neighborhood of East Los Angeles, sometimes called simply the barrio, lies east (surprise!) of the Los Angeles River. Home to the country's largest concentration of Hispanics, this area is where L.A.'s largest population group lives, works, and plays. East L.A.'s modern history starts in the late 18th century when, after 2000 years of occupation, the Gabrieleño Indians were ousted by the Spanish. Mexican and American ranchers moved in during the 19th century, and during the first half of the 20th century, the area became home to Russian, Jewish, Japanese, and Mexican immigrants. By World War II the population was almost exclusively Mexican and so it remains.

Though East L.A. has its problems with gangs and crime, it exudes a sense of cultural pride, and the spirit of Mexico resonates in its vibrant, colorful, and sometimes shabby streets, where vividly hued murals and anger-motivated graffiti adorn the buildings. The best food is usually found in hole-in-the-wall restaurants or at corner burrito stands. And on Saturday and Sunday, along Cesar Chavez Boulevard and adjoining streets, locals line up with ice chests to buy fresh, succulent traditionally made tamales.

SIGHTS

Cesar Chavez Avenue (Brooklyn Avenue), a major thoroughfare in the Boyle Heights district, represents "Little Mexico," a region rich in Mexican restaurants, candy stores, and family shops. If Cesar Chavez Avenue is the heart of the *barrio*, **Whittier Boulevard** is the spine, a neon ganglion charged with electric color. It is here that a guy goes to show off his girl, his car, and himself. Lined with discount stores, *taquerías*, and auto body shops, Whittier is the Sunset Strip of East L.A.

Of course the full flavor of the Chicano community is found among the murals that decorate the streets of East Los Angeles. Exotic in design, vibrant with color, they are a vital representation of the inner life of the *barrio*, a freeform expression of the Mexican people and their 400-year residence in the United States.

HIDDEN ►

A spectacular series of murals adorn the walls of the **Estrada Courts Housing Project**. Here dozens of bright-hued images capture the full sweep of Latin history. ~ Olympic Boulevard between Grande Vista Avenue and Lorena Street.

Two other buildings also provide a panoramic image of Mexican history. In a succession of panels, the **First Street Store** re-

---

THE HEARTBEAT OF A COMMUNITY

Many of the muralists decorating East Los Angeles' streets started at **Plaza de la Raza**. This Chicano cultural center is intimately involved in the artistic life of the community, sponsoring classes in dance, music, theater, and visual arts. For visitors there's a variety of regularly scheduled events. Closed Sunday and from December 14 through January 4. ~ 3540 North Mission Road; 323-223-2475, fax 323-223-1804; www.plazadelaraza.org, e-mail admin@plazaraza.org. Adjacent to the cultural center, **Lincoln Park** features a lake and tree-studded picnic area.

creates prehistoric Mexican society, then progresses through the Aztec area to modern times. ~ 3640 East 1st Street. With a series of surreal tile murals, the nearby **Pan American Bank** carries the saga into the future, portraying Latinos in the post-atomic age. ~ 3626 East 1st Street.

Another color-soaked mural, painted in 1983, "**El Corrido de Boyle Heights**" ("The Ballad of Boyle Heights") captures the community at work and play, with the family, and on the road. A succession of overlapping scenes, it's an anecdotal expression of the *barrio*, done with a flair unique to Chicano culture. ~ Corner of Cesar Chavez Avenue (Brooklyn Avenue) and Soto Street.

DINING

Mexican restaurants are on parade at **El Mercado**, a two-story indoor market adorned with tile floors and colorful murals. Along the mezzanine of this Spanish emporium are chili bars, taco stands, seafood restaurants, and cafés from south of the border. Adding to your dining pleasure, Mexican bands perform love songs and ballads. ~ 3425 East 1st Street; 323-268-3451. BUDGET TO MODERATE.

La Serenta De Garibaldi ranks as one of L.A.'s top Mexican restaurants. Besides more traditional dishes such as fish tacos and enchiladas in tomatillo sauce, daily specials feature fresh fish served with delicate sauces such as avocado, chipotle and *moicatejete*, made with the pungent *epezote* herb. ~ 1842 East 1st Street; 323-265-2887. BUDGET TO MODERATE.

El Tepeyac Café is a hole-in-the-wall eatery with so much soul people migrate across the city to feast on its legendary burritos. Consisting of a small dining room with take-out window and side patio, the place serves everything—*machaca*, tacos, steak *picado*, enchiladas, *chile colorado*, *huevos con chorizo*, and so on. The food is delicious, and the portions are overwhelming. Breakfast, lunch, and dinner are served. Closed Tuesday. ~ 812 North Evergreen Avenue; 323-268-1960. BUDGET.

SHOPPING

For neighborhood shopping in an ethnic environment, just traverse the Macy Street Bridge over the Los Angeles River and enter East Los Angeles. Affectionately known as "Little Mexico," the area around Cesar Chavez Avenue (Brooklyn Avenue) is chockablock with restaurants, markets, bridal shops, and toy stores. **El Mercado** is an enclosed marketplace filled with shops and stalls.

Vendors here sell cowboy boots and Mexican blankets, restaurants serve up tacos *de cabeza* and strolling mariachis create an atmosphere of Old Mexico. ~ 3425 East 1st Street.

NIGHTLIFE · The **Margo Albert Theatre**, part of the Plaza de la Raza arts center, hosts drama, music, and dance programs that relate to Mexican culture. ~ 3540 North Mission Road; 323-223-2475.

The East L.A. theater scene is dominated by the **Bilingual Foundation of the Arts**, which presents plays in English and Spanish. ~ 421 North Avenue 19; 323-225-4044; www.bfatheatre.org.

▼▼▼▼▼▼▼▼▼▼▼▼▼▼▼▼

Echo Park–Silver Lake

Echo Park and Silver Lake were, in the early part of the 20th century, bedroom communities for those working in the city center. Now, just minutes from Downtown by car or bus, the area is populated by a melting pot of cultures and lifestyles. The flats generally comprise apartment buildings and businesses, while the hills are dotted with individually designed houses—many historic, some avant garde, and most built in the last half of the 20th century.

Silver Lake—there actually is a lake—is the kind of neighborhood where punk rockers with multiple body piercings live cheek-by-jowl with up-and-coming attorneys that work Downtown. There's also a significant gay population. In fact, together with West Hollywood, Silver Lake has emerged as one of Los Angeles' major centers of gay culture. This kind of mix makes for a neighborhood cherished by its residents for its free-thinking, accepting attitude and its diverse lifestyles.

Echo Park is mainly a Latino neighborhood, jam-packed with Mexican restaurants, markets, pawn shops, and shabby apartment buildings. On Sunday mornings, however, hip artists and professionals flock to the area's plethora of funky-artsy sidewalk cafés along Sunset Boulevard, where everyone lines up to score a curbside table and wolf down huge breakfasts and designer coffee. Meanwhile, local Latino families pack up picnic lunches and flock to nearby Elysian Park to enjoy a day in the "country" at this green, hilly, eucalyptus-adorned urban park.

SIGHTS For the outdoor-minded, 575-acre **Elysian Park**, the city's second largest park, is a forested region of rolling hills and peaceful glens.

There are picnic areas, meadows planted with exotic palm trees, and numerous nature trails offering views of central Los Angeles and the San Gabriel Valley, as well as basketball, volleyball, and tennis courts. For the sports-minded, the park contains 56,000-seat **Dodger Stadium**, home of the Los Angeles Dodgers. ~ Located near the intersection of Routes 110 and 5; 323-224-1500, fax 323-224-1269; www.dodgers.com.

Nearby, **Echo Park** features a palm-fringed lake complete with footbridge and ducks. There are rental boats (213-847-8524) for exploring the fountain and lotus flowers, which highlight this 15-acre body of water. The lake is stocked with trout and catfish; fishing is allowed, although you need a license. There's also a playground. ~ Glendale Boulevard and Echo Park Avenue; 213-250-3578, fax 213-250-8946.

That circular structure with the imposing white columns across the street is **Angelus Temple**. Modeled after London's Royal Albert Hall, it served the congregation of spiritualist Aimee Semple McPherson during the 1920s and 1930s. Open Sunday and Thursday. ~ 1100 Glendale Boulevard; 213-484-1100; www.angelustemple.org.

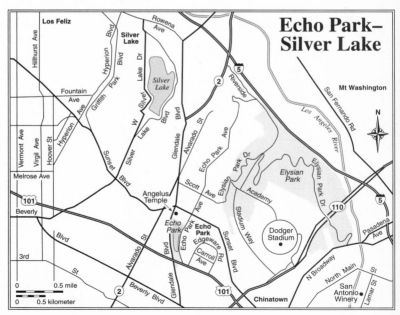

The nearby neighborhood of **Angelino Heights** was the city's first suburb, built during the 1880s on a hill overlooking Downtown and connected to the business district by cable car. Today the once elegant borough, ragged along the edges, still retains vestiges of its glory days. Foremost is the **1300 block of Carroll Avenue**, where a string of gingerbread Victorians have been gussied up in the fashion of the Gay Nineties. Representing Los Angeles' largest concentration of Victorian houses, the street is an outdoor museum lined with turrets, gables, and fanciful woodwork.

Another noteworthy housing colony surrounds the reservoir at **Silver Lake**. Built after World War II, the homes are generally of stucco construction. Since they cover nearby hills, the best way to tour the neighborhood is by winding through the labyrinth of narrow streets that ascends from the lake. ~ Silver Lake Boulevard.

Of architectural note is the row of houses on the **2200 block of East Silver Lake Boulevard**. Designed by Austrian architect Richard Neutra, they are stucco-and-plate-glass structures representative of the International style. Neutra's homes are currently the rage, and Silver Lake real-estate prices have gone sky-high because of the large concentration of such homes. The area is inhabited by young showbiz types, record and TV execs, writers, artists, and musicians who pay premium prices for these mid-20th-century modern homes.

SILVER LAKE MODERNISTS

In the 1920s and '30s modernist architects were drawn to the Silver Lake district, where wealthy, imaginative residents commissioned houses that seemed to defy gravity and convention. Roofs were flat, steel-frame construction was covered with concrete, floor plans were freely arranged, and the extensive use of glass brought the outside in. Many of these structures still stand, including John Lautner's circa-1950 **Silvertop** (2007 Micheltorena Street), with its curved roof and glass walls that take in panoramic views. There are also more than a dozen houses built from the 1930s to the 1960s by the most famous Silver Lake modernist, Richard Neutra. Drive along East Silver Lake Boulevard to find **Treetops** (#2434), **Treweek House** (#2250), **Sokol House** (#2242), and **Yew House** (#2226). Neutra enthusiasts can make arrangements to tour the **Richard & Dion Neutra VDL Research House** (2300 Silver Lake Boulevard; 323-953-0224).

DINING

Sunset Boulevard, particularly around Echo Park and Silver Lake, is a veritable restaurant row. Traveling northeast on this famous street you'll come upon restaurants of every ethnic persuasion. **Taix French Restaurant** is a huge, common-denominator restaurant serving French country cuisine in several dining rooms. The lunch and dinner *cartes* include roast pork, trout almandine, roast duck, and lamb chops. The interior is attractive, if crowded. There's musical entertainment Wednesday through Saturday. ~ 1911 West Sunset Boulevard; 213-484-1265, fax 213-484-0041; www.taixfrench.com. MODERATE TO DELUXE.

◄ HIDDEN

Though this good old no-nonsense coffee shop's been serving tasty and hearty meals for years, **Crest on Sunset** has kept up with the times in the food department, dishing up everything from crab cakes benedict to *huevos rancheros* to biscuits with country gravy. ~ 3725 Sunset Boulevard; 323-660-3645; www. crestonsunset.com. BUDGET.

Burrito King serves superb *frijoles*, as well as a memorable *machaca* burrito consisting of shredded tender beef mixed with sautéed onions and green peppers. Open 'til 1 a.m. for late-night feasts. ~ 2823 Hyperion Avenue; 323-663-9378. BUDGET.

If you like spicy Caribbean flavor in food and atmosphere, make your way over to **Cha Cha Cha**. It's in a rundown East Hollywood neighborhood, but don't let that put you off. A valet will look after your car, and a hip crowd, fired up on *camarones negros*, *sopes*, *empanadas*, and jerk chicken pizza, will hold your attention. ~ 656 North Virgil Avenue; 323-664-7723, fax 323-660-0449. MODERATE.

NIGHTLIFE

The Bavarian-style **Red Lion Tavern**, a friendly German rathskeller, serves lagers in two-liter boots. The German bartenders occasionally initiate impromptu sing-alongs, especially after games at nearby Dodger Stadium. ~ 2366 Glendale Boulevard; 323-662-5337.

There are two small theaters of note in Silver Lake. The **Knightsbridge Theatre,** built in 1927 as a movie palace, is home of the National American Shakespeare Company (they have a sister theater in Pasadena). It performs the Bard's work in both traditional and experimental productions, as well as showcases other classics. ~ 1944 Riverside Drive; 323-667-0955; www.knightsbridge

Text continued on page 86.

Whittier–El Monte Area

Whittier, founded as a Quaker community in 1887, is today simply another Los Angeles bedroom community where the tree-shaded main street, with its historic buildings and meterless parking, is managing to hold its own against strip malls and shopping centers. But what the rest of the country knows about Whittier is that it's the town that raised Richard Nixon. A Richard Nixon pilgrimage? It may sound a bit bizarre, but think about it—a sacred visit to the hometown of the only president who ever resigned from office, "Tricky Dick" himself, the first national leader ever compelled to assure the American public, "I am not a crook."

Anyone who has ever heard a maudlin Nixon speech knows Whittier, where the 37th President of the United States was raised, schooled, and elected to Congress. The **Whittier Chamber of Commerce** is a source of information. Closed weekends. ~ 8158 Painter Avenue, Whittier; 562-698-9554, fax 562-693-2700; www.whittierchamber.com, e-mail carol@whittier chamber.com.

Among the Nixon highlights are **East Whittier Elementary School** (Whittier Boulevard and Gunn Avenue); **Whittier High School** (Philadelphia Street and Pierce Avenue), where young Richard graduated in 1930; and the Spanish-style campus of **Whittier College** (Painter Avenue and Philadelphia Street), from which he received his diploma four years later.

The **Whittier Museum and Historical Society** has displays on local history from the 1800s and early 1900s. There is also a retrospective on Richard Nixon's life, as well as temporary exhibits. The museum is open to the public on Saturday and Sunday. ~ 6755 Newlin Avenue, Whittier; 562-945-3871, fax 562-945-9106; www.whittiermuseum.org, e-mail info@ whittiermuseum.org.

Richard Nixon married Pat Ryan in 1940; after the future President was elected to Congress in 1946, the **Nixon residence** became a modest, low-slung stucco house. Interestingly, none of these places acknowledge the Watergate President. Not to worry, for those of us who remain true believers, each location is an immortal shrine. ~ 14033 Honeysuckle Lane.

The Nixon family store was converted into a gas station, but the **Pat Ryan Nixon House**, where the future First Lady lived when she met her husband, still stands. ~ 13513 Terrace Place.

Of course the true pilgrimage is to the **Richard Nixon Presidential Library and Birthplace,** several miles southeast of Whittier in Yorba Linda. Here you'll find the 900-square-foot home (that "made up in love what it lacked in size") where Nixon was born "on the coldest day of one of the coldest winters in California history." Also here are the garden and gravesite.

The library itself, with barely a book to be seen, is a marvelous succession of movies, interactive videos, and touch-screen presentations that rewrite American history in a fashion that would make even a novelist blush. Admission. ~ 18001 Yorba Linda Boulevard, Yorba Linda; 714-993-3393, 800-872-8865, fax 714-528-0544; www.nixonlibrary.org.

Another famous politician, who eventually died in poverty, made his home nearby. **Pío Pico State Historic Park** contains the 22-room adobe house built by Pío Pico, the last governor of California under Mexican rule, and one of the wealthiest men in Southern California. Surrounded today by freeways and railroad tracks, the home was once a vibrant center of life during the 19th century. Call for guided tour and times. Closed Monday and Tuesday. ~ 6003 Pioneer Boulevard, Whittier; 562-695-1217, fax 562-693-1503.

A natural island in a sea of commerce, **Whittier Narrows Nature Center** is a 419-acre preserve near the San Gabriel and Rio Hondo rivers. Over 290 bird species have been sighted within this quiltwork of rivers, lakes, and open fields. ~ 1000 North Durfee Avenue, South El Monte; 626-575-5523, fax 626-443-5359.

Another point of interest, the **El Monte Museum of History** resides in a classic Spanish-style building that was actually part of a 1936 WPA project. In addition to a typical 19th-century El Monte home, the facility contains representations of the town's old general store, school, and barber shop, as well as an art gallery. Rich in historic lore, the surrounding area was the terminus of the Santa Fe Trail; as a result, the museum has countless photographs, maps, and diaries from the pioneer era. Closed Saturday and Monday. ~ 3150 North Tyler Avenue, El Monte; 626-444-3813, fax 626-444-8142.

The Workman and Temple Family Homestead Museum, also known simply as the Homestead Museum, is an impressive six-acre site, containing the Workman House (a 19th-century adobe), a Victorian-style gazebo, and El Campo Santo, one of the county's oldest private cemeteries. The centerpiece of the park is La Casa Nueva, a 1920s-era Spanish Colonial Revival mansion complete with stained-glass windows, hand-carved ornaments, decorative tiles, and intricate iron fittings. Tours of this complex are offered on the hour from 1 p.m. to 4 p.m. and concentrate primarily on the 1840s, 1870s, and 1920s, when the various buildings were being constructed. Closed Monday and Tuesday. ~ 15415 East Don Julian Road, City of Industry; 626-968-8492, fax 626-968-2048; www.homesteadmuseum.org, e-mail info@homesteadmuseum.org.

Carrying you forward to the tacky architecture of the 1950s, in the equally tacky town of La Puente, is **The Donut Hole**. This drive-through snack bar consists of two structures in the shape of giant donuts. Though these architectural accretions look more like overinflated truck tires than anything edible, visitors drive through the first donut hole, place their orders, then exit via the second donut. Open until midnight for late-night munchies. ~ 15300 East Amar Road, La Puente; 626-968-2912.

theatre.com. The **Celebration Theatre** presents gay and lesbian productions. ~ 7051 Santa Monica Boulevard; 323-957-1884.

Spaceland, which presents mostly live alternative and pop with the occasional deejay night of jungle, house, and techno, has a reputation for offering the surprise big-name artist and sometimes eliminating the cover charge. There's a lounge in the back if you're in the mood for a game of pool. Cover. ~ 1717 Silver Lake Boulevard; 323-661-4380 reservations, 213-833-2843 recorded info; www.clubspaceland.com.

Griffith Park–Los Feliz

Every great city boasts a great city park, and Los Angeles is no exception. Set astride 4000 acres in the Hollywood Hills in the city's northeast corner, Griffith Park is the nation's largest municipal park. Golf courses, hiking trails, pony rides, miniature trains, a merry-go-round, a planetarium, and many other attractions make the park one of the most popular places in town on warm, sunny days.

Los Feliz, the neighborhood adjoining the park, is a combination of pricey and often historic hillside dwellings, apartment buildings, and businesses. Los Feliz was until fairly recently one of Los Angeles' more old-fashioned and sedate neighborhoods. Residents lived in the area for years and frequented shops that had been there since they moved in. But the 1990s saw a shift as old-time businesses were replaced by the new, the hip, and the retro. The area has even been referred to as the New SoHo. Today, punks in tangerine-colored mohawks relax over chai teas at trendy coffee emporiums, while at the next table white-haired matrons sip their decafs.

SIGHTS

There are three main entrances to **Griffith Park** off Los Feliz Boulevard. Fern Dell Drive, on the park's western edge near Western Avenue, winds past a children's playground and a popular picnic area. Vermont Avenue leads directly to the outdoor Greek Theater amphitheater and then to Observation Drive, which leads to the observatory. At the eastern edge, near Route 5, Griffith Park Drive is the most direct route to the merry-go-round, the zoo, the Gene Autry Western Heritage Museum, and Travel Town.

Standing above the urban fray at the southern end of the park is the **Griffith Observatory and Planetarium,** a copper-domed beauty that perfectly represents the public-monument architecture of the 1930s. With its bas-reliefs and interior murals, this eerie site also resembles a kind of interplanetary temple. In fact it has been the setting for numerous science fiction films such as *When Worlds Collide* (1951). The Observatory's most famous appearance, however, was in *Rebel Without a Cause* (1955) when James Dean was confronted by the neighborhood gang.

Apart from a movie setting, the Observatory, which is closed through 2005 for major renovations, will feature a high-tech

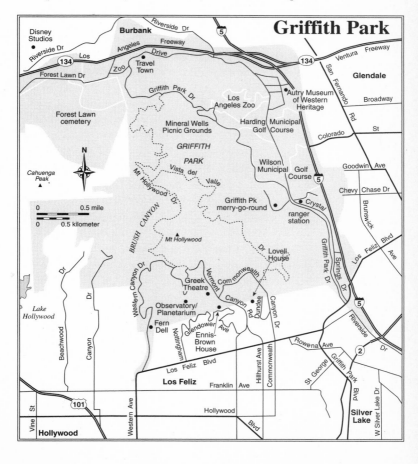

planetarium theater and astronomy exhibits complete with telescopes. A lot of people come simply for the view, which on clear days (in Los Angeles?) extends from the Hollywood Hills to the Pacific. A temporary satellite facility near the L.A. zoo offers mini-planetarium shows, a meteorite exhibit, and a telescopic viewing of the moon and planets at night. Call for details. ~ 2800 East Observatory Road; 323-664-1191, fax 323-663-4323; www.griffithobs.org, e-mail info@griffithobs.org.

Local bird species nest in Fern Dell, a shady glade in Griffith Park with a spring-fed stream. The picnic tables lining the dell create an inviting spot to while away an afternoon. ~ Western Canyon Road.

Toward the southern edge of the park, you'll see the **Griffith Park & Southern Railroad**, a miniature train ride. In the winter, you can ride with Santa. A nearby track offers **pony rides** (closed Monday). Admission. ~ 323-664-6788.

The **ranger station** will provide maps and information while directing you across the street to the **merry-go-round**, a beautiful 1926-vintage carousel. The merry-go-round is open weekends only.

Featuring real life versions of these whirling animals, the **Los Angeles Zoo** is among the highlights of the park. Over 1200 animals inhabit this 113-acre facility, many in environments simulating their natural habitats. The African exhibit houses elephants, rhinos, zebras, and monkeys; Eurasia is represented by tigers; there are jaguars from South America as well as kangaroos and koalas from Australia. Check out its sea lion exhibit slated for inauguration in summer 2004. Admission. ~ 5333 Zoo Drive; 323-644-6400, fax 323-662-9786; www.lazoo.org.

The adjacent **Adventure Island** is where newborn animals are bottle-fed. You can see the baby animals in an exhibition area.

Travel Town is a transportation museum featuring a train yard full of cabooses, steam engines, and passenger cars from the glory days of the railroad. The exhibit also includes a fleet of 1920-era fire trucks and old milk wagons. For the kids there are narrow-gauge train rides (fee). ~ 5200 West Zoo Drive; 323-662-5874.

For Hollywood's version of American history, there's the **Autry Museum of Western Heritage**, located inside the park. The focus here is both on Westerns and the West, and you will see Billy the Kid's gun and Wyatt Earp's badge. There are displays of saloons and stagecoaches, silver saddles, and ivory-handled six-shooters, plus paintings, photos, and film clips of all your fa-

vorite stars, kids. Its nine galleries feature art by Frederic Rem-
ington and Thomas Moran. Closed Monday. Admission. ~ 4700
Western Heritage Way; 323-667-2000, fax 323-660-5721; www.
autry-museum.org.

High on a slope overlooking Los Angeles stands the **Ennis-
Brown House,** a squarerigged, Mayan temple–style home designed
by Frank Lloyd Wright in 1924. You need a reservation to visit.
Closed Sunday. Admission. ~ 2655 Glendower Avenue, Los Feliz;
323-660-0607; www.ennisbrownhouse.org, e-mail ennisbrn@
primenet.com.

The Ennis-Brown mansion resides in the same neighborhood
as the **Lovell House,** a prime example of Richard Neutra's International style of architecture, circa 1929. ~ 4616 Dundee Drive,
Los Feliz.

DINING

Hillhurst Avenue is the Los Feliz area's restaurant row. The Los
Feliz edition of the perennially popular chain, **Louise's Trattoria,**
offers a patio for alfresco dining on California pizzas (try the sausage), salads, homemade pastas (the penne bolognese is simple
but satisfying), lasagne, and chicken entrées. Reliable and affordable. ~ 4500 Los Feliz Boulevard at Hillhurst Avenue; 323-667-
0777. MODERATE.

The tiny, storefront **Trattoria Farfalla** has received its fair
share of praise over the years for simple, but terrific, Italian cooking and reasonable prices. Try tagliolini with shrimp, garlic, and
olive oil, and *insalata farfalla* of romaine and radicchio atop crisp
pizza bread. The place is always crowded, so if you're uncom-
fortable dining almost intimately with strangers, skip it. ~ 1978
Hillhurst Avenue; 323-661-7365, fax 323-661-5956. MODERATE.

Capriccio on Vermont is located toward the eastern edge of
Griffith Park. This little storefront restaurant spills out onto the
wide corner sidewalk on warm evenings, creating a scene reminiscent of Rome or Paris. Try any of the pastas—spaghetti *del
mare,* for example, or Antonio chicken in a light, creamy tomato
sauce. Dinner only. ~ 1757 North Vermont Avenue; 323-662-
5900, fax 323-465-2638. MODERATE.

SHOPPING

You can browse the stacks or snuggle up in a reading chair at
Skylight Books in Los Feliz. This marvelous facility has an extensive selection of foreign and American literature as well as literary periodicals. They also produce a variety of discussions with

and readings by local authors, artists, and community leaders. ~ 1818 North Vermont Avenue; 323-660-1175; www.skylightbooks. com, e-mail skylightbooks@earthlink.net.

NIGHTLIFE The giant 6000-seat **Greek Theatre**, nestled in the rolling hills of Griffith Park, is patterned after a classical Greek amphitheater. The entertainment in this enchanting spot ranges from stellar jazz, classical, pop, and rock music to dance and dramatic performances. Bring a sweater and picnic. ~ 2700 North Vermont Avenue; 323-665-1927; www.nederlander.com/greekbo.html.

Get into the Latin swing of things at **La Fogata**, a sizzling Colombian restaurant and nightclub. Cover. ~ 3000 Los Feliz Boulevard; 323-664-2955.

There's live entertainment every night at **The Derby**, starting between 9:30 and 10:30 p.m. and ranging from rockabilly bands to tap dancing. Call 323-769-5105 for entertainment information. This contemporary club (featuring an oval bar that appeared in *Mildred Pierce*) also offers swing dance lessons Wednesday through Saturday, from 8 to 9 p.m. Cover. ~ 4500 Los Feliz Boulevard at Hillhurst Avenue; 323-663-8979; www.the-derby.com.

North Vermont Avenue, between Hollywood Boulevard and Franklin Avenue, offers some nightlife possibilities. For film offerings in the neighborhood, look to the **Los Feliz Theater.** ~ 1822 North Vermont Avenue at Franklin Avenue; 323-664-2169. **The Dresden**, a stately brick-and-stained-glass restaurant, hosts an elegant piano bar. ~ 1760 North Vermont Avenue; 323-665-4294; www.thedresden.com.

FOUR

Hollywood/Wilshire

Anchored by the Hollywood Hills to the north, Olympic Boulevard to the south, Downtown to the east and Beverly Hills to the west, the sprawling Hollywood–Wilshire area is an eclectic melting pot of infinite variety. Ethnic neighborhoods include Jewish, Korean, Southeast Asian, Filipino, Mexican, and Central American residents, and lifestyles are equally varied, running the gamut from Holocaust survivors to flamboyant cross-dressers. However, the area has gone through many incarnations to reach this point.

It was farm country when Horace and Daeida Wilcox first moved to Cahuenga Valley. Originally part of the Rancho La Brea land grant, the dusty hills lay planted in bell peppers, watermelons, and citrus trees. Then in 1887 Horace had a brainstorm: he subdivided the family farm, Daeida christened the spread "Hollywood," and they put lots on the market for $150 an acre.

By 1910, the cow town's population had grown to 4000 god-fearing, middle-class souls. Like the Wilcoxes, they were staid and sober folk, drawn predominantly from Midwestern stock.

Then came the deluge. The fledgling movie industry—attracted by warm weather and natural locations and conspiring to avoid the royalties levied by Thomas Edison's East Coast company for use of his moving-picture inventions—began relocating to Hollywood. The first studio arrived in 1911. Two years later the trio of Jesse Lasky, Samuel Goldfish (later Goldwyn), and Cecil B. De Mille set up shop. De Mille soon began shooting *Squaw Man*, the first full-length motion picture, in a barn on the corner of Selma Avenue and Vine Street.

The townsfolk termed these studios "gypsy camps" and posted signs declaring, "No dogs, No actors." Movie people were Easterners, morally suspect and in many cases Jewish, defining characteristics guaranteed to stir unease among the local Protestant majority.

But if there is no stopping progress, it is simply impossible to halt a tidal wave. During the 1920s the movie industry became a billion-dollar business, with Hollywood its capital. Picture palaces mushroomed along Hollywood Boulevard beside glamorous restaurants and majestic hotels, and by 1930 the population totaled 150,000.

Hollywood's glory days lasted until the 1960s, when development gave way to decline. The boulevard of dreams became a byway for bikers; Chevys with hydraulic lifters replaced limousines; punks with flaming hair supplanted platinum starlets; and movie studios moved to the San Fernando Valley. Prostitutes worked side streets, leaving the major thoroughfares to hawkers, hustlers, and Hollywood visionaries.

Today, a considerable redevelopment effort has resulted in cleaner streets and sidewalks, particularly along Hollywood Boulevard.

Meanwhile, the corridor along Wilshire Boulevard running between Downtown and Beverly Hills, once a bastion of elegant commercial buildings and homes for the affluent, also began to crumble. Wealthier residents moved to the tony communities of Beverly Hills, Bel Air, and Brentwood while struggling Latino and Asian immigrants flooded the area. Downtown Hollywood became a hangout for the unsavory. Hookers and drug pushers cruised Hollywood Boulevard as the once lavish Wilshire Boulevard buildings fell into disrepair. Today both areas are struggling to recapture at least a modicum of their former glory. Revitalization efforts are afoot in the Wilshire District, and parts of Hollywood Boulevard have been upgraded, as the Hollywood and Highland entertainment complex attests. Meanwhile, West Hollywood has become home to L.A.'s largest gay population.

Hollywood

Despite how tawdry or tired it gets, Hollywood is a legend in its own time. In fact, the word Hollywood has far extended its geographic boundaries and become synonymous with glamour, wealth, and fantasy. This is quite contrast to the reality that is Hollywood, the city. Sizable Latino, Asian, African-American, and Armenian populations have created ethnic neighborhoods here, and the commercial districts are slowly being refurbished. Enough new palm and jacaranda trees have been planted to satisfy preconceived images, new "old Hollywood" light fixtures installed, and private security patrols ensure the safety of (and even answer questions for) Hollywood tourists.

Regardless of the changes, seemingly in spite of itself, the place remains Hollywood, tawdry and tragic, with all its myth and magic. The town that F. Scott Fitzgerald said "can be understood . . . only dimly and in flashes" is still an odd amalgam of truth and tinsel, promise and impossibility, conjuring images of big studios and bright stars.

CENTRAL HOLLYWOOD   It was 1918 when Aline Barnsdall, an enchantingly eccentric oil heiress, purchased an entire hill in Hollywood, planted the 36 acres with olive trees and christened the spot Olive Hill. She next hired Frank Lloyd Wright to design a family home and adjoining arts center. Olive Hill subsequently became **Barnsdall Park,** an aerie studded with olive and conifer trees, from which visitors can survey the entire sweep of Hollywood. ~ 4800 Hollywood Boulevard.

Wright's masterwork became **Hollyhock House,** a sprawling 6200-square-foot home that represents his California Romanza style. Constructed of poured concrete and stucco, the house incorporates a geometric motif based on the hollyhock, Aline Barnsdall's favorite flower. Closed for renovations until spring 2004. ~ Barnsdall Park; 323-913-4157.

Wright also designed the **Barnsdall Arts Center Gallery,** where adult art classes are taught. Call for hours. ~ Barnsdall Park; 323-644-6295.

The nearby **Municipal Art Gallery,** a gray concrete structure built in 1971, offers changing exhibits of Southern California

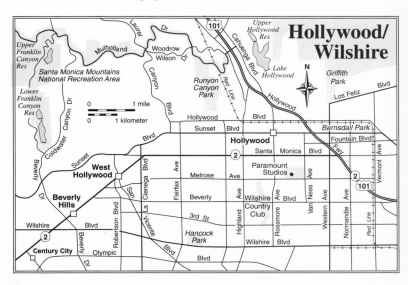

contemporary artwork. While the focus is regional, nearly every arts and crafts medium is represented. Closed Monday and Tuesday. ~ Barnsdall Park; 323-644-6269.

Also part of the Barnsdall Park art complex, the **Junior Arts Center** offers classes for young people. Be sure to see the Holly-wood mural that covers an outside wall of this building. Call for hours. ~ Barnsdall Park; 213-485-4474, fax 213-485-7456.

Not so very long ago, the public wasn't allowed behind the famous wrought-iron gate at **Paramount Studios**. A subject for countless newsreels and Hollywood movies, the portal's most memorable appearance was in *Sunset Boulevard* (1950) when Erich von Stroheim drove Gloria Swanson onto the lot for her tragic encounter with Cecil B. De Mille. (See "Hollywood in Action" for more about studio tours.)

Established during the silent era, Paramount signed stars such as Rudolph Valentino and Clara Bow in the 1920s, Gary Cooper and Marlene Dietrich during the 1930s, and later headlined Bob Hope and Bing Crosby. Today the studio creates TV shows such as "Dr. Phil" and "Charmed," as well as produces blockbuster movies. Unfortunately, with the events of September 11, 2001, the studio and lot remain closed to the public. Tickets to show tapings are still available, though (323-956-1777). Closed week-ends. Admission. ~ 5555 Melrose Avenue; 323-956-1777; www.paramount.com, e-mail info@pde.paramount.com.

Many of these same legends lie buried just north of the stu-dio in **Hollywood Forever Memorial Park**. Surrounded by high walls and shaded with palm trees, the 60-acre greensward is a kind of museum park crowded with Greek statues, Egyptian tem-ples, and Roman memorials. Marble urns and obelisks adorn the place, and the Paramount water tower rises above the south wall.

Along the eastern side of the cemetery, Rudolph Valentino rests in Cathedral Mausoleum, crypt number 1205; Peter Finch is across the aisle in number 1224. Around the nearby pond are the graves of Tyrone Power, Marion Davies, Adolphe Menjou, and the double tomb of Cecil B. De Mille and his wife, Constance Adam De Mille. Next to the Cathedral Mausoleum, a staircase leads to the reflecting pool and tomb of Douglas Fairbanks. ~ 6000 Santa Monica Boulevard.

No one can quite figure how Movieland's most famous address became so prominent. Most of the action occurred elsewhere, but somehow the corner of **Hollywood and Vine** has come to symbolize Hollywood. But Hollywood is good at making the most of fables, so new "skytracker" lights at each of the four corners create an archway of light above the vaunted intersection.

Maybe it's the many radio studios that lined the thoroughfare during the 1930s, or perhaps because the **Pantages Theater** is just down the street. One of the nation's finest art-deco theaters, the Pantages was built in 1930, with a vaulted-ceiling lobby and a monumental auditorium. ~ 6233 Hollywood Boulevard; 323-468-1770, fax 323-468-1718; www.nederlander.com, e-mail concerts@nederlander.com.

Gazing down on all the commotion is the **Capitol Records Building**, a building you have seen in countless photographs. Resembling a squadron of flying saucers piggy-backed on one another, the 13-story structure was actually designed to look like

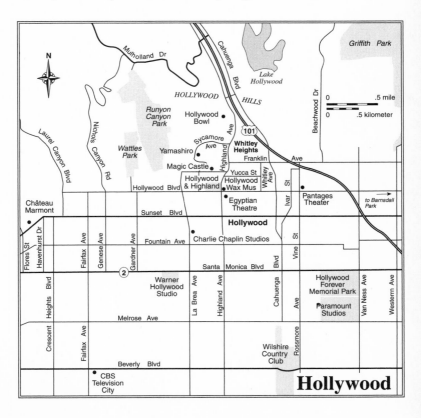

Hollywood

a stack of records with a stylus protruding from the top. ~ 1750 Vine Street.

In a tribute to the great studios once occupying the area, **Home Savings of America** adorned its facade with the names of hundreds of stars and added a tile mural depicting the most note-worthy. The interior contains a marvelous stained-glass window with scenes from Hollywood's early movies. ~ 1500 North Vine Street.

Paramount is the last of the great studios to remain in Hollywood.

Above Hollywood Boulevard, the **1800 block of North Ivar Street** is lined with apartment buildings re-flecting the architecture of the 1920s and 1930s. Na-thaniel West lived in the mock-Tudor **Parua Sed Apart-ments** at #1817 in 1935. Here he wrote screenplays and began work on his great Hollywood novel *The Day of the Locust*. The Mediterranean-style **Alto Nido Apartments** were the fic-tional home of the down-and-out screenwriter played by William Holden in *Sunset Boulevard*. ~ 1851 North Ivar Street.

Eschewing nostalgia, **Los Angeles Contemporary Exhibitions** (LACE), a nonprofit fine-arts center, works with artists to pro-duce and present work in all mediums. Closed Monday and Tuesday; open late on Friday nights. ~ 6522 Hollywood Boule-vard; 323-957-1777, fax 323-956-1777; www.artleak.org, e-mail info@artleak.org.

During the halcyon days of the 1920s, as silent movies gave way to talkies, Hollywood Boulevard was door-to-door with mansions. **The Janes House**, one of the last of this long-vanished breed, is a Queen Anne Victorian complete with turret, gable, and stained-glass windows. This architectural grande belle rests at the end of a plastic shopping mall. Closed Sunday. ~ 6541 Hollywood Boulevard.

Today, Hollywood Boulevard has been taken over by taco vendors, cut-rate video stores, T-shirt and wig shops, and sou-venir stands. More like New York's 42nd Street than the Great White Way, it's a cheap strip where photo galleries take tourists' pictures next to cardboard cutouts of stars.

Throughout this area—extending for two and a half miles along Hollywood Boulevard from Gower Street to La Brea Boule-vard and on Vine Street between Sunset Boulevard and Yucca Street—is the **Walk of Fame**, of star-studded terrazzo, commem-orating notables from the film, television, radio, theater, and music industries. The names of more than 2230 legends appear on brass-rimmed stars embedded in the glittery sidewalk. Pride of Hollywood, it is the only walkway in Los Angeles to be washed several times weekly. Among the stars most frequently sought out by visitors are Marilyn Monroe at 6774 Hollywood Boulevard, James Dean at 1719 Vine Street, John Lennon at 1750 Vine Street, and Elvis Presley at 7080 Hollywood Boulevard. If you've just got to know where your favorite star's star is located, call the **Hollywood Chamber of Commerce.** The Chamber of Commerce also can tell you when the next ceremony will take place to honor a celebrity with a sidewalk star. Closed weekends. ~ 323-469-8311, fax 323-469-2805; www.hollywoodchamber.net, www.explorehollywood.com.

The perfect expression of this high-camp neighborhood is **Frederick's of Hollywood,** a lingerie shop located in an outrageous battleship gray-and-pink art-deco building. With a naughty reputation and a selection of undergarments that leave nothing to the imagination, Frederick's is one of those places we visit in spite of ourselves. Be sure to make your way to the back of the store and visit **Frederick's of Hollywood Lingerie Museum,** rich in Hollywood's version of cultural treasures. On display are a tassels-and-leather bustier from Madonna, the bra Marilyn Monroe wore in *Let's Make Love,* a more modest (but autographed) 32B from Cher, and celebrity undergarments worn by such icons as Mae West and Zsa Zsa Gabor. ~ 6608 Hollywood Boulevard; 323-466-8506, fax 323-464-5149; www.fredericks.com.

The nonprofit film preservation group American Cinematheque had recently agreed to purchase the abandoned **Egyptian Theatre** from the city for a $1 token payment when a 1994 earthquake knocked 40-foot holes in its walls. Earthquake insurance provided seed money for the $13 million restoration of the venerable theater where Cecil B. De Mille's *The Ten Commandments* premiered. Today, with 616 seats instead of the original 2071, the theater presents nightly film retrospectives and a Saturday-and-Sunday afternoon 55-minute history of filmmaking entitled *Forever Hollywood.* ~ 6712 Hollywood Boulevard; 323-466-3456; www.egyptiantheatre.com.

Then there's the **Hollywood Wax Museum,** a melancholy place where you can "see your favorite stars in living wax." Here they are—Marilyn Monroe and Elvis Presley, Clint Eastwood, Sylvester

Stallone and the "Governator" (Arnold Schwarzenegger)—looking just as they would three days after rigor mortis set in, that classic grin or sneer frozen forevermore into a candle with arms. Admission. ~ 6767 Hollywood Boulevard; 323-462-8860, fax 323-462-3993; www.hollywoodwax.com, e-mail contact@holly woodwaxmuseum.com.

Built by Sid Grauman in 1927, **Mann's Chinese Theatre** is a fabulous movie palace, fashioned in a kind of Oriental Baroque style with pagoda roof, stone guard dogs, metal towers, Asian masks, and beautiful bas-reliefs. The interior is equally as lavish with its ornate columns, murals, and Asian vases.

Though the architecture is splendid, the theater is actually known for its sidewalk. Embedded in the cement forecourt are the handprints and footprints of Hollywood's greatest stars. Elizabeth Taylor, Harrison Ford, Susan Sarandon, and Denzel Washington have left their signatures in this grandest of all autograph collections. Not every celebrity simply signed and stepped, however: there are also cement images of Jimmy Durante's nose, Betty Grable's leg, Harpo Marx's harp, and the webbed feet of Donald Duck. ~ 6925 Hollywood Boulevard; 323-464-6266, fax 323-463-0879; www.manntheatres.com.

Butting up against the theater is **Hollywood & Highland**—a mega-entertainment center chock full of restaurants and shops. The Kodak Theatre stands at the heart of the complex and hosts plays, musical performances and the Academy Awards. Also located here is the **Hollywood Visitors Center**. (See "Hooray for Hollywood!" feature in this chapter.) ~ 6801 Hollywood Boulevard; 323-467-6412.

STARRY NIGHTS

Only true night owls will get the full effect of **Night Gallery**, the larger than life–sized series of movie star murals painted on the rolldown security doors of shops on Hollywood Boulevard between Cherokee and Wilcox. The collection consists of almost 40 portraits ranging from Liberace to Harrison Ford. Viewable only at night when stores are closed, these murals were created by Susan Krieg and her team of artists; six muralists, working only between 9 p.m. and 4 a.m., completed the project in two months. Known for her public artworks, often in blighted areas, Krieg's motive is to transform neighborhoods by creating pride in local art.

Hollywood's been around for 80 years, but until the **Holly-**   ◄ HIDDEN
wood Entertainment Museum came on the scene in 1996, there
had never been a museum dedicated solely to the history, technology, and artifacts of Hollywood and the entertainment arts.
The central gallery is a rotunda, where a multimedia presentation about Hollywood is shown at intervals throughout the day.
Radiating from the rotunda are interactive displays employing
interactive computers, video clips, and a few special effects. Visitors
can actually step onto the bridge of the U.S.S. *Enterprise*, one of
the sets from the television series "Star Trek." Then it's on to the
set of "Cheers," whose cast members carved their names into the
bar as a farewell when the show ended. Closed Wednesday from
Labor Day to Memorial Day. Admission. ~ 7021 Hollywood
Boulevard; 323-465-7900; www.hollywoodmuseum.com, e-mail
info@hollywoodmuseum.com.

Despite numerous incarnations, including the most recent as
headquarters for Jim Henson Studios, the **Charlie Chaplin**
Studios have weathered the years relatively unchanged, except
for the statue of Kermit the Frog that proudly adorns the entry-
way. This row of Tudor cottages, built by Chaplin in 1918,
housed the star's sound stage, dressing rooms, carpentry shop,
and stables. The studios currently screen silent movies. ~ 1416
North La Brea Avenue.

HOLLYWOOD HILLS   The lower slopes of the enchanting Santa
Monica Mountains contain some of Los Angeles' most fashionable addresses. These rugged foothills, divorced from the glitter
of Hollywood by serpentine roads, provide a pricey escape valve
from the pressures of Tinseltown. But for those with a car and
an afternoon, it costs no more to explore Hollywood's vaunted
upcountry than to browse Beverly Hills' Rodeo Drive.

Beachwood Canyon, one of the town's prettiest residential
areas, is a V-shaped valley with 1920s- and 1930s-era homes on
either side. First developed as "Hollywoodland" by *Los Angeles*
Times publisher Harry Chandler, the neighborhood is now popular with screenwriters. When Chandler broke ground, he hoped
to create an urban utopia "above the traffic congestion, smoke,
fog, and poisonous gas fumes of the lowlands." (It seems that even
in the 1920s, long before Los Angeles had a name for it, the city
suffered from smog.) ~ Beachwood Drive.

Text continued on page 102.

Hollywood
in Action

The tram is filled with innocent people, a random collection of folks from all walks, some with little kids in tow. Suddenly it is blasted by aliens and hijacked onto a giant spaceship. As the Cyclons prepare to destroy the tram, a laser battle of galactic proportions breaks out.

Escaping one peril, the passengers cross a collapsing wooden bridge, dodge a flash flood and are swept up in an avalanche. This is all child's play compared to the next adventure, when the tram crosses the Brooklyn Bridge with flames erupting, sirens screaming, and King Kong clinging to the trembling girders.

Sound like Hollywood? Actually it's **Universal Studios Hollywood**, a Disneyesque introduction to one of the nation's biggest motion picture and TV facilities. Founded in 1912 when Carl Laemmle, a Bavarian immigrant, converted a chicken farm into a production lot for silent films, Universal is a mammoth 415-acre complex complete with 36 sound stages, a 15-story administration building, and a staff of more than 10,000 filmmakers. Admission. ~ 100 Universal City Plaza, Universal City; 818-508-9600, fax 818-622-0407; www.universalstudios.com.

More like an amusement park than an authentic studio tour, Universal offers visitors an ersatz introduction to Hollywood. The tram passes the locations for classic films such as *My Little Chickadee* (1940) and *The Sting* (1973) and explores the backlot with its street sets of Europe, Texas, New York, and Mexico. If Hollywood is one step away from reality, the Universal Tour is two steps. It's a staging of a staging, a Hollywood version of Hollywood.

Among the most exciting rides at this movie-studio-cum-theme-park are "Jurassic Park—The Ride," "Shrek 4-D," "Back to the Future," "E.T. Adventure," "Revenge of the Mummy—The Ride," "Van Helsing: Fortress of Dracula," and "Terminator2: 3D," based on some of Universal's most popular films. Be prepared for long lines! However, a new service, once offered only to movie stars and public figures, is available—for a steep price. The VIP Experience offers guests a "private tour" of Universal aboard a 15-seat trolley. Walk through props and costume shops, peek inside sound stages and enjoy side-door admittance to the park's signature rides and attractions. But this doesn't come cheaply; expect to pay a pretty penny for one of the limited daily spots on the VIP trolley.

The **NBC Studio Tour** provides a similar view of the television industry. Though only 70 minutes long (in contrast to Universal's half-day extravaganza), it takes guests onto the set of Jay Leno's "Tonight Show" and offers glimpses at other sound stages in use. The wardrobe area, set-construction shop, and make-up room are also on the itinerary. Closed Saturday in winter and Sunday year-round. Admission. ~ 3000 West Alameda Avenue, Burbank; 818-840-3537, fax 818-840-3065; www.nbci.com.

The **Warner Brothers Studios**, by contrast, takes you behind the scenes to see the day-to-day activities of a multimedia complex. It's also home to the Warner Brothers Museum, where memorabilia from the 75-year history of the studio is displayed, including an Oscar awarded for creating Hollywood's first talkie movie, *The Jazz Singer*. No children under the age of eight allowed; tours are mostly technical and educational and change daily. Closed weekends. Admission. ~ 4301 West Olive Avenue, Burbank; 818-954-1744, fax 818-954-2089; www.wbstudio tour.com, e-mail studiotour@warnerbros.com.

Dozens of television programs are taped in Los Angeles. The prime production season runs from August through March. For information on tickets call: **Audiences Unlimited** (818-506-0067); **Paramount Guest Relations** (323-956-1777); **NBC-TV** (818-840-4444).

That's Hollywood!

To advertise "Hollywoodland" the developer erected a huge sign on the hillside. Eventually "land" was removed, the fixture was refurbished, and Chandler's billboard became the **Hollywood Sign**, a 45-foot-tall, 450-foot-long landmark that is now the foremost symbol of Movieland. (Head up Beachwood Drive toward the sign and you'll pass through the stone entrance gates of Hollywoodland at Westshire Drive. Be forewarned: hiking up to the sign can earn you a hefty ticket.) The corner of Gower Street and Sunset Boulevard provides a picture-perfect view of the sign.

Los Angeles has little space for idyllic retreats. One of the city's more placid places is **Lake Hollywood**, a forest-framed reservoir created by the Mulholland Dam. Popular with hikers and joggers, the lake is surrounded by a chain-link fence but still offers splendid views. The reservoir was built in 1925 by Water Commissioner William Mulholland as part of Los Angeles' scandalous water program. Scenes from *Chinatown* (1974), the movie that exposed the civic corruption behind Mulholland's project, were shot around the lake. ~ Southern entrance is at Weidlake Drive; northern entrance is at Lake Hollywood Drive.

For stars living in **Whitley Heights** during the 1920s, life was much like it is in Beverly Hills today. This hilltop neighborhood, with its tile-roofed Mediterranean homes, was the premier residential area for the silent-movie set. Rudolph Valentino lived here, and later stars included Gloria Swanson, Bette Davis, and Janet Gaynor. Today the realm is as unspoiled as it was when H. J. Whitley, a Los Angeles developer with an eye to Europe, first built his "Italian hilltown." To explore the landmark neighborhood, drive up Whitley Avenue to Whitley Terrace and Wedgewood Place, following all three streets as they spiral around the hilltop.

TOWERING LEGENDS

The **sculpture** at the intersection of Hollywood and La Brea boulevards defies simple characterization. It's a gleaming, 30-foot-high gazebo supported at each corner by a statue of a Hollywood legend (Dolores del Rio, Anna May Wong, Mae West, and Dorothy Dandridge) and crowned with what is supposed to be Marilyn Monroe but looks more like an angel atop the Eiffel Tower. Check it out.

One of Hollywood's most enduring symbols is the **Holly-wood Bowl**, a concrete band shell built in 1929. Situated in a sylvan glade called Daisy Dell, the concert hall is an amphitheater within an amphitheater, surrounded by a circle of wooded hills. ~ 2301 North Highland Avenue; 323-850-2000, fax 213-972-7560; www.hollywoodbowl.org.

The Los Angeles Philharmonic performs here and a regular series of concerts is presented. Many movies have used the shell as a backdrop, including *Anchors Aweigh* and the 1937 version of *A Star Is Born*.

The **Hollywood Bowl Museum** presents a fine exhibit of the   ◀ HIDDEN
Bowl's fascinating 75-year history. Display drawers can be opened for a look at vintage programs or letters written by the likes of Aaron Copland and Eugene Ormandy. Listening stations are set up with headphones so you can listen to an 80-year-old recording of soprano Amelita Galli-Curci, a superstar of her day, singing "Caro Nome" from Verdi's *Rigoletto*; or the first open-air recording, made in 1928 of Tchaikovsky's Adagio from *Sleeping Beauty*; or recordings of other artists who've appeared at the Bowl, including Ella Fitzgerald and Paul McCartney. Closed Sunday and Monday. ~ 2301 North Highland Avenue; 323-850-2058, fax 213-972-7560; www.hollywoodbowl.org, e-mail museum@ laphil.org.

A part of Hollywood's history stands just across the street. Back in 1913, a young director named Cecil B. De Mille found a farm town called Hollywood with a horse barn he could use as a studio. The barn, a kind of woodframe keepsake, moved around with De Mille over the years, seeing use as an office, a set, and even a gymnasium for stars like Gary Cooper and Kirk Douglas. It was here that Paramount Pictures was born. Eventually moved to its present site, the historic building became the **Hollywood Heritage Museum**, a showplace dedicated to the era of silent films and containing a replica of De Mille's original office. Open weekends only. Admission. ~ 2100 North Highland Avenue; 323-874-2276, fax 323-789-7281.

If that French Renaissance mansion above Hollywood Boulevard begins to levitate, you'll know the residents are busy at work. The **Magic Castle**, built in 1909, is "the only club in the world devoted to magicians and lovers of magic." Once a private estate, the club now plays host to the Academy of Magical Arts, a members-only organization that includes many of the town's top tricksters. ~ 7001 Franklin Avenue; www.magiccastle.com.

Farther up the hill lies another dream house, a magnificent replica of a Japanese palace called **Yamashiro**. Built of cedar and teak in 1911, the former estate is presently a restaurant complete with ceremonial gardens and a 600-year-old pagoda. Of the many films shot here perhaps the most famous was *Sayonara* (1958), in which Yamashiro was cast as the American Officers' Club. ~ 1999 North Sycamore Avenue; 323-466-5125, fax 323-462-4523; www.yamashirorestaurant.com, e-mail marketing@yamashirorestaurant.com.

From here it's an easy jaunt up Outpost Drive through **Outpost Estates**. Another of Hollywood's picture-perfect neighborhoods, this residential canyon was developed during the 1920s by a creative contractor who placed the utilities underground and built Mediterranean-style homes. The result is a lovely, tree-shaded community, an unpretentious version of Beverly Hills.

HIDDEN ► Tucked into a narrow canyon lies **Wattles Park**, part of the old Gurdon Wattles Estate, a 49-acre preserve. While the Wattles Mansion and formal gardens can be viewed by appointment only, the adjacent park is open on a regular basis. A pond, palm grove, and teahouse occupy the property. ~ 1850 North Curson Avenue; 323-874-4005; www.hollywoodheritage.org.

Château Marmont is a brooding presence amid the glitter. Constructed around 1929 in the pattern of a Norman castle, the place has numbered James Dean, Bob Dylan, and Robert DeNiro among its guests. With its petite gardens, imposing colonnade, and arched-window lobby, the hotel is a study in European elegance. Little wonder it is still favored by Hollywood stars as a hometown hideaway. ~ 8221 Sunset Boulevard; 323-656-1010.

The real spirit of the Hollywood Hills resides in the deep canyons that climb from Hollywood Boulevard into the Santa Monica Mountains. **Nichols Canyon**, a chaparral-coated valley adorned with million-dollar homes, represents one of the toniest parts of town. A narrow two-lane road winds through dense forest to bald heights. ~ Nichols Canyon Road.

Possessing the same cachet and even greater fame, **Laurel Canyon** became known as a hippie hideaway during the 1960s. With

Hooray for Hollywood!

Hollywood & Highland is the latest evidence that Hollywood is coming into a renaissance. An enormous entertainment, shopping, and dining complex, **Hollywood & Highland** is part mall, part theater, and part street scene. Mann's Chinese Theater is here, as is the Kodak Theater (the new home of the Academy Awards), the Grand Ballroom (an upscale venue for catered parties, run by L.A.'s favorite chef, Wolfgang Puck), and a six-screen multiplex cinema. The shopping area features many of the usual suspects (Banana Republic, the Gap) alongside boutiques offering everything from diamonds to blue jeans. The restaurants range from chains like California Pizza Kitchen (323-460-2080) to unique, upscale spots like The Grill on Hollywood (323-856-5530).

This huge outdoor mall dominates the neighborhood and displays a completely different aspect depending on the angle from which you approach it. Coming down Highland Avenue from the north, the enormous four-story Babylonian Arch is the first thing to catch your eye. Its size is impressive, but most arresting is its diagonal positioning. If you enter through the arch, towering above you are two 20-foot pedestals with a life-size elephant sculpture atop each one. Cruising along Hollywood Boulevard traveling east or west, the wraparound, fully animated billboard at the top of the building will make you think you're in the Ginza in Tokyo or Times Square in New York. (The effect is most successful after dark, of course.) Approaching this $615 million dollar extravaganza from underneath, you rise out of the metro station to Hollywood Boulevard, the glittering sidewalk embedded with the names of entertainment stars. The whole complex offers something that's been missing in Hollywood for a long time: glamour. ~ Hollywood Boulevard and Highland Avenue; 323-467-6412; www.hollywoodandhighland.com.

If you like it so much here that you want to stay, you can book a room at the **Renaissance Hollywood Hotel**. With its cool curves and white mirrored facade, this 22-story hostelry evokes the sleek modern design of '50s L.A. Inside, the 637 rooms and suites are appointed in classic '50s fashion, complete with Eames-style chairs and a muted green and yellow color scheme. Amenities include a terrace-top pool and bar, a fitness center, and a restaurant serving eclectic California cuisine. ~ 1755 North Highland Avenue; 323-856-1200, fax 323-856-1205; www.renaissance hollywood.com. ULTRA-DELUXE.

its sinuous side streets and modest bungalows, the wooded vale has a decidedly rustic atmosphere. ~ Laurel Canyon Boulevard.

Both Nichols and Laurel canyons rise sharply into the mountains, eventually reaching the rim of Los Angeles, a 50-mile-long road called **Mulholland Drive**, which extends from Hollywood to Malibu. Tracing a course along the ridge of the Santa Monicas, Mulholland is a spectacularly beautiful road, curving through forests and glades, climbing along sharp precipices, and offering magnificent views of the Los Angeles Basin and San Fernando Valley.

LODGING   The **Hollywood Celebrity Hotel** occupies a 1930s art-deco building located just above Hollywood Boulevard. The 40 guest rooms are nicely refurbished, furnished in neo-deco style and decorated in a Hollywood motif. The rooms are quite spacious and a continental breakfast is included in the rate. There's a sitting room off the lobby. ~ 1775 Orchid Avenue; 323-850-6464, 800-222-7090, fax 323-850-7667; www.hotelcelebrity.com. MODERATE.

The **Orchid Suites Hotel** a few doors down is another 40-unit facility. Lacking the character of its neighbor, it substitutes space and amenities for personality. Every room is a suite and includes a kitchen or kitchenette; there's also an outdoor heated pool. Rooms are fashioned in contemporary style. The building itself is a bland, modern stucco. Reservations strongly recommended. ~ 1753 North Orchid Avenue; 323-874-9678, 800-537-3052, fax 323-874-5246; www.orchidsuites.com, e-mail info@orchidsuites.com. MODERATE.

AUTHOR FAVORITE

The traditional Hollywood hideaway is **Château Marmont**, a Norman-style castle built in 1929. Once favored by Jean Harlow and Howard Hughes, the hotel still lures Hollywood luminaries such as Robert DeNiro, Dustin Hoffman, and Diane Keaton. They come for the privacy and quirky charm of the place, which offers rooms, suites, bungalows, and cottages. Around its beautifully maintained grounds are flower gardens, shade trees, and a heated swimming pool. More than anything, the Marmont possesses cachet, as if the hotel itself were a celebrity, holding within its cloistered lobby a thousand tales of Hollywood. ~ 8221 Sunset Boulevard; 323-656-1010, 800-242-8328, fax 323-655-5311; www.chateaumarmont.com, e-mail reservations@chateaumarmont.com. ULTRA-DELUXE.

Hollywood Boulevard is one of several strips lined with motels. Representative of the species is the **Hollywood Premiere Motel**. This L-shaped building contains standard rooms. There's also an outdoor pool open seasonally. ~ 5333 Hollywood Boulevard; 323-466-1691. BUDGET.

One of Hollywood's best bargains is found at the **Magic Castle Hotel,** a 44-unit establishment next to the famed Magic Castle, a private club for magicians. Suites with fully equipped kitchens are priced moderately and decorated in cool cream tones. They are quite spacious and well maintained. A pool and sundeck are a bonus. ~ 7025 Franklin Avenue; 323-851-0800, 800-741-4915; www.magiccastlehotel.com, e-mail info@magic hotel.com. MODERATE.

Coral Sands Motel is a 58-unit establishment serving the gay community. The guest rooms look out on a central courtyard with pool, jacuzzi, sauna, and exercise area. Each is carpeted wall-to-wall and sentimentally furnished with standard appointments. Continental breakfast is included in the price. Gay-friendly. ~ 1730 North Western Avenue; 323-467-5141, 800-421-3650, fax 323-467-4683; www.coralsands-la.com, e-mail info@coralsands-la. com. BUDGET TO MODERATE.

It's as much a part of Hollywood as the Academy Awards. In fact, the very first Oscars were presented at the **Hollywood Roosevelt Hotel**. Built in 1927, the Spanish Revival building has been completely refurbished and now offers 302 rooms, a restaurant, lounges, and a palm-studded courtyard with pool and hot tub. Priced below many of the city's five-star hotels, this classic caravansary has many features of the finest hostelries. The lobby is a recessed-ceiling affair with colonnades and hand-painted beams. Guest rooms are historic and luxurious. ~ 7000 Hollywood Boulevard; 323-466-7000, 800-950-7667, fax 323-469-7006; www.hollywoodroosevelt.com, e-mail sales@hollywood roosevelt.com. ULTRA-DELUXE.

Jitlada is one of those great ethnic restaurants that L.A. likes to tuck away in minimalls. Just a funky little café, it serves an array of Thai dishes; the most notable are seafood entrées such as squid, mussels, and scallops. Closed Monday. ~ 5233 Sunset Boulevard; 323-667-9809, fax 323-663-3104. BUDGET TO MODERATE.

DINING

HIDDEN ▶

The Hollywood address for righteous soul food is **Roscoe's House of Chicken & Waffles**, a tiny wood-slat café with overhead fans and an easy atmosphere. Ask for an "Oscar" and they'll bring chicken wings and grits; "E-Z Ed's Special" is a chicken liver omelette; and a "Lord Harvey" is a half chicken smothered in gravy and onions. Very hip. ~ 1514 North Gower Street; 323-466-7453, fax 323-962-0278. MODERATE.

La Poubelle means "garbage pail," but it is anything but. This small candlelit restaurant serves up delicate French and Italian cuisine with a style (and a local following) all its own. ~ 5907 Franklin Avenue; 323-465-0807, fax 323-465-0471. MODERATE TO DELUXE.

Popular with entertainers from nearby studios, **Pinot Hollywood and Martini Lounge** is the last word in sleek. From the brick patio with topiary trees and peaked skylight to the pullman booths and green-glass shades, the place is designed with a delicate touch. The American regional cuisine menu changes weekly and offers fresh fish, pasta, pizza, assorted steaks, chops, and chicken for lunch and dinner. No lunch on Saturday. Closed Sunday. ~ 1448 North Gower Street; 323-461-8800; www.patinagroup.com, e-mail hollywood@patinagroup.com. DELUXE.

A cozy Hollywood bungalow has been converted into the fine little restaurant **Off Vine**, known for turning out an eclectic menu of pasta, chicken, and fish. Nothing fancy, but always satisfying. Look for the shark in the roof. ~ 6263 Leland Way, just south of Sunset Boulevard; 323-962-1900, fax 323-962-1969; www.offvine.com. MODERATE TO DELUXE.

The Pig 'N Whistle, complete with soda fountain and an organist, catered to Hollywood legends such as Shirley Temple, Spencer Tracy, and Judy Garland during its heyday from the '20s through the '40s.

Hollywood's oldest restaurant, **Musso & Frank's Grill** is a 1919 original with dark paneling, murals, and red leather booths. A bar and open grill create a clubby atmosphere that reflects the eatery's long tradition. Among the American-style dishes are cracked crab, fresh clams, sea bass, prime rib, roast lamb, plus assorted steaks and chops. Closed Sunday and Monday. ~ 6667 Hollywood Boulevard; 323-467-7788, fax 323-467-3360. MODERATE TO ULTRA-DELUXE.

When the **Pig 'N Whistle** restaurant opened next to the Egyptian Theater in 1927, there were no in-theater concession stands, so the side entrance into the theater's courtyard was used by hungry movie patrons looking for a before- or after-theater meal. By the 1990s, the Pig had deteriorated into a sleazy fast-food joint; fortunately, it was renovated and reopened in 2001. Besides serving lunch and dinner in a relaxed setting, the restaurant is lively at night when the dark, clubby atmosphere attracts a happening bar crowd. ~ 6714 Hollywood Boulevard; 323-463-0000, fax 323-463-0485; www.pignwhistle.com. MODERATE TO DELUXE.

Pink's Famous Chili Dogs is a popular takeout stand that serves hamburgers and tamales. But at Pink's, not ordering a dog slapped with sauce is nearly sacrilegious. For the meat-free among us, vegan dogs are also available. ~ 709 North La Brea Avenue; 323-931-4223, fax 323-935-7465; www.pinkshollywood.com. BUDGET.   ◄ HIDDEN

The fish they serve at **Seafood Village** are not only fresh, they are right there in the display cases of the adjacent market. This nondescript café features several dozen fish dishes plus about a dozen meat entrées; ask about their daily specials. Red snapper, orange roughy, rex sole, sea bass, shark steak, calamari, fried oysters, scallops, shrimp, Alaskan king crab, and Maine lobsters are only some of the offerings. ~ 5732 Melrose Avenue; 323-463-8090. MODERATE.

The celebrity photos covering every inch of **Formosa Cafe** tell a tale of Hollywood that reaches back to the 1940s. This crowded café, originally fashioned from a streetcar, has seen more stars than heaven. Over the years they've poured in from the surrounding studios, leaving autographs and memories. Today you'll find a Chinese restaurant serving low-priced lunches and dinners, a kind of museum with meals. Dinner only; open super-late. ~ 7156 Santa Monica Boulevard; 323-850-9050. BUDGET.

Hollywood's prettiest restaurant is a re-created Japanese palace called **Yamashiro**. Set in the hills overlooking Los Angeles, the mansion was built earlier in the century, modeled after an estate in the high mountains of Japan, and trimmed with ornamental gardens. Dine here and you are surrounded by hand-carved columns, *shoji* screens, and Asian statuary. The courtyard garden contains a waterfall, koi pond, and miniature trees. For dinner they serve a complete Japanese menu as well as Western-style entrées. Dinner only. ~ 1999 North Sycamore Avenue; 323-466-5125. DELUXE TO ULTRA-DELUXE.

SHOPPING Nowhere is the nostalgic heartbeat of Hollywood more evident than along Hollywood Boulevard's Walk of Fame. Most tourist attractions revolve around **Mann's Chinese Theatre**, where the souvenir shops, poster studios, T-shirt stores, and postcard vendors are packed tight as a crowd on opening night. ~ 6925 Hollywood Boulevard; 323-461-3331.

Head over to **Supply Sergeant** and stock up on military and camping gear. A favorite among survivalists, bargain hunters, and pink-coifed punks, this civilian commissary has everything from the subtle to the bizarre. ~ 6664 Hollywood Boulevard; 323-463-4730.

Universal News Agency, reputedly the country's oldest outdoor newsstand, has newspapers and magazines from around the world. ~ 1655 North Las Palmas Avenue; 323-467-3850.

Hollywood Boulevard probably has more bookstores than movie theaters. **Larry Edmunds Bookshop** claims to have the world's largest collection of books and memorabilia on cinema and theater. Closed Sunday. ~ 6644 Hollywood Boulevard; 323-463-3273.

Frederick Mellinger started a tiny mail-order company in 1946 based on the philosophy that "fashion may change but sex appeal is always in style." Today, **Frederick's of Hollywood**, strikingly set in a grey-and-pink art-deco building, continues to entice and enrage onlookers with its fantasy lingerie. ~ 6608 Hollywood Boulevard; 323-466-8506; www.fredericks.com.

The bold exterior of **Soap Plant/Wacko/La Luz de Jesus** hints at the crazy collection of gift items and books within this store. The wild interior is jam-packed with wacky toys and keepsakes, L.A. style. ~ 4633 Hollywood Boulevard; 323-663-0122; www.soapplant.com.

A bigger-than-life mural of Marilyn Monroe marks **Cinema Collectors**. Selling film and television collectibles from every period, they have over 18,000 movie posters and thousands of photos. Closed Sunday. ~ 1507 Wilcox Avenue; 323-461-6516.

HIDDEN ► If Hollywood glamour seems in short supply along the streets of the motion picture capital, a bit of it can be found at the **Cinema Glamour Shop**. Gowns, furs, and other wardrobe items are donated by stars like Julie Andrews, Florence Henderson, and Bob Newhart. You might find a black beaded dress designed by Oleg Cassini ($85), a red Alfred Nipon suit ($125), a white mink jacket ($400), or an original Ferre gown ($95). Closed weekends. ~ 343 North La Brea Avenue; 323-936-9060, fax 323-634-3868.

Reminiscent of the 1930s, the Hollywood Roosevelt Hotel's deco-style **Feinstein's at the Cinegrill** is putting glamour back into Hollywood nightlife. Crème de la crème cabaret entertainers perform here in an intimate, sophisticated atmosphere. Cover. ~ 7000 Hollywood Boulevard; 323-466-7000.

The intimate L-shaped room of the **Gardenia Club** is an ever-popular supper club venue for cabaret entertainers. You don't have to have dinner to attend the show, but sometimes that's the only way to guarantee seating. Reservations required. Cover. ~ 7066 Santa Monica Boulevard; 323-467-7444.

Following a $6 million remodel, Pacific's **El Capitan Theatre** has been returned to its early glory as one of Hollywood's classic theaters. Opened in 1926, the El Capitan is part of the "Cinema District," an eight-block section along Hollywood Boulevard filled with historic landmarks, including several vintage theaters. If you're going to the movies, this is the place! ~ 6838 Hollywood Boulevard; 800-347-6396, www.elcapitantickets.com.

The Palace also has a colorful history dating back to 1927. Today the luxurious complex showcases popular names in rock and jazz, as well as deejay dance nights. Several bars, dancefloors, a restaurant, and an open courtyard add to the luxury. Cover. ~ 1735 North Vine Street; 323-462-3000; www.hollywoodpalace. com, e-mail hpinfo@hollywoodpalace.com.

For sunset panoramas, nothing quite matches **Yamashiro**. Set in a Japanese palace, the lounge overlooks gracious Asian gardens from a perch in the Hollywood Hills. ~ 1999 North Sycamore Avenue; 323-466-5125.

THEATER   Theater in Hollywood varies from tiny storefront establishments to famous stages. In a city filled with actors, the playhouses inevitably are loaded with talent. Professionals from local television and movie studios continually hone their skills on stage, and the area's "equity-waiver" theaters provide an opportunity to see these veterans perform at affordable prices.

The **Hollywood Arts Council** publishes *Discover Hollywood*, calendar listings of all Hollywood theaters. The free, bi-annual publication is available at the Hollywood Visitors Center, or by mailing $2 (postage) to the Council at P.O. Box 931056, Hollywood, CA 90093. ~ 323-462-2355; www.discoverhollywood.com.

To secure tickets for productions, call ticket agencies to charge by phone. Major ticket agencies include **Ticketmaster** (213-480-

3232), **Goodtime Tickets** (323-464-7383), and **Murray's Tickets** (323-234-0123). Or contact the theater directly; day-of-the-event tickets are frequently available for as much as 50 percent off. **Theater LA**'s website offers same-day half-price tickets by using your credit card and paying a service charge for each ticket. ~ www.theatrela.org.

Pantages Theatre, one of Hollywood's largest playhouses, presents major productions, including Broadway musicals. Closed Monday. ~ 6233 Hollywood Boulevard; 323-468-1770; www. nederlander.com, e-mail concerts@nederlander.com.

The refurbished **James Doolittle Theatre**, built in 1926, features top shows from Broadway and London. ~ 1615 North Vine Street. Tickets are available through Telecharge, 800-447-7400.

HIDDEN ► Tucked into a hard-to-find space behind the Egyptian Theatre and down a side street is the **Egyptian Arena Theatre**, home of the Grace Players, one of the better equity-waiver theaters. They offer acting workshops and an irregular season of plays—both original works and classics. ~ 1625 North Las Palmas Avenue; 323-464-1222.

The John Anson Ford Theatre, an outdoor amphitheater, produces jazz, dance, and family programs from June through September. They also house an indoor 87-seat theater that mounts new plays November through April. Closed Monday in summer, Monday and Tuesday in winter. ~ 2580 Cahuenga Boulevard East; 323-461-3673, fax 323-464-1158; www.fordamphi theater.com.

The **Henry Fonda Theatre** also hosts dramatic and musical performances. ~ 6126 Hollywood Boulevard; 323-468-1770; www.henryfondatheater.com.

One of the world's largest natural amphitheaters, seating 18,000, the **Hollywood Bowl** dates back to the 1920s. The concert shell hosts the Los Angeles Philharmonic and features top-bill pop, jazz, and classical concerts. Bring a cushion, sweater, and picnic, and come join the festivities in this park-like setting. ~ 2301 North Highland Avenue; 323-850-2000; www.holly woodbowl.org.

The **Hollywood Palladium**, which once headlined the swing bands of the '40s, now features new wave, rock, international, and Latin groups. ~ 6215 Sunset Boulevard; 323-962-7600.

West Hollywood has always been a bastion of the unconventional and the cutting edge. But since the city was incorporated in 1983, West Hollywood has commanded the lion's share of attention when it comes to all things alternative in Los Angeles—lifestyles, fashion, art and design, entertainment. Progressive, ultra-image conscious (it markets itself as "The Creative City"), a bit impudent, West Hollywood is charged with an energy not found anywhere else in Los Angeles.

West Hollywood

The rest of the world began to notice West Hollywood back in the booming 1980s, when hip clothing boutiques started opening up on a rather dingy stretch of Melrose Avenue. Innovative eateries and galleries followed, and Melrose became *the* retail mecca. Trendiness is fleeting, of course, and Melrose's glam appeal has faded slightly, but West Hollywood's star is still on the rise. For such a small city—1.8 square miles—West Hollywood lays claim to the highest concentration of top-rated restaurants in Los Angeles. Its art galleries exhibit Warhol and Ruscha as well as emerging Caribbean artists. Celebrities from Bette Davis to Jim Morrison to Jerry Seinfeld have called the city home at one time or another. Today, its population of about 35,000 is a dynamic, if curious, mix of gays and lesbians, Russian immigrants, and retirees. And while street parking in West Hollywood is a nightmare, there's something undeniably appealing about this remarkable little city that appeals to just about everybody.

One of the largest parades in California, the Gay Pride Parade and Festival, takes place every June in West Hollywood, drawing hundreds of thousands of celebrants.

SIGHTS

Technically, not all of **Melrose Avenue** is in West Hollywood. But that's being picky. The Melrose attitude—cutting-edge, irreverent, haute-hip, trashy—has always been in keeping with the freewheeling spirit of West Hollywood. A possible signal that things had changed on Melrose was the coming of Starbucks; latex was out and latté was in. But there's still enough of an edge to this street to make it worth a detour (if you can find a parking space). ~ Between La Brea and Fairfax avenues.

The tone of Melrose changes as you move westward, past Fairfax and La Cienega, where very high-end decorator showrooms and fine-art galleries are located. If you need a landmark to lead you through this tony part of town, consider a whale. The

"Blue Whale," to be precise; that's the nickname for the blue-glass monstrosity on Melrose Avenue and San Vicente Boulevard. Formally known as the **Pacific Design Center**, it's a mammoth mall catering to the interior design industry. Since opening in 1975, it has spawned a Green Whale next door. Rumor has it that Moby Blue is pregnant with a Red Whale, due sometime in the next couple of years. Closed weekends. ~ 8687 Melrose Avenue; 310-657-0800, fax 310-652-8576; www.pacificdesigncen ter.com.

Also located in the Pacific Design Center is the **West Hollywood Convention and Visitors Bureau**. ~ 8687 Melrose Avenue; 310-289-2525, 800-368-6020; www.visitwesthollywood.com, e-mail whcvb@visitwesthollywood.com.

The concentration of designer studios and galleries has given a collective moniker—the **Avenues of Art and Design**—to several streets in this area, among them Robertson Boulevard, Almont Drive, and Melrose Avenue. Periodically (every four to eight weeks) several of the galleries host a Saturday evening reception, when a dozen or more are open to the public. Wine, fruit, and cheese are served, and people stroll from one gallery to another. Call the West Hollywood Convention and Visitors Bureau for information about dates for the Saturday night group receptions. ~ 310-289-2525, 800-368-6020; www.visitwesthollywood.com, e-mail whcvb@visitwesthollywood.com.

With as much as one-third of the population thought to be gay and lesbian, West Hollywood is often represented as a "gay city." Of course, the gay and lesbian presence there is a driving force, economically and politically. **Santa Monica Boulevard**, between La Cienega Boulevard and Robertson Boulevard, is the core of the gay community in West Hollywood. This is where you'll find restaurants, bars and nightclubs, retail stores, and other businesses catering to gay and lesbian clientele. (For more information on the gay scene, see "West Hollywood Gay Scene" in this chapter.)

The scene is quite different along **Sunset Boulevard**, which hugs the base of the Hollywood Hills as it snakes through West Hollywood. Known as the Sunset Strip along this stretch, the boulevard really comes alive at night, a pattern that has been repeating itself for decades. During the 1930s and 1940s, the section between Crescent Heights Boulevard and Doheny Drive formed the fabled **Sunset Strip**. Center of Los Angeles night action, it was an avenue of dreams, housing nightclubs like Ciro's, the Trocadero, Mocombo, and the Clover Club. As picture magazines of the times illustrated, starlets bedecked with diamonds emerged from limousines with their leading men. During the 1950s, Ed "Kookie" Byrnes immortalized the street on the television show "77 Sunset Strip."

Today, the two-mile strip is chockablock with the offices of agents, movie producers, personal managers, and music executives. The street's most artistic achievement is the parade of **vanity boards** that captivate the eye with their colors and bold conception. These outsize billboards, advertising the latest movie and record releases, represent the work of the region's finest sign painters and designers. Often done in three dimensions, with lights and trompe l'oeil devices, they create an outdoor art gallery.

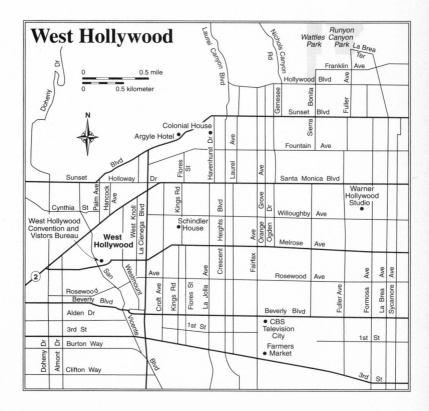

An artist with equal vision was at work here in 1936. That's when architect Robert Derrah built the **Crossroads of the World**. Designed as an oceanliner sailing across Sunset Boulevard, the prow of this proud ship is topped by a tower complete with rotating globe. ~ 6671 Sunset Boulevard.

That streamlined art-deco tower nearby is the old Sunset Tower Apartments, refurbished and rechristened the **Argyle Hotel**. Completed in 1931, this moderne palace contained 46 luxury apartments, leased to luminaries like Errol Flynn, the Gabor sisters, Zasu Pitts, Clark Gable, and Howard Hughes (who seems to have slept in more places than George Washington). ~ 8358 Sunset Boulevard; 323-654-7100, 800-225-2637, fax 323-654-9287; www.argylehotel.com.

Hollywood might be noted for its art-deco towers, but it also contains architectural works by other schools. The **Schindler House**, a house-studio with concrete walls, sliding canvas doors, and sleeping lofts, was designed by Viennese draftsman Rudolph Schindler in 1921. Modeled on a desert camp, the house has been a gathering place for avant-garde architects ever since. The MAK Center for Art and Architecture hosts exhibitions, lectures, and performances here and offers docent tours on Saturday and Sunday. Closed Monday and Tuesday. Admission. ~ 835 North Kings Road; 323-651-1510, fax 323-651-2340; www.makcenter. org, e-mail office@makcenter.org.

F. Scott Fitzgerald fans will want to see the garden court apartments at 1401 North Laurel Avenue where the Roaring '20s novelist spent the final years of his life. Recovering from alcoholism, his career in decline, the author worked here on a film script and his unfinished novel, *The Last Tycoon*.

The **Colonial House** two blocks away was home to celebrities and fictional characters alike. Bette Davis resided in the red brick building, as did Carole Lombard and her husband, William Powell. They were joined, in the imagination of Hollywood novelist Budd Schulberg, by Sammy Glick, the overly ambitious protagonist in *What Makes Sammy Run?* ~1416 North Havenhurst Drive.

The **Nelson House**, where the entire family lived during the 1950s, was used as the model for their TV home on "The Ozzie and Harriet Show." Harriet sold the house several years after Ozzie died in 1975. ~ 1822 Camino Palermo Drive.

The **Los Angeles Conservancy** offers 12 different walking tours of Los Angeles, including Angeline Heights and Highland Park. Tours are held on Saturday at 10 a.m. Reservations required. Fee. ~ 523 West 6th Street, Suite 826, Los Angeles; 213-623-2489, fax 213-623-3909; www.laconservancy.org.

LODGING

Several streamlined and ultramodern hotels are located within a ten-block radius here in West Hollywood. The hallmark of the Mondrian, Bel Âge, Le Parc, Summerfield Suites, and Veladon hotels is the artwork, which hangs seemingly everywhere—in the lobby, public areas, corridors, and guest rooms. You can expect ultramodern furnishings, creative appointments, and personal service at each address.

Ian Schrager spent a fortune renovating his **Mondrian** hotel, transforming a rather dated, cliched property into a surreal temple of contemporary urban style, not to mention attitude. Light, white, and luminescent, the Mondrian sports the "simple chic" look of designer Philippe Starck, who handled the renovation. The hotel's Sky Bar has become the West Hollywood spot to see and be seen. ~ 8440 Sunset Boulevard; 323-650-8999, 800-525-8029, fax 323-650-5215; www.ianschragerhotels.com. ULTRA-DELUXE.

Somewhat more offbeat is the **Wyndham Bel Âge Hotel**. This all-suite hotel offers similar amenities in a complex that is positively laden with artwork. On the rooftop are a pool, jacuzzi, and exercise area. ~ 1020 North San Vicente Boulevard; 310-854-1111, 800-996-3426, fax 310-854-0926; www.wyndham.com. ULTRA-DELUXE.

Located in a quiet residential neighborhood, **Le Parc Suite Hotel De Luxe** offers 154 studio and one-bedroom rooms with a num-

AUTHOR FAVORITE

The elegant **Argyle Hotel**, once the St. James Club, treats guests to an upper-crust club atmosphere. Completed in 1931 as Sunset Towers and now restored to its art-deco magnificence, the Club once was home to screen luminaries from nearby studios. There are 64 beautifully appointed rooms and an on-site restaurant. ~ 8358 Sunset Boulevard; 323-654-7100, 800-225-2637, fax 323-654-9287; www.argylehotel.com. ULTRA-DELUXE.

ber of amenities. Among the facilities are a restaurant, bar, swimming pool, and gym. ~ 733 West Knoll Drive; 310-855-8888, 800-578-4837, fax 310-659-7812; www.leparcsuites.com, e-mail leparcres@aol.com. ULTRA-DELUXE.

Summerfield Suites Hotel features 111 suites with a kitchen, fireplace, and balcony. This establishment also has a rooftop garden with pool, spa, city views, and a café that serves a complimentary breakfast buffet. ~ 1000 Westmount Drive; 310-657-7400, 800-949-6326, fax 310-854-6744; www.summerfieldsuites. com. ULTRA-DELUXE.

Valadon Hotel offers similar accommodations. Among the amenities are laundry facilities and 24-hour room service. You'll find a pool, jacuzzi, and exercise area on the rooftop. ~ 8822 Cynthia Street; 310-854-1114, 800-835-7997, fax 310-657-2623; www.valadonhotel.com. ULTRA-DELUXE.

Another chic Hollywood resting spot, the **Sunset Marquis Hotel and Villas** is a Mediterranean-style hotel frequented by beautiful people with big purses. Guest rooms surround a terrace pool, creating a tropical ambience enhanced by pastel colors and potted plants. The rooms are furnished in contemporary style and range from standard facilities to lavish villas. High in snob appeal, the hotel offers complete amenities. ~ 1200 North Alta Loma Road; 310-657-1333, 800-858-9758, fax 310-652-5300; www.sunsetmarquishotel.com, e-mail reservations@sunsetmarquis hotel.com. ULTRA-DELUXE.

DINING

A mixed bag these days, Melrose Avenue is where you'll find designer fashion boutiques sitting alongside cheap T-shirt outlets, used clothing shops, and specialty stores selling whoopie cushions. Vestiges of the avenue's former glory remain in its excellent restaurants, tucked amid fast-food eateries and theme diners.

The **Moustache Café** was one of the early signs that Melrose was becoming a prominent dining area. Its large enclosed patio is heated on those chilly L.A. evenings Angelenos call winter and Easterners enjoy in short-sleeve shirts. The cuisine is French Continental, featuring striped bass, rack of lamb, and all the other usual suspects. For many, the highlight of the menu is the chocolate soufflé: order yours when you first sit down—it takes about 20 minutes. ~ 8155 Melrose Avenue; 323-651-2111. MODERATE TO DELUXE.

Angeli Caffe/Pizzeria is the archetypal Melrose address. Its high-tech interior is a medley of flying buttresses, wood-slat ceilings, exposed ducts, and whitewashed walls. The menu matches this cutting-edge design with pizza, pasta, calzone, and daily fresh fish specials. No lunch on weekends. ~ 7274 Melrose Avenue; 323-936-9086, fax 323-938-9873. MODERATE.

Try **Tommy Tang's** when next you have an inclination for Thai food and/or sushi. Here you'll find a full sushi bar and an ever-changing gallery of artwork that reflects the trendy crowd. The food is delicious, the portions are small. Happily, everyone is rich. No dinner on Monday. ~ 7313 Melrose Avenue; 323-937-5733, fax 323-937-5781; www.tommytangs.net. MODERATE.

Modern art and pastel walls are also standard issue in the neighborhood's best Chinese restaurant. **Genghis Cohen** serves gourmet dishes to an appreciative crowd at its multiroom complex off Melrose Avenue. Not your ordinary Asian restaurant, specialties here are "scallops on fire," candied shrimp, garlic catfish, soft-shelled shrimp, and "no-name" duck. ~ 740 North Fairfax Avenue; 323-653-0640, fax 323-653-0701. MODERATE TO ULTRA-DELUXE.

When you tire of the tinsel along Melrose Avenue you can always retreat to **Noura Café**, one of the street's few down-home restaurants. Here the food is Middle Eastern with a Mediterranean touch. Just order shish kebab, falafel, grape leaves, or salad at the counter, then enjoy it in a comfortable dining room or out on the patio. For a few dollars more, you can opt for table service. ~ 8479 Melrose Avenue; 323-651-4581, fax 323-651-1375. BUDGET TO MODERATE.

AUTHOR FAVORITE

Duke's is an old favorite watering hole, especially popular with music industry figures. A crowded coffee shop bedecked with posters, it also attracts West Hollywood's underground population. People with purple hair pile into the communal tables, order meatloaf or Chinese vegetables, and settle down for the day. That's what makes Duke's Duke's: it's a scene, a flash, a slice of unreality. A colorful breakfast stop, it features dozens of omelette selections; also hamburgers, sandwiches, diet plates, and a few American dinners. No dinner on weekends. ~ 8909 Sunset Boulevard; 310-652-3100. BUDGET.

Dominick's has a long history of being a Hollywood hotspot. But even though it's a supper club with fine food, the emphasis is the casual trendy atmosphere that attracts the rock crowd. Dinner only. Closed Sunday. ~ 8715 Beverly Boulevard; 310-652-7272. MODERATE TO DELUXE.

Hugo's is a great café for brunch (try one of the pasta or egg dishes). The menu also offers sandwiches and soups. Alfresco dining is available, as is an herb and tea room. ~ 8401 Santa Monica Boulevard; 323-654-3993, fax 323-654-4089; www.hugorestaurant.com. MODERATE.

At **La Boheme**, dining on Cal-French specialties takes on theatrical grandeur under a soaring ceiling and next to an oversized fireplace. The seared ahi with wasabi mashed potatoes is a popular starter. As for entrées, the potato-wrapped halibut with yellow tomato coulis is just one of the possibilities. Dinner only. ~ 8400 Santa Monica Boulevard; 323-848-2360, fax 323-848-9447; www.laboheme-la.com, e-mail boheme-losangeles@global-dining.co.jp. MODERATE TO ULTRA-DELUXE.

Tucked into a cozy storefront space is **Cynthia's**, an altogether delightful spot to dine on updated American comfort food like fried chicken and dumplings, meatloaf, and spicy corn chowder. No lunch on weekends. ~ 8370 West 3rd Street; 323-658-7851, fax 323-658-7535; e-mail cynthiasrestaurant@hotmail.com. MODERATE TO ULTRA-DELUXE.

HIDDEN ►   **Barney's Beanery** is the only place around where you can shoot pool while eating chili, burritos, pizza, ribs, and hamburg-

---

LITERARY L.A.

Since the early 20th century, authors have reveled in exposing the dark underbelly of Los Angeles. Raymond Chandler's hard-boiled private eye Philip Marlowe dealt with the sleaziest L.A. criminals and lived on Franklin Avenue in Hollywood. Latino writer Oscar Zeta Acosta's *The Revolt of the Cockroach People* looks at turmoil in East L.A.'s Chicano community. Nathanael West's *Day of the Locust* portrays the movie industry at its superficial worst, with the novel's grisly conclusion taking place at Mann's Chinese Theater, thinly disguised as Kahn's Persian. Walter Mosley's African-American hero Easy Rawlins combs the seediest corners of South Central and Watts for killers, and in Joan Didion's *Play It as It Lays* Maria Wyeth escapes reality by roaming the Los Angeles freeways.

ers. Or where you can choose from nearly 300 varieties of beer. A dive with character, Barney's has rainbow-colored booths, license plates on the ceiling, and road sign decor. Native funk at low prices. ~ 8447 Santa Monica Boulevard; 323-654-2287, fax 323-654-5123. BUDGET TO MODERATE.

For lunch or weekend brunch, the **Sunset Plaza** stretch of Sunset Boulevard offers several restaurants with sidewalk cafés. ~ 8500–8700 blocks of Sunset Boulevard, between La Cienega and San Vicente boulevards.

L'Orangerie possesses all the pretensions you would expect from one of Los Angeles' finest, most expensive French restaurants. The building has the look of a château, with imposing arches and finials atop the roof. The dining areas are appointed with oil paintings and outsized wall sconces; fresh flowers and the scent of money proliferate. Food, decor, service—all are the finest. The *foie gras* and seafood are flown in fresh from France. Life, or dinner at least, doesn't get much better than this classic French restaurant. Reservations are required (as are jackets for men). Dinner only. Closed Monday. ~ 903 North La Cienega Boulevard; 310-652-9770, fax 310-652-8870; www.lorangerie. com, e-mail lorangerie@lorangerie.com. ULTRA-DELUXE.

SHOPPING

The section of Sunset Boulevard between Crescent Heights Boulevard and Doheny Drive, commonly known as Sunset Strip, is marked by creatively designed billboards announcing the latest Hollywood releases. Amid this skein of signs is a series of star-studded cartoon characters signaling the way to **Dudley Do-Right's Emporium.** Jay Ward's cartoon characters come to life at this Bullwinkle enthusiast's mecca. Closed Sunday, Monday, Wednesday, and Friday. ~ 8200 Sunset Boulevard; 323-656-6550.

Sunset Plaza, a two-block cluster of shops located on Sunset Boulevard between Sunset Plaza Drive and Sherbourne Drive, offers some of the most luxurious shopping on the Strip.

Book Soup, a small but special bookstore, offers a top-notch selection of art books, classic literature, current fiction, and international magazines. ~ 8818 Sunset Boulevard; 310-659-3110; www.booksoup.com.

Step over to **Aahs!** for a selection of greeting cards, informal gifts, and crazy toys. ~ 8878 Sunset Boulevard; 310-657-4221.

Don't worry, you won't miss **Aida's Flowers**. If the festive mural doesn't catch your eye, the character on the corner (dressed as Santa, the Easter Bunny, or Uncle Sam) will flag you down. Once inside, if you dare to enter, you'll find flowers, cards, produce, and piano music in an exotic setting. ~ 1261 North La Brea Avenue; 323-876-6482.

Ultramodern shoppers make a beeline for **Melrose Avenue**. West Hollywood's proving ground for innovative style, Melrose is the smartest street in all L.A., a multiblock mélange of signature boutiques, fresh cuisine restaurants, and heartthrob nightspots. Peopled by visionaries and voluptuaries, it's sleek, fast, and very, very chic. Shops and galleries, with names as trendy as their concepts, come and go with tidal regularity in this super-heated environment. ~ Between Sycamore Avenue and Ogden Drive.

Of course the most futuristic element of all is the past. At **Chic-A-Boom**, the "Mother Lode" of vintage retail, you'll find such shards of American history as a Davy Crockett lamp, a drugstore display from the '50s, toys from the '60s and '70s, vintage *TV Guides*, a huge selection of rock-and-roll posters, plus movie memorabilia. Closed Sunday. ~ 6817 Melrose Avenue; 323-931-7441.

Off The Wall is known for "weird stuff" and unusual 20th-century antiques. You can also pick up some of your favorite vintage advertising signs. Closed Sunday. ~ 7325 Melrose Avenue; 323-930-1185; www.offthewallantiques.com.

Occupying an entire block, **Ron Herman/Fred Segal** is a series of stores within stores. Seeming to specialize in everything, this consumer labyrinth has clothes for men, women, and children, plus lingerie, luggage, shoes, electronic gear, and cosmetics. There's even a café at hand when you tire of browsing or simply become lost. ~ 8100 Melrose Avenue; 323-651-3342.

Gemini GEL is one of the country's top art publishers. Producing limited-edition prints and sculptures, it features two display galleries. Open Saturday by appointment; closed Sunday. ~ 8365 Melrose Avenue; 323-651-0513; www.geminigel.com.

The Bodhi Tree Bookstore is *the* place for books on mysticism, metaphysics, nature, health, and religion. Behind the main store, **The Used Book Ranch** displays used books as well as herbs, teas, and homeopathic remedies. ~ 8585 Melrose Avenue; 310-659-1733; www.bodhitree.com.

The **Beverly Center**, a neon-laced shopping mall, features signature clothing stores, world-class restaurants, and a multiplex entertainment center. Exterior glass-enclosed elevators move shoppers quickly through this eight-story complex. ~ 8500 Beverly Boulevard; 310-854-0070; www.beverlycenter.com.

Gallery 825 is a great place to discover the up and coming while they are still down and out.

Clustered nearby around Robertson Boulevard are several prestigious art galleries. **Margo Leavin Gallery** houses an impressive collection of contemporary American and European art. Closed Sunday and Monday. ~ 812 North Robertson Boulevard; 310-273-0603.

For free travel advice, browse through **Traveler's Bookcase,** a friendly bookstore for people on the move. Here you'll discover a collection of hard-to-find regional titles as well as literature for the new breed of adventure traveler. Take a sojourn on one of the plush couches and flip through a few vacations. ~ 8375 West 3rd Street; 323-655-0575; www.travelbooks.com.

◄ *HIDDEN*

Next door is **Cook's Library**, a speciality bookstore crammed with cookbooks and other food-related literature. Closed Sunday. ~ 8373 West 3rd Street; 323-655-3141.

Another constellation of galleries lies along the 600-to-800-block stretch of North La Cienega Boulevard. Most venerable of all these art centers is **Gallery 825**, which showcases talents from the Los Angeles Art Association. Gallery 825 also offers lectures and workshops. Closed Sunday and Monday. ~ 825 North La Cienega Boulevard; 310-652-8272; www.laaa.org.

The level of talent at the **Comedy Store** is evident from the celebrity signatures covering the building's black exterior and photo-lined interior. The Main Room features the best comedians, the Original Room showcases new talent, and the Belly Room presents a wide range of alternative comics. Cover. ~ 8433 Sunset Boulevard; 323-656-6225; www.thecomedystore.com.

NIGHTLIFE

The ultrahip **Skybar** at the Mondrian hotel features great views for those who want to see and be seen. Reservations required. ~ 8440 Sunset Boulevard; 323-650-8999.

Two long-standing rock clubs dominate Sunset Strip. **Whisky A Go Go** features live music on a nightly basis. Cover. ~ 8901 Sunset Boulevard; 310-652-4202; www.whiskyagogo.com. **The Roxy Theater** headlines known rock-and-roll and alternative rock performers in an art deco–style room. Cover. ~ 9009 Sunset Boulevard; 310-276-2222.

Another one of Hollywood's jazz clubs is **Catalina Bar & Grill**, which draws a relaxed crowd and features name performers. Cover. ~ 6725 Sunset Boulevard; 323-466-2210; www.catalina jazzclub.com.

The Key Club joined the Strip's club lineup in 1997, with a two-level venue for rock, jazz, country, and blues acts. Its in-house restaurant overlooks the stage. Twenty-one and over. Cover. ~ 9039 Sunset Boulevard; 310-274-5800.

Live music at **1020** starts around 7 p.m., Friday and Saturday. ~ In the Wyndham Bel Âge Hotel, 1020 North San Vicente Boulevard; 310-358-7776.

One mainstay in Hollywood nightlife is the coffeehouse. With plump armchairs, weatherbeaten tables and walls covered by contemporary art, the **Insomnia Cafe** serves cappuccino and desserts until the wee hours of the morning. ~ 7286 Beverly Boulevard; 323-931-4943.

The Hard Rock Cafe, a wildly popular gathering place in the Beverly Center, features the loud music and rock memorabilia decor for which this nightclub chain is renowned. ~ 8600 Beverly Boulevard; 310-276-7605; www.hardrock.com.

The **Coronet Theatre** presents comedies, musicals, and occasional dramas. The resident nonprofit theater company, Playwrights' Kitchen Ensemble, hosts an array of interesting workshops. ~ 366 North La Cienega Boulevard; 310-657-7377; www.coronet-theatre.com.

AUTHOR FAVORITE

If you haven't been to the **House of Blues**, you're missing out on one of the best nightspots around. This establishment combines a Delta-inspired restaurant with a live music club. The specialty is blues, although other musical traditions from reggae to rock are also featured. Buddy Guy and Paul Simon have played here as well as Al Green and Melissa Etheridge. The walls at this nightspot are adorned with the portraits of legendary bluesmen including Stevie Ray Vaughan, Robert Johnson, and Albert King. Gospel brunch on Sunday gets the day off to a rousing start. Cover. ~ 8430 Sunset Boulevard; reservations 323-848-5123, box office 323-848-5100; www.hob.com.

The Gig Hollywood headlines live bands seven nights a week: blues, R&B, surf, funk. Settle down in one of the big cushy couches and imagine yourself in your own living room. Twenty-one and over. Cover. ~ 7302 Melrose Avenue; 323-936-4440; www.liveatthegig.com.

There are often as many comedians in the bar as on stage at the **Improv.** This spacious brick-walled club, patterned after the New York original, draws top-name comics such as Drew Carey, as well as local talent. Cover. ~ 8162 Melrose Avenue; 323-651-2583; www.improv.com.

THEATER Small theaters and local playwrights make sections of West Hollywood the Off-Broadway of the West. Dozens of talented companies perform regularly on the following less-known stages.

The Coast Playhouse specializes in original musicals and new dramas. ~ 8325 Santa Monica Boulevard; 323-650-8507. A replica of the British original, the **Globe Playhouse** stages Shakespearean plays in addition to other dramas of historical significance. ~ 1107 North Kings Road; 323-654-5623. The **Matrix Theatre Company** is home to Joseph Stern's award-winning troupe, Actors for Themselves. ~ 7657 Melrose Avenue; 323-852-1445. Comedy and improvisation top the bill at the **Groundling Theatre.** ~ 7307 Melrose Avenue; 323-934-9700.

West Hollywood Gay Scene

West Hollywood did not mysteriously blossom overnight into a gay mecca after the city was incorporated in 1983. Decades ago, gay bars and other establishments that ran the risk of being raided by the Los Angeles Police Department found a more tolerant environment outside the city limits and established themselves in the unincorporated area of West Hollywood. Naturally, many gay men and lesbians settled in, too. Artists, designers, and actors were also drawn to West Hollywood, which helped establish the area's reputation for creativity.

In 1983, residents of the district championed their own destiny and voted to incorporate the City of West Hollywood. Today, few places in the country are as gay-friendly as West Hollywood, and for many gay and lesbian visitors to Southern California, the city has become a destination in its own right. Santa Monica Boulevard, between La Cienega and Robertson boulevards, is the focus of gay life in West Hollywood. Along this stretch of boulevard, restaurants, coffeehouses, bars, clubs, and shops cater to a mainly gay and lesbian clientele.

LODGING   The **Grove Guesthouse** offers just one bright and airy cottage decorated with contemporary leather furniture and high ceilings. There's a distinct home-away-from-home atmosphere here, complete with a pre-stocked pantry from which to create your own meals. As a guest, you have pool and hot tub privileges as well. Hopefully, the oranges on the tree out back will be ready for plucking. Reservations required. ~ 1325 North Orange Grove Avenue; 323-876-7778, 888-524-7683, fax 323-876-0890; www.grove guesthouse.com, e-mail info@groveguesthouse.com. ULTRA-DELUXE.

Located right in the heart of West Hollywood, the **Holloway Motel** is a haven for gays and lesbians. The 22 units are comfortably furnished; suites have full kitchens. ~ 8465 Santa Monica Boulevard; 323-654-2454, 888-654-6400; www.hollowaymotel. com. MODERATE.

Centrally located, the **Ramada West Hollywood** offers classy lodging within its art-deco exterior. Straights and gays alike can be found relaxing on the sundeck and around the heated pool. Rooms are appointed in pastels and contemporary furniture. Suites come equipped with kitchens, wet bars, and sleeping lofts. ~ 8585 Santa Monica Boulevard; 310-652-6400, 800-845-8585, fax 310-652-2135; www.ramadawh.com, e-mail info@ramada wh.com. DELUXE TO ULTRA-DELUXE.

The gay bed-and-breakfast scene is well served by **San Vicente Inn Resort**. This 28-unit complex features an attractive tropical courtyard and a clothing-optional pool, hot tub, and sauna. Rooms and suites may have kitchenettes and shared baths. An expanded breakfast is served poolside. ~ 845 North San Vicente Boulevard; 310-854-6915; e-mail infodesk@sanvicenteinn.com. MODERATE TO ULTRA-DELUXE.

Upon entering **Le Montrose**, guests will be greeted by friendly attendants along with fresh fruit and mineral water. The posh, art nouveau accommodations consist of fireplaces and Nintendo sets; some include full kitchens and balconies. This all-suite hotel also makes it easy to keep fit while traveling. There's a pool, a hot tub, a fully equipped fitness center, free bike use, and a rooftop tennis court with tennis instructors to help you perfect your serve. Afterward, schedule an appointment with the on-staff masseuse to work out those knots. Cookies and milk await guests at check-out time. ~ 900 Hammond Street; 310-855-1115, 800-776-0666, fax 310-657-9192; www.lemontrose.com, e-mail frontdesk@lemontrose.com. ULTRA-DELUXE.

Located inside the French Quarter Market Place is the **French Quarter Restaurant,** festooned with hanging plants among wrought-iron appointments. Breakfast is served all day for those who don't feel like having one of the many choices of sandwiches, steaks, and pasta dishes. Specialties include braised pot roast, glazed King salmon, and blackened chicken penne. Its late hours also make it a great nightspot. Breakfast, lunch, and dinner are served daily. ~ 7985 Santa Monica Boulevard; 323-654-0898, fax 323-656-7898. MODERATE.

DINING

Basix Café is always busy, from morning to night, serving fresh-baked muffins and rolls, as well as sandwiches, grilled chicken, salads, and pastas. It's located on a busy corner, so its sidewalk tables are always a good spot to sit to see and be seen. ~ 8333 Santa Monica Boulevard at Flores Street; 323-848-2460, fax 323-848-2462. MODERATE.

Around the corner is **Marix Tex-Mex.** Margaritas by the pitcher, pretty good Tex-Mex food, and an infectiously festive atmosphere guarantee there's always a wait to get in. ~ 1108 North Flores Street; 323-656-8800. MODERATE.

At **Benvenuto,** dine inside in a warm, cheerful trattoria or outside on the narrow, tented patio. Chicken sausage lasagne, risotto, pizza, and traditional pasta dishes are generally well prepared. An occasional celebrity sighting (Rosie O'Donnell, for ex-

AUTHOR FAVORITE

Mark's serves elegant California cuisine in a casual, contemporary setting. Along with tasty entrées such as grilled rare ahi with sesame-ginger sauce, there are Maryland crab cakes with corn purée and tomato-basil sauce, and turkey-vegetable potstickers. Advance reservations are the smart way to go on "half-price Mondays." Dinner only; Sunday brunch. ~ 861 North La Cienega Boulevard; 310-652-5252, fax 310-652-0295; www.marksrestaurant.com, e-mail marksresla@aol.com. MODERATE TO DELUXE.

ample) adds to the fun. No lunch on Monday, Saturday and Sunday. ~ 8512 Santa Monica Boulevard at La Cienega Boulevard; 310-659-8635, fax 310-659-8638. MODERATE.

A large gay crowd shows up for Argentine tantalizers at the **Tango Grill**—authenticity furnished courtesy of the owner, who's from Buenos Aires. The brick walls, Mexican tile floors, and wooden tables do much for the South American atmosphere, and diners may choose to take their sizzling dishes out on the patio under large umbrellas. Chicken, seafood, beef, and vegetables are marinated in special blends of citrus juice and garlic. ~ 8807 Santa Monica Boulevard; 310-659-3663. BUDGET TO MODERATE.

More upscale but equally popular with West Hollywood's gay population is **Café D'Etoile**. The cuisine here is a Continental mix of pasta, steak, chicken, and roast pork dishes, and the decor is a mix of antique furniture and contemporary artwork. ~ 8941½ Santa Monica Boulevard; 310-278-1011. MODERATE TO DELUXE.

You'll find sandwiches, salads, burgers, chicken, and pastas prepared in a variety of ways at **The Abbey**. Although the regulars tend to be gay men, lesbians and straight couples frequently come to chat over coffee and a huge assortment of desserts and martinis (which, by the way, outnumber the regular menu). Outdoor seating is available. Open for breakfast, lunch, and dinner. ~ 692 North Robertson Boulevard; 310-289-8410, fax 310-289-8429. BUDGET TO MODERATE.

HIDDEN ► **Bossa Nova** amounts to a slip of a restaurant, a bunch of outdoor tables, and a booming take-out business. The owner describes the aromatic cuisine as Brazilian-Salvadoran, with specialties that include shrimp and cheese inside deep-fried dough and Brazilian sausage with grilled onions and yucca. ~ 685 North Robertson Boulevard; 310-657-5070, fax 310-657-0358. BUDGET.

TICKET TO LOUNGE

A neighborhood bar located in the heart of West Hollywood, **Mother Lode** is ideal for those looking for a cozy place to hang out and have a stout or two. Nightly deejays spin tunes ranging from rock-and-roll to dance music; ironically, there's no dancefloor to let loose on. But the crowd, which mainly consists of gay men, doesn't seem to mind. Sunday and Thursday also features karaoke. ~ 8944 Santa Monica Boulevard; 310-659-9700.

Not only is **A Different Light** a "full service gay and lesbian book-store," it also serves as a focal point for West Hollywood's gay population, complete with community bulletin board and an on-going schedule of events. ~ 8853 Santa Monica Boulevard; 310-854-6601.

Specializing in erotica, **The Pleasure Chest** offers an unparalleled array of leather goods, lingerie, latex clothing, novelties, and gay literature. ~ 7733 Santa Monica Boulevard; 323-650-1022; www.nocost.com.

Two former clubs (and $2 million) created **Ultra Suede at the Factory,** a 15,000-square-foot danceclub. Plush couches in the back lounge are a good resting spot away from the exuberance of the dancefloor. Discotheque inspired, the driving beat at this happening place favors music from the past few decades, particularly the '80s and '90s. Open Wednesday, Friday, and Saturday. ~ 661 Robertson Boulevard; 310-659-4551; www.factorynightclub.com/ultra-suede.htm.

The Abbey is another popular gay hangout. ~ 692 North Robertson Boulevard; 310-289-8410.

Rage Restaurant and Bar is a spacious all-gay dance club that spills onto the sidewalk; inside there are outrageous videos plus sounds ranging from house and high-energy music to alternative rock. Cover Tuesday/Wednesday and Thursday/Friday. ~ 8911 Santa Monica Boulevard; 310-652-7055.

It is primarily gay men who frequent **Micky's,** a West Hollywood nightspot that offers dancing to a deejay video. Occasional cover. ~ 8857 Santa Monica Boulevard; 310-657-1176; www.mickys.com.

The Palms is the oldest women's bar in Los Angeles. It features pool playing, a dancefloor, music videos, a deejay and something going on every night of the week. Cover. ~ 8572 Santa Monica Boulevard; 310-652-6188.

Wilshire District

Though Wilshire Boulevard actually extends from Downtown to the Pacific, the Wilshire District encompasses the stretch from Downtown to the Beverly Hills city limits. Developed during the 1890s by H. Gaylord Wilshire, a socialist with an ironic knack for making money in real estate, it was originally a tony area whose buildings exhibited some of the most creative and elaborate architectural features of the day. As the affluent moved west, the area deteriorated, many of these architectural wonders fell into disrepair, and a seedy element moved in.

Today the area is home to an assortment of ethnic groups and, since the 1990s, an on-going revitalization effort has been working to return the area to at least some semblance of its former glory. Not surprisingly, the farther west and closer to Beverly Hills one travels, the better the neighborhood.

SIGHTS

WESTLAKE/MACARTHUR PARK In the 19th century, when Westlake was a wealthy enclave west of Downtown, gingerbready Victorian confections were the norm. Today a few still remain along the **800 and 1000 blocks of South Bonnie Brae Street**, including the particularly dramatic Queen Anne at 818 and its onion-domed neighbor.

MacArthur Park, a 32-acre greensward bisected by Wilshire Boulevard, is one of Los Angeles' oldest parks and has seen better days. This formerly pristine area, with its lake and palm-fringed island, is more likely to be inhabited by truant teenagers and senior citizens on social security than the affluent. The once-elegant Sheraton Townhouse Hotel has been turned into affordable housing, the area is plagued by drug-related problems, and the park's lake is frequently littered with trash. Still, it remains an urban green space where immigrant mothers sit in shady picnic areas while their children frolic on the playground and the elderly enjoy a game of chess in the sun. ~ Alvarado Street between 6th and 7th streets.

An art deco masterpiece built in 1929, for decades the **Bullocks Wilshire** building housed a high-end Los Angeles department store chain. Today this stunning copper-sided tower, where wealthy Angeleno grandmothers used to take their granddaughters to lunch in the "Tea Room," is occupied by Southwestern University School of Law. ~ 3050 Wilshire Boulevard; 213-738-8240, fax 213-738-1205.

The Asian answer to gentrification is evident in **Koreatown**, a burgeoning neighborhood that has redefined the Wilshire District. Colorful storefronts, refurbished cottages, and Korean calligraphy have transformed the entire area into a unique enclave.

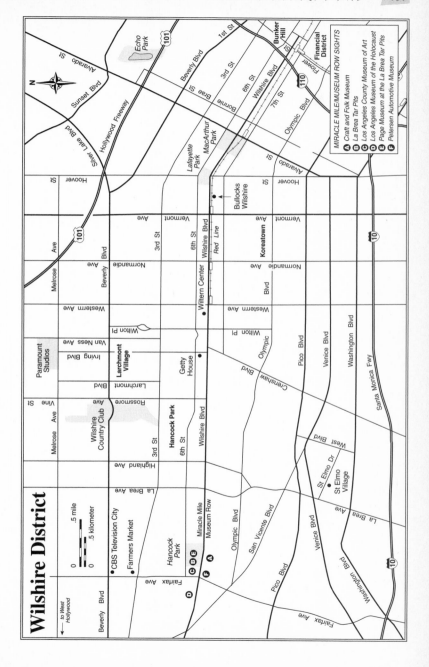

Wilshire District

0 .5 mile
0 .5 kilometer

MIRACLE MILE/MUSEUM ROW SIGHTS

Ⓐ Craft and Folk Museum
Ⓑ La Brea Tar Pits
Ⓒ Los Angeles County Museum of Art
Ⓓ Los Angeles Museum of the Holocaust
Ⓔ Page Museum at the La Brea Tar Pits
Ⓕ Petersen Automotive Museum

~ Centered between 4th Street and Olympic Boulevard, Western Avenue, and Vermont Avenue.

In fact, if you take a long drive down Pico Boulevard or Olympic Boulevard from the Harbor Freeway (Route 110) to Fairfax Avenue, you'll pass through a succession of **ethnic neighborhoods** including Indonesian, Japanese, Taiwanese, Vietnamese, and Thai sections.

LARCHMONT VILLAGE Within spitting distance of El Royale, the apartment building on Rossmore Avenue where Mae West lived is a small enclave of shops and restaurants called **Larchmont Village**. With the introduction of such national chains as Koo Koo Roo, Noah's Bagels, and Blockbuster, the village has lost a little of its upscale small-town charm. Still, some of the long-time mom-and-pop businesses, such as Cafe Chapeau and Landis General Store, continue to hang on, and the tree-lined boulevard is still an appealing place to meet for a latte at a sidewalk café.

An art-deco masterpiece, the Wiltern Center is a towering building with wings flaring from either side. Built in 1931, it is covered in green terra cotta. ~ 3780 Wilshire Boulevard.

From Larchmont Village, it's a short few blocks to **South Wilton Place**, a historical district of modest California bungalows dating from the early part of the 20th century. ~ South Wilton Place at Beverly Boulevard.

HANCOCK PARK/LA BREA AVENUE The residential architecture of **Hancock Park** includes posh estates once owned by the Crocker, Huntington, and Doheny families. Developed during the 1920s, this well-tended neighborhood contains a variety of architectural styles. With wide boulevards and manicured lawns, it's a perfect place for a Sunday drive (even on a Tuesday). ~ Between Wilshire Boulevard and Melrose Avenue, centered around the Wilshire Country Club.

One of the highlights of the district, politically if not architecturally, is the **Getty House**. A 1921 Tudor home with leaded-glass windows and slate roof, it is the official residence of the mayor of Los Angeles. ~ 605 South Irving Boulevard.

HIDDEN ▶ **MID-CITY** St. Elmo Village marks another breed of neighborhood entirely. Here a complex of cottages has been transformed into a kind of creative art center. The simple bungalows are painted primary colors and adorned with murals and sculptures. Containing private residences and art studios, the settlement is luxuriously landscaped. Some houses are open to the public. ~ 4830 St. Elmo Drive; 323-931-3409, fax 323-931-2065; www. stelmovillage.org, e-mail stelmovillage@earthlink.net.

MIRACLE MILE/MUSEUM ROW Back in the 1920s and 1930s the showcase for commercial architecture rested along the **Miracle Mile**. That was when an enterprising developer turned the area into a classy corridor for shops and businesses. The magnificent art-deco towers that lined the strip still survive, particularly between the 5200 and 5500 blocks of Wilshire, but Wilshire's early glory has faded as the area has changed from popular to historic. ~ Wilshire Boulevard between La Brea and Fairfax avenues.

The West's largest museum is a multibuilding complex with an international art collection. Providing a thumbnail tour of the entire history of art, the **Los Angeles County Museum of Art** ranges from pre-Columbian gold objects and African masks to post–World War II minimalist works. Stops along the way include sculpture, paintings, and stained-glass windows from the Middle Ages; a Renaissance gallery featuring Rembrandt and other Masters; Impressionist paintings by Cézanne, Gauguin, and Monet; and early-20th-century creations by Magritte, Chagall, and Miró. The Pavilion for Japanese Art houses the well-known Shin'enkan collection of paintings, as well as Japanese screens, scrolls, ceramics, and sculpture. The entire complex is beautifully laid out around a central courtyard adorned with terra-cotta pillars and four-tiered waterfall. Closed Wednesday. Admission (free the second Tuesday of the month). ~ 5905 Wilshire Boulevard; 323-857-6000; www.lacma.org, e-mail publicinfo@lacma.org.

Dedicated to works created by hand, the **Craft and Folk Museum** draws its exhibits from a wide range of subjects, showcasing objects such as the handcrafted furniture of Sam Aloof, mechanical toys, and masks of Mexico. Closed Monday and Tuesday. Admission (free the first Wednesday of the month). ~ 5814 Wilshire Boulevard; 323-937-4230.

Beauty gives way to the beast at the nearby **Page Museum at the La Brea Tar Pits**. This paleontological showplace features displays of mammoths, mastodons, and ground sloths. There are also extinct camels, ancient horses, and ancestral condors. Admission (free the first Tuesday of the month). ~ 5801 Wilshire Boulevard; 323-934-7243, fax 323-933-3974; www.tarpits.org, e-mail info@nhm.org.

Altogether, there are more than 200 varieties of other creatures that fell victim to the **La Brea Tar Pits**, which surround the museum. Dating to the Pleistocene Era, these oozing oil pools trapped birds, mammals, insects, and reptiles, creating fossil deposits that are still being discovered by scientists. Indians once used the tar to caulk boats and roofs. Today you can wander past the pits, which bubble menacingly with methane gas and lie covered in globs of black tar.

Wilshire Boulevard, conceived in the emerging age of the automobile as a linear downtown, is part of the automotive history of Los Angeles. Wide store windows were set close to the sidewalk and street so their contents could be easily seen from a passing car. Large rear entrances to parking lots accommodated the automobile. So it's an altogether appropriate site for the **Petersen Automotive Museum**, which devotes its four floors to automotive history through a series of dioramas, rotating special exhibits of cars, and art related to the automobile. There's also a children's Discovery Center to keep the little ones occupied. Closed Monday. Admission. ~ 6060 Wilshire Boulevard; 323-930-2277, fax 323-930-6642; www.petersen.org, e-mail info@petersen.org.

Still retaining its luster and heritage is **Carthay Circle**, a cluster of small 1930s-era homes. This antique neighborhood is shaped more like a triangle than a circle. The Spanish stucco and art-deco homes create an island surrounded by streets streaming with traffic. ~ Bounded by Fairfax Avenue and Wilshire and San Vicente boulevards.

HIDDEN ►   L.A.'s vernacular architecture is alive and well at **Tail O' The Pup**, a hot dog stand shaped like (what else?) a hot dog. Created in 1945, the hot dog stands in humorous contrast to its well-heeled neighbors. ~ 329 North San Vicente Boulevard; 310-652-4517.

OY TOGETHER NOW

A favorite gathering place of the Jewish community is the intersection of Fairfax and Oakwood avenues. Here one corner supports a mural depicting Jewish life in Los Angeles and another corner contains **Above the Fold**, which sells periodicals from around the world. ~ 370 North Fairfax Avenue; 323-935-8525.

The oldest holocaust museum in the United States, the **Los** ◄ **HIDDEN**
Angeles Museum of the Holocaust is filled with images from the
Nazi extermination camps. The ovens of Buchenwald, the gas
chambers of Auschwitz, and skeletal figures from other camps
are captured in terrifying detail. The photos portray masses being
executed; tiny children, their hands in the air, surrounded by
storm troopers; and a mother being shot while clutching a child in
her arms. Many of the docents are Holocaust survivors with personal stories to recount as they lead visitors through these har-
rowing halls. Closed Saturday. ~ 6006 Wilshire Boulevard; 323-
761-8170, fax 323-761-8174; www.lamuseumoftheholocaust.
org, e-mail rjagoda@jewishla.org.

Nearby, **Fairfax Avenue** is the center of the city's Jewish community. Since World War II this middle-class neighborhood has
been a local capital for Los Angeles Semites. Filled with delica-
tessens, bakeries, and kosher grocery stores, it is occupied by
Orthodox, Hasidic, and Reform Jews. ~ Located between Beverly
Boulevard and Melrose Avenue.

Back in 1934, local farmers paid 50 cents a day to come to
Fairfax Avenue and 3rd Street and sell produce out of the backs
of their trucks. Over the years, the **Farmers Market** developed into
an open-air labyrinth of stalls, shops, and grocery stands. Purists
weren't happy when the adjacent Grove shopping and entertainment complex gobbled up some of the market's property; still,
over 70 businesses remain, selling everything from handmade
English toffee to free-range poultry. ~ 6333 West 3rd Street; 323-
933-9211, fax 323-549-2145; www.farmersmarketla.com.

The Grove, a distinctly more urban annex, features additional shopping and dining, as well as a movie complex (this is
L.A., after all). A replica of the old Los Angeles Red Car trolley
ferries visitors between the Market and The Grove. ~ 6333 West
3rd Street; 323-933-9211, fax 323-549-2145; www.farmersmar
ketla.com, e-mail info@farmersmarketla.com.

Best Western, The Mayfair Hotel, located on the fringes of the   **LODGING**
Downtown district, is a 295-room hostelry. Built in 1927 and
beautifully refurbished, it offers a touch of luxury at a price lower
than the five-star hotels. There's a restaurant and lounge as well
as an attractive skylit lobby. The guest rooms are average size and

feature contemporary furnishings, textured wallpaper, and pastel color schemes. ~ 1256 West 7th Street; 213-484-9789, 800-821-8682, fax 213-484-2769; www.mayfairla.com, e-mail mayfair @mayfairla.com. MODERATE.

In the Beverly, Wilshire and 3rd Street neighborhood, the **Beverly Plaza Hotel** is a charming boutique hotel with 98 rooms. It offers a fitness center, two saunas, and a pool. Perhaps its most appealing feature is the location, which is within walking distance of shopping and good restaurants. ~ 8384 West 3rd Street; 323-658-6600; www.beverlyplazahotel.com, e-mail info@beverly plazahotel.com. DELUXE.

A refurbished 1920s-era art-deco building, the **Wilshire Royale Howard Johnson Plaza Hotel** has been transformed into a contemporary 200-room facility. The lobby is a beamed-ceiling affair with piano, fresh flowers, and upholstered armchairs. Rooms have tile baths and standard furnishings. Restaurant, lounge, pool, and spa are additional facilities. This historic hotel is an excellent choice. ~ 2619 Wilshire Boulevard; 213-387-5311, 800-421-8072, fax 213-380-8174; www.hojola.com, e-mail ho jola@hojola.com DELUXE.

Wilshire Crest Inn is one of those terribly modern hotels with track lighting, black trim, and fabric wall coverings. The 33 rooms, built around an interior courtyard, are done in oak and furnished with platform beds. The color scheme, naturally, is pastel. There's a dining room where continental breakfast is served and a sitting area complete with potted plants and trimly upholstered armchairs. The hotel is conveniently located near Wilshire Boulevard in the Fairfax district. ~ 6301 Orange Street; 323-936-5131, 800-654-9951, fax 323-936-2013. MODERATE.

DINING   **WESTLAKE/MACARTHUR PARK**   The coming of the Metrorail to MacArthur Park revived the fortunes of long-loved **Langer's**. For hungry central-city office workers, their beloved pastrami sandwiches are now just a quick subway ride away. Closed Sunday. ~ 704 South Alvarado Street; 213-483-8050, fax 213-483-7171. BUDGET TO MODERATE.

The reason for the balcony at **La Fonda** becomes stirringly evident every evening when Los Camperos strike up a Spanish song. One of the city's best mariachi bands, they lure dinner guests by the dozens to this hacienda-style restaurant. In addition to the sound of Los Camperos, diners enjoy the flavor of Veracruz-style shrimp, steak *picado*, chicken flautas, and *chile verde*. Dinner only. Closed Monday. ~ 2501 Wilshire Boulevard; 213-380-5055, fax 213-386-2569. MODERATE TO DELUXE.

Also consider **La Fonda Antioqueña**, a Columbian restaurant that comes recommended by a former Consul General of Colombia. Here you will discover about 15 different platters, each prepared with South American flair. This intriguing ethnic restaurant offers everything from fish, chicken, beef, and pork dishes to liver and tongue. For an adventure in south-of-the-border dining, La Fonda Antioqueña is the place. ~ 4903 Melrose Avenue; 323-957-5164. MODERATE.

The interior of **Casa Carnitas** is tiny but overwhelming. Colorful as an old mission chapel, the walls are covered with murals portraying Mayan warriors. Naturally, the food is Yucatecan and includes a variety of beef, chicken, and shrimp dishes prepared with tasty *ranchera* sauce. Considering the imaginative decor and low prices, Casa Carnitas is an excellent find. ~ 4067 West Beverly Boulevard; 323-667-9953. BUDGET.

Tommy's Hamburgers is a Los Angeles landmark. In fact at last count there were 23 such landmarks. But the original Tommy's, dating back to 1946, is at 2575 West Beverly Boulevard. Here you can enjoy "while you watch" service as they prepare hamburgers, hot dogs, and tamales before your hungry eyes. Open 24 hours, this is the place where they give you paper towels instead of napkins and still charge cheap prices. (Ain't L.A. amazing?) ~ 2575 West Beverly Boulevard; 213-389-9060; www.originaltommys. com. BUDGET.

◄ *HIDDEN*

One of Koreatown's best restaurants is a multiroom complex named **Dong Il Jang**. The place contains several dining rooms as

THE WURST IS THE BEST

L.A.'s best known delicatessen lies at the heart of the Jewish neighborhood around Fairfax Avenue. **Canter's**, a casual 24-hour restaurant and bar, doubles as local landmark and ethnic cultural center. As you might have guessed, lox and bagels, hot pastrami, corned beef, and matzo ball soup are the order of the day. ~ 419 North Fairfax Avenue; 323-651-2030, fax 323-651-4835. BUDGET TO MODERATE.

well as a sushi bar, each decorated with bamboo screens and Asian statuary. The Korean dinners include *maewoon tahng* (spicy codfish casserole), *kalbi* (marinated ribs), and *jun bok juk* (abalone porridge). A complete offering of Japanese dishes is also presented. ~ 3455 West 8th Street; 213-383-5757. MODERATE TO DELUXE.

HIDDEN ►

LARCHMONT VILLAGE Very popular with neighborhood regulars, **La Luna** offers a quiet, atmospheric spot for a low-key meal of grilled vegetables topped with goat cheese, spaghetti *misto funghi* (wild mushrooms and garlic–white wine sauce), risotto *frutti di mare*, *vitello* (veal), *pollo* (chicken), or thin-crust pizza. No lunch on Sunday. ~ 113 North Larchmont Boulevard; 323-962-2130, fax 310-962-4816. MODERATE TO ULTRA-DELUXE.

Well-known for its Thai cuisine, **Chan Dara** is a modern restaurant with a mirrored bar and brass-rail dining room. Specialties vary from spicy barbecue to vegetable entrées. Patio dining is available. ~ 310 North Larchmont Boulevard; 323-467-1052; www.chandara.com, e-mail chandarett@loop.com. MODERATE.

HANCOCK PARK/LA BREA AVENUE **Campanile**, something of a foodie shrine for years now, offers what is probably the best contemporary American cooking in the city. Mark Peel and Nancy Silverton are nearly cult heroes—he for his rustic originality in turning out grilled meats and fish, aromatic soups, and zesty vegetables, she for her unmatched skill at baking great breads and desserts. The setting is quite lovely, too—a glass-roofed courtyard with a tiled fountain. Dinner and Saturday and Sunday brunch served. ~ 624 South La Brea Avenue; 323-938-1447; www.cam

AUTHOR FAVORITE

A restaurant inside a flower shop is unique enough, but it's the clever concoctions, healthfully prepared, that account for the popularity of **Flora Kitchen**. Sandwiches and salads are the specialties, with ingredients such as olive tapenade, roasted peppers, fresh herbs, buffalo mozzarella, and fresh ahi tuna. They do breakfast, lunch, and dinner as well as cappuccino and espresso. Flora also does a booming gourmet takeout business, and you can pick up fresh flowers at the same time. They have beer and wine as well. Only brunch is served on Sunday. ~ 460 South La Brea Boulevard; 323-931-9900, fax 323-938-7941. MODERATE.

panilerestaurant.com, e-mail campanile@campanilerestaurant.
com. DELUXE TO ULTRA-DELUXE.

The **Sonora Café** is a Southwestern restaurant decorated with
earth tones and *viga* ceilings. The patio in front is covered with
wrought-iron latticework. Lunch and dinner include fajitas, duck
tamales, chicken tostadas, and blue-corn enchiladas. There are
also fresh fish and steak dishes. Outdoor seating with a view of
the city skyline is available. No lunch on weekends. ~ 180 South
La Brea Avenue; 323-857-1800, fax 323-857-1601; www.sonora
cafe.com. MODERATE TO DELUXE.

FAIRFAX DISTRICT Eclectic Asian delicacies are served up at
Buddha's Belly, a simple feng shui-ed restaurant. Even the traditional foods come with a twist, such as fried rice with cara-
melized garlic cloves and Japanese salad dressing that tingles
with chiles. Diners can watch all the action in the wide-open
kitchen from either tables or the counter. ~ No lunch on Sunday.
7475 Beverly Boulevard; 323 931-8588. BUDGET.

◄ *HIDDEN*

The **Authentic Cafe** is truly trendy, but the food merits its popularity. Its eclectic array is really tasty: try the designer pizzas,
Szechuan fire dumplings, wood-grilled Yucatán chicken, or *chi-
laquiles*. There's a full bar and weekend brunch. Closed Monday.
~ 7605 Beverly Boulevard; 323-939-4626, fax 323-931-7929;
www.authenticcafe.com, e-mail authcafe@earthlink.net. MODER-
ATE TO DELUXE.

Farmers Market, a sprawling open-air collection of vendor
stands, is a good spot to visit and an even better place to eat. The
takeout stands lining each corridor dispense burritos, egg rolls,
jambalaya, corned beef, hot dogs, crêpes, and every other type
of ethnic food imaginable. Simply order at the counter, then find
a table in the sun. ~ 6333 West 3rd Street; 323-933-9211, fax 323-
954-4229; www.farmersmarketla.com, e-mail farmersmarketla.
com. BUDGET TO MODERATE.

Loteria Grill, a tiny Farmers Market taco stand, serves food
that's a long way from the usual Mexican-American fare.
Specialties include such intriguing choices as ceviche tostadas on
handmade tortillas and dark mole poblano enchiladas. ~ Farmers Market Stall 6333; West 3rd Street; 323 930-2211. BUDGET.

◄ *HIDDEN*

In the Farmers Market area, **Sofi Greek Restaurant** is a family-run Greek restaurant with a potful of grandmother's recipes.
Open for lunch and dinner, they serve moussaka in the dining

room or out on the patio. No lunch on Sunday. ~ 8030¾ West 3rd Street; 323-651-0346, fax 323-651-0347. MODERATE TO DELUXE.

HIDDEN ►   **SOUTH OF WILSHIRE**   Favored among savvy locals, **Rosalind's West African Cuisine** serves plantains, yam balls, and *akara* (deep-fried black-eyed peas). Main courses include Niger-style goat (sautéed with African herbs and spices), sautéed beef with onions and herbs, and groundnut stew (with nuts, beef, chicken, and spices). Enhancing the exotic cuisine is a complete wall mural depicting a waterfall on the Nile river. ~ 1044 South Fairfax Avenue; 323-936-2486, fax 323-936-1997. MODERATE.

SHOPPING   The city's burgeoning **Koreatown** is a warren of small shops and markets, each brightly painted in the calligraphy of the East. While many sell Korean foodstuffs and cater to local clientele, each provides a small glimpse into the life of this energetic community. ~ Centered between 4th Street and Olympic, Western, and Vermont avenues.

A spate of art galleries and restaurants attracts shoppers along **La Brea Avenue**. **Jan Baum Gallery** presents national and international contemporary art exhibits. Closed Sunday and Monday. ~ 170 South La Brea Avenue; 323-932-0170; www.janbaum.com. **Jack Rutberg Fine Arts** features modern paintings, drawings, sculptures, original prints, and museum-quality collectibles. Closed Sunday and Monday. ~ 357 North La Brea Avenue; 323-938-5222.

The La Brea corridor, as the area between Wilshire Boulevard and Melrose Avenue is called, is home to a collection of innovative galleries.

Along Wilshire Boulevard, stop in at the gift shop at the **Los Angeles County Museum of Art**, where you'll find art books, photographic items, and graphic reproductions. Closed Wednesday. ~ 5905 Wilshire Boulevard; 323-857-6146.

Nearby Fairfax Avenue, the center of L.A.'s Jewish community, is a neighborhood steeped in religious tradition and filled with delis, bakeries, and kosher grocery stores. **Canter's**, with its sumptuous baked goods and delicious sandwiches, is by far the most popular deli in the district. ~ 419 North Fairfax Avenue; 323-651-2030.

NIGHTLIFE   The Mexican food may be good at **El Cholo**, but the famed margaritas really draw the crowds to this lively bar scene. ~ 1121 South Western Avenue; 323-734-2773; www.elcholocafe.com.

Tom Bergin's, a traditional Irish pub dating to the 1930s, was voted one of the top 100 bars in the United States by *Esquire* magazine. Judging from the 7500 patron-inscribed shamrocks mounted on the wood-paneled walls, the regular crowd confirms *Esquire*'s vote. ~ 840 South Fairfax Avenue; 323-936-7151; www. tombergins.com.

The **Wiltern Theatre** opened its doors in 1931 as a Warner Brothers movie house. Now restored to its art-deco splendor, the terra-cotta structure is a center for the performing arts. Rock and classical music, drama, and opera programs are regularly scheduled. ~ 3790 Wilshire Boulevard; 213-380-5005.

A beautiful 1927 Renaissance-style building, the **Wilshire Ebell Theatre** is the setting for television specials and live theater, opera, and dance presentations. ~ 4401 West 8th Street; 323-939-1128; www.ebellla.com.

You'll want to jump and jive at the **Atlas Supper Club,** a snazzy supper club showcasing jazz, swing, salsa, and cabaret acts. Cover on Friday and Saturday, and for special events. ~ 3760 Wilshire Boulevard; 213-380-8400.

The **Los Angeles County Museum of Art** (LACMA) presents an ongoing series of outdoor jazz concerts on Friday evenings (free), film screenings on Friday and Saturday evenings (admission), and Sunday afternoon music concerts (free). ~ 5905 Wilshire Boulevard; 323-857-6000; www.lacma.org, e-mail publicinfo@lacma.org.

FIVE

The Westside

Like Horace Greeley's proverbial pioneer, wealth in Los Angeles has gone west. As Los Angeles' population mushroomed and the burgeoning automobile culture produced more and better roads, anyone who could afford to moved away from the city center. While areas crumbled in their wake, the rich and wannabe rich kept moving toward the sea until they could go no further. Today, the Westside, the area starting in Beverly Hills and ending with Pacific Palisades, contains Los Angeles' most sought-after real estate. Cultural diversity is defined here not so much by race and class as by whether one is already rich or simply striving to be.

Beverly Hills and Bel Air are exclusive colonies marked by manicured lawns, gated mansions, world-famous restaurants, and designer shops. But they were not always like this.

Back in 1844, a Spanish woman named Maria Rita Valdez acquired controlling interest over 4500 acres of sagebrush and tumbleweed that would later become Beverly Hills. Luckily she spent only $17.50 on the transaction. One shudders to think what the same property would cost today, but at the time the land was of little worth. Even by the turn of the 20th century it consisted only of lima bean fields, sheep meadows, and a few isolated farmhouses. Plans for wheat cultivation, oil drilling, and a community of German immigrants failed. Finally, in 1912, a group of entrepreneurs, struggling to sell this barren real estate, happened on the idea of building a big hotel to publicize their new housing development. Happily, the fledgling movie industry was already attracting people to neighboring Hollywood, and the Beverly Hills Hotel became a rendezvous for rising stars.

What really secured the community's future, however, was the decision of the undisputed King and Queen of Hollywood, Douglas Fairbanks and Mary Pickford, to build their palace on a hill above the hotel in 1920. Within a few years

Gloria Swanson, Charlie Chaplin, Rudolph Valentino, Buster Keaton, John Barry-more, and Will Rogers were neighbors. The dusty farmland, now a town named Beverly Hills, had finally blossomed.

Bel Air, developed during the 1920s by an entrepreneur with a sense of ele-gance, was originally subdivided into plots of several acres, guaranteeing that only the wealthy would need apply. At first even movie people, many of whom were Jewish, were excluded from this elite area. Then during the Depression, with other businesses dying while Hollywood flourished, Bel Air's greed proved stronger than its bigotry. Movie stars began moving in en masse and by the 1940s were rapidly becoming the area's most notable residents.

Although Brentwood and Pacific Palisades offer less history and are a bit more low-key and eclectic, rents are still high, real estate prices heart-stopping, and the shops exclusive and expensive. In Westwood, more than 35,000 UCLA students are squeezed into one of the most valuable real estate districts in the na-tion, an area that was little more than ranch land in the early 20th century. The original commercial area, known simply as "The Village" by students and locals, was developed during the 1920s as a Mediterranean-style complex with shops and restaurants. While this campus town is an odd mix of blocky apartment buildings, high-rise condominiums, older residences, and mundane office towers, nearby Century City, a former film studio, has been transformed into a futuristic landscape with plazas, greenswards, and vaulting high-rises.

Culver City and West Los Angeles are about as affordable as it gets on the Westside. Businesses here cater to those who live on a weekly paycheck and eth-nic restaurants serve inexpensive and tasty meals. But if you wanted to buy a house here, you'd better be prepared to pay $250,000 and up for a fixer-upper.

Beverly Hills

Nowhere in Los Angeles are people better coifed, made up, and dressed than in downtown Beverly Hills. Even the air smells expensive as these perfumed and groomed men and women breeze along the boulevards, headed for the city's most exclusive stores and restaurants.

It's a rags-to-riches town with a lot of Horatio Alger stories to tell. The world capital of wealth and glamour, Beverly Hills is a place in which driving a BMW makes you a second-class citizen and where the million-dollar houses are in the poorer part of town. This community with more gardeners per capita than any other United States city is one of the few spots outside Texas where flaunting your money is still considered good taste. A facelift here is as common as a haircut, and some of the residents look like they've been embalmed for the past 30 years.

Still, it's Beverly Hills, the town that simply oozes wealth, style, and success. From all over the world hopefuls come here to share the seemingly gold-paved streets with the absurdly rich as they fantasize about one day being part of this exclusive group.

SIGHTS It seems only fitting that the gateway to this posh preserve should be along **Santa Monica Boulevard**, a greenbelt with an exotic array of plant life. Each block of this blooming corridor is alive with a variety of vegetation. Trees are closely pruned, shrubs carefully shaped, and the flowers are planted in a succession of colorful beds. Most impressive of all is the landscape of cactus and succulents between Camden and Bedford drives. ~ Between Doheny Drive and Wilshire Boulevard.

Rising near the center of the promenade is **Beverly Hills City Hall**, a Spanish Baroque structure capped with a tile cupola. The foyer of this 1932 building has a recessed ceiling with scroll ornaments and hand-painted panels. ~ North Rexford Drive and Santa Monica Boulevard.

A contemporary commentary on City Hall, the adjacent **Beverly Hills Civic Center** features a stepped design in Spanish deco style. The tile trim and palm landscape further reflect the earlier building.

By contrast, the **U.S. Post Office** is an Italian Renaissance structure of brick and terra cotta. Built in 1933, the interior contains WPA-type murals popular during the Depression. ~ 9300 Santa Monica Boulevard.

Canon Drive, another horticultural corridor, is a parade of palms stretching for four blocks between Santa Monica and Sunset boulevards. The 80-foot trees lining this august street are Mexican and California sand palms.

To help find your way around the winding streets of this hillside community, the **Beverly Hills Visitors Bureau** provides printed information. Closed weekends. ~ 239 South Beverly Drive; 310-248-1015, 800-345-2210; www.beverlyhillsbehere.com.

Regardless of its famous faces and stately residences, Beverly Hills has a single address that symbolizes the entire community. **Rodeo Drive**, where wannabes walk with the wealthy, represents one of the most fashionable strips in the world of shopping. This gilded row extends only from the 200 to 400 block, but within that enclave are shops whose names have become synonymous with style.

From May through December, catch the classic-style **Beverly Hills Trolley** at Rodeo Drive and Dayton Way for a docent-led tour of the posh downtown area. Fee. ~ 310-285-2438.

Surprisingly, little of the architecture is noteworthy. Among the artistic exceptions is the 1928 beaux-arts **Regent Beverly Wilshire,** which anchors the avenue. ~ 9500 Wilshire Boulevard.

Frank Lloyd Wright's **Anderton Court,** created during the 1950s, projects a fractured effect with each part angling in a different direction, as if the building were about to split in pieces like a child's block pile. Holding it together is a Guggenheim-type circular ramp that curves past multiple levels of shops to a jagged metal tower. ~ 332 North Rodeo Drive.

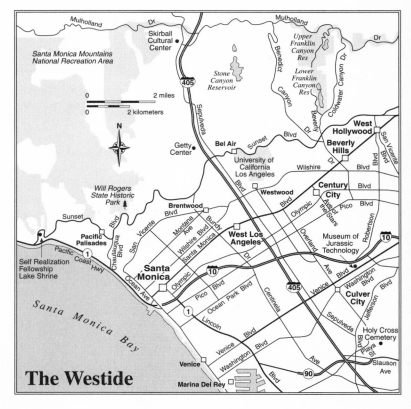

The Westide

Just beyond the commercial district stands the **O'Neill House**, an art nouveau confection reminiscent of the work of Spanish architect Antonio Gaudi. ~ 507 North Rodeo Drive.

For years Hollywood's chief gossip factory was the **Beverly Hills Hotel**, a pink Mission Revival building dating to 1912. During the 1930s the hotel's Polo Lounge attracted Darryl Zanuck, Will Rogers, and other polo enthusiasts. Later its private bungalows became trysting places for celebrities. (Marilyn Monroe reportedly entertained John and Robert Kennedy in a very private bungalow here.) Howard Hughes, Marilyn Monroe, and Sophia Loren rented them. John Lennon and Yoko Ono holed up for a week here, and Elizabeth Taylor and Richard Burton made love and war. Today the hotel's manicured grounds are tropically landscaped and well worth visiting, even when the stars are not out. ~ 9641 Sunset Boulevard; 310-276-2251, 800-283-8885, fax 310-281-2905; www.thebeverlyhillshotel.com, e-mail sales@beverlyhillshotel.com.

The most famous homes in Beverly Hills may be those of the stars, but its most intriguing residence is the **Spadena House**. Built in 1921 as a movie set and office, this "Witch's House" resembles something out of a fairy tale. Its sharp peaked roof, mullioned windows, and cobweb ambience evoke images of Hansel and Gretel. ~ 516 Walden Drive.

By calling in advance you can tour the **Virginia Robinson Gardens**, a six-acre estate landscaped with king palm trees and a variety of gardens. The home here, which is part of the tour, is the oldest house in Beverly Hills, a 1911 Mediterranean Revival structure. Open Tuesday through Friday, by appointment only. Admission. ~ 310-276-5367, fax 310-276-5352.

ANNALS OF THE AIRWAVES

If you missed President Franklin D. Roosevelt's first fireside chat in 1933, don't despair. It, along with other events of historical and cultural importance, can be seen and heard at the **Museum of Television & Radio**. You can access over 100,000 TV and radio programs from the '20s to the '90s. This sleek, three-story, classic-modernist building, designed by Richard Meier, is the outpost of the Museum of Television & Radio in Manhattan. Closed Monday and Tuesday. ~ 465 North Beverly Drive; 310-786-1000, fax 310-786-1086; www.mtr.org.

Greystone Park is the site of a 55-room English Tudor manor built during the 1920s by oil tycoon Edward L. Doheny. Although the house is closed to the public, visitors can stroll through the 18-acre grounds and perhaps take in a summer concert and occasional theater performance (June through September). ~ 905 Loma Vista Drive; 310-550-4654, fax 310-858-9238; www.beverlyhills.org.

Despite its standing as one of the wealthiest communities in the nation, Beverly Hills offers at least one low-cost lodging facility. The **Beverly Terrace Hotel** is a 39-unit facility, with accommodations typical of motel digs. Among the amenities are a pool and a restaurant that serves lunch and dinner. The choice location is less than a block from Melrose Avenue. Continental breakfast and free parking are included. ~ 469 North Doheny Drive; 310-274-8141, 800-842-6401, fax 310-385-1998; www.beverlyterracehotel.com, e-mail bthotel@aol.com. MODERATE.

LODGING

Located within easy walking distance of Rodeo Drive and Century City, **The Peninsula Beverly Hills** sets the tone for your stay with its light, cream-colored lobby where large windows look out on gardens and a fountain by day and crystal chandeliers cast a soft glow after dark. The 196 guest rooms feature marble baths, French doors, king-size beds, overstuffed chairs, and armoires containing satellite TVs. Guests for whom money is truly no object can opt for one of the 16 villa suites, some with private spas, terraces, and fireplaces. ~ 9882 South Santa Monica Boulevard; 310-551-2888, 800-462-7899, fax 310-788-2319; www.peninsula.com, e-mail pbh@peninsula.com. ULTRA-DELUXE.

Comprising two former apartment houses and the late Beverly Carlton Hotel, whose guest register included such industry legends as Mae West and Marilyn Monroe, the **Avalon Hotel** is one of the hippest and hottest places to stay in Beverly Hills. The mid-20th-century architecture, complete with kidney-shaped pool, cries retro chic. The 86 rooms, suites, and studios are also coolly decorated, and outfitted with VCRs, CD players, and fax machines; a number have private balconies. ~ 9400 West Olympic Boulevard; 310-277-5221, 800-535-4715, fax 310-277-4928; www.avalonbeverlyhills.com. DELUXE.

◄ HIDDEN

On a knoll overlooking Beverly Hills is the **Loews Beverly Hills Hotel,** a 12-story building with 137 rooms. The hotel of-

Text continued on page 150.

Hollywood Legends

The favorite sport in Beverly Hills has always been stargazing. Synonymous with glamour, wealth, and fame, the town has been home to actors since the era of silent films. In fact, the best way to trace Hollywood's past is by driving through Beverly Hills.

LOVE—HOLLYWOOD STYLE Starting at the intersection of Rodeo Drive and Santa Monica Boulevard, drive nine blocks northwest on Santa Monica to North Palm Drive and turn left. That Elizabethan cottage on your right at 508 North Palm Drive was home to **Marilyn Monroe and Joe DiMaggio** in 1954 during their stormy marriage. The couple moved in around April, but by September, when Marilyn was filming *The Seven Year Itch,* the tumultuous tie had already been broken. Continue two blocks up Palm, turn left on Elevado Avenue and then right on North Maple Drive, to see the home of a couple who had a happier and far more enduring marriage. If **George Burns and Gracie Allen**'s place at 720 North Maple Drive looks familiar, that's because a model of the home was used for their 1950s TV show.

TAYLOR–TODD MANSION Beverly Hills is nothing if not the story of marriages. The bond between **Elizabeth Taylor and Mike Todd** ended tragically in 1958 when Todd's plane crashed over New Mexico. The couple was occupying the Mediterranean-style mansion at 1330 Schuyler Road when the movie producer died. To find it, from George and Gracie's house continue a block north on Maple to Sunset Boulevard; turn right, go two blocks to Hillcrest and make a U-turn to go west on Sunset; take the next right onto Mountain Drive. Take the next right onto Schuyler Road, which skirts **Greystone Park** (page 147); turn right onto Doheny Road, then left to get back on Schuyler. The Taylor-Todd mansion is at Schuyler and Cerrocrest Drive.

LANA'S LOVE NEST **Lana Turner**'s relationship with mobster Johnny Stompanato didn't last long, either. It seems that after Stompanato threatened Turner's life during a heated argument, her daughter Cheryl Crane stabbed him to death in their prim Colonial house at 730 North Bedford Drive. The even more heated trial that followed drew tremendous press coverage and exposed secrets of the star's love life. To see the scene of the crime, after driving back down the hill to Sunset Boulevard, turn right and drive four blocks west to Beverly Drive. Turn left, drive one block south past Will Rogers Memorial Park, and turn right onto Lomitas Avenue. Three blocks down, turn left on Bedford Drive, where the Lana Turner house is on your left in the middle of the block.

NORTH ROXBURY DRIVE   Continue to the end of the block, turn left on Elevado Avenue, then left again at the next block to drive up North Roxbury Drive, a residential street trimmed with trees and lined with 1930s-era estates that celebrities once called home. **Marlene Dietrich** lived in the squarish, art-deco mansion at 822. **Jimmy Stewart** set up residence in the brick Tudor house just across Sunset at 918, while **Lucille Ball** lived at 1000 and **Jack Benny** lived next door at 1002. Benny's brick Colonial home, like Burns and Allen's house, was sometimes filmed in his television show.

CITIZENS HEARST AND GARBO   Continue north on Roxbury Drive as it curves around to the right and becomes Hartford Way. At 1700 Lexington Road, where Hartford and Lexington intersect, is the mansion that newspaper baron William Randolph Hearst purchased during the 1920s for his mistress, **Marion Davies**. Later in the decade **Greta Garbo** and her parrot, four cats, and a chow chow moved into the neighborhood at 1027 Chevy Chase Drive. To get there, backtrack one block on Hartford to Benedict Canyon Drive, turn right, drive one block, and turn left.

TOWER ROAD AND GREEN ACRES   One block farther north on Benedict Canyon Drive, veer right onto Tower Road, which also saw its share of stars. **Juliet Prowse** lived behind the mullioned windows at 1136; **Arthur Rubinstein** occupied 1139; and actor **Spencer Tracy** called 1158 Tower Road home. Two blocks farther north on Benedict Canyon Drive, turn left on Greenacres Drive, where Green Acres, the estate of silent film comedian **Harold Lloyd** at 1740 Green Acres Place, has been reduced to a mere five acres. When Lloyd moved here in 1928 the grounds included 20 acres and were planted with 12 gardens, each following a different theme. The house he occupied until his death in 1971 has 44 rooms, including 26 bathrooms.

FALCON LAIR   Continuing up Benedict Canyon Road, take the second left onto Cielo Drive and follow it to Bella Drive, then turn left and look for the mansion at 1436, where **Rudolph Valentino** sought seclusion from his adoring fans in 1925 by moving here to Falcon Lair (named for his movie *The Hooded Falcon*), a magnificent mansion appointed with Renaissance art, oriental carpets, and medieval armor. Little did the young actor realize when he finally found his retreat that he would die from ulcers the next year.

fers a range of amenities including an outdoor swimming pool, health club, and restaurant. The lobby has an airy feel with a front desk inlaid with onyx and mother of pearl. ~ 1224 South Beverwil Drive; 310-277-2800, 800-421-3212, fax 310-277-5470; www. loewshotels.com. ULTRA-DELUXE.

An intimate and stylish alternative is **Maison 140**. A brick Colonial-style structure, it was once owned by silent film star Lillian Gish. Today, each of the 45 guest rooms is furnished in Asian and French vintage style; all have private baths, cable TV, and mini-refrigerators. Add a friendly staff and a comfortable lobby to round out this fine small Beverly Hills hotel. ~ 140 South Lasky Drive; 310-281-4000, 800-432-5444, fax 310-281-4001; www.maison140.com. DELUXE TO ULTRA-DELUXE.

The **Mosaic Hotel** is an elegant boutique hostelry on a residential street just off Wilshire Boulevard. Rooms are outfitted with king beds, warm wood furniture, plush bedding and marble bathrooms, as well as amenities such as robes, hairdryers, CD players and internet connection; some have private decks that overlook the pool surrounded by lush foliage. You'll also find an exercise room as well as a bar. Breakfast, lunch and dinner are served in the restaurant. ~ 125 South Spalding Drive; 310-278-0303, 800-463-4466, fax 310-278-1728; www.mosaichotel.com, e-mail reservations@ mosaichotel.com. ULTRA-DELUXE.

Small and elegant, **Raffles L'Ermitage** is tucked away on a quiet tree-lined street. Only the discreet sign reveals that it's a hotel. A rooftop garden terrace with a 360-degree view has a heated pool and private cabanas for guests' use. Although Raffles L'Ermitage is expensive, you're not dollared to death. ~ 9291 Burton Way; 310-278-3344, 800-800-2113, fax 310-278-8247; www.lermitage hotel.com. ULTRA-DELUXE.

The Regent Beverly Wilshire Hotel, a 1928 beaux-arts building, is another grand old hotel in Beverly Hills. Located at the foot of Rodeo Drive, this landmark features a Wilshire wing with 147 rooms and suites and an adjacent Beverly wing, built during the 1970s. Guest rooms in the Wilshire wing are quite spacious, designed with flair, and possess the character that makes this a great hotel. The 248 rooms and suites in the newer wing are decorated in a Southern California contemporary style. Both sections draw on a full line of amenities, including shops, restaurants, lounges, fitness center, and pool. ~ 9500 Wilshire Boulevard; 310-

275-5200, 800-427-4354, fax 310-274-2851; www.fourseasons. com. ULTRA-DELUXE.

DINING

The place to nosh in Beverly Hills is **Nate 'n' Al Deli**, a traditional delicatessen with a complete assortment of kosher dishes. There are bagels, sandwiches on rye and pumpernickel, and a smoked fish plate that includes lox, cod, and whitefish. ~ 414 North Beverly Drive; 310-274-0101, fax 310-274-0485. MODERATE.

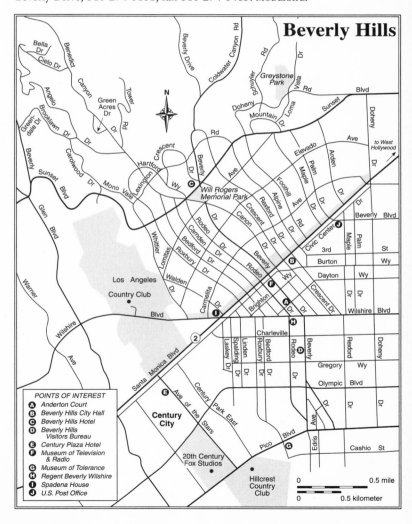

Beverly Hills

POINTS OF INTEREST
- **A** Anderton Court
- **B** Beverly Hills City Hall
- **C** Beverly Hills Hotel
- **D** Beverly Hills Visitors Bureau
- **E** Century Plaza Hotel
- **F** Museum of Television & Radio
- **G** Museum of Tolerance
- **H** Regent Beverly Wilshire
- **I** Spadena House
- **J** U.S. Post Office

With an exterior that looks like a shiny chrome Airstream trailer and an interior full of turquoise- and apricot-colored formica and vinyl, the kitschily retro **Airstream Diner** is about the last place you'd expect to find in Beverly Hills. Diners perch on garden gnome–supported stools, wolfing down such over-the-top creations as the Hunka, Hunka Burnin' Love pancakes that come with peanut butter, chocolate chips, and bananas, drizzled with caramel sauce. Kids can make their own peanut-butter-and-jelly sandwiches, and meatloaf takes on a new meaning when covered in cumin ketchup. ~ 9601 Santa Monica Boulevard; 310-550-8883. BUDGET TO MODERATE.

Neapolitan-style pizzas are topped with the freshest ingredients and pasta dishes are graced with lovingly homemade sauces at **Da Pasquale**. This traditional trattoria serves tasty meals with less pretense and for less money than most Beverly Hills eateries. No lunch on Saturday. Closed Sunday. ~ 9749 Little Santa Monica Boulevard; 310-859-3884. MODERATE.

HIDDEN ▶

Owned and frequented by celebrities, minimalist in decor, **Maple Drive** has emerged as one of Beverly Hills' top trysts. You can dine on a number of American/Continental tidbits while catching the flash and dance of Hollywood on parade. There's live jazz Tuesday through Saturday nights, and a jazz brunch on Sunday. No lunch on Saturday. ~ 345 North Maple Drive; 310-274-9800; www.mapledriverestaurant.com, e-mail info@mapledriverestaurant.com. DELUXE TO ULTRA-DELUXE.

Gourmet food, chic surroundings, and beautiful people combine to make **Prego** a popular rendezvous. This Italian trattoria

AUTHOR FAVORITE

Most Beverly Hills restaurants are places to be seen; **Kate Mantílini** is a place to see. A kind of *Star Wars* diner, this 21st-century rendezvous is an artwork in steel and tile. Jagged edges and angular beams are everywhere; a boxing mural covers an entire wall; and in the center a sundial/skylight rises from floor to dome. For dinner there's rotisserie chicken, meatloaf, lamb shank, frogs' legs, a half dozen steaks, and fresh fish daily. Open for breakfast, lunch, and dinner on weekdays; brunch, lunch, and dinner only on weekends. ~ 9101 Wilshire Boulevard; 310-278-3699, fax 310-273-0863; www.gardensonglendon.com. MODERATE TO ULTRA-DELUXE.

serves pizza, pasta, and several entrées. Among the pizzas are calzones, folded pizzas with smoked mozzarella, and stracchino cheese pizzas. Pasta dishes include *fusilli con luganega* (corkscrew noodles with sausage); entrées feature Italian sausage, veal chops, and fresh fish. The kitchen is open to view and the decor consists of modern artwork along brick walls, track lights, and hardwood trim. No lunch on Sunday. ~ 362 North Camden Drive; 310-277-7346, fax 310-858-7879; www.spectrumfoods.com. MODERATE TO DELUXE.

A Los Angeles institution, **Trader Vic's**, the last of the Polynesian-themed restaurants popular in the 1950s and '60s, is a veritable South Seas fantasy. Kitschy tropical decor and umbrella drinks served in coconut shells may be old school, but the bar is packed with trendy martini drinkers, and the Asian-style food is first rate. Dinner only. ~ 9876 Wilshire Boulevard; 310-276-6345; www.tradervics.com. DELUXE.

Ranking among Los Angeles' finest restaurants, **La Scala** is an intimate and well-appointed dining room. Upholstered booths add to an elegant interior where oil paintings are combined with decorative plates. The gourmets and celebrities frequenting this address also come for the excellent Italian cuisine. Among the entrées are spaghetti *alla* cognac, filet mignon, and fresh fish dishes. Closed Sunday. ~ 434 North Canon Drive; 310-275-0579, fax 310-246-9099. MODERATE TO ULTRA-DELUXE.

With the possible exception of Berkeley's Chez Panisse, **Spago** is California's most famous restaurant (owner and celebrity chef Wolfgang Puck helped originate California cuisine). Spago's incarnation in Beverly Hills, just north of Wilshire Boulevard, offers many of the original restaurant's signature dishes like smoked salmon pizza, but also a slate of new entrées. You can enjoy selections from their daily-changing menu while dining on the open-air patio. No lunch Sunday. ~ 176 North Canon Drive; 310-385-0880. DELUXE TO ULTRA-DELUXE.

SHOPPING

Without doubt, the capital of consumerism is Beverly Hills. In the mythic order of things, this gilded neighborhood is a kind of shopper's heaven, where everything sparkles just out of reach.

At the heart of the capital lies the "golden triangle," an exclusive shopping district bounded by Wilshire Boulevard, Rexford Drive, and Santa Monica Boulevard. The heart within the heart is, you guessed it, **Rodeo Drive**. World-famous designer showcases like Gucci, Van Clef and Arpels, Cartier, Louis Vuitton, Giorgio, and Ralph Lauren are part of the scenery on Rodeo Drive. Some are soooo exclusive they open only by appointment.

> Often the fun of shopping in Beverly Hills (especially if you're on a budget) is in the people watching.

The breathtaking etchings of Rembrandt are among the rare selections at **Galerie Michael**. ~ 430 North Rodeo Drive; 310-273-3377; www.galeriemichael.com.

The **Rodeo Collection** houses designer boutiques that carry Stephanie Anais and Thalian designs. ~ 421 North Rodeo Drive; 310-858-7580.

The **Barakat** collection of jewelry features an amazing combination of Old World antiquities spanning the globe. This magnificent shop also holds an extensive pre-Columbian art collection. Even the catalog is a collector's item. Closed Sunday. ~ 405 North Rodeo Drive; 310-859-8408; www.barakatgallery.com.

Among the town's chic spots is **Giorgio Armani Boutique**, home of Giorgio perfume and an array of haute couture. ~ 436 North Rodeo Drive; 310-271-5555.

Frances Klein Antique & Estate Jewelry could be the world's most exclusive mom-and-pop store; and there may be enough fine jewelry here to make it the world's first mom-and-pop museum. Closed Sunday. ~ 310 North Rodeo Drive; 310-273-0155.

Tiffany & Co. continues to awe and inspire. ~ 210 North Rodeo Drive; 310-273-8880.

Two Rodeo is a $200-million cobblestone mall featuring about two dozen shops. Built along three levels, it's a brass-door-and-antique-street-lamp promenade reminiscent of a European boulevard. ~ Corner of Rodeo Drive and Wilshire Boulevard.

Beverly Hills supports several dozen art galleries, many located along Rodeo Drive. Most galleries stay open until 10 p.m.

Some of the country's most famous department stores line Wilshire Boulevard between the 9600 and 9900 blocks. **Neiman Marcus** (310-550-5900) and **Saks Fifth Avenue** (310-247-9419) are only part of this elite company.

"Little" Santa Monica Boulevard has less formal, less expensive shops, such as **Susanna**, which features custom-made haute-couture designs for day and evening wear. Closed Sunday. ~ 9647 Little Santa Monica Boulevard; 310-276-7510.

South Robertson Boulevard is home to dozens of small boutiques. At **Lisa Kline,** you can browse through an array of vintage and new clothing for women. ~ 136 South Robertson Boulevard; 310-246-0907.

NIGHTLIFE

For a European-style disco, check out the scene at **Orsini's.** Every Thursday through Sunday, a deejay spins lively dance tunes to the delight of the crowd. Cover. ~ 9575 West Pico Boulevard; 310-277-6050.

The late-night drinking and dancing Beverly Hills elite goes to **Joya.** This classy dance place really rocks on Wednesday nights and weekends, when a deejay plays everything from hip-hop to R&B. Closed Monday. ~ 242 North Beverly Boulevard; 310-274-4440, fax 310-274-2611.

Bel Air

Beverly Hills, at least the flatland section, seems downright middle-class in comparison with the palatial estates nestled in the hills of Bel Air. The most famous of the famous in the movie industry have lived and still live in multi-roomed palaces hidden behind towering hedges and walls and guarded by elaborate gates.

SIGHTS

Except for a country club and a super-luxury hotel, Bel Air is strictly a residential area (albeit L.A.'s most expensive and exclusive). If you are a classic movie fan, however, there are a couple of homes here not to be missed. **Humphrey Bogart and Lauren Bacall,** who met on the set of *To Have and Have Not* in 1944, settled down together in a brick Colonial house in Bel Air. Bogey was 25 years older than Bacall, but they became one of America's most legendary couples, starring together in *The Big Sleep* (1946), *Dark Passage* (1947), and *Key Largo* (1948). ~ 232 South Mapleton Drive.

The stone mansion at 750 Bel Air Road served for eight seasons as the "Beverly Hillbillies" House. This French estate was the prime-time home for one of television's oddest families.

A real-life family, **Judy Garland** and her mother, lived in the red brick house located at 1231 Stone Canyon Road. The childhood star of *The Wizard of Oz* built the place in 1940, equipping it with a badminton court, pinball machines, and her own top-floor suite.

LODGING   Los Angeles' most Eden-like address lies in a forested canyon
surrounded by peach and apricot trees. A classic country inn, the
Hotel Bel-Air is an exclusive 91-room complex and private haven
for show business celebrities and European royalty. The 1920s
Mission-style buildings are shaded by a luxuriant garden of silk
floss trees and redwoods. A stream tumbles through the property, creating small waterfalls and a pool with swans. All around
is a mazework of archways and footbridges, colonnades, and
fountains. Numbering among the nation's finest hotels, the Bel-
Air also provides an oval swimming pool, a gym, a gourmet
restaurant, a lounge, and a patio terrace. ~ 701 Stone Canyon
Road; 310-472-1211, 800-648-4097, fax 310-476-5890; www.
hotelbelair.com, e-mail info@hotelbelair.com. ULTRA-DELUXE.

DINING   Commercial establishments are rare in residential Bel Air. Finding a restaurant with reasonable prices is even more challenging,
especially as you ascend the hills—the farther you climb, the
higher the prices become.

At **Four Oaks Restaurant** you encounter a French restaurant
that's comfortable and understated. This intimate dining room is
illuminated through skylights and features a brick patio for dining alfresco. The constantly evolving fare consists of organically
grown ingredients prepared in a modern French-American style.
Reservations recommended. Closed Monday. ~ 2181 North Beverly Glen Boulevard; 310-470-2265, 877-804-2788, fax 310-475-
5492; www.fouroaksrestaurant.com. DELUXE TO ULTRA-DELUXE.

The restaurant at the Hotel Bel-Air—**The Restaurant**—is so
low-key it doesn't even have a name. This is no glitzy, glamorous
monument to gastronomy. At the end of a graceful arcade in the
hotel's Mission-style main building, its understated decor soothes
diners who settle into comfortable Queen Anne chairs. A menu
of topnotch Continental/American food caters to the worldly, well-
heeled patron looking for a traditional meal in a comfortable atmosphere. Breakfast, lunch, and dinner are served, with brunch
on Sunday. ~ 701 Stone Canyon Road; 310-472-1211, 800-648-
4097, fax 310-476-5890; www.hotelbelair.com. ULTRA-DELUXE.

NIGHTLIFE   Hidden in a forested Bel Air canyon, **The Bar** at the Hotel Bel-
Air is the perfect place for an intimate cocktail. Piano music from
this wood-paneled den wafts onto the patio and out across the

garden, waterfall, and pond. ~ 701 Stone Canyon Road; 310-472-1211, fax 310-476-5890; www.hotelbelair.com.

Prior to June 12, 1994, mention Brentwood and the few who had heard of it conjured up images of a tony Westside neighborhood near Santa Monica. After that Sunday night, mention Brentwood and the world remembers the scandal of O.J. Simpson and his murdered wife Nicole. After the infamous trial, the Simpson house was bulldozed and another mansion built in its place, while Nicole's condo complex underwent a facelift. Brentwood shortly returned to its former upscale and quiet self.

Brentwood

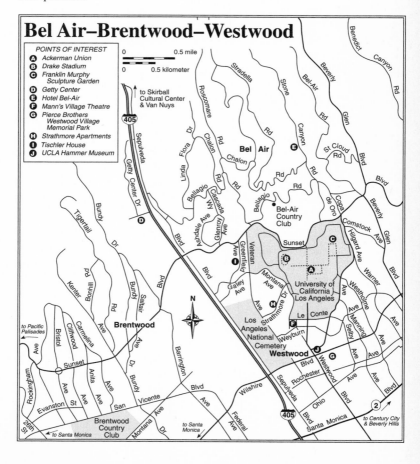

Bel Air–Brentwood–Westwood

POINTS OF INTEREST

Ⓐ Ackerman Union
Ⓑ Drake Stadium
Ⓒ Franklin Murphy Sculpture Garden
Ⓓ Getty Center
Ⓔ Hotel Bel-Air
Ⓕ Mann's Village Theatre
Ⓖ Pierce Brothers Westwood Village Memorial Park
Ⓗ Strathmore Apartments
Ⓘ Tischler House
Ⓙ UCLA Hammer Museum

Brentwood differs from its neighbor Bel Air in that, while it has its share of wall-, gate-, and hedge-protected mansions, it also has plenty of apartment buildings, condos, restaurants, and shops. While property values are still staggering, there are houses to be had for less than $1 million and condos for under $500,000. This makes Brentwood a hot place for the striving-to-be-rich to live.

SIGHTS

High on a hilltop in the Santa Monica Mountains, the **Getty Center** resembles some kind of postmodern fortress. And with its own freeway exit, to boot. The Getty Center commands attention, like a castle on a hill, a white, gleaming presence on the landscape. Visitors arrive via trams to the Arrival Plaza and continue by foot up the steps to the Entrance Hall—a series of five pavilions connected by glass walkways that provide views of the surrounding hillsides. Visitors can make up their own route through the museum and view the Getty's superb collection of pre-20th-century European sculpture and paintings, French decorative arts, European master drawings, illuminated manuscripts, and photography. Painting galleries on the upper floors have skylights whose louvers admit natural light, approximating the conditions under which pictures were painted and exhibited before the advent of electricity. Closed Monday and major holidays. Parking fee, $5. ~ 1200 Getty Center Drive; 310-440-7300, fax 310-440-7760; www.getty.edu.

> Make sure to wander through the Getty Center's central garden, an impressive array of natural wonders as captivating as the art collection itself.

Farther north, the **Skirball Cultural Center** presents a range of visual, literary and performing arts focused on the Jewish Experience. The museum displays include exhibits on the Torah and the Jewish holy days. The archaeology of the Middle East is also represented in a series of artifacts. One imaginative exhibit features simulated dig sites as well as a cut-away that shows how different strata of a hill contain remnants from earlier and earlier civilizations. Closed Monday. Admission. ~ 2701 North Sepulveda Boulevard; 310-440-4500, fax 310-440-4595; www.skirball.org, e-mail info@skirball.org.

One of Hollywood's most infamous families, **Joan Crawford** and her *Mommie Dearest* daughter Christina, lived in the sprawling Brentwood house at 426 North Bristol Avenue. Crawford moved here in 1929 with her first husband, Douglas Fairbanks, Jr., divorced him in 1934, and went on to marry three more husbands while raising four adopted children. Following the death of her last husband she sold the place in 1959.

During the 1930s, **Shirley Temple** and her family moved into the Brentwood mansion at 209 North Rockingham Road. The young actress had already blossomed into the country's archetypal little girl, destined to play the curly-haired beauty in over 20 films and then to become, incongruously, a right-wing politician as an adult.

Commercial establishments in this well-heeled community center **SHOPPING** around San Vicente Boulevard, a beautiful tree-lined street. **P. J. London** is Brentwood's ultimate resale shop, offering designer clothes handed down from wealthy Westside and Malibu residents. ~ 11661 San Vicente Boulevard; 310-826-4649; www.pj london.com.

Brentwood Country Mart, a village-style shopping complex, features several dozen stores. Closed Sunday. ~ 26th Street and San Vicente Boulevard; 310-395-6714.

del Mano Gallery displays three-dimensional artwork and fine crafts by American artists. Here you'll find a beautiful collection of ceramics, blown glass, and other media. Closed Monday. ~ 11981 San Vicente Boulevard; 310-476-8508; www.delmano.com.

▼ ▼ ▼ ▼ ▼ ▼ ▼ ▼ ▼ ▼ ▼

Westwood

Westwood has the unique distinction of having a transient population of people under 30 that is almost as large as that of the area's full-time residents. This gives the town an air of vitality and hipness that would likely be absent otherwise. Westwood boomed when one of the nation's largest and finest universities, UCLA, opened in 1929, and still remains the place where students go to sip designer coffees at sidewalk cafés and see the latest flick. In striking contrast to the low-rise, old-timey village are the towering high-rise businesses and condos on Wilshire Boulevard.

A sense of the old Westwood pervades **Westwood Village**, near the **SIGHTS** university. Here you can stroll past a succession of shops, many located in 1920s-era buildings of brick and wood. The Village's true identity, however, is revealed on Friday and Saturday nights when major movies are previewed and the place becomes a world of bumper people, with traffic gridlocked and crowds milling everywhere. ~ Centered around Westwood Boulevard.

Of Westwood's countless movie houses, the most inventive by far is **Mann's Village Theatre,** with its lofty tower and Spanish Moderne design. Built in 1931, the landmark features elevated pillars, ornamental scrollwork, and a free-standing box office. ~ 961 Broxton Avenue; 310-208-5576. The proximity of the 1937 **Mann's Bruin Theatre** across the street makes this the city's busiest crosswalk. ~ 948 Broxton Avenue; 310-208-8998.

Just across Le Conte Avenue from this cinema center lies the UCLA **Campus,** an impressive 419-acre enclave. A true multiversity, UCLA has 13 libraries and boasts over 70 separate departments. The grounds are a labyrinth of grand staircases and brick walkways leading past over 100 buildings that (as on most major campuses) constitute an architectural hodge-podge. Next door to classic structures are blocky metal-and-glass highrises reflective of the Bauhaus movement; modern masterpieces stand cheek-by-jowl with utilitarian monstrosities. ~ 310-825-4321, fax 310-206-8460; www.ucla.edu.

To navigate this enormous tree-shaded campus, hop on the **Campus Express,** a campus shuttle service. ~ 310-206-2908.

Ackerman Student Union represents the center of campus activity. **Kerckhoff Hall** next door is the only Gothic-style building on campus, a brick imitation of King Edward VII's Westminster chapel.

The geographic center of UCLA lies along the quadrangle at the top of **Janss Steps.** Anchoring the corners of the quad are the school's original buildings, magnificent Italian Romanesque structures dating to 1929. **Royce Hall,** a cloister-like building with twin towers and loggia, contains a public auditorium. The **Fowler Museum of Cultural History,** located next to Royce Hall, offers a changing series of exhibitions on world arts and cultures. Closed Monday and Tuesday. ~ 310-825-4361, fax 310-206-7007; www.fowler.ucla.edu, e-mail fowlerws@arts.ucla.edu.

Powell Hall across the rectangle is an ornate, gargoyled Moorish masterwork housing the UCLA **Film and Television Archive Research and Study Center.** This important cultural resource, known as the second largest film and TV archive in the country, has a collection of over 220,000 movies and television shows dating as far back as the silent film era. With advance notice, visitors can view many of the archive films at no charge (as long as they're working on a specific research project). Closed weekends. ~ 310-206-5388, fax 310-206-5392; www.cinema. ucla.edu, e-mail arsc@ucla.edu.

Prettiest place on the entire campus is the **Franklin Murphy Sculpture Garden**, a five-acre park planted with jacaranda trees. Among the more than 70 artworks adorning this greensward are pieces by Arp, Calder, Matisse, Moore, and Rodin. ~ Located near the University Research Library.

Because of its reputation as a university town, Westwood's beautiful residential areas are frequently overlooked. Explore the neighborhood just west of campus and you'll discover the **Tischler House**, a contemporary home designed by Austrian architect Rudolph Schindler in 1949. With a geometric layout and plate-glass prow, the home is like a ship moored in a hillside port. ~ 175 South Greenfield Avenue.

The **Strathmore Apartments**, located several blocks away, were built by Schindler's Viennese colleague, Richard Neutra, in 1937. Among the former tenants of this glass-and-stucco court were Orson Welles and Clifford Odets. ~ 11005 Strathmore Drive.

Nearby you'll encounter the UCLA **Hammer Museum**, which features lithographs and sculptures by Honoré Daumier as well as paintings by Rembrandt, Van Gogh, Monet, Cassatt, and Chagall. The Hammer also features contemporary artists in all visual media. Closed Monday. Admission. ~ 10899 Wilshire Boulevard; 310-443-7000, fax 310-443-7099; www.hammer.ucla.edu, e-mail hammerinfo@arts.ucla.edu.

In the same building as the Hammer Museum, you'll find the **Grunwald Center for the Graphic Arts**. Dedicated to "works on paper," the collection contains more than 35,000 prints, drawings, and photos. There are works by Dürer, Cézanne, Toulouse-

AUTHOR FAVORITE

sights The **Mildred Mathias Botanical Garden**, an enchanted spot in the southeastern corner of the UCLA campus, displays nearly 4000 plant species within its eight-acre domain. Focusing on tropical and subtropical vegetation, the glade is filled with lilies and rhododendrons, palms, and cactus. Visits to the **Hannah Carter Japanese Garden**, a Kyoto-style rock garden with teahouse and footbridges, can be arranged through the visitors center. It's about a mile from campus in Bel Air.

Lautrec, and Picasso, as well as contemporary artists such as June Wayne and Carlos Almaraz. Open by appointment only; closed weekends. ~ 310-443-7076, fax 310-443-7099; www.hammer. ucla.edu.

HIDDEN ▶

Tucked away, ironically, behind the Avco cinema complex on Wilshire Boulevard in Westwood is **Pierce Brothers Westwood Village Memorial Park**. This small cemetery is the final resting place for an impressive number of Hollywood legends, including Marilyn Monroe, Dean Martin, Natalie Wood, Burt Lancaster, Peggy Lee, Walter Matthau, and Jack Lemmon. ~ 1218 Glendon Avenue; 310-474-1579.

LODGING

Just one block from the UCLA campus, the **Hotel Claremont** has 53 rooms. These are plain, clean accommodations that share a large lobby. ~ 1044 Tiverton Avenue; 310-208-5957, 800-266-5957, fax 310-208-2386. BUDGET.

The **Royal Palace Westwood** next door offers 36 guest rooms, many with kitchens. These units are also well maintained and feature private patios. ~ 1052 Tiverton Avenue; 310-208-6677, 800-631-0100, fax 310-824-3732; www.royalpalacewestwood. com, e-mail lahotels@earthlink.net. MODERATE.

Nearby **Hilgard House Hotel** is a spiffy brick building with 47 rooms and six suites. Accommodations in this three-story structure are furnished with facsimile antiques, plushly carpeted, and attractively decorated with wall hangings; many come equipped with jacuzzi tubs. A complimentary continental breakfast is included. ~ 927 Hilgard Avenue; 310-208-3945, 800-826-3934, fax 310-208-1972; www.hilgardhouse.com, e-mail reservations@ hilgardhouse.com. DELUXE.

Directly across the street, but a big step uptown, stands the **W Los Angeles**, a 16-floor, all-suite hotel. There are restaurants and lounges steps away from a sumptuous lobby, two pools set in a landscaped garden, plus a complete work-out facility. ~ 930 Hilgard Avenue; 310-208-8765, 877-946-8357, fax 310-824-0355; www.whotels.com. ULTRA-DELUXE.

DINING

Sepi's Giant Submarines makes the best submarine sandwiches on the West Side. Half a sandwich is a meal for most humans. ~ 10968 Le Conte Avenue; 310-208-7171. BUDGET.

Farther out on Westwood Boulevard, proceeding south from the UCLA campus, there is a string of ethnic restaurants worth trying. **La Bruschetta** serves high Italian cuisine. This gourmet address is filled along several walls with wine racks. Vibrant artwork of recent vintage decorates the place. No lunch on weekends. ~ 1621 Westwood Boulevard; 310-477-1052. MODERATE TO DELUXE.

You'll find cafeterias at Ackerman Student Union (310-825-2311) and the North Campus Student Center (310-206-0720). The food will fill your stomach without emptying your purse; beyond that I guarantee nothing. ~ BUDGET.

The flavor is Persian at **Shamshiry Restaurant**, a pleasant restaurant with latticework booths and hanging plants. The shish kebab and other Middle Eastern dishes, served at lunch and dinner, are reasonably priced. ~ 1712 Westwood Boulevard; 310-474-1410, fax 310-474-3396. MODERATE.

Enjoy *tandoori* chicken and a host of curry dishes prepared in **India's Oven**. It isn't the Taj Mahal—at lunch and dinner you'll dine from plastic plates, but at these prices, who can complain? Closed Monday. ~ 11645 Wilshire Boulevard; 310-207-5522, fax 310-820-1467. BUDGET TO MODERATE.

SHOPPING

Westwood might house UCLA, but this highrise city is a far cry from the typical campus town. Among its cosmopolitan attributes is a shopping district large enough to wear a hole in any shopper's shoes (and purse). **Westwood Village**, adjacent to UCLA, is the Westside's premier shopping and entertainment district. Designed with the pedestrian in mind, "the village" is frequented by college crowds and fashionable Westside residents alike. Student-oriented shops devoted to books, clothes, and accessories combine with cafés and first-run movie theaters to keep the district hopping day and night. ~ Westwood Boulevard.

Bookstores, of course, are a Westwood specialty. Large chain stores and small specialty shops proliferate throughout the neighborhood. Browse the 2000 to 2300 blocks of Westwood Boulevard, affectionately known as "Booksellers Row."

NIGHTLIFE

Westwood Village, located at the heart of Westwood a few strides from the UCLA campus, bubbles with nighttime activity. Students and moviegoers crowd the sidewalks and spill into the streets. While many are headed to the first-run movie theaters for which this college town is known, some frequent the local clubs.

Geffen Playhouse, a 500-seat Egyptian-style "event theater," produces classic plays and often showcases West Coast and world premieres. ~ 10886 Le Conte Avenue; 310-208-5454; www.geffenplayhouse.com.

The **UCLA Center for the Performing Arts** holds perform-ances on campus. ~ 405 Hilgard Avenue; 310-825-4401; www.cto.ucla.edu.

West Los Angeles

West Los Angeles is about as close to an ethnically and economically diverse area as there is on the Westside. Occupying the land south of Westwood and Brentwood, west of Century City and east of Santa Monica, the area is filled with businesses, apartment buildings, and mod-est homes. This is where the Westsiders do their discount shop-ping, buy furniture and major appliances, and go for reasonably priced meals at one of the area's ethnic restaurants.

Nearby Culver City is an unpretentious little town filled with early-20th-century bungalows and local businesses. It is also the self-proclaimed "Motion Picture Capital of the World," having produced more than half the movies released in the United States during the 1930s and '40s. Today it is enjoying a resurgence of its former glory, thanks to the new recording and independent film studios that have moved there.

SIGHTS

The consequences of intolerance are the focus of the **Museum of Tolerance.** Here enlightening displays reveal the terrible impact of prejudice throughout history; from Nazi Germany to segrega-tion in America. The center utilizes modern multimedia techniques to create stunning audio, visual, and interactive presentations. Computers quiz observers about social justice and responsible citizenship. Holocaust survivors speak daily of their experiences. Closed Saturday. Admission. ~ 9786 West Pico Boulevard, West Los Angeles; 310-553-8403, 800-900-9036, fax 310-553-4521; www.museumoftolerance.com.

Cowboys may be buried on Boot Hill, but movie stars are in-terred in a site overlooking the MGM studios. The celebrities in **Holy Cross Cemetery** have one thing in common—they were all Catholic. Rosalind Russell of *Auntie Mame* fame is here along with Bing Crosby, Jimmy Durante, and Charles Boyer. Bela Lugosi rests nearby; the most macabre tombstone, however, is

Living on Tokyo Time

Tucked away between a freeway and a police station is a hidden slice of Japan right in West L.A. Looking like many other commercial/residential areas in L.A., the only clue to the street's ethnicity are the Japanese characters on business signs. Still, the restaurants, markets, nurseries, and shops on Sawtelle Boulevard between Missouri and Olympic are about as Japanese as you can get without actually buying a ticket to Tokyo.

Yamaguchi Bonsai Nursery, on Sawtelle since the 1920s, is the place to go for award-winning bonsai. ~ 1905 Sawtelle Boulevard; 310-477-7274. **Happy Six** sells all sorts of contemporary women's casual wear from Hello Kitty T-shirts to brightly colored plastic flip-flops. ~ 2111 Sawtelle Boulevard. For more traditional Japanese imports like ceramics and kimonos, stop by **Satsuma Oriental Imports**. ~ 2029 Sawtelle Boulevard; 310-473-3946.

Get past the intriguing merchandise and you'll discover that what really shines along Sawtelle Boulevard are the restaurants. Traditional food ranging from curry to sushi and tempura to noodles is served in restaurants that run the gamut from simply elegant to basic and brightly lit. **Hide Sushi** is no secret to Westsiders who have been lining up to eat the freshest raw fish available at this traditional sushi house for over 20 years. ~ 2040 Sawtelle Avenue; 310-477-7242. BUDGET TO MODERATE. Conversely, non-traditional **2117** is a hidden treasure of a restaurant, with an inspired chef who creates French-fusion Japanese dishes such as Japanese Tia snapper carpaccio with fired noodles. ~ 2117 Sawtelle Boulevard; 310-477-1617. MODERATE.

If you'd rather eat your Japanese delicacies on the run, head to the **Japanese Deli**, where authentic products come direct from Japan. ~ 2130 Sawtelle Boulevard; 310-575-3300. At the **Safe & Save Market**, the freshest seafood available is sliced up by an expert fish cutter. ~ 2030 Sawtelle Boulevard; 310-479-3810.

And don't leave Sawtelle without indulging in that favorite Japanese pastime, karaoke. For an hourly rate, karaoke aficionados can warble to their hearts content at **Yuu Yuu Karaoke Studio**. ~ 2130 Sawtelle Boulevard; 310-479-1477.

that of Sharon Tate Polanski and her unborn son Paul, murdered in 1969 by the Charles Manson gang. (Rosalind Russell's grave is marked by the large crucifix near the center of the park; most of the other resting places are near the "grotto" to the left of the entrance.) ~ 5835 West Slauson Avenue, Culver City.

HIDDEN ▶ Also in Culver City is one of the most original museums Los Angeles County has to offer. The **Museum of Jurassic Technology** is idiosyncratic, to say the least. It had been flying under the radar since its inception in the early '90s until the museum's curator and founder, David Wilson, received a MacArthur Grant in 2001. Nothing about the plain front of the nondescript building would give you any hint as to the wonders within. Without insider information or a tip from one of the cognoscente, it's doubtful anyone would venture inside. Every exhibit here, no matter how odd, is substantiated with "authentic" and thorough scholarship, yet the museum constantly challenges one's perception of the credibility of its displays, blurring the line between fantasy and reality with a huge degree of whimsy. Along with the permanent collection, there are changing exhibits, such as microscopic still lifes constructed entirely out of the scales of butterflies and diatoms. Closed Monday through Wednesday. ~ 9341 Venice Boulevard, Culver City; 310-836-6131, fax 310-287-2267; www.mjt.org, e-mail mjt@mjt.org.

If Beverly Hills is the ultimate in residential communities, Century City represents the final word in business centers. Bland as a three-piece suit, this 180-acre highrise heaven is built of office towers and broad boulevards.

The **Century Plaza Hotel** is a twin-tower city in itself, an over 700-room hotel that vies with Century City's other metal-and-glass palaces for prominence.

What today is a corporate version of Las Vegas was once the fabled backlot of 20th Century Fox. While the studio still holds ground in part of the city, it has lost the glamour of its glory days and is closed to the public.

LODGING   **Hotel Del Capri** is a bright, cozy complex complete with two tiers of guest rooms encircling a pool terrace, and more suites and rooms in an adjoining tower. The lobby and many of the 79 guest rooms contain modern curvilinear furniture. Many of the tile bathrooms include jacuzzi bathtubs; continental breakfast is

served in your room or out by the pool; all suites have kitchenettes; all the beds are adjustable. In sum, a very attractive establishment. ~ 10587 Wilshire Boulevard, West Los Angeles; 310-
474-3511, 800-444-6835, fax 310-470-9999; www.hoteldelcapri.
com. DELUXE.

DINING

For standard old American fare, head out to **The Apple Pan**, a
clapboard cottage that contains a single U-shaped counter. Renowned for great burgers, The Apple Pan also serves sandwiches
(as in ham, Swiss cheese, and tuna salad) and pies (as in apple,
berry, and pecan). Closed Monday. ~ 10801 West Pico Boulevard, West Los Angeles; 310-475-3585. BUDGET.

◀ HIDDEN

Mr. Cecil's California Ribs is one of the last places you'd expect to find on the Westside. The exterior looks like a cartoon
character–festooned moonshiner's still, and the food is heart
stopping. Still, the unadorned barbecued St. Louis baby back and
beef ribs are delicious, as are the grilled corn, hushpuppies, and
cole slaw that accompany them. ~ 12244 West Pico Boulevard,
West Los Angeles; 310-442-1550. BUDGET.

◀ HIDDEN

You may have to wait for a table at **La Serenata Gourmet**.
This cheery Mexican eatery specializes in fresh fish and gorditas
(cornmeal pockets filled with shrimp). ~ 10924 Pico Boulevard,
West Los Angeles; 310-441-9667. BUDGET TO MODERATE.

SHOPPING

Westside Pavilion, an urban mall, is a glass atrium affair that spans
Westwood Boulevard and contains over 100 shops. Department
stores anchor this triple-tiered mall. ~ 10800 West Pico Boulevard,
West Los Angeles; 310-474-6255; www.westsidepavilion.com.

Boys and girls with dreams of the great outdoors can chart a
course to **Adventure 16, Inc**. Catering to the wilderness enthusiast, this shop can outfit you for rock climbing and backpacking.

AUTHOR FAVORITE

The pungent garlicky aroma that wafts through **Versailles** is almost as tantalizing as the succulent chicken, shrimp, and shredded roast
pork that produces it. Main courses are served with traditional rice and
black beans in a colorful decor that's as close to Havana as you'll get in
Los Angeles. ~ 10319 Venice Boulevard, Culver City; 310-558-3168;
www.versaillescubanfood.com. BUDGET.

The inventory for adventurers includes clothing, camping equipment, luggage, and travel gear. ~ 11161 West Pico Boulevard, West Los Angeles; 310-473-4574; www.adventure16.com.

For specialty foods at discount prices, there's no place quite like **Trader Joe's**, with its endless array of nuts, cheeses, wines, and gourmet items. ~ 10850 National Boulevard, West Los Angeles; 310-470-1917.

Westside Pavilion in West Los Angeles was designed by the architects of the 1984 Olympics.

Shopping in Culver City, on the other hand, centers around **Fox Hills Mall**, a modern, 140-store center anchored by large department stores. ~ Slauson Avenue and Sepulveda Boulevard; 310-390-5073. There are more dads than lads at **Allied Model Trains**, a toy wonderland and replica of the Los Angeles Union Station that's filled with every type of model train imaginable. Closed Sunday except in December. ~ 4411 South Sepulveda Boulevard, Culver City; 310-313-9353; www.alliedmodeltrains.com.

Westchester Faire Antique Mall, a massive marketplace, houses about 70 shops selling antiques, collectibles, and jewelry. ~ 8655 South Sepulveda Boulevard, Westchester; 310-670-4000. **The Place and Company**, one of the best resale stores in the city, carries a large selection of top-designer fashions. Closed Sunday. ~ 8820 South Sepulveda Boulevard, Westchester; 310-645-1539.

Over in Century City, where broad boulevards and highrise buildings rest on the former lot of 20th Century Fox, there's a 100-store mall complete with boutiques, markets, crafts shops, and international food pavilions. **Westfield Shoppingtown Century City** sprawls across 18 acres, counting among its more glamorous addresses Louis Vuitton, Coach, Kenneth Cole, Tiffany & Co. and the Metropolitan Museum of Art Store. ~ 10250 Santa Monica Boulevard, Century City; 310-553-5300.

NIGHTLIFE The "equity-waiver" **Odyssey Theatre** offers avant-garde productions by a variety of playwrights. ~ 2055 South Sepulveda Boulevard, West Los Angeles; 310-477-2055.

San Francisco Saloon and Grill is a small, intimate bar. Wood paneling, historic photos of San Francisco, and comfortable surroundings create a sense of intimacy. ~ 11501 West Pico Boulevard, West Los Angeles; 310-478-0152.

HIDDEN ▶

A formerly 1950s-type dive, the **Arsenal Restaurant & Lounge** has been reinvented as a hip nightspot. Divided into three rooms (a happening bar, a cozy red-boothed dining room, and an open-air "smoking" patio), the music is loud—there's a deejay on the weekends—and the crowd youngish and lively. ~ 12012 West Pico Boulevard, West Los Angeles; 310-575-5511.

▾▾▾▾▾▾▾▾▾▾▾

Pacific Palisades

Pacific Palisades, known to residents as simply "The Palisades," is the latest Westside refuge for superstars and tycoons. Not all the homes are mansions here— there are plenty of modest bungalows, condos, and apartments— but prices are still sky high. The tree-lined village area is pristine, the shops and restaurants understated, and the residents non-flashily rich and famous. If you're lucky, you might catch sight of Tom Hanks and family at a local street fair or Angela Lansbury at Gelson's, the local upscale supermarket.

SIGHTS

◀ *HIDDEN*

At first glance, the **Self Realization Fellowship Lake Shrine** is an odd amalgam of pretty things. Gathered along the shore of a placid pond are a Dutch windmill, a houseboat, and a shrine topped with something resembling a giant artichoke. In fact, the windmill is a chapel, the houseboat is a former stopping place of yogi and Self Realization Fellowship founder Paramahansa Yogananda, and the oversized artichoke is a golden lotus arch-way near which some of Indian leader Mahatma Gandhi's ashes are enshrined. A strange but potent collection of icons in an evocative setting, the Fellowship is a meditation garden open to people of any religion. Closed Monday. ~ 17190 Sunset Boulevard; 310-454-4114, fax 310-459-7461; www.yogananda-srf.org.

Several miles inland at **Will Rogers State Historic Park**, on a hillside overlooking the Pacific, you can tour the ranch and home of America's greatest cowboy philosopher. Will Rogers, who started as a trick roper in traveling rodeos, hit the big time in Hollywood during the 1920s as a kind of cerebral comedian whose humorous wisdom plucked a chord in the American psyche.

From 1928 until his tragic death in 1935, the lariat laureate occupied this 31-room home with his family. The house is de-ceptively large but not grand; the woodframe design is basic and unassuming, true to Will Rogers' Oklahoma roots. Similarly the interior is decorated with Indian rugs and ranch tools. Western knickknacks adorn the tables and one room is dominated by a full-sized stuffed calf which Rogers utilized for roping practice. Well worth visiting, the "house that jokes built" is a simple expression of a vital personality. Admission. The house is undergoing a major restoration that is scheduled to be completed in late 2005. ~ 1501 Will Rogers State Park Road; 310-454-8212, fax 310-459-2031.

BEACHES & PARKS

WILL ROGERS STATE HISTORIC PARK 🚶 🚴 🐎 The former ranch of humorist Will Rogers, this 186-acre spread sits in the hills of Pacific Palisades. The late cowboy's home is currently undergoing restoration until late 2005 and is not open to visitors, although there are hiking trails leading around the property and out into adjacent Topanga Canyon State Park. Facilities include picnic areas, a museum (also undergoing restoration), and restrooms. Day-use fee, $5 per vehicle. ~ 1501 Will Rogers State Park Road, Pacific Palisades; 310-454-8212, fax 310-459-2031.

WILL ROGERS STATE BEACH 🚴 🏊 🚶 Simple and homespun he might have been, but Will Rogers was also a canny businessman with a passion for real estate. He bought up three miles of beachfront property that eventually became his namesake park. It's a sandy strand with an expansive parking lot running the length of the beach. Route 1 parallels the parking area and beyond that rise the sharp cliffs that lend Pacific Palisades its name. The South Bay Bike Trail makes its northernmost appearance here. You'll find good swimming, and surfing is best in the area where Sunset Boulevard meets the ocean. Lifeguards are on duty. Facilities include restrooms, volleyball courts, and playgrounds. Day-use fees vary from $5 to $10, depending on crowds expected. ~ Located south along Route 1 from Sunset Boulevard in Pacific Palisades; 310-305-9545.

SIX

Westside Beaches

L.A.'s Westside beaches call to the hip, active, and creative. There's a devil-may-care feeling here, a relaxed and casual ambiance that belies stress or worry. In truth, many residents are extended beyond their means by heart-stopping mortgages, and striving to reach economic goals befitting the area is stressful at best. Still, this is a happening place where visitors can see everything from movie stars to street performers and bask in the sun-drenched shadow of its tanned, confident, and successful residents.

Extending to the very edge of the sea, the Santa Monica Mountains are a succession of rugged peaks that create Los Angeles' most varied terrain. Part of the Transverse Range, they are the only mountains in California running east and west. Along the coast, bald peaks frame white-sand beaches and crystal waters and flourishing kelp beds attract abundant sea life and make for excellent fishing and skindiving, while the mountains provide a getaway for hikers and campers.

Lying along a narrow corridor between the Santa Monicas and the sea is Malibu, that quintessential symbol of California, a rich, glamorous community known for its movie stars and surfers. Once inhabited by Chumash Indians, whose skeletal remains are still occasionally uncovered, Malibu escaped Los Angeles' coastal development until 1928, when the aging widow who controlled the region like a personal fiefdom finally succumbed to the pressures of progress and profit. Within a few years it became a haven for Hollywood. Stars like Ronald Colman and John Gilbert found their paradise on the sands of Malibu. Like figures out of The Great Gatsby, they lived insouciant lives in movie-set houses. Hollywood's rich and famous still flock to Malibu today, where they live in beachfront mansions at the edge of the Pacific.

By the 1960s, artists and counterculturists, seeking to flee a town that in turn had become too commercial, expensive, and crowded, left Malibu for the outlying mountains. In Topanga Canyon they established freeform communities, under-mined in recent years by breathtaking real-estate prices, but still retaining vestiges of their days as flower children retreats.

Neighboring Santa Monica was originally developed as a beachside resort in 1875. Back in 1769, explorer Gaspar de Portolá had claimed the surrounding area for the Spanish crown. Over the years this royal domain has served as a major port, retirement community, and location for silent movies. Today Santa Monica is a bastion of expensive, architecturally diverse houses, designer-coffee emporiums, and left-wing politics.

Venice began as an early-1900s attempt to re-create its Italian namesake. Built around plazas and grand canals, it was originally a fashionable resort town with oceanfront hotels and an amusement park. Today studios and galleries have replaced roller coasters and gondolas in this eccentric and eclectic place where freethinkers of all ages and incomes coexist. Unconventional and colorful, this is where bohemians go to the beach, roller-skating is an art form, and weightlifting a way of life.

While Venice has miraculously evaded money-hungry developers, Marina del Rey is the result of them. It was well into the 20th century, 1962 to be exact, that Marina del Rey, the largest manmade small- boat harbor in the world, was cre-ated. Defined by nondescript architecture and ho-hum eateries, the Marina is not particularly enthralling. On an up note, however, restaurants do have those ma-rina views, and the area buzzes on weekends, when the bike path is crowded with cyclists and the marina is a maze of sailboats.

Malibu

Malibu is a 27-mile-long ribbon lined on one side with pearly beaches and on the other by the Santa Monica Mountains. Famed as a movie star retreat and surfer's heaven, it is one of America's mythic communities. It has been a favored spot among Hollywood celebrities since the 1920s, when a new highway opened the region and film stars like Clara Bow and John Gilbert publicized the idyllic community. By the 1950s, Malibu was rapidly developing and becoming nationally known for its rolling surf and freewheeling lifestyle. The 1959 movie *Gidget* cast Sandra Dee and James Darren as Malibu beach bums and the seaside community was on its way to surfing immortality.

Today surfers by the dozens hang ten near the pier, just south of where movie and television greats live behind locked gates in lavish mansions on stretches of sand that are off-limits to normal folk. That lack of access may change however, as there's a move-ment afoot to make these hitherto "private" beaches public.

Today blond-mopped surfers still line the shore and celebrities continue to congregate in beachfront bungalows. Matter of fact, the most popular sightseeing in Malibu consists of ogling the homes of the very rich. **Malibu Road**, which parallels the waterfront, is a prime strip. To make it as difficult as possible for common riffraff to reach the beach, the homes are built townhouse-style with no space between them. It's possible to drive for miles along the water without seeing the beach, only the backs of baronial estates. Happily there are a few accessways to the beach, so it's possible to wander along the sand enjoying views of both the ocean and the picture-window palaces. Among the Malibu beach accessways is one that local wags named after the "Doonesbury" character Zonker Harris.

What's amazing about these beachfront colonies is not the houses, but the fact that people insist on building them so close to the ocean that every few years several are demolished by high surf while others sink into the sand.

One of Malibu's loveliest houses is open to the public. The **Adamson House**, located at Malibu Lagoon State Beach is a stately Spanish Colonial Revival–style structure adorned with ceramic tiles. With its bare-beam ceilings and inlaid floors, the house is a study in early-20th-century elegance. The building is

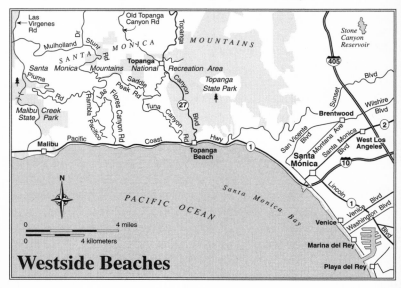

Westside Beaches

surrounded by landscaped grounds, which border the beach at
Malibu and overlook a lagoon alive with waterfowl and are
open to the public. Though there is an admission for the house,
there is no fee to stroll the gardens. Closed Sunday through Tuesday. Admission. ~ 23200 Pacific Coast Highway; 310-456-8432.

Another seafront attraction is the **Malibu Pier**. Storm damage has closed the pier, and it's ironic that in this ultra-privileged
community, a lack of funding has kept the necessary repairs from
being made. ~ 23000 Pacific Coast Highway.

LODGING   There are several motels scattered along the coastal highway in
Malibu, two of which I can recommend. **Topanga Ranch Motel**
is a 30-unit complex that dates back to the 1920s. Here are cute
little cottages painted white with red trim and clustered around
a circular drive. Granted they're somewhat timeworn, but each is
kept neat and trim with plain furnishings and little decoration. A
few have kitchens. A good deal for a location right across the highway from the beach. ~ 18711 Pacific Coast Highway; 310-456-
5486, fax 310-456-1447; www.topangaranchmotel.com, e-mail
raycraig@earthlink.net. MODERATE.

At **Casa Malibu Inn on the Beach**, you'll be in a 21-room facility with two suites that actually overhangs the sand. Located
smack in the center of Malibu, the building features a central
courtyard with lawn furniture and ocean view, oceanfront red-
brick patio plus a balcony dripping with flowering plants. The
rooms are decorated in an attractive but casual fashion; some have
private balconies, fireplaces, kitchens, and/or ocean or garden
views. ~ 22752 Pacific Coast Highway; 310-456-2219, 800-831-
0858, fax 310-456-5418; www.casamalibu.com, e-mail casamal
ibu@earthlink.net. MODERATE TO ULTRA-DELUXE.

The **Malibu Beach Inn** is posh and each of its 47 guest rooms
offers spectacular ocean views from private balconies. Minibars
round out the amenities. Some rooms feature jacuzzis and fireplaces. The location on the beach, one block from the Malibu
Pier, makes this an ideal getaway. ~ 22878 Pacific Coast Highway; 310-456-6444, 800-462-5428, fax 310-456-1499; www.
malibubeachinn.com, e-mail reservations@malibubeachinn.com.
ULTRA-DELUXE.

At the northern Zuma Beach end of Malibu, you'll find the
16-room **Malibu Country Inn** perched atop a hillside above Pa-

cific Coast Highway. Draped in bougainvillea, this property also has four suites and a restaurant. Since the inn isn't directly on the beach, only some of the rooms have partial ocean views; but all have unobstructed mountain views, private decks, coffee makers, and a floral-wicker decor scheme. The suites include fireplace and spa tub. There's a small pool surrounded by a garden of roses and other flowers and herbs. Continental breakfast at the restaurant is included. ~ 6506 Westward Beach Road at Pacific Coast Highway; 310-457-9622, 800-386-6787, fax 310-457-1349; www.malibucountryinn.com, e-mail info@malibucountry inn.com. DELUXE TO ULTRA-DELUXE.

DINING

The **Reel Inn Restaurant** is my idea of heaven—a reasonably priced seafood restaurant. Located across the highway from the beach, it's an oilcloth restaurant with an outdoor patio and a flair for serving good, healthful food at low prices. Among the fresh fish lunches and dinners are salmon, snapper, lobster, and swordfish. ~ 18661 Pacific Coast Highway; 310-456-8221, fax 310-456-3568. BUDGET TO DELUXE.

For a possible celebrity sighting over your whole-wheat pancakes with strawberries and bananas, try **Coogie's Beach Cafe**. ~

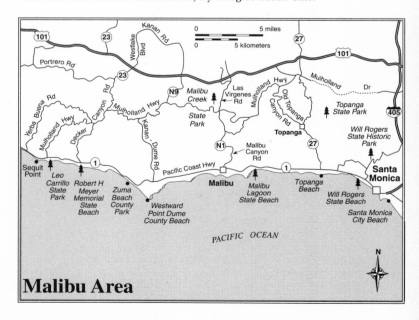

Malibu Area

Malibu Colony Plaza, 23700 Pacific Coast Highway; 310-317-1444, fax 310-317-1446. BUDGET TO MODERATE.

Cutting-edge Continental cuisine can be found at **Granita**, where chef Wolfgang Puck's culinary cohorts whip up original creations. Watch as they prepare grilled ahi tuna with wasabi puree, sesame asparagus and Chinese black bean sauce. Yow! The marble terrazo tile gives an underwater effect. Dinner only; brunch on weekends. Closed Monday. ~ Malibu Colony Plaza; 310-456-0488, fax 310-456-8317; www.wolfgangpuck.com, e-mail granita@wolfgangpuck.com. DELUXE TO ULTRA-DELUXE.

There's nothing fancy about **Malibu Fish & Seafood**. It's just a fish-and-chips stand across the highway from the beach with picnic tables under a covered patio outside, but the menu includes such tantalizing specialties as ahi tuna burgers and steamed lobster. The price is hard to beat when you add the ocean view. ~ 25653 Pacific Coast Highway; 310-456-3430, fax 310-456-8017. BUDGET TO DELUXE.

BeauRivage Mediterranean Restaurant, another gourmet gathering place, located across the highway from the ocean, boasts a cozy dining room and ocean-view terrace. With exposed-beam ceiling, brick trim, and copper pots along the wall, it has the feel of a French country inn. The dinner menu, however, is strictly Mediterranean. In addition to several pasta dishes, including gnocchi al pesto and linguine with clams, tomatoes, and garlic, there is New Zealand rack of lamb, Long Island duckling, Norwegian salmon, antelope, wild boar, and grilled Italian bass. Dinner and

A SIDE ORDER OF ENLIGHTENMENT, PLEASE

Up in the Santa Monica Mountains, high above the clamor of Los Angeles, rests the **Inn of the Seventh Ray**. A throwback to the days when Topanga Canyon was a hippie enclave, this mellow dining spot serves organic "energized" foods to "raise your body's light vibrations." Entrées include buckwheat mushroom terrine and baked young leeks, asparagus and golden beet vichyssoise sauce. There is also a selection of fresh seafood, duckling, and lamb dishes. Open for lunch and dinner, the restaurant features dining indoors or outside on a pretty, tree-shaded patio, where coyotes can often be seen from your table. Far out. ~ 128 Old Topanga Canyon Road, Topanga; 310-455-1311, fax 310-455-0033; www.innoftheseventh ray.com. DELUXE TO ULTRA-DELUXE.

Sunday brunch served. ~ 26025 Pacific Coast Highway; 310-456-5733, fax 310-317-1589; www.beaurivagerestaurant.com, e-mail beaurivagemalibu@aol.com. MODERATE TO ULTRA-DELUXE.

The quintessential Malibu dining experience is **Geoffrey's**, a clifftop restaurant overlooking the ocean. The marble bar, white-washed stucco walls, stone pebble tiles, and flowering plants exude wealth and elegance. The entire hillside has been landscaped and beautifully terraced, creating a Mediterranean atmosphere. The menu, a variation on California cuisine, includes grilled filet mignon with a roasted shallot and Granny Smith cabernet reduction, and lobster bruschetta. The lunch and dinner menus are almost identical and on Saturday and Sunday they also serve brunch. The setting, cuisine, and high prices make Geoffrey's a prime place for celebrity gazing. ~ 27400 Pacific Coast Highway; 310-457-1519, 800-927-4197, fax 310-457-7885; www.geoffreys malibu.com, e-mail gmalibu@earthlink.net. DELUXE TO ULTRA-DELUXE.

When you're out at the beaches around Point Dume or elsewhere in northern Malibu, there are two adjacent roadside restaurants worth checking out. **Coral Beach Cantina** is a simple Mexican restaurant with a small patio. The menu contains standard south-of-the-border fare. ~ 29350 Pacific Coast Highway; 310-457-5503. BUDGET TO MODERATE.   ◄ *HIDDEN*

Over at **Zuma Sushi** they have a sushi bar and table service. In addition to the house specialty there are tempura and teriyaki dishes. Like its neighbor, this is a small, unassuming café. Dinner only. ~ 29350 Pacific Coast Highway; 310-457-4131. BUDGET TO MODERATE.   ◄ *HIDDEN*

For a good meal near the beach there's **Neptune's Net Seafood**. Located across the highway from County Line Beach (at the Los Angeles–Ventura county border), it's a breezy café frequented by surfers. Fresh seafood, live lobster, sandwiches, burgers, and clam chowder, as well as oyster, shrimp, clam, and scallop baskets fill the bellies here. Ocean views at beach-bum prices. Closed one week before Christmas. ~ 42505 Route 1; 310-457-3095, fax 310-457-6314; www.neptunesnetseafood.com. BUDGET TO DELUXE.   ◄ *HIDDEN*

Zuma Canyon Orchids offers elegant, exquisite prize-winning orchids that can be shipped anywhere in the world. If you call   **SHOPPING**

Santa Monica Mountains

When you've had your fill of Malibu's sand and surf, take a detour from Route 1 up into the Santa Monica Mountains. This chaparral country filled with oak and sycamore forests offers sweeping views back along the coast. As long as you remember which direction the water is (south), it's hard to get lost no matter how crazily the roads wind and twist. But if you descend on the wrong side of the mountains—that is, the north side—into the vast suburban sprawl of the San Fernando Valley, it can be an all-day challenge to find your way back around the mountains to Los Angeles. You'll find a fair amount of solitude if you take this drive on a weekday; on weekends you can expect traffic and full parking lots.

TOPANGA CANYON   Topanga Canyon Boulevard (Route 27), perhaps the best known of these mountain roads, turns off Route 1 five miles west of Santa Monica, or eight miles east of the village of Malibu, near the temporarily closed J. Paul Getty Villa. It curves gradually up the rocky canyon to the rustic town of **Topanga**. Back in the '60s this was a fabled retreat for flower children. Even today vestiges of the hippy era remain in the form of health food stores, New Age shops, and organic restaurants. Many of the woodframe houses are handcrafted, and the community still vibrates to a slower rhythm than coastal Malibu and cosmopolitan Los Angeles. Turn right in town on Entrada Road to go for a walk in **Topanga State Park** (see below), the world's largest wilder-

ahead for a reservation, they will even provide a tour of the greenhouses. Closed Sunday. ~ 5949 Bonsall Drive; 310-457-9771; www.zumacanyonorchids.com.

Up in the secluded reaches of Topanga Canyon there are numerous artists and craftspeople who have traded the chaos of the city for the serenity of the Santa Monica Mountains. Craft shops come and go with frustrating regularity here, but it's worth a drive into the hills to see who is currently selling their wares.

NIGHTLIFE   For some easy listening, check out the scene at **BeauRivage Mediterranean Restaurant**. There's a piano player Monday through Thursday. A cozy bar and fireplace add charm to the scene. ~ 26025 Pacific Coast Highway; 310-456-5733; www.beaurivage restaurant.com.

ness located entirely within the boundaries of a major city. The gentlest and prettiest trails for a short hike start at Trippet Ranch near the park entrance. There's a parking fee.

MULHOLLAND HIGHWAY   To reach the top of the world, retrace your route from Entrada a short distance back down Topanga Boulevard to where Old Topanga Canyon Road forks off to the northwest. Turn right, follow this road for about five miles to the intersection with Mulholland Highway, and turn left. With its panoramic views of the Los Angeles Basin and San Fernando Valley, Mulholland is justifiably famous. On weekend nights, Mulholland Drive (as it's known in town) is a rendezvous for lovers and a drag strip for daredevil drivers, but the rest of the time you'll find it a sinuous country road far from the madding mobs. If you have time and don't mind paying another parking fee, **Malibu Creek State Park** (page 180), near the junction of Mulholland and Las Virgenes/Malibu Canyon Road, has a creek, a lake, lava rock formations, and miles of hiking trails.

KANAN DUME ROAD   Depending on how far you want to drive, any of the several roads that turn off Mulholland to the left will bring you out of the mountains at a nice beach; staying on Mulholland all the way to the end will, too. Our favorite is Kanan Dume Road, which comes out at **Westward Point Dume County Beach** (page 181). A great spot to while away the remainder of the afternoon, it's just 19 miles from Santa Monica on Route 1.

Malibu is largely a bedroom community; it's not known for wild nightlife, unless it's a private party at one of the beachfront homes in the colony. For music, theater, dance, and art, Pepperdine University's **Smothers Theater** offers performances and exhibitions by visiting artists. ~ 24255 Pacific Coast Highway; 310-506-4522; www.pepperdine.edu/cfa.

TOPANGA STATE PARK 🚶 🚲 🐎 Not much sand here, but you will find forests of oak and fields of rye. This 10,000-plus-acre hideaway nestles in the Santa Monica Mountains above Pacific Palisades. Along the 36 miles of hiking trails and fire roads are views of the ocean, San Gabriel Mountains, and San Fernando Valley. There are meadows and a stream to explore. The park climbs from 200 to 2100 feet in elevation, providing an introduc-

**BEACHES
& PARKS**

tion to one of Los Angeles' few remaining natural areas. Biking is restricted to the fire roads. Facilities include trails, picnic areas, and restrooms. Parking fee, $4. ~ From Route 1 in Malibu take Topanga Canyon Road up to Entrada Road. The park is at 20825 Entrada Road; 310-455-2465, fax 310-455-7085.

▲ There are eight hike-in sites, tents only; $2 per person per night.

TOPANGA BEACH 〰 🏃 🏄 ⛵ This narrow sand corridor extends for over a mile. The adjacent highway breaks the quietude, but the strand is still popular with surfers and those wanting to be close to Malibu services. The swimming is good; surfing and windsurfing are excellent around Topanga Creek. Lifeguards are on duty; facilities include restrooms, showers, picnic tables, and barbecues. Parking fee, $5. ~ Route 1, near Topanga Canyon Road in Malibu; 310-451-2906, fax 310-458-6445.

MALIBU CREEK STATE PARK 🏃 🚴 🏇 〰 ⛵ Once the location site for *M*A*S*H* and the original *Planet of the Apes*, this 7000-acre facility spreads through rugged, virgin country in the Santa Monica Mountains. Among its features are over 80 miles of hiking trails, four-acre Century Lake, and Malibu Creek, which is lined with willow and cottonwood. In spring the meadows explode with wildflowers; at other times of the year you'll encounter squirrels, rabbits, mule deer, coyotes, and bobcats. The bird life ranges from aquatic species such as ducks and great blue herons along the lake to hawks, woodpeckers, quail, and golden eagles. The lava hills, sloping grasslands, and twisted sedimentary rock formations make it an intriguing escape from the city. Facilities here include picnic areas, restrooms, and showers. Day-use fee, $5. ~ Located off Mulholland Highway at 1925 Las Virgenes Road, Calabasas; 818-880-0367, fax 818-706-3869.

▲ There are 60 sites for tents and trailers or RVs (no hookups); $15 per night. No wood fires. Reservations: 800-444-7275.

MALIBU LAGOON STATE BEACH 🏃 〰 🏃 ⛵ Not only is there a pretty beach here but an estuary and wetlands area as well. You can stroll the white sands past an unending succession of lavish beachfront homes, or study a different species entirely in the park's salt marsh. Here Malibu Creek feeds into the ocean, creating a rich tidal area busy with marine life and shorebirds. The surfing is world-renowned. This is also a very popular spot for swimming; lifeguards are on duty most of the year. Facilities include picnic areas and restrooms. Day-use fee, $5. ~ Pacific Coast Highway at Cross Creek Road in Malibu; 818-880-0350.

WESTWARD POINT DUME COUNTY BEACH 🏃 🚲 🏊 🎣   ◀ HIDDEN
🏃 🚣 This long narrow stretch is really a southerly continuation of Zuma Beach. Unlike its neighbor, it is conveniently located away from the highway and bordered by lofty sandstone cliffs. For white sand serenity this is a choice spot. Matter of fact, on the far side of Point Dume you'll encounter what was once a popular nude beach in **Pirate's Cove**. Swimming is good, but beware of dangerous currents. Surfing is good along Westward Beach and off Point Dume. Lifeguards are on duty and restrooms are available. Parking fee, $7. ~ The park entrance is located near the southern entrance to Zuma Beach County Park; take Westward Beach Road off of Route 1 about six miles west of Malibu. To reach the beach at Pirate's Cove, take the trail over the Point Dume Headlands; 310-457-2525, fax 310-457-1632.

ZUMA BEACH COUNTY PARK 🏊 🎣 🏃 🍴 🚣 🚻 This
long, broad beach is a study in the territorial instincts of the species. Los Angeles County's largest beach park, it is frequented in one area by Latinos; "Vals," young residents of the San Fernando Valley, have staked claim to another section, while families and students inhabit another stretch (Zuma 3 and 4). Not as pretty as other Malibu beaches, Zuma offers more space and better facilities, such as restrooms, lifeguards, playgrounds, volleyball courts, and proximity to restaurants and stores. Swimming and surfing are good; for information on surf conditions, call 310-457-9701. Parking fee, $7. ~ Route 1, approximately six miles west of Malibu; 310-457-2525, fax 310-457-1632.

> ◆◆◆◆◆◆◆◆◆◆◆◆◆◆◆◆◆◆◆◆◆◆◆
> Look for the natural tunnel under lifeguard tower #3 at Leo Carrillo State Park.

ROBERT H. MEYER MEMORIAL STATE BEACHES 🏃 🏊 This
unusual facility consists of three separate pocket beaches—**El Pescador**, **La Piedra**, and **El Matador**. Each is a pretty strand with sandy beach and eroded bluffs. Together they are among the nicest beaches in Malibu. My favorite is El Matador with its rock formations, sea stacks, and adjacent Malibu mansions. Use caution swimming at these beaches; there are unstationed lifeguards Memorial Day to Labor Day. Facilities include toilets. Access to

the beaches is by stairs and short, steep trails. Parking for all beaches is $2. ~ Route 1, about 11 miles west of Malibu; 818-880-0350, fax 818-880-6165; e-mail info@csp-angeles.com.

LEO CARRILLO STATE PARK 🏃 ⛵ 🎣 🏄 ⚓ Extending more than a mile, this white-sand corridor rests directly below Route 1. Named after Leo Carrillo, the TV actor who played sidekick Pancho in "The Cisco Kid," the beach offers tidepools and interesting rock formations. Nicer still is **Leo Carrillo North Beach,** a sandy swath located just beyond Sequit Point and back-dropped by a sharp bluff. This entire area is a prime whale-watching site from February through April. At the south end of this 1600-acre park people have been known to bathe in the buff—but beware, if caught you will be cited. Facilities here include limited picnic areas, restrooms, showers, and lifeguards. Swimming and surfing are good; the best waves break around Sequit Point, and there's also excellent surfing a few miles north at **County Line Beach.** Day-use fee, $5. ~ On Route 1 about 14 miles west of Malibu. There's access to Leo Carrillo Beach North from the parking lot at 35000 Pacific Coast Highway; 818-880-0350; e-mail info@csp-angeles.com.

▲ There are 136 sites for tents and trailers or RVs (no hook-ups); $15 per night. Reservations: 800-444-7275.

▼▼▼▼▼▼▼▼▼▼
Santa Monica

It's possible to walk for miles on the concrete biking and walking path along Santa Monica's fluffy beach, past pastel-colored condominiums and funky wood-frame houses. Roller skaters and bicyclists galore crowd the byways and chess players congregate at the picnic tables.

A middle-class answer to mod Malibu, Santa Monica started as a seaside resort in the 1870s, when visitors bumped over long, dusty roads by stagecoach from Los Angeles. After flirting with the film industry in the age of silent movies, Santa Monica reverted in the 1930s to a quiet beach town that nevertheless was notorious for the gambling ships moored offshore. It was during this period that detective writer Raymond Chandler immortalized the place as "Bay City" in his brilliant Philip Marlowe novels.

Today Santa Monica is *in.* Its cleaner air, cooler temperatures, pretty beaches, and attractive homes have made it one of the most popular places to live in Los Angeles. It's the town that seems to have it all, with restaurants that range from world-class and expensive to ethnic and cheap, and shops that accommodate every taste and income. Still, all is not perfect in paradise—critics of the town council's liberal politics have dubbed it "The People's Republic of Santa Monica," and so far no one's been able to solve the problem of how to cope with the growing number of street people.

Despite these problems, people from around the world crowd to Santa Monica. On the weekends Palisades Park, along Ocean Avenue overlooking the Pacific, is filled with Eastern Europeans soaking up the rays while they play card games on portable ta-

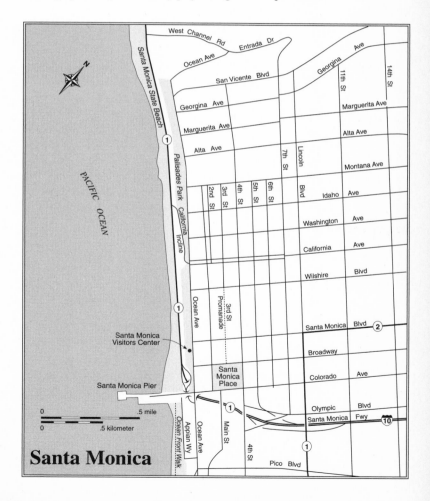

bles. Young British transplants work at the town's restaurants and pubs. And, when the temperatures soar, the beach is jammed with Latino families from the barrio looking for relief from the heat.

SIGHTS   Highlight of the beach promenade (and perhaps all Santa Monica) is the **Santa Monica Pier**. No doubt about it, the place is a scene. Acrobats work out on the playground below, surfers catch waves offshore, and street musicians strum guitars. And I haven't even mentioned the official attractions. There's a late-19th-century carousel with hand-painted horses that was featured in that cinematic classic, *The Sting*. There are video parlors, pinball machines, skee ball, bumper cars, and a restaurant. ~ Located at the foot of Colorado Avenue.

At the Santa Monica Pier is **Pacific Park**, a family amusement park featuring 12 rides, 21 amusement games and an oceanfront food plaza. Reaching up to 55 feet in height, the Santa Monica West Coaster cruises around the park at 35 miles per hour and makes two 360-degree turns. The nine-story-high Ferris wheel offers a bird's-eye view of the beach and coastline. Other attractions include adult and kid bumper cars and a slew of kiddie rides. ~ 380 Santa Monica Pier; 310-260-8744, fax 310-260-8748; www.pacpark.com.

From here it's a jaunt up to the **Santa Monica Visitors Center** information kiosk. Here are maps, brochures, and helpful workers. ~ 1400 Ocean Avenue; 310-393-7593, 800-544-5319, fax 310-319-6273; www.santamonica.com, e-mail info@santamonica.com.

The booth is located in **Palisades Park**, a pretty, palm-lined greensward that extends north from Colorado Avenue more than a mile along the sandstone cliffs fronting Santa Monica beach. One of the park's stranger attractions here is the **Camera Obscura**, a periscope of sorts through which you can view the pier, beach, and surrounding streets. ~ In the Senior Recreation Center, 1450 Ocean Avenue.

For 25 cents, the **Tide Shuttle** takes you through the heart of Santa Monica's tourist zone, from Main Street to the Santa Monica Pier and the Third Street Promenade. It also stops at many beachfront hotels. Running every 15 minutes, the shuttle is a great way to visit the city's central attractions. Maps and schedules are available at the visitor center and most central hotels.

For a glimpse into Santa Monica's past, take in the **California Heritage Museum**. Heirlooms and antiques are housed in a grand American Colonial Revival home. The mansion dates to 1894 and is furnished entirely in period California pieces. There are photo archives, historic artifacts galore, and rotating exhibits of decorative and fine arts. Closed Monday and Tuesday. Admission. ~ 2612 Main Street; 310-392-8537, fax 310-396-0547.

Sympathetic as it is to liberal politics, Santa Monica is nonetheless an extremely wealthy town. In fact, it's a fusion of two very different neighbors, mixing the bohemian strains of Venice with the monied elements of Malibu. For a look at the latter influence, take a drive from Ocean Avenue out along **San Vicente Boulevard**. This fashionable avenue, with its arcade of magnolias, is lined on either side with lovely homes. But they pale by comparison with the estates you will see by turning left on **La Mesa Drive**. This quiet suburban street boasts a series of marvelous Spanish Colonial, Tudor, and contemporary-style houses.

LODGING

Ocean Avenue, which runs the length of Santa Monica, paralleling the ocean one block above the beach, boasts the most hotels and the best location in town. Among its varied facilities are several generic motels. These are all-American-type places furnished in veneer, carpeted wall-to-wall, and equipped with telephones and color televisions. If you book a room in one, ask for quiet accommodations since Ocean Avenue is a busy, noisy street.

A reasonably good bargain is the **Bayside Hotel**. Laid out in motel fashion, this two-story complex offers plusher carpets and

AUTHOR FAVORITE

Shutters on the Beach, perched directly on Santa Monica Beach, is cozy and sedate. The lobby has two large fireplaces and the 198 gray-and-white rooms are well appointed with dark walnut furniture. Most rooms have coastal views; all feature, yes, shutters, as well as marble baths with jacuzzis. The hotel has a lovely pool terrace, two restaurants, and an oceanview bar. ~ 1 Pico Boulevard; 310-458-0030, 800-334-9000; www.shuttersonthebeach.com, e-mail info@shuttersonthebeach.com. ULTRA-DELUXE.

plumper furniture than motels hereabouts. More important, it's just 50 yards from the beach across a palm-studded park. Some rooms have ocean views and fully equipped kitchens. ~ 2001 Ocean Avenue; 310-396-6000, 800-525-4447, fax 310-396-1000; www.baysidehotel.com, e-mail info@baysidehotel.com. MODERATE TO DELUXE.

Just off Ocean Avenue and a little quieter than most, the **Sea Shore Motel** has 19 guest rooms and one suite located two blocks from the beach and within walking distance of all Santa Monica sights. The rooms have terra-cotta tile floors, granite counter tops, and refrigerators. There's a sundeck and off-street parking. ~ 2637 Main Street; 310-392-2787, fax 310-392-5167; www.seashore motel.com, e-mail reservations@seashoremotel.com. MODERATE.

Of course the ultimate bargain is found at **Hostelling International—Santa Monica**. This four-story, dorm-like structure boasts 30,000 square feet, room for 228 beds. There are several common rooms, internet kiosks, a central courtyard, and a kitchen. In addition to facilities for independent travelers, the hostel has set aside nine private rooms for couples. ~ 1436 2nd Street; 310-393-9913, 800-909-4776, fax 310-393-1769; www. hiusa.org, e-mail reserve@hiusa.org. BUDGET TO MODERATE.

Despite its location on a busy street, **Channel Road Inn** conveys a cozy sense of home. Colonial Revival in style, built in 1910, this sprawling 14-room bed and breakfast offers guests a living room, library, and dining room as well as a jacuzzi and hillside garden. The guest rooms vary widely in decor—some traditional, others contemporary; some florid, others demure. ~ 219 West Channel Road; 310-459-1920, fax 310-454-9920; www. channelroadinn.com, e-mail info@channelroadinn.com. DELUXE TO ULTRA-DELUXE.

The **Viceroy Hotel** looks the part of a contemporary Southern California hotel. Across the street from the beach, this sprawling 163-room facility boasts a pool, exercise room, and patio. There's a restaurant off the lobby as well as a lounge. ~ 1819 Ocean Avenue; 310-451-8711, 800-622-8711, fax 310-394-6657; www.viceroysantamonica.com. ULTRA-DELUXE.

Think of sunflowers backdropped by a deep blue Mediterranean sky. That's what the **Hotel Oceana Santa Monica** evokes. From its magnificent oceanfront setting to its lush courtyard planted with fragrant flowers, this exquisite hotel—reminiscent of the beauty of the Côte d'Azur—is a lesson in understated elegance. The lobby is decorated with a wrought-iron registration desk and floor-to-ceiling murals. Each guest suite comes with a fully equipped kitchen and is individually decorated in a French-impressionist style. The amenities include room service from Wolfgang Puck's Cafe, a fitness center, and a swimming pool. ~ 849 Ocean Avenue; 310-393-0486, 800-777-0758, fax 310-458-1182; www.hoteloceana.com, e-mail beth@hoteloceana.com. ULTRA-DELUXE.

The **Loews Santa Monica Beach Hotel**, a creamy yellow structure contemporary Victorian," features a mock turn-of-the-20th-century design. Its spectacular five-story glass atrium lobby and most of the 340 rooms provide views of the famed Santa Monica Pier. Rooms are furnished in rattan and wicker and offer special amenities. Non-beachies love the oceanview indoor/outdoor pool. ~ 1700 Ocean Avenue; 310-458-6700, fax 310-458-6761; www.loewshotels.com. ULTRA-DELUXE.

Hotel Shangri-La is private, stylish, and nothing short of beautiful. A 1939 art-deco building with a facade like the prow of a steamship, the 55-room home-away-from-paparazzi is completely up-to-date. The art moderne–era furniture has been laminated and lacquered and each appointment is a perfect expression of the period. Located on the palisades one block above Santa Monica Beach, many rooms sport an ocean view and have a kitchen. There's no pool or restaurant, but the hotel has a sundeck, serves continental breakfast and afternoon tea, and is close to the beach, shops, and pier. ~ 1301 Ocean Avenue; 310-394-2791, 800-345-7829, fax 310-451-3351; www.shangrila-hotel.com. DELUXE TO ULTRA-DELUXE.

DINING

Santa Monica is a restaurant town. Its long tradition of seafood establishments has been expanded in recent years by a wave of

GOURMET GHETTO

Every type of cuisine imaginable is found on the bottom level of **Santa Monica Place**. This multitiered shopping mall has an entire floor of take-out food stands. It's like the United Nations of dining, where everything is affordably priced. ~ On Broadway between 2nd and 4th streets. BUDGET.

ethnic and California cuisine restaurants. While some of the most fashionable and expensive dining rooms in L.A. are right here, there are also many excellent, inexpensive cafés. Generally you'll find everything from the sublime to the reasonable located within several commercial clusters—near the beach along Ocean Avenue, downtown on Wilshire and Santa Monica boulevards, and in the chic, gentrified corridors of Main Street and Montana Avenue.

One of the best places in Southern California for stuffing yourself with junk food while soaking up sun and having a whale of a good time is the **Santa Monica Pier**. There are taco stands, fish-and-chips shops, hot dog vendors, oyster bars, snack shops, pizzerias, and all those good things guaranteed to leave you clutching your stomach. The prices are low to modest and the food is amusement park quality. ~ At the foot of Colorado Avenue.

There's a sense of the Mediterranean at the sidewalk cafés lining Santa Monica's Ocean Avenue: palm trees along the boulevard, ocean views in the distance, and (usually) a warm breeze blowing. Any of these bistros will do (since it's atmosphere we're seeking), so try **Ivy at the Shore**. It features a full bar, serves espresso, and, if you want to get serious about it, has a full lunch and dinner menu with pizza, pasta, steaks, and Cajun dishes. ~ 1541 Ocean Avenue; 310-393-3113, fax 310-458-9259. ULTRA-DELUXE.

In business since the 1950s, **Chez Jays** is a Santa Monica institution. It's a sort of chic dive where aging surfers rub elbows with high-profile Hollywood stars. To say that the decor is unpretentious is an understatement, but the no-nonsense steaks are always tender and tasty and the seafood unfailingly fresh. Owner Jay Fiondella, a legend in his own right, still seats customers and just may regale you with tales of his colorful life if asked. The bar is always jam-packed with an eclectic array of locals. No lunch on Monday. ~ 1657 Ocean Avenue; 310-395-1741; www.chezjays.com. MODERATE.

Big, bustling, and always busy, **Ocean Avenue Seafood** is Santa Monica's premier fish restaurant. Lengthy selections of fresh regional fish change daily, and the large noisy bar is almost always crowded with the cocktail set and diners waiting for tables. Oyster lovers won't want to miss Oyster Hour (4 to 6 p.m. Monday through Friday and 3 to 5 p.m. Saturday and Sunday), when the oyster bar serves up the freshest oysters available for 99 cents per oyster. If the din in the main dining room is too

Third Street
Promenade

One of the liveliest and hippest places in Santa Monica is the **Third Street Promenade**. A three-block-long pedestrian-only street, it's always jam-packed with people and crackling with energy. Topiary dinosaur fountains, stores, restaurants, and movie theaters share space with street vendors and performers. Sit on a bench or a restaurant patio long enough and you'll see everything from straight-laced seniors in sensible shoes to teenagers with spiked purple hair and multiple body piercings.

The Promenade gains its carnival atmosphere in part from its street performers. Traditional Chinese jugglers twirl plates on poles, balancing them on every available body part from feet to foreheads. Expert swing dancers decked out in 1940s fashions look like they just stepped out of a WWII canteen. And singers and musicians of varying abilities play the Promenade, hoping to be discovered by an influential music producer on the lookout for new talent.

While there are plenty of places to shop, the Promenade is essentially a place to see and be seen. The abundance of alfresco dining options is great for enjoying the Southern California weather and watching the action. Everything from falafel to gravlax can be scarfed up at a table with a view.

Transplanted New Yorkers will feel right at home at **The Broadway Deli**. Traditional Jewish fish dishes and stacked-high corned beef sandwiches offer a little slice of Manhattan. Take out or eat in—the choice is yours. ~ 1457 Third Street Promenade; 310-451-0616. MODERATE.

As for nightlife, the **Monsoon Café**'s long bar is the scene of happy-hour well drinks, house wines, and $2.50 beers, and $3 Asian *pupus*. On Wednesdays, the place dances to a salsa beat, and weekends offer live entertainment that runs the gamut from reggae to R&B. ~ 1212 Third Street Promenade; 310-576-9996.

Just a couple of storefronts off the Promenade, **Houston's** is the place to rub elbows with L.A.'s young, hip professionals. You'll have to yell to be heard, but the food is good and the bar is hopping. ~ 202 Wilshire Boulevard; 310-576-7558. MODERATE TO DELUXE.

much, book a table on the enclosed patio. ~ 1401 Ocean Avenue; 310-394-5669, fax 310-394-7322; www.oceanave.com, e-mail dmunyon@kingsseafood.com. DELUXE.

A number of excellent eateries line Santa Monica's vaunted Third Street Promenade. This three-block-long walkway, filled with movie theaters and located in the downtown district, boasts some of the best coffeehouses and restaurants in the area.

Gotham Hall serves California cuisine, including free-range chicken marsala and seared ahi tuna. But the real show here is the decor—from the oblong mirrors and wavy-looking paint job in hues of aqua and pink on the walls to the purple pool tables and spotlights shining at odd angles from the beamed ceiling, this restaurant's look couldn't be more unique. Dinner only. ~ 1431 Third Street Promenade; 310-394-8865, fax 310-395-7040; www. gothamhall.com. MODERATE TO DELUXE.

If steak-and-kidney pie, bangers and mash, or shepherds' pie sound appetizing, head over to **Ye Olde King's Head**. You won't see a king's head on the wall of this British pub, but you will find British memorabilia alongside photographs of the celebrities who inhabit the pub. Like you, they are drawn here by the cozy ambience and the lively crowd. ~ 116 Santa Monica Boulevard; 310-451-1402, fax 310-393-6869; www.yeoldekingshead.com, e-mail ruth88@earthlink.net. MODERATE.

In the world of high chic, **Chinois on Main** stands taller than most. Owned by famous restaurateur Wolfgang Puck, the fashionable dining room is done in nouveau art deco–style with track lights, pastel colors, and a central skylight. The curved bar is hand-painted; contemporary artworks adorn the walls. Once you drink in the glamorous surroundings, move on to the menu, which includes Shanghai lobster with curry sauce, whole sizzling catfish, and grilled Szechuan beef. The appetizers and other entrées are equal in originality, a medley of French, Chinese, and California cuisine. This is an excellent restaurant with high standards of quality. No lunch Saturday through Tuesday. ~ 2709 Main Street; 310-392-9025, fax 310-396-5102; www.wolfgangpuck.com. DELUXE TO ULTRA-DELUXE.

HIDDEN ▶

The spot for breakfast in Santa Monica is **Rae's Restaurant**, a diner on the edge of town several miles from the beach. With its formica counter and naugahyde booths, Rae's is a local institution, always packed. The breakfasts are hearty American-style feasts complete with biscuits and gravy. At lunch they serve the usual selection of sandwiches and side orders. Come dinner time they have fried shrimp, liver, fried chicken, steaks, and other platters at prices that seem like they haven't changed since the place opened in 1958. ~ 2901 Pico Boulevard; 310-828-7937. BUDGET.

The word's spread about **Louise's**. A friendly trattoria atmosphere, creative Italian fare, and reasonable prices account for its popularity. ~ 1008 Montana Avenue; 310-394-8888. MODERATE.

There's no denying that the tariff at quietly elegant **Melisse** is steep, but the exquisite service and food make it one of the Westside's finest eateries. A gracious and ever-present, but unhovering, waitstaff serves up perfectly cooked, French-inspired dishes such as wild king salmon with lima bean purée, lamb stew on vegetable risotto, and white corn raviolis with truffles. Dinner only. ~ 1104 Wilshire Boulevard; 310-395-0881, fax 310-395-3810; www.melisse.com, e-mail mail@melisse.com. ULTRA-DELUXE.

◄ HIDDEN

There are many who believe the dining experience at **Michael's** to be the finest in all Los Angeles. Set in a restored stucco structure and decorated with original artworks by David Hockney and Jasper Johns, it is certainly one of the region's prettiest dining rooms. The menu is French-American, with original entrées such as squab on duck liver, and scallops with papaya, shallots, and chevril. At lunch there is grilled salmon with a tomato-basil vinaigrette, Alaskan halibut with fava beans, chanterelle and citrus nage, and several elaborate salads. Haute cuisine is the order of the evening here. The artistry that has gone into the restaurant's cuisine and design have permanently established Michael's reputation. There is a cozy lounge and a garden terrace. No lunch Saturday. Closed Sunday. ~ 1147 3rd Street; 310-451-0843, fax 310-394-1830. ULTRA-DELUXE.

◆◆◆

FOR LOVERS OF LIBERAL LANGUAGE . . .

There is one shop in particular that exemplifies Santa Monica's liberal politics. **Midnight Special Bookstore** specializes in politics and social sciences. Rather than current bestsellers, the window displays might feature books on Latin America, world hunger, Africa, or disarmament. ~ 1450 2nd Street; 310-393-2923; www.msbooks.com, e-mail books@ms books.com.

SHOPPING   Montana Avenue is Santa Monica's version of designer heaven, making it an interesting, if inflationary, strip to shop. From 7th to 17th Street, chic shops and upscale establishments line either side of the thoroughfare.

Brenda Himmel, an elegant stationary and gift store, just oozes refinement and good taste. While they sell buttery-leather journals, photo albums, and engagement books, and sterling silver picture frames, their forte is custom invitations and stationary. Almost nothing is impossible (provided you can afford it), from creative and colorful personally designed kids' birthday invitations to monogrammed note cards on the finest paper available. ~ 1126 Montana Avenue; 310-395-2437.

Check out the lively Sunday morning Farmer's Market held on the grounds of the California Heritage Museum. You'll find live music, food booths, crafts, and local produce. ~ 2612 Main Street.

For men's and women's fashion sportswear, try **Weathervane For Men**. ~ 1132 Montana Avenue; 310-395-0397.

Across the street, but no relation, is another **Weathervane**, this one featuring high-end designer casual clothing for women. Owner Jan Brilliot opened her shop in 1974, long before Montana Avenue had all the buzz. She journeys twice yearly to Paris and Italy looking for clothing that makes a statement. And her store certainly does with its architectural features and provocative art. You feel the thought and care that's gone into every detail. Closed Sunday. ~ 1209 Montana Avenue, Santa Monica; 310-393-5344.

Though they carry elegant traditional styles as well, **A. Mason** will offer you a look at worldwide cutting-edge fashion with their presentation of creations for women by emerging international talent. The emphasis in this special store is on originality. ~ 1511 Montana Avenue, Santa Monica; 310-394-7179.

Room with a View is a sort of Bed, Bath & Beyond for the rich. Exuding class, with its wooden floors, thick carpets, and potpourri aroma, the shop sells all sorts of high-end household accessories. The linens are nothing but the best; sheets have lofty thread counts, and towels are luxuriously fluffy. Combined with to-die-for table settings and gleaming silver accent pieces, this is a place that makes credit card max-out a definite possibility. ~ 1600 Montana Avenue; 310-998-5858.

Browse **Main Street** and you'll realize that Montana Avenue is only a practice round. Block after block of this thoroughfare is filled with trendy fashion and stylish shops.

The shopper's parade stretches most of the length of Main Street, but the center of action resides around the 2700 block. **Galleria Di Maio** is an art-deco mall with several spiffy shops including **Suji**, which carries fun, romantic women's clothing. ~ 2525 Main Street; 310-396-7614.

For designer labels at a fraction of their original cost, **The Address Boutique** is the place to go. The rich and famous from the nearby communities of Brentwood and Bel Air bring their hardly worn couturier clothes and accessories here to be resold. Why buy new when you can get a $1494 Vera Wang knit dress and jacket for $395 or a $2500 ivory satin Valentino gown for a mere $350? ~ 1116 Wilshire Boulevard; 310-394-1406; www. theaddressboutique.com.

◄ HIDDEN

The last of Santa Monica's several shopping enclaves is in the center of town. Here you'll find **Santa Monica Place**, a mammoth triple-tiered complex with about 140 shops. This flashy atrium mall has everything from clothes to books to luggage to leather work, jewelry, toys, hats, and shoes. ~ On Broadway between 2nd and 4th streets; 310-394-1049; www.santamonicaplace.com.

Step out from this glittery gathering place and you'll immediately encounter the **Third Street Promenade,** a three-block walkway lined on either side with shops, upscale cafés, and movie theaters. ~ Located between Broadway and Wilshire Boulevard.

Well-run and well-stocked, **Hennessey & Ingalls Bookstore** has almost any book you could think of covering the visual arts. Whether it's weaving or architecture, they either have it or can order it. Anyone who has any interest at all in the arts will find this a seductive place to hang out and peruse the beautiful coffee table books. ~ 1254 Third Street Promenade; 310-458-9074.

For the outward bound, **California Map & Travel Center** has it all—maps, directories, and guidebooks. Or, if you're planning a little armchair traveling at home, there are globes and travelogues. ~ 3312 Pico Boulevard; 310-396-6277; www.mapper.com.

The lively Third Street Promenade has several spots to enjoy a drink, but if you have your dancing shoes on, stop by **Gotham Hall.** Deejays spin hip-hop, dance, and house music in the Moroccan-

NIGHTLIFE

style lounge Thursday through Saturday. Cover. ~ 1431 Third Street Promenade; 310-394-8865.

Ye Olde King's Head might be the most popular British pub this side of the Thames. From dart boards to dark wood walls, trophy heads to draft beer, it's a classic English watering hole. Known throughout the area, it draws crowds of locals and expatriate Brits. ~ 116 Santa Monica Boulevard; 310-451-1402, fax 310-393-6869; www.yeoldekingshead.com, e-mail ruth88@earthlink.net.

McCabe's Guitar Shop is a folksy spot with live entertainment on weekends. The sounds are almost all acoustic and range from Scottish folk bands to jazz to blues to country. The concert hall is a room in back lined with guitars; performances run Friday through Sunday. Cover. ~ 3101 Pico Boulevard; 310-828-4497; www.mccabes.com.

For a raucous good time, try **O'Briens**. This bar is a loud, brash place that draws hearty crowds. There are live bands nightly, ranging from Irish rock to Texas blues. The decor is what you'd expect from an Irish pub, with old pictures and beer signs hanging from the walls. Cover on Friday and Saturday. ~ 2941 Main Street; 310-396-4725, fax 310-399-7514.

For blues, R&B, soul, and jazz, try **Harvelle's**, which hosts local acts nightly. Cover. ~ 1432 4th Street; 310-395-1676; www. harvelles.com.

BEACHES & PARKS

SANTA MONICA CITY BEACH ⚓ 🏊 🎣 If the pop song is right and "L.A. is a great big freeway," then truly Santa Monica is a great big beach. Face it, the sand is very white, the water is very blue, the beach is very broad, and they all continue for miles. From Venice to Pacific Palisades, it's a sandbox gone wild. Skaters, strollers, and bicyclists pass along the promenade, sunbathers lie moribund in the sand, and volleyball players perform acrobatic shots. At the center of all this stands the Santa Monica Pier with its amusement park atmosphere. If it wasn't right next door to Venice this would be the hottest beach around. Lifeguards are on duty; facilities include picnic areas, restrooms, and snack bars. Swimming and surfing are good, and anglers usually opt for the pier. Parking fee, $7. ~ Route 1, at the foot of Colorado Avenue; 310-458-8374.

SANTA MONICA MOUNTAINS NATIONAL RECREATION AREA
🚶 🚵 🐎 One of the few mountain ranges in the United States

to run transversely (from east to west), the Santa Monicas reach for 50 miles to form the northwestern boundary of the Los Angeles basin. This federal preserve, which covers part of the mountain range, encompasses about 153,000 acres between Routes 1 and 101, much of which is laced with hiking trails (about 500 miles); in addition to high country, it includes a coastal stretch from Santa Monica to Point Mugu. Considered a "botanical island," the mountains support chaparral, coastal sage, and oak forests; mountain lions, golden eagles, and many of California's early animal species still survive here. ~ Several access roads lead into the area; Mulholland Drive and Mulholland Highway follow the crest of the Santa Monica Mountains for about 50 miles from Hollywood to Malibu. The National Park Service visitor center is at 401 West Hillcrest Drive, Thousand Oaks; 805-370-2301, fax 805-370-1850; www.nps.gov/samo.

▲ There is a group campground that accommodates 10 to 50 people; $2 per person, 10 person minimum. Reservations required.

Venice

Venice, California, was the dream of one man, a tobacco magnate named Abbot Kinney. He envisioned a "Venice of America," a Renaissance town of gondoliers and single-lane bridges, connected by 16 miles of canals. After convincing railroad barons and city fathers, Kinney dredged swampland along Santa Monica Bay, carved a network of canals, and founded this dream city in 1905. The place was an early-20th-century answer to Disneyland with gondola rides and amusement parks. The canals were lined with vaulted arches and rococo-style hotels.

> Venice, to quote Bob Dylan, represents "life and life only," but a rarefied form of life, slightly, beautifully askew.

Oil spelled the doom of Kinney's dream. Once black gold was discovered beneath the sands of Venice, the region became a landscape of drilling rigs and oil derricks. Spills polluted the canals and blackened the beaches. In 1929, the city of Los Angeles filled in most of the canals, and during the subsequent decades Venice more resembled a tar pit than a cultural center.

But by the 1950s, latter-day visionaries—artists and bohemians—rediscovered "Kinney's Folly" and transformed it into an avant-garde community. It became a magnet for Beats in the 1950s and hippies during the next decade. Musician Jim Morrison of The Doors lived here and Venice developed a reputation as a center for the cultural renaissance that Abbot Kinney once envisioned. Today the creative energy of Venice is hard to stifle. The town is filled with galleries and covered by murals, making it one of the region's most important art centers.

On weekends, Venice is where the action is. Along the broad concrete path that runs from the Venice pier toward Santa Monica, an amazing amalgamation of street performers and retailers set up shop. Skimpily clad Pamela Anderson lookalikes on roller blades whiz by conservatively dressed tourists from the Midwest, while yuppies rub elbows with street people. There is perhaps nowhere in L.A. where the city's ethnic and lifestyle diversity is more evident. In the carnival atmosphere, this eccentric mix of players can have its fortunes told, eat corn dogs, marvel at skateboarding demonstrations, see a guy swallow fire, or buy a $3 T-shirt. It's Venice at its best and most outrageous.

SIGHTS   The revolution might have sputtered elsewhere, but in Venice artists seized control. City Hall has become the **Beyond Baroque Literary Arts Center**, housing a library and bookstore devoted to small presses. Closed Sunday and Monday. ~ 681 Venice Boulevard; 310-822-3006; www.beyondbaroque.org.

Next door, the former **Venice Police Station** is home to SPARC, or the Social and Public Art Resource Center. Some of the jail cells of this imposing 1929 art deco–style building have been converted into an art gallery. The holding pen is intact and you'll walk through an iron door to view contemporary artwork by mostly local alternative, cutting-edge artists. The center also houses a gift shop and the UCLA/SPARC Cesar Chavez Digital Mural Lab. Closed Saturday and Sunday except by appointment. ~ 685 Venice Boulevard; 310-822-9560, fax 310-827-8717; www.sparcmurals.org, e-mail sparc@sparcmurals.org.

Both the Venice City Hall and Police Station are great places to learn about what's going on in the community. Also consider the **Venice Chamber of Commerce**. If you can find someone there (which is not always easy), you can obtain maps, brochures, and answers. ~ 583¾ North Venice Boulevard, Suite C; 310-396-7016, fax 310-314-7641.

The commercial center of Venice rests at the intersection of Windward Avenue and Main Street. Windward was the central boulevard of Kinney's dream city, and the Traffic Circle, marked today by a small sculpture, was to be an equally grand lagoon. Continue along Windward Avenue to the arcades, a series of Italian-style colonnades that represent one of the few surviving elements of old Venice.

What's left of **Kinney's canals** can be found a few blocks south of Windward between Venice and Washington boulevards. Here three small canals flanked by two larger ones comprise an enclave of charming bungalows and showy mini-mansion remodels. Strains of opera or jazz float out of open windows as resident ducks, squawking loudly, paddle along the canals and joggers run along the narrow walkways and over small arched wooden bridges.

The heart of modern-day Venice pulses along the **boardwalk**, a two-mile strip that follows Ocean Front Walk from Washington Street to Rose Avenue. **Venice Pier**, an 1100-foot fishing pier, anchors one end. The pier is renovated with excellent lighting and coin-operated telescopes for lovely views of the Strand. Between

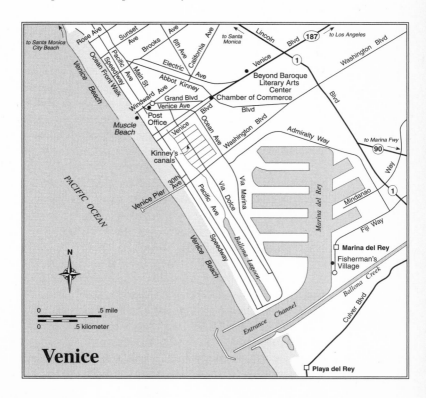

Venice

Washington Street and Windward Avenue, the promenade is bordered by a palisade of beachfront homes, two- and three-story houses with plate-glass facades. ~ Ocean Front Walk and Washington Boulevard.

Walking north, the real action begins around 18th Avenue, at **Muscle Beach,** where rope-armed heavies work out in the world-class weight pen, smacking punching bags and flexing their pecs, while gawking onlookers dream of oiling their bodies and walking with a muscle-bound strut.

The rest of the boardwalk is a grand open-air carnival that you should try to visit on the weekend. It is a world of artists and anarchists, derelicts and dreamers, a vision of what life would be if heaven were an insane asylum. Guitarists, jugglers, conga drummers, and clowns perform for the crowds. Kids on roller skates and bicycles whiz past rickshaws and unicycles. Street hawkers and panhandlers work the unwary while singers with scratchy voices pass the hat. Vendors dispense everything from corn dogs to cotton candy, T-shirts to wind-up toys.

LODGING

HIDDEN ▶

There's nothing quite like **The Venice Beach House**. That may well be because there are so few bed-and-breakfast inns in the Los Angeles area. But it's also that this is such a charming house, an elegant and spacious California craftsman–style home built in 1911 by Warren Wilson. The living room, with its beam ceiling, dark wood paneling, and brick fireplace, is a masterwork. Guests also enjoy a sunny alcove, patio, and garden. The stroll to the Venice boardwalk and beach is only one-half block. The nine guest rooms are beautifully appointed and furnished with antiques; each features patterned wallpaper and period artwork. I can't recommend the place highly enough. ~ 15 30th Avenue; 310-823-1966, fax 310-823-1842; www.venicebeachhouse.com, e-mail reservations@venicebeachhouse.com. DELUXE TO ULTRA-DELUXE.

HIDDEN ▶

The **Cadillac Hotel**, a renovated art-deco throwback, is located right on the Venice strand. The rooms aren't lavish, but they're as close to the beach as you're going to get, and the facade and lobby are decorated in eye-catchingly crazy colors and patterns. Some good deals can be had here, particularly during the winter. ~ 8 Dudley Avenue; 310-399-8876, fax 310-399-4536; www.thecadillachotel.com. BUDGET TO MODERATE.

Murals of Venice & Santa Monica

Nowhere is the spirit of Venice and Santa Monica more evident than in the murals adorning their walls. Both seaside cities house major art colonies, and numerous galleries and studios make them important centers for contemporary art.

Over the years, as more and more artists made their homes here, they began decorating the twin towns with their art. The product of this creative energy lives along street corners and alleyways, on storefronts and roadways. Crowded with contemporary and historic images, these murals express the inner life of the city.

Murals adorn nooks and crannies all over Venice. You'll find a cluster of them around Windward Avenue between Main Street and Ocean Front Walk. The interior of the **Post Office** is adorned with public art. There's a trompe l'oeil mural nearby on the old St. Marks Hotel that beautifully reflects the street along which you are gazing. Don't miss the woman in the upper floor window. ~ Windward Avenue and Main Street. On the other side of the building, facing the ocean, **Venice Reconstituted** depicts the unique culture of Venice Beach. ~ Windward Avenue and Speedway.

At last count Santa Monica boasted about two dozen outdoor murals. Route 1, or Lincoln Boulevard, is a corridor decorated with local artworks. **John Muir Woods** portrays a redwood forest. ~ Lincoln and Ocean Park boulevards. **Early Ocean Park and Venice Scenes** captures the seaside at the turn of the 20th century. ~ Located two blocks west of Lincoln Boulevard along Kensington Road in Joslyn Park.

Ocean Park Boulevard is another locus of creativity. At its intersection with the 4th Street underpass you'll encounter **Whale of a Mural**, illustrating whales and underwater life common to California waters, and **Unbridled**, depicting a herd of horses fleeing from the Santa Monica Pier carousel. One of the area's famous murals awaits you at Ocean Park Boulevard and Main street, where **Early Ocean Park** vividly re-creates scenes from the past.

For more information or a tour of these and other murals, contact the **Social and Public Art Resource Center**. ~ 685 Venice Boulevard; 310-822-9560; www.sparcmurals.org. The **Santa Monica Cultural Affairs Division** can also help. ~ 310-458-8350; www.arts.santamonica.org. Los Angeles has earned a reputation as the mural capital of the United States, making this tour a highpoint for admirers of public art.

Also consider the **Best Western Marina Pacific Hotel & Suites**. Located in the recreational center of Venice only 200 feet from the sand, this three-story, 88-unit hostelry has a small lobby and café downstairs. The guest rooms are spacious, nicely furnished, and well maintained; all have refrigerators, hairdryers, coffee-makers, and irons. Very large one-bedroom suites, complete with kitchen and fireplace, are also available. All rooms have small balconies. Amenities include a coin laundry. ~ 1697 Pacific Avenue; 310-452-1111, 800-421-8151, fax 310-452-5479; www.mp hotel.com, e-mail info@mphotel.com. DELUXE TO ULTRA-DELUXE.

For the international hostel-hopper, Venice Beach is a veritable heaven by the ocean. The **Venice Beach Cotel**, located right on the beach, offers both private and shared rooms. Passports are required at check-in. ~ 25 Windward Avenue; 310-399-7649, fax 310-399-1930; www.venicebeachcotel.com, e-mail reservations @venicebeachcotel.com. BUDGET.

Hostel California features ten units with shared baths: six dorm-style rooms hold six beds, four rooms are available for couples. Other amenities include kitchen and laundry facilities. Reservations are not taken for private rooms. ~ 2221 Lincoln Boulevard; 310-305-0250, fax 310-305-8590; www.hostelcalifornia.net, e-mail hoca90291@aol.com. BUDGET.

DINING

The best place for finger food and junk food in all Southern California might well be the **boardwalk** in Venice. Along Ocean Front Walk are vendor stands galore serving pizza, frozen yogurt, hamburgers, falafel, submarine sandwiches, corn dogs, etc.

Regardless, there's really only one spot in Venice to consider for dining. It simply *is* Venice, an oceanfront café right on the **HIDDEN ►**   boardwalk, **The Sidewalk Café**. Skaters whiz past, drummers

---

PARKING POINTERS

Parking in Venice, especially on hot summer weekends, can be a pain, and an expensive one at that. Street parking close to the beach cannot be found after 10 or 11 in the morning; lots closest to the beach will charge between $9 and $12 per car. If you don't mind a bit of walking, try your luck in the public lots at Venice Boulevard and Pacific Avenue; a day of parking here should cost between $7 and $10. The best advice: come early and be patient.

beat rhythms in the distance, and the sun stands like a big orange wafer above the ocean. Food is really a second thought here, but eventually they're going to want you to spend some money. So, on to the menu . . . breakfast, lunch, and dinner are what you'd expect—omelettes, sandwiches, hamburgers, pizza, and pasta. There are also fresh fish dishes plus specialty salads, steak, spicy chicken, and fried shrimp. Validated parking is a block away in the lot at Market and Speedway. ~ 1401 Ocean Front Walk at Horizon Avenue; 310-399-5547, fax 310-399-4512. MODERATE.

Take a walk down the boardwalk to **Venice Bistro**. This beach-front establishment is a casual dining room with a tile floor and brick walls. Cozy and comfortable, it features a menu that includes hamburgers, salads, pasta, and some Mexican dishes. There's a full bar. ~ 323 Ocean Front Walk; 310-392-7472. BUDGET TO MODERATE.

Or check out **Jody Maroni's Sausage Kingdom**, a beach stand with over a dozen types of sausage, all natural. There's sweet Italian, Yucatán chicken, Louisiana hotlinks, and, of course, Polish. All sausages are served with grilled onions and peppers on a poppy-seed roll. Breakfast served daily. Open until sunset; closed on rainy days. ~ 2011 Ocean Front Walk; 310-822-5639, fax 310-348-1510; www.jodymaroni.com, e-mail info@jodymaroni.com. BUDGET.

Amuse Cafe is cozily ensconced in a bright yellow house. The specialties here include such tasty treats as pork ribs and roasted pepper vichyssoise with watercress. The menu changes often, but you'll also find pasta, poultry, and steak. Closed Monday. ~ 796 Main Street; 310-450-1956; www.amusecafe.com. MODERATE.

◄ *HIDDEN*

The landing ground for Venetians is a warehouse dining place called **The Rose Café**. There's a full-scale deli, bakery counter, and a restaurant offering indoor seating and outdoor patio service. The last serves lunch and dinner daily from a reasonably priced menu that may include entrées like linguine with smoked salmon, sautéed chicken, and a good selection of vegetarian dishes. A good spot for pasta and salad, The Rose Café, with its wall murals and paintings, is also a place to appreciate the vital culture of Venice. Call for hours. ~ 220 Rose Avenue; 310-399-0711, fax 310-396-2660. BUDGET TO MODERATE.

◄ *HIDDEN*

In the mood for Asian cuisine? **Hama Restaurant** is a well-respected Japanese restaurant in the center of Venice. The place features an angular sushi bar, a long, narrow dining room, and a patio out back. The crowd is young and the place is decorated to reflect Venice's vibrant culture. There are paintings on display representing many of the area's artists. In addition to scrumptious sushi, Hama offers a complete selection of Japanese dishes including tempura, teriyaki, and sashimi. ~ 213 Windward Avenue; 310-396-8783, fax 310-392-9456. ULTRA-DELUXE.

HIDDEN ► At **Pam's Place** chef-owner Pam Klingliang cooks up made-to-order spicy Thai delicacies. Specialties served in this colorfully decorated restaurant include shrimp with roasted chiles, coconut custard, and some of the best *pad Thai* in town. No lunch on Sunday. ~ 636 Venice Boulevard; 310-301-8002. MODERATE.

"American comfort cooking"—barbecued pork ribs with ribbons of collard greens; roast chicken with a side of coffee-flavored barbecue sauce; fried calamari served with chipotle-pepper dipping sauce; calf's liver with pancetta; and iceberg lettuce with a creamy bleu-cheese dressing, for example—that's what **James' Beach** is all about. Frequented by the Venice arts-and-letters crowd, this art-filled restaurant (Billy Al Bengston designed the interior) offers daily dinner specials that are well conceived and reasonably priced. Dinner and weekend brunch; lunch Wednesday through Friday. ~ 60 North Venice Boulevard; 310-823-5396, fax 310-823-5397. MODERATE TO ULTRA-DELUXE.

Chef Joseph Manzare returns to L.A. (from Globe San Francisco) as chef/co-owner of **Globe Venice Beach**. When last in the Southland, he was head chef at Spago before it moved to Beverly Hills. The California cuisine menu features seafood, pasta, pizza, and mesquite-grilled T-bone. All is done with imagination and skill. No lunch on Saturday and Sunday. ~ 72 Market Street; 310-392-8720, fax 310-399-5953. MODERATE TO ULTRA-DELUXE.

SHOPPING To combine slumming with shopping, be sure to wander the **boardwalk** in Venice. Ocean Front Walk between Windward and Ozone avenues is lined with low-rent stalls selling beach hats, cheap jewelry, sunglasses, beach bags, and souvenirs. You'll also encounter **Small World Books**, a marvelous beachside shop crammed with fiction, mysteries (novels, that is), poetry, and other books. ~ 1407 Ocean Front Walk; 310-399-2360; www.small worldbooks.com, e-mail info@smallworldbooks.com.

L.A. Louver is one of Venice's many vital and original galleries. It represents David Hockney, R. B. Kitaj and other contemporary

American and European artists. Closed Sunday and Monday. ~
45 North Venice Boulevard; 310-822-4955, fax 310-821-7529;
www.lalouver.com, e-mail info@lalouver.com.

Philip Garaway Native American Art specializes in museum-   ◄ HIDDEN
quality antique American Indian art, 19th-century Navajo blankets, antique rugs, vintage kachina dolls, Western American
Indian basketry, and Pueblo pottery dating from A.D. 700 to the
20th century. By appointment only. ~ Venice; 310-577-8555, fax
310-577-8557; e-mail philipgaraway@earthlink.net.

The **Beyond Baroque Literary Arts Center**, a clearinghouse
for local talent, has a bookstore and sponsors poetry readings,
dramatic revues, lectures, and concerts. It's located in the old Venice City Hall. Closed Sunday
and Monday. ~ 681 Venice Boulevard; 310-822-
3006; www.beyondbaroque.org.

A covey of art galleries
and antique shops lines
the 1200 to 1500
blocks of West
Washington Boule-
vard in Venice.

The town's erstwhile jail, the **Social and Public Art
Resource Center**, or SPARC, has a store offering Latin
American and Southwestern folk art as well as a selection
of art books, prints, and cards. ~ 685 Venice Boulevard; 310-
822-9560; www.sparcmurals.org.

NIGHTLIFE

The **Townhouse**, set in a '20s-era speakeasy, has live music occasionally. Otherwise, you can stop by for a drink or a game of darts
or pool. Occasional cover. ~ 52 Windward Avenue; 310-392-4040.

The **Venice Bistro** features a different style of live music every
night—bluegrass, blues, rock, acoustic, folk—and there's never a
cover charge. Call ahead for the schedule. ~ 323 Ocean Front
Walk; 310-392-7472.

The **Sidewalk Café** is also a popular nightspot and gathering
place, more for its central location than anything else. ~ 1401
Ocean Front Walk; 310-399-5547.

For an unusual way to spend the evening in the summer
months, ask **Malibu Ocean Sports** about their moonlight kayak
tours around Marina del Rey. The evening can include dinner at
one of the marina's restaurants. ~ 310-456-6302; www.malibu
kayaks.com.

VENICE BEACH 🚴 🏊 🏄 ⛵ This broad white-sand corridor runs the entire length of Venice and features Venice Pier. But
the real attraction—and the reason you'll find the beach described
in the "Dining," "Sights," and "Shopping" sections—is the board-

**BEACHES
& PARKS**

walk. A center of culture, street artistry, and excitement, the board-walk parallels Venice Beach for two miles. As far as beach facilities, you'll find restrooms, showers, lifeguards, playgrounds, basket-ball courts, weightlifting facilities ($5 to use), a bike path, and handball and paddle ball courts. If you can tear yourself away from the action on the boardwalk, the swimming and surfing are good here, too. Closed on rainy days. ~ Ocean Front Walk in Venice parallels the beach; 310-399-2775, fax 310-577-1046.

Marina del Rey

What could be more appropriate to a city famous for illusion than the world's largest manmade small boat harbor. South of Venice and Washington Boulevard, Marina del Rey—known simply as "The Marina" by locals—was dismissed from its mid-1960 beginnings as land of the shallow and phony. Filled with condos, overpriced apartments, and undistinguished restaurants, in its heyday in the 1970s it was known as a haven for Hugh Hefner wannabes with bared chests and gold medallions who languished in hot tubs with their "Baywatch"-type beach-bunny girlfriends. It's mellowed a bit since then, and some of the eateries are actually worth visiting, but this is still a slick, false-fronted kind of place with little character.

SIGHTS Over 6000 pleasure boats and yachts dock at the manmade small-boat harbor here, the largest in the world. Private charters, dinner, dance and Sunday champagne brunch cruises are provided by **Hornblower Cruises & Events**. ~ 13755 Fiji Way; 310-301-9900, 800-668-4322; www.hornblower.com, e-mail md@hornblower.com.

The entire region was once a marsh inhabited by a variety of waterfowl. Personally, I think they should have left it to the birds. Marina del Rey is an ersatz community, a completely fabricated place where the main shopping area, **Fisherman's Village**, resembles a New England whaling town, and everything else attempts to portray something it's not. ~ 13755 Fiji Way; 310-823-5411.

Playa del Rey, on the other hand, is an unpretentious beach town that time seems to have passed by. Separated from The Marina by the hotly contested Ballona Wetlands and the break-water, its residents are staunchly protective of their town. How long they can hold out against developers remains to be seen however, particularly since the adjacent, hitherto undeveloped

Hughes Aircraft land is being quickly turned into a huge condominium complex.

Situated a few blocks from a broad, pleasant beach, the **Inn at Playa del Rey** abuts the Ballona Wetlands, one of the last wetlands habitats in Southern California. With 21 rooms and suites, many with fireplaces and whirlpool tubs, the gray-and-white clapboard inn looks more like a New England beach house than a California B&B. Bicycles are available for guests' use, and the outdoor jacuzzi is a popular feature. In addition to a full breakfast, owner Susan Zolla provides afternoon wine and cheese. ~ 435 Culver Boulevard, Playa del Rey; 310-574-1920, fax 310-574-9920; www.innatplayadelrey.com, e-mail info@innatplayadelrey.com. DELUXE TO ULTRA-DELUXE.

Café Del Ray stands out among Marina del Rey's mostly underwhelming eateries with food that is definitely a couple of steps above any of the other harborside restaurants. Featuring dishes that are French with Asian overtones, specialties run the gamut from Thai shellfish sausage to Grand Marnier chocolate soufflé. ~ 4451 Admiralty Way; 310-823-6395; www.calcafe.com/cafe_del_rey. DELUXE.

DOCKWEILER STATE BEACH 🚲 🏖 🏃 🎣 🚣 It's long, wide, and has fluffy white sand—what more could you ask? Rather, it's what less can you request. Dockweiler suffers a minor problem. It's right next to Los Angeles International Airport, one of the world's busiest terminals. Every minute planes are taking off, thundering, reverberating, right over the beach. To add insult to infamy, there is a sewage treatment plant nearby. Nevertheless, swimming and surfing are good, fires are permitted, and fishing is good from the jetties. You'll also find picnic areas and restrooms. Parking fee, $5 to $6.75. ~ At the foot of Imperial Highway, along Vista del Mar Boulevard, Playa del Rey; 310-322-4951, fax 310-726-0371.

▲ There is an RV park with 82 sites with full hookups and 35 without; $13 to $25 per night. Reservations are recommended and are accepted 7 to 90 days in advance.

SEVEN

Santa Catalina Island

There's something surprising about finding a little slice of the Mediterranean sitting in the middle of the sea just a short ferry ride from the urban sprawl of L.A. Along its 54 miles of shoreline, Santa Catalina Island offers sheer cliffs, pocket beaches, hidden coves, and some of the finest skin diving anywhere. To the interior, mountains rise sharply to over 2000 feet in elevation. Island fox, black antelope, and over 400 bison range the island while its waters teem with marlin, swordfish, and barracuda. Happily, this unique habitat is preserved for posterity and adventurous travelers by an arrangement under which 86 percent of the island lies undeveloped, protected by the Santa Catalina Conservancy. Avalon, the famous coastal resort enclave, is the only town on the island. The rest is given over to mountain wilderness and pristine shoreline.

As romantic as its setting is the history of the island. Originally part of the Baja coastline, it broke off from the mainland eons ago and drifted 100 miles to the northwest. Its earliest inhabitants arrived perhaps 4000 or 5000 years ago, leaving scattered evidence of their presence before being supplanted by the Gabrieleño Indians around 500 B.C. A society of sun worshippers, the Gabrieleños constructed a sacrificial temple, fished island waters, and traded ceramics and soapstone carvings with mainland tribes, crossing the channel in canoes.

Juan Rodríguez Cabrillo discovered Catalina in 1542, but the place proved of such little interest to the Spanish that, other than Sebastian Vizcaíno's exploration in 1602, they virtually ignored it. By the 19th century, Russian fur traders, attracted by the rich colonies of sea otters, succeeded in exterminating both the otters and the indigenous people. Cattle and sheep herders took over the Gabrieleños' land while pirates and smugglers, hiding in Catalina's secluded coves, menaced the coast. Later in the century, Chinese laborers were secretly landed on the island before being illegally carried to the mainland.

Other visionaries, seeing in Catalina a major resort area, also took control. After changing hands several times, the island was purchased in 1919 by William Wrigley, Jr. The Wrigley family—better known for their ownership of a chewing gum company and the Chicago Cubs baseball team—developed Avalon for tourism and left the rest of the island to nature. Attracting big-name entertainers and providing an escape from urban Los Angeles, Avalon soon captured the fancy of movie stars and wealthy Californians. Today the island is popular with Angelinos who are looking for a nearby getaway, be it a day or a week, while tourists enjoy the novelty of visiting a laidback and rural island just a short ferry ride away from the hustle and bustle of the rest of L.A.

Avalon

Cruising into the port of Avalon on a sunny California day is about as blissful as it gets. Boats fill the harbor, wooden houses dot the hillsides, and the narrow streets of the tiny downtown are filled with low-rise, early-20th-century buildings. Tiny Avalon is only one square mile so, though no cars are allowed except those belonging to islanders, it's easy to get around by either renting a bicycle or golf cart, or by hoofing it.

In the summer months, the place swarms with bathing-suited tourists strolling along the promenade next to the small beach, which is jammed with sunbathers and sand castle–building kiddies. Funky beach houses become summer rentals for L.A. families looking for a nearby, safe place for a vacation. In the winter, many of the souvenir shops and food stands close up, and the town takes on a somnambulistic air. On a clear, sunny, brisk winter day there's nowhere better to chill out than sitting at a harborside restaurant, sipping a margarita and chatting with the locals.

SIGHTS

Set in a luxurious amphitheater of green mountains, **Avalon** is like a time warp of Southern California early in the 20th century. The architecture is a blend of Mediterranean and Victorian homes as well as vernacular structures designed by creative locals who captured both the beautiful and whimsical.

From the ferry dock you can wander **Crescent Avenue**, Avalon's oceanfront promenade. Stroll out along the **Avalon Pleasure Pier**, located at Crescent Avenue and Catalina Street, for a view of the entire town and its surrounding crescent of mountains. Located along this wood plank promenade are food stands, the harbormaster's office, and bait-and-tackle shops. The **Catalina Island Visitors Bureau and Chamber of Commerce** has an information center here that will help orient you to Avalon and the island. ~ #1 Green Pier; 310-510-1520, fax 310-510-7606; www.catalina. com, e-mail info@visitcatalina.org.

Among the pier kiosks is a ticket booth offering guided tours in a **semi-submersible vessel** out to a nearby cove filled with colorful fish and marine plant life. Known as Catalina's "undersea gardens," the area is crowded with rich kelp beds and is a favorite haunt of spotted and calico bass, golden adult Garibaldi, and leopard sharks. **Santa Catalina Island Company** has tours in the day and also at night when huge floodlights are used to attract sea life. In the summer they seek out the spectacular flying fish that seasonally inhabit these waters. They also offer coastal cruises and inland motor tours. Drop by their visitor information center. ~ 423 Crescent Avenue; 310-510-2000, 800-626-1496, fax 310-510-2300; www.scico.com.

Farther along the waterfront, dominating the skyline, sits the **Avalon Casino**. A massive circular building painted white and capped with a red tile roof, it was built in 1929 after a Spanish Moorish design. What can you say other than that the place is famous: it has appeared on countless postcards and travel posters. The ballroom has heard the big band sounds of Count Basie and Tommy Dorsey and the entire complex is a study in art deco with fabulous murals and tile paintings. ~ On Casino Way at the end of Crescent Avenue; 310-510-2000, 800-626-1496, fax 310-510-2300; www.scico.com.

Downstairs is the **Catalina Island Museum**, which holds a varied collection of local artifacts. Of particular interest is the contour relief map of the island, which provides an excellent perspective for anyone venturing into the interior. The museum also features an award-winning interactive exhibit chronicling the history of steamship transportation. Closed Thursday from January through March. Admission. ~ Avalon Casino; 310-510-2414, fax 310-510-2780; e-mail catalinaislmuseum@catalinaisp. com.

Another point of particular interest, located one and a half miles inland in Avalon Canyon, is the **Wrigley Memorial and Botanical Garden**, a tribute to William Wrigley, Jr. The monument, an imposing 130-foot structure fashioned with glazed tiles and Georgia marble, features a spiral staircase in a solitary tower. The gardens, a showplace for native island plants, display an array

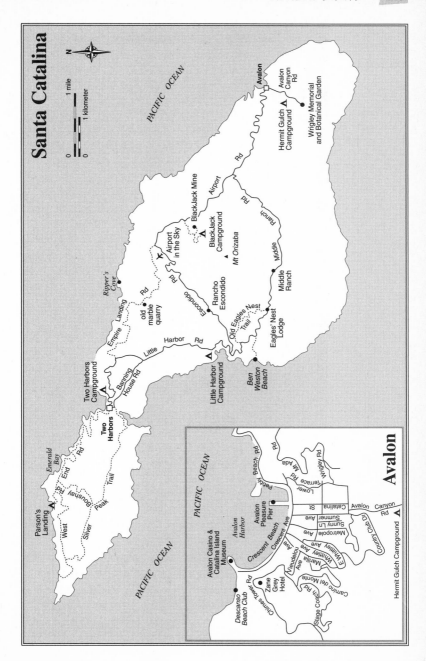

Santa Catalina

N

0   1 mile
0   1 kilometer

PACIFIC OCEAN

Avalon
Avalon Canyon Rd
Hermit Gulch Campground
Wrigley Memorial and Botanical Garden

BlackJack Mine
Airport in the Sky
BlackJack Campground
Mt Orizaba
Airport Rd
Ranch Rd
Middle Ranch Rd

Ripper's Cove
old marble quarry
Empire Landing Rd
Escondido Rd
Rancho Escondido
Old Eagles' Nest Trail
Eagles' Nest Lodge
Middle Ranch

Little Harbor Rd
Banning House Rd
Two Harbors Campground
Two Harbors
Little Harbor Campground
Ben Weston Beach

Emerald Bay
West End Rd
Boushay Rd
Silver Peak Trail
Parson's Landing

PACIFIC OCEAN

Avalon

PACIFIC OCEAN

Pebble Beach Rd
Mt Ada
Wrigley Rd
Lower Terrace Rd
Catalina St
Avalon Canyon Rd
Metropole Ave
Sumner Ave
Sunny Ln
E Whitley Ave
Whitley Ave
Marilla Ave
Vieudelou Ave
Crescent Ave
Camino del Monte
Avalon Pleasure Pier
Crescent Beach
Avalon Harbor
Country Club Dr
Hermit Gulch Campground

Avalon Casino & Catalina Island Museum
Descanso Beach Club
Chimes Tower Rd
Zane Grey Hotel
Stage Coach Rd
5th Rd

of succulents and cactus. Admission. ~ 1400 Avalon Canyon Road; 310-510-2288; e-mail wmgarden@catalinas.net.

LODGING   One fact about lodging in Catalina everyone seems to agree upon is that it is overpriced. Particularly in the summer, when Avalon's population swells from about 3200 to over 10,000, hotels charge stiff rates for rooms. But what's a traveler to do? The island is both pretty and popular, so you have no recourse but to pay the piper.

> Gold fever swept Santa Catalina in 1863 as miners swept onto the island, but the rush never panned out.

It's also a fact that rates jump seasonally more than on the mainland. Summer is the most expensive period, winter the cheapest, with spring and fall somewhere in between. Weekend rates are also sometimes higher than weekday room tabs and usually require a two-night minimum stay.

The last fact of life for lodgers to remember is that since most of the island is a nature preserve, most hotels are located in Avalon.

Low-price lodgings are as rare as snow in Avalon. But at the **Hotel Atwater** you'll find accommodations to suit all budgets. The newer wing offers 26 country-style rooms in the deluxe-to-ultra-deluxe range. The older part of the hotel has wicker chairs and blond wood furniture. Besides, it has a friendly lobby with oak trim and tasteful blue furniture, plus dozens of rooms to choose from. Closed mid-November to April. ~ 125 Sumner Street; 310-510-1788, 800-322-3434, fax 310-510-1673; www.scico.com. MODERATE TO ULTRA-DELUXE.

One of Santa Catalina's most popular hotels is the **Pavilion Lodge,** a 73-room facility on Avalon's waterfront street. Designed around a central courtyard, it offers guests a lawn and patio for sunbathing. The rooms contain modern furniture, ceramic tile flooring, and Italian bedding. If you want to be at the heart of downtown in a comfortable if undistinguished establishment, this is the place. ~ 513 Crescent Avenue; 310-510-1788, fax 310-510-2073; www.scico.com. ULTRA-DELUXE.

Plainly put, the **Hotel Vista del Mar** is a gem. Each of the 15 spacious Mediterranean-style rooms is decorated in soft pastels and features a wet bar, fireplace, and full tiled bath. All surround an open-air atrium courtyard lobby, where guests enjoy ocean breezes and views from comfortable wicker rockers. One smaller room is priced deluxe, while courtyard rooms command ultra-deluxe rates. ~ 417 Crescent Avenue; 310-510-1452, 800-601-

3836; www.hotel-vistadelmar.com, e-mail vista@catalinas.net.
DELUXE TO ULTRA-DELUXE.

Farther along the same street is **Hotel Villa Portofino** with 35
rooms situated around a split-level brick patio. The accommodations are small but have been stylishly decorated with modern
furniture, dressing tables, and wallpaper in pastel shades. There
are tile baths with stall showers; a few have tubs. The oceanview
suites have marble tubs. A small lobby downstairs has been finished with potted plants and marble. ~ 111 Crescent Avenue;
310-510-0555, 888-510-0555, fax 310-510-0839; www.hotel
villaportofino.com, e-mail vpstaff@catalinaisp.com. DELUXE TO
ULTRA-DELUXE.

It's a big, bold, blue and white structure rising for five levels
above the hillside. **Hotel Catalina** has been a fixture on the Avalon skyline since 1892. The 32-unit, completely non-smoking facility features a comfortable lobby complete with overhead fans,
plus a sundeck and jacuzzi. The sleeping rooms are small but
comfy with standard furnishings; many offer ocean views and all
the rooms have ceiling fans, small refrigerators, and VCRs. There
are also four trim little cottages that are warmly decorated. A
bright, summer atmosphere pervades the place. ~ 129 Whittley
Avenue; 310-510-0027, 800-540-0184, fax 310-510-1495; www.
hotelcatalina.com, e-mail jarneson@catalinaisp.com. MODERATE
TO DELUXE.

La Paloma Cottages, a rambling complex consisting of several
buildings, features a string of eight contiguous cottages. These are
cozy units with original decor and comfortable furnishings. There
are also six larger family units (with kitchens) available in a nearby
building. Set on a terraced street in a quiet part of town, La Paloma is attractively landscaped. There are no phones or daily maid
service in the rooms. However, at **Las Flores,** an addition to the
original hotel, you can get pricier rooms with maid service, phones,
and a whirlpool bath to boot. ~ 326 Sunny Lane; 310-510-0737,
800-310-1505, fax 310-510-2424; www.catalina.com/lapaloma.
html, e-mail lapaloma@catalinaisp.com. ULTRA-DELUXE.

Best Western Catalina Canyon Resort and Spa is a chic, modern 72-room complex complete with pool, jacuzzi, sauna, restaurant, and bar. This Mediterranean-style hotel sits on a hillside in
Avalon Canyon. The grounds are nicely landscaped with banana
plants and palm trees. Each guest room is furnished in an upscale

beach style with wrought iron and granite, adorned with art prints, and decorated in a motif of natural colors. ~ 888 Country Club Drive; 310-510-0325, 800-253-9361, fax 310-510-0900; www.pacificahost.com ULTRA-DELUXE.

The romantic **Hotel St. Lauren** rises with a pink blush a block from the sand above Catalina's famed harbor. The Victorian-style hotel is a honeymoon paradise, with 42 spacious rooms and jacuzzi tubs in minisuites. ~ Metropole and Beacon streets; 310-510-2299, 800-645-2496, fax 310-510-1369; www.stlauren.com. DELUXE TO ULTRA-DELUXE.

DINING

As with Catalina hotels, there are a few points to remember when shopping for a restaurant. Prices are higher than on the mainland. With very few exceptions the dining spots are concentrated in Avalon; services around the rest of the island are minimal. Also, business is seasonal, so restaurants may vary their schedules, serving three meals daily during summer and weekends but only dinner during winter. The wisest course is to check beforehand.

Original Antonio's Deli is a hole-in-the-wall, but a hole-in-the-wall with panache. It's chockablock with junk—old pin-up pictures, record covers, dolls, and trophies. There's sawdust on the floor and a vague '50s theme to the place. The food—pizza, pasta, and hot sandwiches—is good, filling, and served daily at lunch and dinner. "Come on in," as the sign suggests, "and bask in the ambience of the decaying 1950s." ~ 114 Sumner Avenue; 310-510-0060; e-mail antonios@catalinaisp.com. BUDGET TO MODERATE.

HIDDEN ▶

The Beachcomber Café is a local gathering place located right on the beach. It's hard to match the views from the patio of this simple café. This is one place in Catalina that's open for breakfast, lunch, and dinner year-round. For lunch you can dine on vegetable platters, tacos, tostadas, salads, and sandwiches while gazing out at the pier and harbor. The dinner menu offers buffalo burgers, fried shrimp, teriyaki chicken, and steak. ~ 306-B Crescent Avenue; 310-510-1983, fax 310-510-1205. MODERATE TO DELUXE.

The other half of the vintage stucco-and-red-tile building housing the Busy Bee is the site of **Armstrong's Seafood Restaurant and Fish Market**. The interior is trimly finished in knotty pine and white tile with mounted gamefish on the walls. Since the establishment doubles as a fish market you can count on fresh seafood. The menu is the same at lunch and dinner with only the portions and prices changing. Mesquite-grilled dishes include mahimahi, scallops, swordfish, skewered shrimp, and steak. They also feature lobster, ahi, and orange roughy. You can dine indoors or on the patio right along the waterfront, making Armstrong's reasonable prices a bargain. ~ 306-A Crescent Avenue; 310-510-0113, fax 310-510-0266; www.armstrongseafood.com. MODERATE TO ULTRA-DELUXE.

No one sails to Santa Catalina Island searching for bargains. Everything here has been shipped from the mainland and is that much more expensive as a result.

Café Prego, a small Italian bistro complete with oil-cloth tables and stucco arches, comes highly recommended. The specialties are seafood and pasta; you'll find a menu offering fresh swordfish, sea bass, halibut, and snapper, plus manicotti, rigatoni, lasagna, and fettuccine. There are also steak and veal dishes at this waterfront nook. It features good food and a cozy ambience. Dinner only. ~ 609 Crescent Avenue; 310-510-1218, fax 310-510-2997; e-mail pregocafe@catalinaisp.com. MODERATE TO ULTRA-DELUXE.

For a step upscale head down the street to **Ristorante Villa Portofino**, where you'll find pink stucco walls and candlelit tables set off by flowers. With art-deco curves and colorful art prints the place has a Mediterranean feel. The Continental cuisine includes several veal dishes, scampi, grilled filet mignon, lobster, and a selection of pasta dishes. This is the place for a romantic meal. Dinner only. Closed in January. ~ 101 Crescent Avenue; 310-510-2009; www.hotelvillaportofino.com. MODERATE TO ULTRA-DELUXE.

SHOPPING

The town of Avalon has a row of shops lining its main thoroughfare, Crescent Avenue, and other stores along the streets running up from the waterfront. Within this commercial checkerboard are also several mini-malls, one of which, **Metropole Market Place**, is a nicely designed complex. ~ Crescent and Whitney avenues.

Half the stores in town are souvenir or curio shops. I'd wait 'til you return to that shopping metropolis 26 miles across the sea.

NIGHTLIFE

Like all other Catalina amenities, nightspots are concentrated in Avalon. The **Chi Chi Club** is the hottest danceclub on the island with live and deejay music (ranging from Top-40 and hip-hop to retro) and an enthusiastic crowd. Live comedy shows are offered on summer weekends. Cover on weekends. ~ 107 Sumner Avenue; 310-510-2828.

Also check the schedule for **Avalon Casino**. This fabulous vintage ballroom still hosts big bands and most of the island's major events. The Avalon also shows films at night in its restored golden-era motion picture theater. ~ Located at the end of Crescent Avenue; 310-510-2000.

BEACHES & PARKS

If you are planning to camp on Catalina, there are a few things to know. First, there is a fee for camping and reservations are a must (reservation numbers are listed under the particular park).

In addition to designated beaches, camping is permitted in many of the island's coves. These are undeveloped sites with no facilities; most are readily accessible by boat. Patrolling rangers collect the fees here.

For information on hiking permits, camping, and transportation to campgrounds, contact the **Santa Catalina Island Conservancy** (125 Claressa Avenue, Avalon; 310-510-1421; www.catalina conservancy.org), **Two Harbors Enterprises** (P.O. Box 5086, Two Harbors; 310-510-4250), or the agent at **Two Harbors Campground** (310-510-2800) who seems to know just about everything relating to camping in the area.

CRESCENT BEACH About as relaxing as Coney Island, this beach is at the center of the action. Avalon's main drag parallels the beach and a pier divides it into two separate strips of sand. Facing Avalon Harbor, the strand is flanked on one side with a ferry dock and along the other by the famous Avalon Casino. Full service facilities (including restrooms, showers, and beach rentals) are available on the street adjacent to the beach; lifeguards are also on duty. Fishing is good from the pier, and the harbor provides protection from the surf, making it an excellent swimming area. ~ Along Crescent Avenue in Avalon; 310-510-1520.

DESCANSO BEACH CLUB Somehow the appeal of this private enclave escapes me. A rock-strewn beach on the far side of the Avalon Casino, it seconds as a mooring facility for sailboats. Granted, there is a rolling lawn dotted with palm trees and the complex is nicely surrounded by hills. But with all the commotion at the snack bar and volleyball courts it's more like being on an amusement pier than a beach. Besides that, you have to pay to get onto the beach. Once there, you'll find good

Touring Catalina
sans Rental Car

When it comes time to venture further afield, you'll find that traveling around Santa Catalina Island is more complicated than it first seems. Preserving nature is probably what the island's caretakers had in mind when they made driving cars illegal on Catalina for non-residents. While golf carts are allowed in Avalon, visitors must navigate the remainder of the island's roads by two wheels, two feet, or a shuttle.

You can hike or bicycle to most places on the island, although permits are required outside Avalon. They can be obtained from the **Santa Catalina Island Conservancy**. ~ 125 Claressa Avenue; 310-510-2595; www.catalinaconservancy.org. Permits are also available at **The Airport in the Sky**. ~ 310-510-0143. You can also call **Two Harbors Visitors Services**. ~ P.O. Box 5086, Two Harbors, CA 90704; 310-510-0303.

Brown's Bikes rents bicycles, tandems, mountain bikes, and kids' bikes. Maps and helmets are included. ~ 107 Pebbly Beach Road; 310-510-0986. In Avalon proper, rent golf carts from outfits like **Island Rentals**. ~ 125 Pebbly Beach Road; 310-510-1456. You can also try **Catalina Auto Rental**, which rents golf carts as well as mountain bikes. Bike rentals include helmets. ~ 301 Crescent Avenue; 310-510-0111. There are also taxis in town.

Catalina Safari Bus provides a shuttle service to Two Harbors. ~ 310-510-2800, 800-785-8425. Santa Catalina Island Conservancy, the agency charged with overseeing the island, shuttles visitors to the airport and provides jeep tours.

swimming, a restaurant, horseshoes, Ping-Pong tables, restrooms, a playground, and showers. ~ Located off Crescent Avenue past Casino Way; 310-510-1226.

HERMIT GULCH CAMPGROUND 🚶 🚴 This grassy field, dotted with palm and pine trees, is the only campground serving the Avalon area. Located up in Avalon Canyon inland from the beach, it provides a convenient and inexpensive way to visit Avalon and utilize its many services. There are pretty views of the surrounding hills and hiking trails are nearby. Facilities include picnic areas, restrooms, and showers. ~ Located on Avalon Canyon Road a mile from downtown Avalon; 310-510-8368, fax 310-510-2698; www.scico.com/camping.

▲ There are extensive camping facilities, ranging from tent cabins to basic camping to equipment rentals. There are 43 tent sites, $12 per person per night. Reservations are recommended in July and August.

Catalina's Outback

Once out of the town of Avalon, Catalina Island is much as it was when the Gabrieleños lived here. In the Two Harbors area, sinkholes of the gold mines that flourished here in the 1860s are still evident, while the Civil War barracks, built in 1863, are now in use by the Isthmus Yacht Club. Two Harbors is also where the majority of diving and snorkeling takes place, while safari-van tours into the island's rugged interior provide spectacular cliffside views and a chance to meet the island's thriving bison population up close and personal. The island's backcountry offers great hiking on everything from goat trails to fire roads and allows the opportunity to see all sorts of wildlife, including wild boar, deer, and rattlesnakes.

SIGHTS

The most exhilarating sightseeing excursion in Avalon lies in the hills around town. Head out Pebbly Beach Road along the water, turn right on **Wrigley Terrace Road**, and you'll be on one of the many terraces that rise above Avalon. The old **Wrigley Mansion** (currently The Inn on Mt. Ada, Wrigley Road), an elegant estate with sweeping views, was once the (ho hum) summer residence of the Wrigley family.

Other scenic drives on the opposite side of town lie along Stage and Chimes Tower roads. Here you'll pass the **Zane Grey Hotel**, a 1926 pueblo adobe that was formerly the Western novel writer's home. ~ 199 Chimes Tower Road; 310-510-0966, fax 310-510-1340; www.zanegreypueblohotel.com.

Both routes snake into the hills past rocky outcroppings and patches of cactus. The slopes are steep and unrelenting. Below you blocks of houses run in rows out to a fringe of palm trees and undergrowth. Gaze around from this precarious perch and you'll see that Avalon rests in a green bowl surrounded by mountains.

Regardless of how you journey into Catalina's outback, there's only one way to get there, **Airport Road**. This paved thoroughfare climbs steadily from Avalon, offering views of the rugged coast and surrounding hills. Oak, pine, and eucalyptus dot the hillsides as the road follows a ridgetop with steep canyons falling away on either side. **Mt. Orizaba**, a flat-topped peak which represents the highest point on the island, rises in the distance.

A side road out to BlackJack Campground leads past **BlackJack Mine**, a silver mine closed since early in the century. Today little remains except tailing piles and a 520-foot shaft. Then the main road climbs to Catalina's **Airport in the Sky**, a small landing facility located at 1600-foot elevation.

From the airport you might want to follow a figure eight course in your route around the island, covering most of the island's roads and taking in as much of the landscape as possible (beyond the airport all the roads are dirt). Just follow Empire Landing Road, a curving, bumping track with side roads that lead down past an **old marble quarry** to **Ripper's Cove**. Characteristic of the many inlets dotting the island, the cove is framed by sharply rising

UNDERWATER WONDERS

Giant kelp forests, rocky reefs, wrecks, and plenty of marine life make scuba diving in Catalina extremely appealing. Plus, the water is much clearer here than off the mainland, and excellent diving locations are within walking distance of the shoreline. The easiest-to-reach dive spots are on the lee side of the island, where currents are gentler. Divers can expect to encounter horn sharks, moray eels, octopi, and calico bass—and may even experience the thrill of having a seal or sea lion as a diving partner. Fans of wreck diving will find a 163-foot yacht and a 70-foot schooner off Casino Point Marine Dive Park.

hills. There's a boulder-and-sand beach here and a coastline bordered by interesting rock formations.

Two Harbors, at the intersection of the figure-eight's loops, is a half-mile wide isthmus connecting the two sections of Catalina Island. A small fishing pier, several tourist facilities, and a boat harbor make this modest enclave the only developed area outside Avalon.

From here **West End Road** curves and climbs, bends and descends along a rocky coast pocked with cactus and covered by scrub growth. There are Catalina cherry trees along the route and numerous coves at the bottom of steep cliffs. Not for the faint-hearted, West End Road is a narrow, bumpy course that winds high above the shore.

Anchored off **Emerald Bay** are several rock islets crowded with sea birds. From **Parson's Landing**, a small inlet with a brown-gray sand beach, dirt roads continue in a long loop out to the west end of the island, then back to Two Harbors.

Catalina possesses about 400 species of flora, some unique to the island, and is rich in wildlife. Anywhere along its slopes you are likely to spy quail, wild turkey, mountain goats, island fox, mule deer, and wild boar. Bison, placed on the island by a movie company filming a Western way back in the 1920s, graze seemingly everywhere. En route back toward Avalon, Little Harbor Road climbs into the mountains. From the hilltops around **Little Harbor** you can see a series of ridges that drop along sheer rockfaces to the frothing surf below.

Take a detour up to **Rancho Escondido**, a working ranch that boards champion Arabian horses. There's an arena here where

AUTHOR FAVORITE

Banning House Lodge, is an early-20th-century hunting lodge. Set in the isthmus that connects the two sections of Santa Catalina, it's a low-slung shingle building with a dining room and a mountain-lodge atmosphere. The living room boasts a brick fireplace. The guest rooms are trimly and individually decorated with throw rugs and wood furniture. The lodge provides an excellent opportunity to experience the island's outback. Continental breakfast is served in the lodge's breakfast room. ~ Two Harbors; 310-510-4228, fax 310-510-1303; www.scico.com. DELUXE TO ULTRA-DELUXE.

trainers work these exquisite animals through their paces, and a "saddle and trophy room" filled with handcrafted riding gear as well as prizes from major horse shows.

Back at Little Harbor, Middle Ranch Road cuts through a mountain canyon past **Middle Ranch**, a small spread with livestock and oat fields. En route lies **Eagles' Nest Lodge,** a stagecoach stop dating to 1890. Numbered among the antique effects of this simple woodframe house are wagon wheels and a split-rail fence. Carry on to Airport Road then back to Avalon, completing this easy-eight route around an extraordinary island.

LODGING

Rare and incredible is the only way to describe **The Inn on Mt. Ada.** Nothing on the island, and few places along the California coast, compare. Perched on a hillside overlooking Avalon and its emerald shoreline, this stately hostelry resides in the old Wrigley mansion, a 7000-square-foot Georgian Colonial home built by the chewing gum baron in 1921. A masterwork of French doors and elegant columns, curved ceilings, and ornamental molding, the grande dame is beautifully appointed with antiques and plush furnishings. The entire ground floor—with rattan-furnished sitting room, oceanfront veranda, formal dining room, and spacious living room—is for the benefit of visitors. Wine and hors d'oeuvres are served in the evening and there's a full breakfast and lunch served to guests and a limited number of visitors. The wonder of the place is that all this luxury is for just six guest rooms, two of which have semiprivate terraces, guaranteeing personal service and an atmosphere of intimacy. The private rooms are stylishly furnished in period pieces and adorned with a creative selection of artwork. The room fee includes a golf cart for transportation. Reserve at least two months in advance. Closed Christmas eve and Christmas day. ~ 398 Wrigley Road, P.O. Box 2560, Avalon, CA 90704; 310-510-2030, 800-608-7669, fax 310-510-2237; www.catalina.com/mtada. ULTRA-DELUXE.

DINING

Buffalo Springs Station, situated up in the mountains at 1600 feet, is part of Catalina's Airport in the Sky complex. This facility serves egg dishes, hot cakes, buffalo burgers, and a variety of sandwiches. There's not much to the self-service restaurant itself, but it adjoins a lobby with stone fireplace and a tile patio that overlooks the surrounding mountains. Breakfast, lunch, and early dinner are served. ~ 310-510-2196, fax 310-510-2140. BUDGET.

HIDDEN ►   Catalina's remotest dining place is the **Harbor Reef Restaurant,** located way out in the Two Harbors area. This rambling establishment has a dining room done in nautical motif with fish nets and shell lamps. There's also an adjoining patio for enjoying the soft breezes that blow through this isthmus area. Fresh seafood and fresh fish are to be expected, of course, as are steak and pasta dishes. Reservations are recommended. ~ Two Harbors; 310-510-4235, fax 310-510-8690. MODERATE TO ULTRA-DELUXE.

Next to the Harbor Reef Restaurant there's an adjoining **snack bar** serving three meals daily; breakfast and lunch in winter months. It offers egg dishes, sandwiches, burgers, pizza, and burritos. ~ Two Harbors. BUDGET.

BEACHES & PARKS   **BLACKJACK CAMPGROUND** 🏃 🚲 Situated at 1600 feet elevation, this facility sits on a plateau below Mt. BlackJack, the island's second-highest peak. It's a lovely spot shaded by pine and

HIDDEN ►   eucalyptus trees and affording views across the rolling hills and out along the ocean. Among backcountry facilities this is about the least popular on the island. The campground has picnic areas, toilets, and showers. ~ Located south of The Airport in the Sky off Airport Road. Seasonal shuttle available from Avalon to BlackJack Trail Junction; 310-510-2800, fax 310-510-7254; www.scico.com/camping.

▲ There is a hike-in campground with 10 sites; $12 per person per night. Reservations are required.

BEN WESTON BEACH 🏃 ⛵ 🏊 〰️ A favorite among locals, this pewter-colored beach is surrounded by rocky hills. Located at the end of a long canyon road, it is serene and secluded. Avalon residents come here to flee the tourists, so you might consider making it your hideaway. This is a day-use beach only. Fishing

---

CIRCLE OF SEASONS

One thing to remember about Catalina is that perhaps more than any other spot along the California coast, its tourism is seasonal. The season, of course, is summer, when mobs of people descend on the island. During the winter months everything slows down, storms wash through intermittently, and some facilities close. Spring and fall, when the crowds have subsided, the weather is good, and everything is still open, may be the best seasons of all.

and swimming are good, and it is one of the island's best spots for surfing. Facilities are limited to toilets. ~ Located about two miles south of Little Harbor off Middle Ranch Road.

LITTLE HARBOR CAMPGROUND 🏊 🎣 🚣 ⛱ On the southwest shore of the island, this camp sits near a sandy beach between rocky headlands. It's studded with palm trees and occasionally filled with grazing bison, making it one of the island's prettiest facilities. In addition, Shark Harbor, a section of Little Harbor, is excellent for shell collecting and bodysurfing. Fishing, swimming, and skindiving are good here; facilities include picnic areas, toilets, and cold showers. ~ Located about seven miles east of Two Harbors along Little Harbor Road; 310-510-2800, fax 310-510-7254; www.scico.com/camping.

▲ The campground has a 150-person maximum (tents only); $12 per person per night.

TWO HARBORS CAMPGROUND 🥾 🚴 🏊 🎣 🚣 ⛱ Set along a series of terraces above a brown sand beach, this facility is adjacent to the services at Two Harbors. It's also a convenient base camp from which to hike out along the island's west end. Facilities include picnic areas, restrooms, and showers. The fishing and swimming are good, and the colorful waters here make skindiving especially rewarding. ~ Located next to Two Harbors in Little Fisherman's Cove; 310-510-2800, fax 310-510-7254; www. scico.com.

▲ The facilities here are extensive and include 45 tent sites and 13 tent cabins with added amenities, a 24-hour-a-day ranger, and more. Prices vary; call for information.

PARSON'S LANDING 🥾 🚴 🏊 🎣 ⛱ The most remote of Catalina's campgrounds, this isolated facility sits along a small brown-gray sand beach with grass-covered hills in the background. Fishing, swimming, and skindiving are all good; facilities include picnic areas and toilets. The beach is ideal for shell combing, amethyst and beach glass. ~ Located seven miles west of Two Harbors along West End Road; 310-510-2800, fax 310-510-7254; www.scico.com.

▲ The campground holds a maximum of 45 people; there are 8 tent-only sites; $12 per person per night, plus $9 the first night.

EIGHT

South Bay Beaches

While Westside beaches cater to ridiculously rich movie stars, liberals, artists, and the outrageous, the South Bay beaches are the bastion of wealthy suburbanites, conservatives, surfers, and the moderate middle class. There's a strong blue-collar presence here, particularly in San Pedro and Long Beach, and the general feeling is more Middle America than La-La-Land. Despite being the less flashy L.A. beach area, the south coast towns that stretch from Manhattan Beach to Long Beach still have plenty of variety. The economy depends mainly on commercial shipping and tourism, while residents include millionaires, immigrant fishermen and surfers.

The South Bay beaches of Manhattan, Hermosa, and Redondo are home of the quintessential Southland beach culture. This is the surfing center of the Los Angeles coastal region: think sun, sand, and Beach Boys songs. Like most of the coastal communities, the South Bay didn't take off as a beach resort until the turn of the 20th century, after railroad lines were extended from the city center to the shore, several decades after downtown Los Angeles experienced its 1880s population boom. Today this strip of coast is home to Los Angeles International Airport.

Travel south and blond-haired surfers give way to wealthy suburbanites. The Palos Verdes Peninsula is an expensive and pristine slice of suburbia where lawn sculptures are replaced by grazing thoroughbreds. Rambling million-dollar houses sit on expansive lots, and residents take advantage of the area's natural beauty on bridle paths, golf courses, tennis courts, and nature preserves. One of Los Angeles' prettiest seascapes, the Palos Verdes Peninsula is a region of striking geologic contrasts, where a series of 13 marine terraces, interrupted by sheer cliffs, descend to a rocky shoreline. For 15 miles the roadway rides high above the surf past tidepools, rocky points, a lighthouse, and secluded coves.

Travel farther south and you encounter San Pedro and Long Beach, industrial enclaves that form the port of Los Angeles, a world center for commerce and shipping. Embodying 35 miles of heavily developed waterfront, the port is a maze of inlets, islets, and channels protected by a six-mile breakwater. It is one of the world's largest manmade harbors; over $79 billion in cargo crosses its docks every year. Despite all this hubbub, the harbor supports over 125 fish species and over 90 types of birds, including several endangered species.

The great port dates to 1835, when a small landing was built on the shore. Following the Civil War, an imaginative entrepreneur named Phineas Banning developed the area, brought in the railroad, and launched Los Angeles into the 20th century. Originally an amusement center complete with airship, carousel, and sword swallowers, Long Beach became one big oil field during the 1920s. That's when wildcat wells struck rich deposits and the region was transformed into a two-square-mile maze of derricks. Even today the offshore "islands" hide hundreds of oil wells.

In addition to being a major port and manufacturing center, Long Beach is the site of a naval base and a revitalized tourist center, home to the retired ocean liner *Queen Mary* and the Aquarium of the Pacific. It also contains the neighborhood of Naples, a system of islands, canals, and footbridges reminiscent of Italy's gondola cities.

Commercial fishing, another vital industry in Long Beach and San Pedro, supports an international collection of sailors. Mariners from Portugal, Greece, and elsewhere work the waterfront and add to the ethnic ambiance.

Manhattan/Hermosa/Redondo Beaches

The birthplace of California's beach culture lies in a string of towns on the southern skirt of Santa Monica Bay—Manhattan Beach, Hermosa Beach, and Redondo Beach. It all began here in the South Bay with George Freeth, "the man who can walk on water." It seems that while growing up in Hawaii, Freeth resurrected the ancient Polynesian sport of surfing and transplanted it to California. Equipped with a 200-pound, solid wood board, he introduced surfing to fascinated onlookers at a 1907 event in Redondo Beach.

It wasn't until the 1950s that the surfing wave crested. The surrounding towns became synonymous with the sport and a new culture was born, symbolized by blond-haired, blue-eyed surfers committed to sun, sand, and the personal freedom to ride the last wave. By the 1960s, a group of local kids called The Beach Boys were recording classic beach songs.

Manhattan Beach is the most pristine and yuppified town, with million-dollar houses resting along the Strand and upscale restaurants and boutiques lining the commercial area. Hermosa Beach is the most easy-going of the group with casual, sometimes funky restaurants and bars that cater to the beach set. Redondo Beach, the most industrial of the three towns, has the biggest pier area and specializes in sportfishing trips. Sightseeing spots are rather scarce in these beach towns. Basically, this is the place for surfing, sunning, swimming, and soaking up the laidback atmosphere.

SIGHTS   The **Manhattan Beach Pier**, which extends extends 900 feet from the beach, is the site of the **Roundhouse Marine Studies Lab and Aquarium**, a community marine science center full of local sea creatures. A mini-reef tank, shark tank, and touch tank make this a great place to take kids. ~ At the west end of Manhattan Beach Boulevard, Manhattan Beach; 310-379-8117, fax 310-937-9366; www.roundhousemb.com.

From here, you can saunter along **The Strand**. This pedestrian thoroughfare borders a broad beach and passes an endless row of bungalows, cottages, and condominiums. It's a pleasant walk, with shops and restaurants once you cross into Hermosa Beach.

At Hermosa's **Municipal Pier** waves wash against the pilings. Beneath the wood plank walkway, sea birds dive for fish. These sights and sounds are repeated again and again on the countless piers that line the California coast. Less grandiose than the pier farther south in Redondo Beach, this 1320-foot concrete corridor is simply equipped with a snack bar and bait shop. From the end you'll have a sweeping view back along Hermosa Beach's low skyline. ~ Located at the foot of Pier Avenue, Hermosa Beach.

In Redondo Beach, **Fisherman's Wharf** is home to surfcasters and hungry seagulls. Walk out past the shops, salt breeze in your face, and you can gaze along the waterfront to open ocean.

The other sightseeing diversion in these parts is the stroll. The stroll, that is, along the beach. **Esplanade** in Redondo Beach is a wide boulevard paralleling the waterfront. Wander its length and take in the surfers, sunbathers, and swimmers who keep this resort town on the map. Or walk down to the waterline and let the cool Pacific bathe your feet.

Wide and wonderful, the beach is lined by beautiful homes with plate-glass windows that reflect the blue hues of sea and sky. Together, these oceanfront walkways link the South Bay towns in a course that bicyclists can follow for miles.

The **Sea View Inn at the Beach** is a compound of five buildings a block up from the beach. Accommodations range from single and double rooms to suites to apartment-style units with kitchens. You'll find comfortable furniture, refrigerators, microwaves, and air conditioning in every room; many have ocean views and balconies. In addition, it is close to the surf and lodging is rare in

LODGING

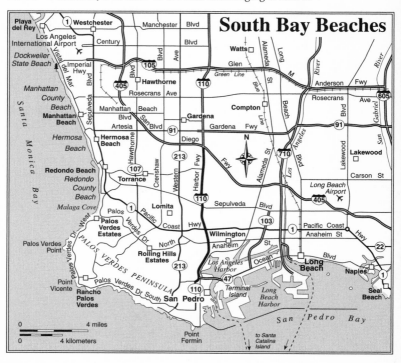

South Bay Beaches

these parts. The inn offers complimentary bikes, boogie boards, towels and beach umbrellas and chairs. ~ 3400 Highland Avenue, Manhattan Beach; 310-545-1504, fax 310-545-4052; www. seaview-inn.com, e-mail info@seaview-inn.com. MODERATE TO ULTRA-DELUXE.

At the **Hi View Motel**, you're only a step away from the beach, shopping malls, and restaurants. There are 21 standard guest rooms and 4 studio apartments (these are ultra-deluxe in price and rent by the week) for rent. ~ 100 South Sepulveda Boulevard, Manhattan Beach; 310-374-4608, fax 310-937-9542; e-mail reservations@hiviewmotel.com. BUDGET TO MODERATE.

The best bargain on lodging in South Bay is found at **Sea Sprite Motel & Apartments**. Located right on Hermosa Beach, this multibuilding complex offers oceanview rooms with kitchenettes at moderate to deluxe prices. The accommodations are tidy, well furnished, and fairly attractive. There is a swimming pool and sundeck overlooking the beach. The central shopping district is just two blocks away, making the location hard to match. You can also rent suites at deluxe prices or a two-bedroom beach cottage at an ultra-deluxe price. Be sure to ask for an oceanview room in one of the beachfront buildings. ~ 1016 The Strand, Hermosa Beach; 310-376-6933, fax 310-376-4107; www.seaspritemotel.com, e-mail questions@seaspritemotel.com. MODERATE TO ULTRA-DELUXE.

One of the few Southern California beach hotels that is actually on the beach, the **Beach House at Hermosa** is a beautifully appointed, elegant three-story affair that offers 96 loft suites complete with fireplace, CD player, television, and continental breakfast. ~ 1300 The Strand, Hermosa Beach; 310-374-3001, 888-895-4559, fax 310-372-2115; www.beach-house.com, e-mail tw@beach-house.com. DELUXE TO ULTRA-DELUXE.

The Portofino Hotel and Yacht Club is a big, brassy hotel set on King Harbor. The 163 units are decorated in contemporary fashion and look out either on the ocean or the adjoining marina. There is a decorous lobby as well as a waterside swimming pool and a restaurant; other facilities are nearby in the marina. ~ 260 Portofino Way, Redondo Beach; 310-379-8481, 800-468-4292, fax 310-372-7329; www.hotelportofino.com, e-mail reservations@theportofino.net. ULTRA-DELUXE.

Route 1 barrels through Los Angeles' beach towns and serves as the commercial strip for generic motels. As elsewhere, these facilities are characterized by clean, sterile rooms and comfortable, if unimaginative surroundings.

The Ramada Ltd. features 40 rooms with refrigerators, microwaves, and TVs. Some of the rooms have jacuzzis. This establishment rests two blocks from the beach. Continental breakfast is included. ~ 435 South Pacific Coast Highway, Redondo Beach; 310-540-5998, fax 310-543-9828. BUDGET TO DELUXE.

Located within walking distance of the beach, the **Starlite Motel** offers 20 standard, motel-style units. ~ 716 South Pacific Coast Highway, Redondo Beach; 310-316-4314. BUDGET TO MODERATE.

DINING

Café Pierre is an excellent choice for adventurous gourmets. Black chairs and cherry wood furnishings create a contemporary but warm atmosphere. You can feast on flamed filet mignon Roquefort, striped bass filet niçoise, and homemade pasta. Daily specials may include stuffed swordfish or venison. No lunch on Saturday and Sunday. ~ 317 Manhattan Beach Boulevard, Manhattan Beach; 310-545-5252, fax 310-546-6072; www.cafe pierre.com. MODERATE TO DELUXE.

No restaurants line the Strand in Manhattan Beach, so you'll have to make do with the pier's snack shop or hike up the hill into town, where you'll find **Mama D's Original Italian Kitchen** just around the corner. It has the feel of a genuine neighborhood eatery. There's usually a wait for supper, but the occasional tray of warm garlic bread, fresh from the oven, passed among the prospective diners reminds you why you're in line. Entrées include

FRESH FROM THE SEA

Fish lovers will find the freshest catches at the seafood markets on the southern end of Redondo Beach's horseshoe-shaped pier. Tanks are filled with live shellfish, while halibut, red snapper, and other fish are delivered direct from local boats. For those who want to picnic on the spot, live crabs are steamed to order in giant cauldrons and served with a side of drawn butter and a wooden mallet for cracking; cement tables spread with clean newspaper make cracking a snap. Adjacent food stands sell beer and soft drinks, as well as other types of fast food.

homemade ravioli, lasagna with *diablo* sauce, and *cioppino* with linguine. The thin New York–style pizza is a perennial favorite. ~ 1125-A Manhattan Avenue, Manhattan Beach; 310-546-1492. BUDGET TO MODERATE.

HIDDEN ►

There is excellent thin-crust pizza at **Pedone's**. Popular with the beach crowd, it's a good spot for a quick meal in a convenient locale. ~ 1332 Hermosa Avenue, Hermosa Beach; 310-376-0949. BUDGET TO MODERATE.

In addition to serving good Asian food, **Thai Thani** is an extremely attractive restaurant. Black trim and pastel shades set off the blond wood furniture and etched glass. There are fresh flowers all around plus a few well-placed wall prints. The lunch and dinner selections include dozens of pork, beef, vegetable, poultry, and seafood dishes. Unusual choices like spicy shrimp coconut soup, whole pompano smothered in pork, and whole baby hen make this a dining adventure. No lunch on the weekend. ~ 1109 South Pacific Coast Highway, Redondo Beach; 310-316-1580, fax 310-316-0812. BUDGET TO MODERATE.

A wider than usual selection of healthy dishes—not to mention the surfboard decor—sets the **GoodStuff Restaurant** at the entrance to Riviera Village apart from other restaurants in the area (there are also branches in Manhattan Beach and Hermosa Beach). The menu features a full range of meat, fish, and vegan entrées, salads, and sandwiches. There's even heart-healthy options for the not *quite* vegetarian such as ground turkey enchiladas. ~ 1617 Pacific Coast Highway, Redondo Beach; 310-316-0262, fax 310-316-3182; www.eatgoodstuff.com. BUDGET TO MODERATE.

The capital of "in" dining around the South Bay is **Chez Melange**. As the name suggests, and as current trends demand,

AUTHOR FAVORITE

The Comedy & Magic Club features name acts nightly. Many of the comedians are television personalities with a regional, if not national, following. Jay Leno, for instance, frequently tests his new "Tonight Show" material on the club's Sunday-night crowd. The supper club atmosphere is upscale and appealing. There's a showroom that features star memorabilia. Reservations are required. Closed Monday. Cover. ~ 1018 Hermosa Avenue, Hermosa Beach; 310-372-1193, fax 310-379-2806; www.comedymagicclub.com.

the cuisine is eclectic, thanks to its on-site cooking school. You'll find a hip crowd ordering everything from caviar to sushi to Cajun meatloaf. ~ 1716 Pacific Coast Highway, Redondo Beach; 310-540-1222, fax 310-316-9283; www.chezmelange.com, e-mail melangeinc@aol.com. MODERATE TO ULTRA-DELUXE.

In downtown Redondo Beach, just a couple blocks from the water, are several small restaurants serving a diversity of cuisines.

Petit Casino, a French bakery, serves quiche, soups, salads, and sandwiches (including the French standard, *croque monsieur*). ~ 1767 South Elena Avenue, Redondo Beach; 310-543-5585. BUDGET.

A family-run, longtime Redondo Beach favorite, **Captain Kidd's Fish Market and Restaurant** has live crabs and lobsters, fresh shrimp and clams, and at least 18 kinds of fresh fish. Pick what you want and they'll cook it to order, whether charbroiled, panfried, deep-fried, or simmered into a chowder, gumbo, jambalaya, or Italian-style cioppino stew. There's indoor and outdoor seating at the harbor's edge. ~ 209 North Harbor Drive, Redondo Beach; 310-372-7703, fax 310-379-1531; www.captain kidds.com, e-mail rmatey1@captainkidds.com. BUDGET TO MODERATE.

SHOPPING

If they weren't famous Pacific beach communities, the South Bay enclaves of Manhattan, Hermosa, and Redondo beaches would seem like small-town America. Their central shopping districts are filled with pharmacies, supply shops, and shoe stores. There are a few places of interest to folks from out of town.

In Manhattan Beach, Manhattan Beach Boulevard is traversed by Highland and Manhattan avenues.

Shops in Hermosa Beach concentrate along Pier and Hermosa avenues, especially where they intersect.

In Redondo Beach, scout out Catalina Avenue, particularly along its southern stretches.

NIGHTLIFE

Locals bemoan the passing of Manhattan Beach's funky old La Paz Bar, a victim of urban gentrification that was recently turned into a parking lot. Since then, the surfer and beach-bum crowd from the La Paz has gravitated to the **Shellback Tavern** to carry on the endless beach party with tacos and burgers, loud music, cheap beer, and elbow-to-elbow tanned bodies. ~ 116 Manhattan Beach Boulevard, Manhattan Beach; 310-376-7857.

◄ HIDDEN

The Lighthouse Café spotlights blues, reggae, rock-and-roll, and funk bands; the different styles draw vastly different crowds. Cover on Friday and Saturday. ~ 30 Pier Avenue, Hermosa Beach; 310-372-6911; www.thelighthousecafe.net.

BEACHES & PARKS

MANHATTAN COUNTY BEACH 🚴 🛶 🏃 🏊 ⛵ Back in those halcyon days when their first songs were climbing the charts, the Beach Boys were regular fixtures at this silvery strand. They came to swim and check out the scene along The Strand, the walkway that extends the length of Manhattan Beach. What can you say, the gentlemen had good taste—the surfing here is some of the best in Southern California; the prime spot hereabouts is perhaps El Porto, located at the northern end of the beach. This sand corridor is wide as a desert, fronted by an aquamarine ocean and backed by the beautiful homes of the very lucky. If that's not enough, there's a fishing pier and an adjacent commercial area door-to-door with excellent restaurants. The swimming here is good, and the surfing is tops. Other facilities include restrooms, lifeguards, and volleyball courts. ~ At the foot of Manhattan Beach Boulevard, Manhattan Beach; 310-372-2166, fax 310-372-6902.

Surfers pay homage to the original surfer dude, Hawaiian George Freeth, by draping colorful leis around his statue at Redondo Beach Pier.

HERMOSA BEACH 🚴 🛶 🏃 ⛵ One of the great beaches of Southern California, this is a very, very wide (and very, very white) sand beach extending the entire length of Hermosa Beach. Two miles of pearly sand are only part of the attraction. There's also The Strand, a pedestrian lane that runs the length of the beach; Pier Avenue, an adjacent street lined with interesting shops; a quarter-mile fishing pier; and a local community known for its artistic creativity. Personally, if I were headed to the beach, I would head in this direction. The swimming is good and the surfing is very good around the pier and all along the beach. Lifeguards are on duty, and facilities include restrooms, volleyball courts, and a playground. Parking fee, $5. ~ At the foot of Pier Avenue, Hermosa Beach; 310-372-2166, fax 310-372-6902; www.watchwater.com.

REDONDO BEACH 🚴 🛶 🏃 🏊 ⛵ Surfers know this strand and so should you. Together with neighboring Hermosa and Manhattan beaches, it symbolizes the Southern California beach scene. You'll find a long strip of white sand bordered by a hillside carpeted with ice plants. In addition to surfers, the area is populated by bicyclists and joggers, while anglers cast from the nearby piers. Not surprisingly, fishing is particularly good from nearby Fisherman's Wharf. The swimming at Redondo is good, and surfing is even better. Facilities include restrooms, lifeguards, and volleyball courts. ~ Along the Esplanade, Redondo Beach; 310-372-2166, fax 310-372-6902.

Palos Verdes Peninsula

Though Portuguese explorer Juan Cabrillo first described the area in 1542, the peninsula was home to the Gabrieleño Indians until 1827, when Don Dolores Sepulveda received 75,000 acres in an original land grant. By 1913, a consortium of New York investors owned most of the property, which it planned to divide into large estates. However, the first homes didn't start appearing here until the mid-20th century. Today it is an upscale residential neighborhood overlooking one of Southern California's loveliest stretches of coastline. Residents embrace an active lifestyle: Equestrian and hiking trails wind through lovely tree-shaded areas past pristine homes on large lots, and golfers try their luck on Los Angeles' only oceanfront golf course.

SIGHTS

The forces of nature seem to dominate as you proceed out along the Palos Verdes Peninsula from San Pedro. Follow 25th Street, then Palos Verdes Drive South and encounter a tumbling region where terraced hills fall away to sharp coastal bluffs.

As you turn **Portuguese Bend**, the geology of this tumultuous area becomes startlingly evident when the road begins undulating through landslide zones. The earthquake faults that underlie the Los Angeles basin periodically fold and collapse the ground here. To one side you'll see the old road, fractured and useless. Even the present highway, with more patches than your favorite dungarees, is in a state of constant repair.

Of course the terrible power of nature has not dissuaded people from building here. Along the ridgetops and curving hills below are colonies of stately homes. With its rocky headlands, tidepool beaches and sun-spangled views, the place is simply so magnificent no one can resist.

Most lordly of all these structures is the **Wayfarers Chapel,** a simple but extraordinary center designed by the son of Frank Lloyd Wright. Nestled neatly into the surrounding landscape, the sunlit chapel is built entirely of glass and commands broad views of the terrain and ocean. With its stone altar and easy repose the chapel was built to honor Emanuel Swedenborg, the 18th-century Swedish philosopher and mystic. A visitors center designed by Wrights's son, Eric Lloyd Wright, also graces the grounds. ~ 5755 Palos Verdes Drive South, Rancho Palos Verdes; 310-377-1650, fax 310-377-8589; www.wayfarers chapel.org, e-mail harveyt@wayfarerschapel.org.

> Malaga Cove is nicknamed "RAT" beach because it's "right after Torrance."

The **Point Vicente Lighthouse** rises farther down the coast, casting an antique aura upon the area. While the beacon is not open to the public, the nearby **Point Vicente Interpretive Center** offers a small regional museum. This is a prime whale-watching spot in the winter when onlookers gather in the adjacent park to catch glimpses of migrating gray whales. (At press time, the center was closed for soil remediation work and construction; call ahead for reopening information.) Admission. ~ 31501 Palos Verdes Drive West, Rancho Palos Verdes; 310-377-5370, fax 310-544-5294; www.palosverdes.com/rpv.

HIDDEN ▶

For a vision of how truly beautiful this region is, turn off Palos Verdes Drive West in Palos Verdes Estates and follow Paseo Lunado until it meets the sea at **Lunada Bay.** This half-moon inlet, backdropped by the jagged face of a rocky cliff, looks out upon an unending expanse of ocean. Steep paths lead down to a rocky shoreline rich in tidepools.

The road changes names to Paseo del Mar but continues past equally extraordinary coastline. There is a series of open fields and vista points along this shoreline preserve where you can gaze down from the blufftop to beaches and tidepools. Below, surfers ride the curl of frothing breaks and a few hardy hikers pick their way goat-like along precipitous slopes.

The setting is decidedly more demure at the **South Coast Botanic Garden.** This 87-acre garden is planted with exotic vegetation from Africa and New Zealand as well as species from other parts of the world. Admission. ~ 26300 South Crenshaw Boulevard, Palos Verdes; 310-544-6815, fax 310-544-6820; www. southcoastbotanicgarden.org.

Restaurants are a rare commodity along the Palos Verdes Peninsula. You'll find a cluster of them, however, in the Golden Cove Shopping Center. Granted, a mall is not the most appetizing spot to dine, but in this case who's complaining?

The Admiral Risty is one of those nautical cliché restaurants decorated along the outside with ropes and pilings and on the interior with brass fixtures. Know the type? Normally I wouldn't mention it, but the place has a full bar, a knockout view of the ocean, and happens to be the only member of its species in the entire area. My advice is to play it safe and order fresh fish (or never leave the bar). The menu is a surf-and-turf inventory of fish (prepared four ways), steak, chicken, and so on. Dinner and Sunday brunch. ~ 31250 Palos Verdes Drive West, Rancho Palos Verdes; 310-377-0050; www.admiral-risty.com, e-mail wayne@admiral-risty.com. DELUXE TO ULTRA-DELUXE.

For genuine elegance, make lunch or dinner reservations at **La Rive Gauche**, an attractively appointed French restaurant. With its upholstered chairs, brass wall sconces, and vintage

Palos Verdes Peninsula

travel posters, this cozy candlelit dining room is unique to the peninsula. The three-course dinner menu is a study in classic French cooking including veal chop with *foie gras* and truffles, duck à l'orange, and a selection of fresh seafood like Norway salmon and John Dory. A pianist adds to the romance. The lunch offerings, while more modest, follow a similar theme. In sum, gourmet cuisine, warm ambience, and a world-class wine list. No lunch on Monday. ~ 320 Tejon Place, Palos Verdes Estates; 310-378-0267, 888-646-8166, fax 310-373-5837. MODERATE TO ULTRA-DELUXE

BEACHES & PARKS

ABALONE COVE SHORELINE PARK The Palos Verdes Peninsula is so rugged and inaccessible that any beach by definition will be secluded. This gray-sand hideaway is no exception. It sits in a natural amphitheater guarded by sedimentary rock formations and looks out on Catalina Island. There are tidepools to ponder and a marine ecological reserve to explore, and the fishing and swimming are good. For surfing, try the east end of the cove. There are also picnic areas, restrooms, and lifeguards on weekends, holidays, and in summer. Parking fee, $5. ~ Off Palos Verdes Drive South in Rancho Palos Verdes. From the parking lot a path leads down to the beach; 310-377-1222.

TORRANCE BEACH This beach is a lengthy stretch of bleach-blond sand guarded on one flank by the stately Palos Verdes Peninsula and on the other by an industrial complex and colony of smokestacks. Just your average middle-class beach; it's not one of my favorites, but it has the only white sand hereabouts. Also consider adjacent **Malaga Cove**, noted for tidepools, shells, and rock-hounding. Prettier than its pedestrian partner, Malaga Cove is framed by rocky bluffs. At Torrance there are restrooms, some concession stands, and lifeguards; around Malaga Cove you're on your own. Fishing for corbina is good at both beaches, and surfing is generally good (but better in winter) at Malaga Cove with steady, rolling waves ideal for beginners. For swimming I recommend Torrance, where lifeguards are on duty year-round. Parking fee, $5. ~ Paseo de la Playa in Torrance parallels the beach. To reach Malaga Cove, walk south from Torrance toward the cliffs; 310-372-2166, fax 310-372-6902.

Overlooking the busy Port of Los Angeles, one of the
largest deep-water ports in the nation, San Pedro lies at
the eastern end of the rocky Palos Verdes Peninsula. In
1542, Portuguese explorer Juan Cabrillo named it "Bay of
Smokes," inspired by the hillside fires of the Gabrieleño Indians;
San Pedro was given its current name by Spanish navigator
Sebastian Vizcaino in 1602. The city began to develop its reputation as a major port in the mid-19th century, when the railroad
came to town. Almost 100 years later, during World War II, Fort
MacArthur was built on the bluff to protect the bustling harbor
from invasion. Now the fort houses a small museum and a youth
hostel, and all manner of boats—from tankers to fishing vessels
to cruise ships—steam in and out of the bay in peace.

San Pedro

The Los Angeles Harbor, a region of creosote and rust, is marked
by 28 miles of busy waterfront. This landscape of oil tanks and
cargo containers services thousands of ships every year.

SIGHTS

Head over to the **22nd Street Landing** and watch sportfishing
boats embark on high-sea adventures. Then wander the waterfront and survey this frontier of steel and oil. Here awkward,
unattractive ships glide as gracefully as figure skaters and the
machinery of civilization goes about the world's work with a
clatter and boom. The most common shorebirds are cargo cranes.
~ At the foot of 22nd Street.

◀ HIDDEN

Ports O' Call Village, a shopping mall in the form of a 19th-
century port town, is home to several outfits conducting harbor
cruises. ~ The entrance is at the foot of 6th
Street; 310-732-7696. The boats sail around the
San Pedro waterfront and venture out for glimpses
of the surrounding shoreline; for information, call
Spirit Cruises. ~ Ports O' Call Village; 310-548-8080;
www.spiritdinnercruises.com.

San Pedro is a departure
point for the Catalina
Express Shuttleboats
to Santa Catalina
Island. ~ 800-897-
7154.

Moored serenely between two bustling docks is the
S.S. Lane Victory. This World War II cargo ship, a 455-foot-long
National Historic Landmark, offers weekend cruises from mid-
July to mid-September as well as daily tours. Admission. ~ Berth
94; 310-519-9545, fax 310-519-0265; www.lanevictoryship.com.

For more of our history on the sea, stop by the **Los Angeles
Maritime Museum**. This dockside showplace displays models

of ships ranging from fully rigged brigs to 19th-century steam schooners to World War II battleships. Exhibits include a comprehensive display on the history of commercial (hard-hat) diving in Los Angeles Habor. Closed Monday. ~ Berth 84; 310-548-7618, fax 310-832-6537; www.lamaritimemuseum.org, e-mail museum@lamaritimemuseum.org.

HIDDEN ► Another piece in the port's historic puzzle is placed several miles inland at the **Phineas Banning Residence Museum**. This imposing Greek Revival house, built in 1864, was home to the man who dreamed, dredged, and developed Los Angeles Harbor. Today Phineas Banning's Mansion, complete with a cupola from which he watched ships navigate his port, is furnished in period pieces and open for guided tours. Closed Monday and Friday. ~ 401 East M Street, Wilmington; 310-548-7777; www.banningmuseum.org.

By definition any shipping center is of strategic importance. Head up to **Fort MacArthur** and discover the gun batteries with which World War II generals planned to protect Los Angeles Harbor. From this cement-and-steel compound you can inspect the bunkers and a small military museum, then survey the coast. Once a site of gun turrets and grisly prospects, today it is a testimonial to the invasion that never came. ~ Angel's Gate Park, 3601 South Gaffey Street; 310-548-2631; www.ftmac.org, e-mail director@ftmac.org.

Nearby, you can visit the **Bell of Friendship**, which the people of South Korea presented to the United States during its 1976 bicentennial. Housed in a multicolor pagoda and cast with floral and symbolic images, it rests on a hilltop looking out on Los Angeles Harbor and the region's sharply profiled coastline.

Down the hill at the **Cabrillo Marine Aquarium**, there is a modest collection of display cases with samples of shells, coral, and shorebirds. Several dozen aquariums exhibit local fish and marine plants, and there's a large outdoor touch tank. Closed Monday. ~ 3720 Stephen M. White Drive; 310-548-7562, fax 310-548-2649; www.cabrilloaq.org, e-mail info@cabrilloaq.org.

Nearby, 1200-foot **Cabrillo Fishing Pier** stretches into the Pacific from Cabrillo Beach, where on a clear day you can see Santa Catalina.

Of greater interest is **Point Fermin Park**, a 37-acre blufftop facility resting above spectacular tidepools and a marine preserve. The tidepools are accessible from the Cabrillo Marine Aquarium, which sponsors exploratory tours, and via steep trails from the park. Also of note (though not open to the public) is the **Point Fermin Lighthouse,** a unique 19th-century clapboard house with a beacon set in a rooftop crow's nest. From the park plateau, like lighthouse keepers of old, you'll have open vistas of the cliff-fringed coastline and a perfect perch for sighting whales during their winter migration. ~ 805 Paseo del Mar; 310-548-7756; e-mail parkoffice@sanpedro.com.

Then drive along Paseo del Mar, through arcades of stately palm trees and along sharp sea cliffs, until it meets 25th Street. The sedimentary rocks throughout this region have been twisted and contorted into grotesque shapes by tremendous geologic pressures.

Hostelling International—Los Angeles South Bay is located in the Army barracks of old Fort MacArthur. Set in Angel's Gate Park on a hilltop overlooking the ocean, it's a pretty site with easy access to beaches. Men and women are housed separately in dorms but couples can be accommodated. Kitchen facilities are provided. Reservations are highly recommended from June through August. ~ 3601 South Gaffey Street, Building 613; 310-831-8109, fax 310-831-4635; e-mail hisanpedro@aol.com. BUDGET.

LODGING

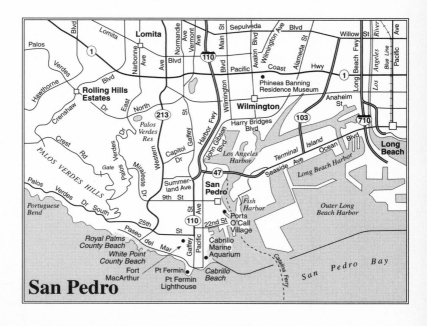

San Pedro

San Pedro also has several chain hotels designed to serve the needs of departing or returning cruise ship passengers. Perhaps the most distinctive among them is the **Holiday Inn San Pedro**, which captures the flavor of a traditional European hotel. Behind the columned facade with its faux mansard roof are individually decorated Victorian-style rooms; some have kitchenettes. Two-room suites with harbor views and fireplaces are available. ~ 111 South Gaffey Street; 310-514-1414, 800-248-3188, fax 310-831-8262; www.holi dayinnsanpedro.com. MODERATE TO DELUXE.

Extending along 6th Street between Mesa Street and Harbor Boulevard is the Sportswalk, featuring plaques dedicated to Olympic medalists as well as great collegiate and professional athletes.

DINING

The vintage shopping mall at **Ports O' Call Village** is Los Angeles Harbor's prime tourist center. It's situated right on the San Pedro waterfront and houses numerous restaurants. Try to avoid the high-ticket dining rooms, as they are overpriced and serve mediocre food to out-of-town hordes. But there are a number of take-out stands and ethnic eateries, priced in the budget and moderate ranges, which provide an opportunity to dine inexpensively on the water. ~ The entrance is at the foot of 6th Street; 310-732-7696.

HIDDEN ►

Of course local anglers rarely frequent Ports O' Call. The old salts are over at **Canetti's Seafood Grotto**. It ain't on the waterfront, but it is within casting distance of the fishing fleet. Which means it's the right spot for fresh fish platters at good prices. Dinner Friday and Saturday; breakfast and lunch all week. ~ 309 East 22nd Street; 310-831-4036. MODERATE.

Trade the Pacific for the Aegean and set anchor at **Papadakis Taverna**. The menu features moussaka, Greek-style cheese dishes, lamb baked in pastry, grilled contessa shrimp in tomato and feta and occasional specials like stuffed eggplant, fresh seafood, and regional delicacies. Dinner only. ~ 301 West 6th Street; 310-548-1186. MODERATE TO ULTRA-DELUXE.

SHOPPING

Los Angeles Harbor's answer to the theme shopping mall craze is **Ports O' Call Village**, a mock 19th-century fishing village. There are clapboard stores with shuttered windows, New England–style structures with gabled roofs, and storehouses of corrugated metal. Dozens of shops here are located right on the water, giving you a chance to view the harbor while browsing the stores. It's one of those hokey but inevitable places that I swear to avoid but always seem to end up visiting. ~ The entrance is at the foot of 6th Street; 310-732-7696, fax 310-547-5389.

Landlubbers can enjoy a quiet drink on the waterfront at **Ports O' Call Restaurant**. In addition to a spiffy oak bar, they have a dockside patio. ~ Ports O' Call Village; 310-833-3553.

NIGHTLIFE

CABRILLO BEACH 〜 The edge of Los Angeles harbor is an unappealing locale for a beach, but here it is, a two-part strand, covered with heavy-grain sand and bisected by a fishing pier. One half faces the shipping facility; the other half looks out on the glorious Pacific and abuts on the Point Fermin Marine Life Refuge, a rocky corridor filled with outstanding tidepools and backdropped by dramatic cliffs. You'll also find restrooms, showers, picnic areas, lifeguards, an aquarium, a playground, and volleyball courts. Fires are permitted. Fishing can be done from the pier, and for surfing try the beach-front and near the jetty; this area is a windsurfing mecca. People do swim here, but I saw a lot of refuse from the nearby shipping harbor. After heavy rains, storm drainage increases the bacteria count; stick to the oceanside during these times. If you like tide-pooling, beeline to Cabrillo—if not, there are hundreds of other beaches in the Golden State. Parking fee, $6.60. ~ 3720 Stephen M. White Drive; 310-372-2166, fax 310-372-6902.

BEACHES & PARKS

ROYAL PALMS COUNTY BEACH 〜 Situated at the base of a sedimentary cliff, this boulder-strewn beach gains its name from a grove of elegant palm trees. This was an erstwhile hub of elegant activity in the 1920s; the Royal Palms country club and a Japanese-owned resort presided here until a violent storm de-stroyed them in 1939. Today the guests of honor are surfers and tidepoolers. While the location is quite extraordinary, I prefer an-other beach, Point Fermin Park's **Wilder Annex**, located to the east. This little gem also lacks sand, but is built on three tiers of a cliff. The upper level is decorated with palm trees, the middle tier has a grassy plot studded with shady magnolias, and the bottom floor is a rocky beach with promising tidepools and camera-eye views of Point Fermin. Fishing is good at both parks, but swimming is not recommended. Surfing is popular at Royal Palms, where there are lifeguards, and off White Point, a peninsula separating the two parks. Snorkelers and divers take advantage of Diver's Cove, at the far east end of the parking lot. Facilities are limited to restrooms. Day-use fee, $6. ~ Both parks are located along Paseo del Mar in San Pedro. Royal Palms is near the intersection with Western Avenue and Wilder Annex is around the intersection with Meyler Street; 310-372-2166, fax 310-372-6902.

Long Beach

Anchoring the southern end of Los Angeles County is Long Beach, one of California's largest cities (the fifth-largest, in fact). Back in the Roaring Twenties, after oil was discovered and the area experienced a tremendous building boom, Long Beach became known as "The Coney Island of the West." Boasting five and a half miles of beachfront and a grand amusement park, it was a favorite spot for daytripping Angelenos.

Several decades of decline followed, but in more recent years the metropolis launched a redevelopment plan dubbed the Queensway Bay Development. The star of this facelift is the Aquarium of the Pacific. Together with the *Queen Mary* and Shoreline Village, the aquarium rounded out an oceanfront triumvirate of family-oriented attractions, each of which is accessible to the others by a water taxi called the AquaBus.

Today Long Beach ranks together with neighboring San Pedro as one of the largest manmade harbors in the world and is a popular tourist destination. It's a revealing place, a kind of social studies lesson in modern American life. Travel Ocean Boulevard as it parallels the sea and you'll pass from quaint homes to downtown skyscrapers to fire-breathing smokestacks.

SIGHTS

For a dynamic example of what I mean, visit the enclave of **Naples** near the south end of town. Conceived early in the 20th century, modeled on Italy's fabled canal towns, it's a tiny community of three islands separated by canals and linked with walkways. Waterfront greenswards gaze out on Alamitos Bay and its fleet of sloops and motorboats. You can wander along bayside paths past comfortable homes, contemporary condos, and humble cottages. Fountains and miniature traffic circles, alleyways and boulevards, all form an incredible labyrinth along which you undoubtedly will become lost.

Adding to the sense of old Italia is the **Gondola Getaway**, a romantic hour-long cruise through the canals of Naples. For a hefty price (less, however, than a ticket to Italy), you can climb aboard a gondola, dine on hors d'oeuvres, and occasionally be serenaded with Italian music. Reservations of up to three weeks in advance are strongly suggested. ~ 5437 East Ocean Boulevard, Naples; 562-433-9595; www.gondola.net.

Housed in a converted skating rink, the **Museum of Latin American Art** is the only museum in the western United States to exclusively exhibit contemporary art from Latin America. The museum store also features the works of Latin American artists. For children there are hands-on art-making workshops on Sunday. Closed Monday. Admission. ~ 628 Alamitos Avenue; 562-437-1689, fax 562-437-7043; www.molaa.com, e-mail info@molaa.com.

For a touch of early Spanish/Mexican culture, plan on visiting the region's old adobes. Built around 1800 with walls more than two feet thick, the adobe core of **Rancho Los Alamitos** is one of Southern California's oldest remaining houses. In its gardens, which cover more than three acres, are brick walkways and

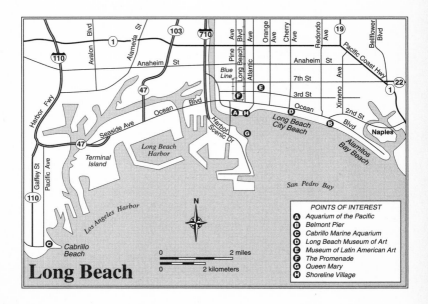

Long Beach

POINTS OF INTEREST

- A Aquarium of the Pacific
- B Belmont Pier
- C Cabrillo Marine Aquarium
- D Long Beach Museum of Art
- E Museum of Latin American Art
- F The Promenade
- G Queen Mary
- H Shoreline Village

a variety of majestic trees. You can tour old barns (housing draft horses, sheep, and chickens), a blacksmith shop, and a feed shed. There's also a chuck wagon with a coffeepot still resting on the wood-burning stove. Closed Monday and Tuesday. ~ 6400 Bixby Hill Road (enter at guard gate at Palo Verde and Anaheim); 562-431-3541, fax 562-430-9694; rancholosalamitos.com, e-mail info@rancholosalamitos.com.

Rancho Los Cerritos, a two-story Monterey Colonial home built in 1844, once served as headquarters for a 27,000-acre ranch. Now the adobe is filled with Victorian furniture and reflects the families and workers who lived and worked on the ranch in the 19th century. The site includes historic gardens, a California history research library and an orientation exhibit. Closed Monday and Tuesday. ~ 4600 Virginia Road; 562-570-1755, fax 562-570-1893; www.ranchoscerritos.org.

The Pacific Ocean may be Long Beach's biggest natural attraction, but many birds in the area prefer the **El Dorado Nature Center.** Part of the 450-acre El Dorado East Regional Park, this 103-acre wildlife sanctuary offers one- and two-mile hikes past two lakes and a stream. About 150 bird species as well as numerous land animals can be sighted. Though located in a heavily urbanized area, the facility encompasses several ecological zones. There's also a quarter-mile paved, handicapped-accessible nature trail. Closed Monday. Parking fee. ~ 7550 East Spring Street; 562-570-1745, fax 562-570-8530; www.ci.long-beach.ca.us/park/index.htm.

Another side of Long Beach is the steel-and-glass downtown area, where highrise hotels vie for dominance. The best way to tour this crowded commercial district is to stroll **The Promenade,** a six-block brick walkway leading from 3rd Street to the waterfront. There's a **tile mosaic** (Promenade and 3rd Street) at the near

AUTHOR FAVORITE

sights

The **Long Beach Museum of Art** is a must. Dedicated to the past 300 years of design and decorative arts, this museum has ever-changing exhibits, bluff-top gardens, and an oceanview café. Closed Monday. Admission, except for the first Friday of every month. ~ 2300 East Ocean Boulevard; 562-439-2119, fax 562-439-3587; www.lbma.org; e-mail tours@lbma.org.

end portraying an idyllic day at the beach complete with sail-boats, sunbathers, and lifeguards. Visit the **Long Beach Area Convention & Visitors Bureau**, home to maps, brochures, and other bits of information. Open daily in summer; closed Saturday and Sunday at other times. ~ 1 World Trade Center, Suite 300; 562-436-3645, 800-452-7829, fax 562-435-5653; www.visitlong beach.com, e-mail staff@longbeachcvb.org.

The latest addition to Long Beach's popular waterfront attractions is **The Pike at Rainbow Harbor.** Located on 18 acres beside the Aquarium of the Pacific, The Pike features a slew of restaurants and places to play, including a pedestrian bridge over Shoreline Village Drive, a carousel, Ferris wheel and movie theater and video arcade.

Cross Ocean Boulevard and you'll arrive at a park shaded with palm trees and adjacent to **Shoreline Village**, a shopping center and marina disguised as a 19th-century fishing village. ~ 407 Shoreline Village Drive.

Another aspect of Long Beach rises in the form of oil derricks and industrial complexes just across the water. To view the freighters, tankers, and warships lining the city's piers, gaze out from the northern fringes of Shoreline Village.

Fittingly, the climax of a Long Beach tour comes at the very end, after you have experienced the three phases of urban existence. Just across the Los Angeles River, along Harbor Scenic Drive ("scenic" in this case meaning construction cranes and cargo containers), lies one of the strangest sights I've ever encountered. The first time I saw it, peering through the steel filigree of a suspension bridge, with harbor lights emblazoning the scene, I thought something had gone colossally wrong with the world. An old-style ocean liner, gleaming eerily in the false light, appeared to be parked on the ground. Next to it an overgrown geodesic dome, a kind of giant aluminum breast, was swelling up out of the earth.

Unwittingly I had happened upon Long Beach's top tourist attraction, the *Queen Mary*, once the world's largest ocean liner. Making her maiden voyage in 1936, the **Queen Mary** was the pride of Great Britain. Winston Churchill, the Duke and Duchess of Windsor, Greta Garbo, and Fred Astaire sailed on her, and during World War II, she was converted to military service.

Today she is the pride of Long Beach, a 1000-foot-long "city at sea" transformed into a floating museum and hotel that brilliantly re-create shipboard life. An elaborate walking tour carries you down into the engine room (a world of pumps and propellers), out along the decks, and up to each level of this multistage behemoth. There's a parking fee and admission to the ship (the admission fee is waived for hotel guests).

The *Queen Mary* carried so many troops across the Atlantic Ocean that Adolf Hitler offered $250,000 and the Iron Cross to the U-boat captain who sank her.

The *Queen Mary* is expertly refurbished and wonderfully laid out, an important addition to the Long Beach seafront and the anchor attraction for Queen Mary Seaport, which also includes the **Queen Mary Seawalk** shopping and dining area. Her neighbor is the world's largest clear-span geodesic dome. The dome once housed Howard Hughes' *Spruce Goose*, the largest plane ever built. Admission. ~ 1126 Queen's Highway; 562-435-3511, 800-437-2934, fax 562-437-4531; www.queenmary.com, e-mail attractions@queenmary.com.

The **Aquarium of the Pacific**, located at the waterfront Rainbow Harbor in downtown Long Beach, has three major permanent galleries designed to lead visitors on a "journey of discovery" through the waters of the Pacific Ocean. The journey begins in the temperate waters of Southern California and Baja, and includes tidepools and endangered sea turtles. The Bering Sea is the focus of the exhibit representing the icy waters of the northern Pacific, which are inhabited by sea otters, a giant octopus, and spider crabs. The coral reefs and lagoons of Palau in Micronesia are spotlighted in the Tropical Pacific Gallery, which also features the huge Tropical Reef exhibit, where microphone-equipped scuba divers swim along with schools of brilliant fish and sharks, answering questions for visitors. There's also an outdoor lagoon where visitors can touch sharks and a lorikeet forest where visitors can handfeed colorful birds. Admission. ~ 100 Aquarium Way; 562-590-3100, fax 562-590-3109; www.aquariumofpacific.org, e-mail info@lbaop.org.

Long Beach's latest effort to draw tourists is the Soviet-built submarine **Scorpion**, which is docked alongside the *Queen Mary*. Visitors enter through the forward hatch of the 300-foot Foxtrot-class Russian sub, then squeeze their way along corridors for a look through the periscope and a self-guided tour of the torpedo room, crew quarters, and communications center. Admission. ~ 1126 Queen's Highway; 562-435-3511.

The **AquaBus**, a water taxi service, links the city's main waterfront attractions—the aquarium, Shoreline Village, the *Queen Mary*, Catalina Express, and the convention center—with daily service. ~ 800-429-4601.

Long Beach is also a departure point for the **Catalina Express** shuttle boats to Santa Catalina Island. Reservations recommended. ~ 310-519-1212, 800-897-7154; www.catalinaexpress.com.

Beyond all the shoreline hubbub, the venerable Pacific gray whales migrate along the "Whale Freeway" between late December and mid-April, and several enterprises in Long Beach offer whale-watching opportunities. The **Long Beach Area Convention & Visitors Bureau** can put you in touch with a whale-watching operator. ~ 800-452-7829; www.visitlongbeach.org, e-mail staff@ longbeachcvb.org.

LODGING

The **Beach Plaza Hotel** has 40 units, some with ocean views, many offering kitchens and all with easy access to the beach. Each room is furnished in contemporary fashion. There's a pool and jacuzzi. ~ 2010 East Ocean Boulevard; 562-437-0771, 800-485-8758, fax 562-437-0900; www.beachplazahotel.net, e-mail yeman eh@verizon.com. MODERATE

Granted I'm a fool for gimmicks, but somehow the opportunity to stay aboard a historic ocean liner seems overwhelming. Where else but at the **Hotel Queen Mary** can you recapture the magic of British gentility before World War II? What other hotel offers guests a "sunning deck"? Staying in the original staterooms of this grand old ship, permanently docked on the Long Beach waterfront, you are surrounded by the art-deco designs for which the *Queen Mary* is famous. Some guest rooms are small (this *is* a ship!) and dimly illuminated through portholes, but the decor is classic. There are also restaurants, lounges, and shops on board. ~ 1126 Queen's Highway; 562-435-3511, 800-437-2934, fax 562-437-4531; www.queenmary.com, e-mail reservations@ queenmary.com. DELUXE.

DINING

One of the first small brewery/restaurants in the Long Beach area, the **Belmont Brewing Company** brews pale and amber ales, seasonal beers, and a dark, rich porter—Long Beach Crude—

that closely resembles the real stuff pumped from nearby coastal oil derricks. Gourmet pizzas, fresh seafood, steaks, and pastas are served in the dining area, at the bar, and outside on the patio. I'd opt for the patio where you can enjoy watching the sun set over the water. Breakfast is served on the weekends. ~ 25 39th Place; 562-433-3891, fax 562-434-0604; www.belmontbrewing. com. MODERATE.

HIDDEN ▶ Southern cooking at the **Shenandoah Café** is becoming a tradition among savvy shore residents. The quilts and baskets decorating this understated establishment lend a country air to the place. Add waitresses in aprons dishing out hot apple fritters and it gets downright homey. Dinner and Sunday brunch are special events occasioned with "riverwalk steak" (filet in mustard caper sauce), prime rib, salmon on wild-rice pancake, gumbo, "granny's fried chicken," and Texas-style beef brisket. Try it! No breakfast or lunch Monday through Saturday. ~ 4722 East 2nd Street; 562-434-3469, fax 562-438-4299; www.shenandoahcafe.com, e-mail info@shenandoahcafe.com. MODERATE TO ULTRA-DELUXE.

HIDDEN ▶ **The Porch Cafe**, a gay-owned restaurant that serves great breakfasts and lunches, is a favorite with the town's large gay and lesbian population, as well as with straight folks who also appreciate the generous portions and reasonable prices. The breakfast special of eggs, French toast, bacon, and orange juice is available for under $6. No dinner. Closed Wednesday. ~ 2708 East 4th Street; 562-433-0118. BUDGET.

In downtown Long Beach the **King's Pine Avenue Fish House** is a prime spot for seafood. The private booths and dark wood trim lend an antique atmosphere to this open-kitchen establishment. The seafood platters are too numerous to recite (besides, the menu changes daily); suffice it to say that you can have them baked, broiled, sautéed, or grilled. For those not keen on seafood, there are also pasta, pizza, and chicken. ~ 100 West Broadway; 562-432-7463, fax 562-435-6143; www.kingsfishhouse. com. MODERATE TO DELUXE.

Back in the world of good eats and frugal budgets, **Acapulco Mexican Restaurant & Cantina** offers standard as well as innovative dishes. Tacos, burritos, and enchiladas are only the beginning; this comfortable eatery also serves several Mexican-style seafood dishes. ~ 6270 East Pacific Coast Highway; 562-596-3371, fax 562-431-0290. MODERATE.

What more elegant a setting in which to dine than aboard the *Queen Mary*. There you will find everything from snack kiosks to coffee shops to first-class dining rooms. The **Promenade Café** offers a reasonably priced menu of chicken, steak, and seafood dishes. They also have salads and sandwiches. The café is a lovely art-deco restaurant featuring period lamps and stunning views. Breakfast, lunch and dinner served. ~ 1126 Queen's Highway; 562-499-1595, fax 562-432-7674; www.queenmary.com. MODERATE TO DELUXE.

For a true taste of regal life aboard the old ship, cast anchor at **Sir Winston's**, the *Queen Mary*'s most elegant restaurant. The Continental and California cuisine in this dining emporium includes rack of lamb, veal medallion, muscovy duck, venison, châteaubriand, broiled swordfish, and Australian lobster. Sir Winston's is a wood-paneled dining room with copper-rimmed mirrors, white tablecloths, and upholstered armchairs. The walls are adorned with photos of the great prime minister and every window opens onto a full view of Long Beach. A semiformal dress code is enforced and jackets are requested. Reservations required. Dinner only. ~ 1126 Queen's Highway; 562-499-1657, fax 562-432-7674; www.queenmary.com, e-mail sirwinstons@ queenmary.com. ULTRA-DELUXE.

The best street shopping in Long Beach is in Belmont Shore along East 2nd Street. This 15-block strip between Livingston Drive and Bayshore Avenue is a gentrified row. Either side is lined with art galleries, book shops, boutiques, jewelers, and import stores.   **SHOPPING**

For **vintage-store and antiques** shoppers, Redondo Avenue, East Broadway, and East 4th Street in downtown Long Beach have nearly two dozen stores where you can find everything from Bauer

AUTHOR FAVORITE

The Reef on the Water is rambling, ramshackle, and wonderful. Built of rough-sawn cedar, it sits along the waterfront on a dizzying series of levels. The Continental American cuisine includes such contemporary choices as seafood collage and jumbo shrimp scampi. For the traditionalists, there are steaks, pasta, and swordfish. There's also Sunday brunch. ~ 880 Harbor Scenic Drive; 562-435-8013, fax 562-432-6823; www.specialtyrestaurants.com. MODERATE TO DELUXE.

pottery to antique furniture to Depression glass to beaded sweaters. Look for a copy of the Long Beach Antique and Vintage Shopping Guide to help you map out your itinerary.

Shoreline Village is one of those waterfront malls Southern California specializes in. With a marina on both sides, the buildings are New England–style shingle and clapboard structures designed to re-create an Atlantic Coast port town. ~ 407 Shoreline Village Drive; 562-435-2668; www.shorelinevillage.com.

There are more than half a dozen stores onboard the **Queen Mary**. There is a fee charged to board the ship. Concentrated in the Piccadilly Circus section of the old ship are several souvenir shops as well as stores specializing in artifacts and old-fashioned items. Perhaps the prettiest shopping arcade you'll ever enter, it is an art-deco masterpiece with etched glass, dentil molding, and brass appointments. ~ 1126 Queen's Highway; 562-435-3511; www.queenmary.com.

Adjacent to the *Queen Mary*, the **Queen Mary Seawalk** is a shopping plaza styled after a 19th-century British village and offering a variety of speciality and souvenir shops.

NIGHTLIFE **Panama Joe's Grill & Cantina** cooks Thursday through Sunday night. The bands are R&B ensembles, rock groups, and assorted others, which create an eclectic blend of music. Your average Tiffany-lamp-and-hanging-plant nightspot, the place is lined with sports photos and proudly displays an old oak bar. ~ 5100 East 2nd Street; 562-434-7417, fax 562-434-7810; www.panamajoes.com.

E. J. Malloy's is a small sports bar with a comfortable pub-style interior including a long wood bar, brick walls, and plenty of televisions for watching a Lakers game with the locals. There's a fireplace, bar, and patio seating. The sports fans can get loud and rambunctious on game nights. ~ 3411 East Broadway; 562-433-3769, fax 562-987-3580.

Located right along the promenade in downtown Long Beach is **The Blue Café**. This tavern serves up live blues, swing, and alternative music seven nights a week and tasty dishes from the deli and grill. Hip hustlers hang out upstairs where there are plenty of billiard tables and a karaoke lounge on Friday nights. Closed Monday. Cover. ~ 210 Promenade North; 562-983-7111, fax 562-901-3057; www.thebluecafe.com.

No matter how grand, regardless of how much money went into its design, despite the care taken to assure quality, any Long Beach nightspot is hard pressed to match the elegance of the **Observation Bar** aboard the *Queen Mary*. Once the first-class bar for this grand old ship, the room commands a 180° view across the bow and out to the Long Beach skyline. The walls are lined with fine woods, a mural decorates the bar, and art-deco appointments appear everywhere. The bar features live jazz as well as rock-and-roll on the weekends.

> Protected from the ocean by a peninsula and breakwater, Bayshore Beach faces the waterfront community of Naples; you can catch gondola rides through Naples' canals.

If live music is not your thing, you can always adjourn aft to **Sir Winston's Piano Bar**, a cozy and elegant setting decorated with memorabilia of the WWII British leader. ~ 1126 Queen's Highway; 562-499-1657.

GAY SCENE   A long-time favorite is **Ripples**, which has a dance-club upstairs and a bar downstairs. There's also a pool table and patio. Live entertainment on Saturday and Sunday. Cover. ~ 5101 East Ocean Boulevard; 562-433-0357; www.clubripples. com. **Mineshaft** has pool tables, pinball machines, and live dee-jay music Tuesday, Friday and Saturday. ~ 1720 East Broadway; 562-436-2433.

The Falcon is a gay bar complete with a CD player and dart boards. ~ 1435 East Broadway; 562-432-4146.

ALAMITOS PENINSULA   The ocean side of this slender salient offers a pretty sand beach looking out on a tiny island. Paralleling the beach is an endless string of woodframe houses. The sand corridor extends all the way to the entrance of Alamitos Bay where a stone jetty provides recreation for anglers, occasional surfers, swimmers, and climbers with sturdy hiking shoes. Facilities include restrooms, lifeguards in summer, and volleyball courts; the paved bike path leading to Aquarium of the Pacific begins here. ~ Located along Ocean Boulevard between 54th Place and 72nd Place; park at the end of the road; 562-570-3100, 562-570-3109.

BEACHES & PARKS

BAYSHORE BEACH   This hook-shaped strand curves along the eastern and southern shores of a narrow inlet. Houses line the beach along most of its length. Protected from surf and tide, this is a safe, outstanding spot for swimming, and conditions are perfect for windsurfing. At the corner of Bayshore and Ocean there are basketball and handball courts as well as kayak and sailboat rentals. Restrooms are available at the beach; lifeguards in summer only. ~ Located along Bayshore Avenue and Ocean Boulevard; 562-570-3215, fax 562-570-3247.

LONG BEACH CITY BEACH 🚲 ⛵ 🎿 🚶 🛶 🏊 🎣 They don't call it Long Beach for nothing. This strand is broad and boundless, a silvery swath traveling much of the length of town. There are several islets parked offshore. Along the miles of beachfront you'll find numerous facilities and good size crowds. **Belmont Veterans Memorial Pier**, a 1300-foot-long, hammer-head-shaped walkway, bisects the beach and offers fishing services. Fishing is good from the pier, where halibut and sea bass are common catches, and the beach is protected by the harbor break-water, making for safe swimming. Along the beach you'll find restrooms, lifeguards, a snack bar, a playground, and volleyball courts. A paved bike path along Long Beach City Beach leads to the Aquarium of the Pacific. ~ Located along Ocean Boulevard between 1st and 72nd places. Belmont Pier is at Ocean Boulevard and 39th Place; 562-570-3100, 562-570-3109.

NINE

Pasadena Area

Tucked between L.A.'s Downtown district and the lofty San Gabriel Mountains lies the San Gabriel Valley. Extending east from the San Fernando Valley toward San Bernardino, this former orange-growing empire has developed into a suburban realm noted for its wealth, botanic gardens, and smog.

Back in 1771, when 14 soldiers, two priests, and several mule drivers founded a mission in San Gabriel, they laid claim to an outpost that controlled the entire countryside, including Los Angeles Pueblo. The priests became land barons as the region was divided into vineyards, cattle ranches, and olive groves. In the mid-19th century, American settlers further transformed the valley into an oasis of lemon and orange trees.

By the late 19th century, Pasadena was supplanting San Gabriel as the cultural heart of the San Gabriel Valley. Boasting an ideal climate, it billed itself as a health lover's paradise and became a celebrated resort area. Its tree-trimmed boulevards were lined with beaux-arts, Mediterranean, Italian Renaissance, and Victorian houses, making the town a kind of open-air architectural museum.

Eventually visitors became residents, hotels were converted to apartments, and gradually paradise became suburbia. In the 1920s, the suburbs starting spreading west from Pasadena. Suddenly houses were popping up in agricultural areas, and La Cañada, Glendale, and Burbank became fast-growing towns. By mid-century, Columbia, Warner Brothers, and other television and movie studios moved to Burbank, and the western portion of the San Gabriel Valley began rivaling that celluloid center on the far side of the Hollywood Hills. Despite the show-biz element, Burbank and Glendale—lacking Pasadena's old wealth and sophistication—are Middle America–type communities, home to subdivisions, blue-collar workers, and striving executives.

For years, Pasadena's overweening wealth and stubborn sense of tradition left the town with a reputation for stodgy conservatism. The Beach Boys captured the sense of the place with their 1964 hit record, "The Little Old Lady from Pasadena." In recent years, the proverbial little old ladies are being outnumbered by the younger set, and things in Pasadena are livening and loosening up. This is at least partially due to a revitalized Old Town that rocks after dark, while a zany addition to the parade scene is a motley gathering of "briefcase drill teams" and "lawnmower marching groups," known as the Doo Dah Parade.

Pasadena

Pasadena is the unofficial cultural center of the San Gabriel Valley. The town was incorporated in 1886, and its early years included the initiation of a mid-winter festival that was to become The Tournament of Roses; the founding of Throop Polytechnic Institute, which became California Institute of Technology (or Caltech); and the building of many outstanding houses designed by some of the country's finest architects.

During the 1920s, Pasadena gained a reputation as a tourist center and winter resort for the wealthy. The tourist industry nose-dived during the Depression, however, and it took World War II to put Pasadena on the path to modern industrial growth, thanks in part to Caltech and the Jet Propulsion Laboratory.

In the 1950s, '60s, and '70s, the town developed a reputation for a diverse population ranging from the conservative and dowdily clad wealthy to economically depressed African Americans. Pasadena's Old Town fell into disrepair, and the town seemed to lack a center both physically and philosophically.

In recent years, however, the renewal of Old Town has helped to bring back a sense of vitality. Hip restaurants, clubs, and coffeehouses call to night owls, while culture vultures can overdose on world-class museums and trendy galleries. Staid no more, Pasadena has managed once again to reinvent itself and emerge as a vibrant part of the L.A. landscape.

SIGHTS   Not so many years ago, Pasadena's **Old Town** historic core was an eyesore of decaying old buildings. Old Town today has been transformed into one of the liveliest districts in Southern California. Small-scale brick buildings dating from the late 19th century have been renovated and now house cafés, restaurants, and shops. The arrival of high-profile national retailers like Pottery Barn, Gap, Williams-Sonoma, and Barnes & Noble has introduced a shopping-mall feel to this charming historic district. But sidewalk cafés and plenty of pedestrians create a very satisfying street scene. Plenty of parking helps draw crowds, too. Most Old Town businesses open around 11 a.m. and remain open well into the evening, when Old Town is at its liveliest. ~ Bordered by Holly and Green streets, Pasadena Avenue, and Arroyo Parkway.

Orienting visitors to the old and the new is the **Pasadena Convention and Visitors Bureau.** Closed Sunday. ~ 171 South Los Robles Avenue, Pasadena; 626-795-9311, 800-307-7977, fax 626-795-9656; www.pasadenacal.com, e-mail cub@pasadenacal. com. They will tell you that the best place to begin touring the town is **Pasadena City Hall**, a 1925 Baroque building with a spectacular tile dome. A prime example of the city's classical architecture, the edifice features a colonnaded courtyard with fountain and formal gardens. ~ 100 North Garfield Avenue, Pasadena.

The **Pasadena Public Library**, completed two years later, is a Renaissance-style building with sufficient palm trees and red roof tiles to create a quintessentially Southern California setting. ~ 285 East Walnut Street, Pasadena; 626-744-4052, fax 626-585-8396. The **Pasadena Post Office** is a 1913 Italian Renaissance beauty. ~ 281 East Colorado Boulevard, Pasadena. Another point of local pride is the **Pasadena Civic Auditorium**, an attractive building that dates from 1932. ~ 300 East Green Street, Pasadena; 626-449-7360, fax 626-395-7132.

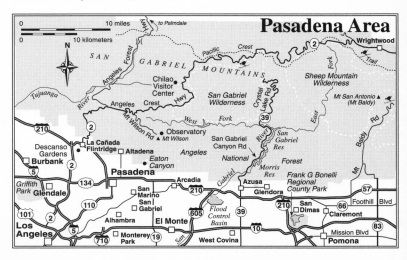

The public sector can never compete with its private counterpart when money is concerned. Pasadena displays its real wealth on the west side of town, where civic gives way to civilian.

HIDDEN ►

First stop at the **Pacific Asia Museum**, a Chinese palace–style building originally owned by an eccentric Pasadena art dealer. Dedicated to Asian and Pacific Island art and culture, the museum showcases 18th-century Japanese paintings and Southeast Asian ceramics. The museum boasts 15,000 objects in its permanent collection and an 8000-volume research library. Take time to contemplate the Chinese garden and koi fish pond in the courtyard. Closed Monday and Tuesday. Admission. ~ 46 North Los Robles Avenue, Pasadena; 626-449-2742, fax 626-449-2754; www.pac asiamuseum.org, e-mail info@pacificasiamuseum.org.

Even the gardens at the Norton Simon Museum are landscaped with 19th- and 20th-century sculptures by Rodin and Henry Moore.

Then drive out Colorado Boulevard, route of the Rose Parade held every New Year's Day, to the **Norton Simon Museum**. Housed in this odd edifice, which looks more like it was planned by a camera maker than an architect, is one of the finest collections of European and Asian art in the country.

Touring the Simon's 38 galleries and picturesque gardens is like striding through time and space. The works span 2000 years, traveling from ancient India and Southeast Asia to the world of contemporary art. The Old Masters are represented by Rembrandt, Rubens, and Raphael. There are Goya etchings, 17th-century watercolors, and pieces by Cézanne and van Gogh. Closed Tuesday. ~ 411 West Colorado Boulevard, Pasadena; 626-449-6840, fax 626-796-4978; www.nortonsimon.org, e-mail art@nortonsimon.org.

Art on a grander scale is evident at the **Colorado Street Bridge**, an antique causeway arching high above an arroyo. ~ Colorado Boulevard west of Orange Grove Boulevard, Pasadena. Not far from this engineering wonder, the old Wrigley mansion, a splendid Italian Renaissance–style estate, now serves as the **Tournament House**, headquarters of the Rose Bowl game and Rose Parade. The house itself captures the spirit of its early years. Guided tours are available every Thursday from February through August. Situated on four princely acres, the gardens are open daily. ~ 391 South Orange Grove Boulevard, Pasadena; 626-449-4100, fax 626-449-9066; www.tournamentofroses.com, e-mail rosepr@earthlink.net.

Another estate with meaning is the imposing 1906 edifice of the Fenyes Mansion that plays host to the **Pasadena Historical Museum**. Containing furnishings and keepsakes from Pasadena's early days, this beaux-arts house with an Edwardian interior was once home to the Finnish Consul. As a result the museum expresses a second theme: Finland, represented on the grounds, a facsimile 16th-century farmhouse, and an exhibit of Finnish folk art. There's also a lovely garden on-site. Docent-guided tours are offered Wednesday afternoon. Closed Monday and Tuesday. Admission. ~ 470 West Walnut Street, Pasadena; 626-577-1660, fax 626-577-1662; www.pasadenahistory.com.

Humbling all these estates is **The Gamble House**, jewel of   ◄ HIDDEN
Pasadena, a Craftsman-style bungalow designed by the famous architectural firm of Greene and Greene in 1908. Heavily influenced by such Japanese innovations as overhanging roofs and pagoda flourishes, the wood shingle home is a warm blend of hand-rubbed teak and Tiffany glass. Built for the Cincinnati-based Gamble (as in Procter & Gamble) family, the house displays crafted woodwork and the original furnishings. A veritable neighborhood of these elegantly understated Greene and Greene bungalows lines the **Arroyo Terrace** loop next to The Gamble House. Closed Monday through Wednesday; afternoon tours of-

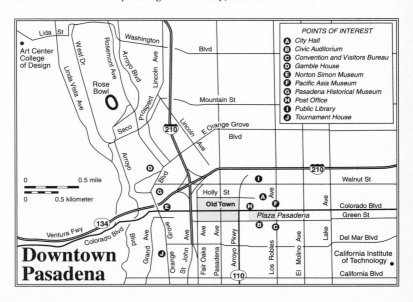

POINTS OF INTEREST
- **A** City Hall
- **B** Civic Auditorium
- **C** Convention and Visitors Bureau
- **D** Gamble House
- **E** Norton Simon Museum
- **F** Pacific Asia Museum
- **G** Pasadena Historical Museum
- **H** Post Office
- **I** Public Library
- **J** Tournament House

Downtown Pasadena

fered Thursday through Sunday. The bookstore is open daily. Admission. ~ 4 Westmoreland Place, Pasadena; 626-793-3334, fax 626-577-7547; gamblehouse.usc.edu, e-mail gamblehs@usc.edu.

To continue the architectural tour, follow nearby **Prospect Boulevard** and **Prospect Crescent** along their tree-lined courses. The neighborhood entranceway and several local structures were designed by Charles and Henry Greene, the brothers who fashioned the Gamble House. Another architect, one Frank Lloyd Wright, enters the picture at **La Miniatura** (the Millard House), an unusual assemblage of crosses and concrete blocks resembling a pre-Columbian tower. ~ 645 Prospect Crescent.

Grandest of all the area's architectural achievements is the **Rose Bowl**. Built in 1922, this 92,542-seat stadium is the home of UCLA's football team and the site of the New Year's Day clash between the Big Ten and the Pac-10. ~ 1001 Rose Bowl Drive, Pasadena; 626-577-3100, fax 626-405-0992; www.rosebowl stadium.com.

The future greats of the art world reside up the hill at the **Art Center College of Design**. An excellent school of art and design, the college has galleries displaying work by both students and established artists. It also rests on 175 hillside acres that provide marvelous views of Pasadena and the San Gabriel Mountains. ~ 1700 Lida Street, Pasadena; 626-396-2200, fax 626-795-0578; www.artcenter.edu.

Students with a more scientific bent are cracking the books at **Caltech**, an internationally renowned science and engineering school whose faculty and alumni have won 30 Nobel Prizes and whose faculty once included Richard Feynman. These hallowed halls, in case you were wondering, were modeled after a Spanish Colonial style. There are campus tours Monday through Friday. ~ California Institute of Technology Visitors Center, 315 South Hill Avenue, Pasadena; 626-395-6327; www.caltech.edu, e-mail www@caltech.edu.

LODGING   Motel row in Pasadena lies along Colorado Boulevard, route of the famous Rose Parade. **Pasadena Central Travelodge**, a 53-unit stucco complex, is typical of the accommodations. It offers standard rooms with cinderblock walls, stall showers, wall-to-wall carpeting, and other basic amenities. ~ 2131 East Colorado

Boulevard, Pasadena; 626-796-3121, 800-578-7878, fax 626-793-4713. BUDGET.

The revered 1907 **Ritz-Carlton Huntington Hotel & Spa** is situated on 23 manicured acres. This 392-room hotel combines modern amenities with the style and charm of another era. There's an Olympic-size swimming pool (reputed to be the first in California) to exercise in, a spa to relax in, or you can wander the hotel's Japanese and Horseshoe gardens. If you are seeking Old World elegance, this is the address. ~ 1401 South Oak Knoll Avenue, Pasadena; 626-568-3900, 800-241-3333, fax 626-568-1842; www.ritzcarlton.com. ULTRA-DELUXE.

For a great buy, try **Burger Continental**, a congested and crazy café where you order at the counter, then dine indoors or on a patio. Portions are bountiful and the prices ridiculously low. But it's not only the huge, low-priced menu that keeps this establishment packed—the belly dancing shows also draw crowds, Thursday through Sunday evening and at Sunday brunch. In addition to hamburgers they serve steaks, seafood, sandwiches, and an enticing array of Middle Eastern dishes. Breakfast, lunch, and dinner are served daily. ~ 535 South Lake Avenue, Pasadena; 626-792-6634, fax 626-792-8520; www.burgercontinental.com, e-mail mail@burgercontinental.com. BUDGET TO MODERATE.

DINING

◀ *HIDDEN*

You can people watch from the sidewalk dining area while feasting on delectable dishes at the **Crocodile Café**. Try the Chinese pot stickers to start. The Cobb salad is also very tasty. Inside seating is a little noisy, but the food makes up for it. Highly rec-

AUTHOR FAVORITE

If you are the former head chef at L'Orangerie and the person who replaced Wolfgang Puck at Les Anges when he left to open Spago, you can rightfully name your restaurant after yourself. That is exactly what Hideo "Shiro" Yamashiro did. **Restaurant Shiro** combines French and Asian influences to produce an everchanging menu that might include lamb chops marinated in mint and garlic, scallops in ginger and lime sauce, and steamed whitefish with capers. Dinner only. Closed Monday and Tuesday. ~ 1505 Mission Street, South Pasadena; 626-799-4774. MODERATE TO ULTRA-DELUXE.

ommended. ~ 140 South Lake Avenue, Pasadena; 626-449-9900, fax 626-449-6968. BUDGET TO MODERATE.

Tucked away in an art-deco building on a side street, **Bistro 45** is a gathering spot for Pasadena's "elegancia." The airy high-tech atmosphere, pastel walls, and contemporary art match the handsomely presented French (with just a dash of Californian) cuisine. The menu includes roasted chicken with fresh herbs and garlic, grilled ahi, and grilled beef tenderloin. No lunch on weekends. Closed Monday. ~ 45 South Mentor Avenue, Pasadena; 626-792-2535, fax 626-792-2676; www.bistro45.com. DELUXE TO ULTRA-DELUXE.

Pasadena Brewing Co., with its plasma televisions and specialty brews and martinis, is a happening place for the sports-minded bar crowd. Don't think standard pub grub, though; entrées at this microbrewery/restaurant include such creative dishes as guava-glazed barbecued ribs and lavender-smoked salmon. No lunch on Monday. ~ 42 South DeLacey Avenue, Pasadena; 626-405-0404. MODERATE.

Specializing in Mandarin and Szechuan cuisine, **Panda Inn** is a dimly lit restaurant with Chinese prints. The spicy Szechuan dishes include hot braised shrimp, sweet and pungent chicken, spicy bean curd, and twice-cooked pork. There are also chow mein, egg foo yung, and noodle entrées, as well as a full inventory of Mandarin-style beef, fowl, seafood, and vegetable dishes. ~ 3488 East Foothill Boulevard, Pasadena; 626-793-7300, fax 626-793-2781; www.pandainn.com. MODERATE.

HIDDEN ► Don't be fooled by the unpretentious decor and reasonable prices. **Akbar Cuisine of India** serves traditional and creative Indian dishes such as ginger-marinated lamb chops and mint chicken kabobs. ~ 44 North Fair Oaks Boulevard, Pasadena; 626-440-0309, fax 626-577-9919; www.akbarcuisineofindia.com. BUDGET.

Any town as wealthy and prone to gentrification as Pasadena is bound to have numerous California-cuisine cafés. One of note is **Parkway Grill**, a brick-wall-and-bare-beam restaurant decorated with track lights and stained glass. The antique bar is hardwood; the kitchen, *naturalement*, sits in the center of the complex, completely open to view. The chefs prepare gourmet pizza and pasta dishes such as black linguini with popcorn shrimp, spicy Thai tagliatelle and forest mushroom ravioli. Entrées include catfish in lime-soy sauce, mesquite-grilled filet mignon, and

Afternoon Tea

Considering the Pasadena area's genteel beginnings, it's no surprise that this is the place to go for afternoon tea. Expect fine English bone china, scones and cream, and the finest teas at the best of the area's tea emporiums.

Perhaps the most elegant (and certainly the most expensive) afternoon tea is served at the **Ritz-Carlton Huntington**'s lobby lounge. Tea is poured from sparkling silver teapots while a harpist strums soothing melodies. Though the experience is guaranteed to make tea goers feel like royalty, the price isn't for the budget-minded. High tea costs $24, while the Royal Tea, which includes champagne, will set you back $32. No tea service Monday through Wednesday. ~ 1401 South Oak Knoll Avenue, Pasadena; 626-568-3900. DELUXE.

At Mary and Edward Fry's **Rose Tree Cottage**, a Pasadena institution for over two decades, afternoon tea is all about being pampered. The setting is reminiscent of an English country inn, with Liberty of London linens and homemade scones and shortbread. The tea is Fry's special blend, and Edward, a transplanted Brit, always serves the whole extravaganza dressed in his tuxedo. Reservations required. No tea service Monday. ~ 828 East California Boulevard, Pasadena; 626-793-3337, fax 626-793-8125; www.rosetreecottage.com. MODERATE.

Tea aficionados can indulge in a simple cuppa at **Turnabout Teacup**, or have a full-blown afternoon tea. Sipping tea and nibbling on scones in this unpretentious establishment with its flowery decor is like being transported to an English village tea room. Closed Sunday and Monday. ~ 1432 Foothill Boulevard, La Cañada; 818-790-3342. BUDGET TO MODERATE.

High tea at the **Rose Garden Tea Room** at the Huntington Library, Art Collections & Botanical Gardens is a little like being time machined back to Agatha Christie's England. Waitresses in traditional black dresses with starched white aprons and caps serve tea from silver pitchers, while scones and cream are delivered to the table. Served in what was originally Henry Huntington's bowling and billiard room (redecorated, of course), purists may object to the accompanying dazzling array of finger sandwiches and bite-sized pastries being served buffet style, but still, the fare is delicious and the setting lovely. Reservations required. Closed Monday. ~ 1151 Oxford Road, San Marino; 626-683-8131; www.huntington.org/tearoom.html. MODERATE.

oak oven–roasted garlic chicken with goat cheese, potato purée and fig chutney. No lunch Saturday or Sunday. ~ 510 South Arroyo Parkway, Pasadena; 626-795-1001, fax 626-796-6221. DELUXE TO ULTRA-DELUXE.

Italian food is hot in Pasadena. There's always an exuberant and bustling crowd in Old Town's popular *ristorantes*.

For alfresco dining, be sure to delve into the pleasures of **Sorriso**. Decorated with a stunning art collection, this trattoria-style eatery serves authentic Italian cuisine. Try their delicious *linguine saporose* (linguine served with a zesty tomato sauce and lightly breaded pan-fried calamari and shrimp). The food is outstanding, and the ambience is *molto* Italian. ~ 168 West Colorado Boulevard, Pasadena; 626-793-2233, fax 626-796-8392; www.sorrisopasadena.com. MODERATE TO DELUXE.

At **Mi Píace**, the cuisine is exquisite. Try their chicken lasagne with a sweet pepper cream sauce, and you'll be very *contento*. The airy interior is further enhanced by simple pine-colored chairs, a wrought-iron bar, and fresh flowers. ~ 25 East Colorado Boulevard, Pasadena; 626-795-3131. MODERATE.

Regional Italian cuisine is the name of the game at **Il Fornaio**. Will it be Tuscany, Sicily, or Sardinia? The menu changes monthly, but there are always wood-fired pizzas and mesquite-grilled steaks, chicken, and seafood. With its white marble floors, a fashionable bar, and sleek, contemporary Italian feel, this eatery comes highly praised. Patio dining is also available. ~ Located on the northwest corner of Colorado Boulevard and Fairoaks Avenue, Pasadena; 626-683-9797, fax 626-683-0789; www.ilfornaio.com. DELUXE.

SHOPPING Shopping in the San Gabriel Valley centers around Pasadena. **South Lake Avenue,** the oldest and once the most prestigious shopping district in town, had its origins in 1947 when Bullocks department store opened for business. Today the venerable establishment has been replaced by **Macy's.** ~ 626-792-0211.

Stop by **The Colonnade**, a small arcade that houses **Kokila's Boutique.** At this shop you'll find natural fiber fashions for women. ~ 626-584-1157. Closed Sunday. **Burlington Arcade,** modeled after The Burlington in London, is another elegant gallery of specialty shops. ~ 380 South Lake Avenue.

Just west of South Lake Avenue, visit a charming group of English-style cottages. One is the **Rose Tree Cottage**, where you can browse for fine British imports or enjoy afternoon tea in a traditional setting. Reservations for tea should be made one week in advance. Closed Monday. ~ 828 East California Boulevard, Pasadena; 626-793-3337; www.rosetreecottage.com.

Another major Pasadena shopping district lies along **Colorado Boulevard**, the town's main artery and the route of the annual Rose Parade. **Vroman's Bookstore,** one of the area's oldest and finest bookstores, is among the revered shops along this boulevard. ~ 695 East Colorado Boulevard, Pasadena; 626-449-5320.

Touted as the world's largest swap meet, the Rose Bowl Flea Market is held on the second Sunday of each month. You'll find everything from collectibles to contemptibles. Admission. ~ 1001 Rose Bowl Drive, Pasadena; 323-560-7469.

The pride of the Boulevard is Pasadena's **Paseo Colorado**, three blocks of open-air shopping with over 100 stores, restaurants, and businesses, as well as a 14-screen multiplex movie theater. Unlike Old Towne there is plenty of parking. ~ On Colorado Boulevard through to Green Street, between Los Robles and Marengo avenues; 626-795-8891.

Old Town Pasadena is a lively historic district that is the pride of the city. ~ Bordered by Holly and Green streets, Pasadena Avenue, and Arroyo Parkway.

Travelers will want to stop in at **Distant Lands**, one of the finest travel-related bookstores anywhere. In addition to travel literature, they also carry a complete selection of travel clothing, accessories, and luggage. ~ 56 South Raymond Avenue, Pasadena; 626-449-3220, 800-310-3220; www.distantlands.com, e-mail distantlands@earthlink.net.

Pasadena Antique Center & Annex, the city's largest gallery of shops, houses more than 130 antique dealers. Among them is **Djanet**, with a collection of antique glassware, and **Things of Interest**, specializing in Mission-style furniture and accessories. ~ 480 South Fair Oaks Avenue, Pasadena; 626-449-7706.

The colorful exterior of **The Folk Tree** will inevitably draw you in to see the shop's amazing collection of folk art. Originating from Mexico and South America, the inventory includes a fascinating collection of dolls. Tours are available. ~ 217 South Fair Oaks Avenue, Pasadena; 626-795-8733; www.folktree.com.

For more international folk art, head three doors down to **The Folk Tree Collection**, where there's a large selection of folk art, jewelry, and clothing from all over the world, as well as changing art exhibits. ~ 199 South Fair Oaks Avenue, Pasadena; 626-793-4828; www.folktree.com.

NIGHTLIFE   Like almost everything else in the San Gabriel Valley, the entertainment scene centers around Pasadena.

The Ice House presents new and established comedians every night. Another section of the 1920s-era ice house, **The Ice House Annex**, features stand-up comedy. Closed Monday. Cover. ~ 24 North Mentor Avenue, Pasadena; 626-577-1894.

Barney's Ltd., an old-style saloon with village charm and friendly spirit, pours over 80 brands of beer from all over the world. ~ 93 West Colorado Boulevard, Pasadena; 626-577-2739.

Or consider the **Pasadena Playhouse**, a historic theater that has been the birthplace for numerous stars of stage and screen. A multitude of performances are produced in the 680-seat space. ~ 39 South El Molino Avenue, Pasadena; 626-356-7529; www. pasadenaplayhouse.org.

▼▼▼▼▼▼▼▼▼▼
San Marino

Originally a Spanish land grant, this former rancho was purchased by railroad baron Henry E. Huntington in the early part of the 20th century. In 1919, Huntington and his wife turned their estate, including his collections of rare books, art, and plants, into a collections-based research and educational institution that is today the stunning Huntington Library, Art Collections, and Botanical Gardens. The beautiful residential area surrounding the Huntington complex is filled with large, architecturally interesting, and expensive homes that house the area's elite.

SIGHTS

HIDDEN ►

El Molino Viejo, the Old Mill, represents a vital part of the area's Spanish tradition. Built in 1816 by Indians from San Gabriel Mission, it was Southern California's first water-powered grist mill. Only the millstones remain from the actual mill, but the building, an adobe beauty with red-tile roof, is still intact. With its courtyard setting and flowering fruit trees, the place is thoroughly enchanting. Down in the basement you'll find a working scale model of the mill's machinery. Closed Monday. ~ 1120 Old Mill Road, San Marino; 626-449-5458.

One of the Southland's most spectacular complexes and certainly the premier attraction in the San Gabriel Valley is the **Huntington Library, Art Collections, and Botanical Gardens**. This incredible cultural preserve was once presided over by a single individual, Henry E. Huntington (1850–1927), a shrewd tycoon who made a killing in railroads and real estate, then consolidated his fortune by marrying the widow of his equally rich uncle.

The focal point of Huntington's 207-acre aesthetic preserve, the **Huntington Gallery**, was originally his home. Today the mansion is dedicated to 18th- and 19th-century English and French art and houses one of the finest collections of its kind in the country. Gainsborough's "Blue Boy" is here, as well as paintings by Turner and Van Dyck, tapestries, porcelains, and furniture. Another gallery contains Renaissance paintings and French sculpture from the 18th century; the **Virginia Steele Scott Gallery of American Art**, housed in an enchanting building, traces American painting from 1730 to the mid-1900s.

Moving from oil to ink, and from mansion to mansion, the **Huntington Library** contains one of the world's finest collections of rare British and American manuscripts and first editions. Representing nine centuries of literature, the exhibit includes a Gutenberg bible, the Ellesmere Chaucer (a handpainted manuscript dating from 1410), classics such as Ovid's *Metamorphosis* and Milton's *Paradise Lost*, and latter-day works by James Joyce and Henry James. The Founding Fathers are present with original manuscripts by Washington, Franklin, and Jefferson; and the

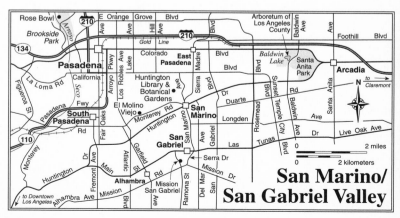

San Marino/San Gabriel Valley

American Renaissance is evident in the literary works of such classic authors as Poe, Hawthorne, and Twain.

This describes only some of the *buildings* on the property! There are also the grounds, a heavenly labyrinth of gardens ranging from a verdant jungle setting to the austerely elegant **Desert garden**. Rolling lawns are adorned with Italian statuary and bordered by plots of roses and camellias. The **Shakespeare garden** is filled with plants mentioned by the playwright; the **Japanese garden** features an arched bridge, koi pond, and 19th-century house. The first phase—three acres out of twelve—of what will be one of the largest classical **Chinese gardens** built outside of China will be completed in 2004. A 90,000-square-foot addition to the library will be finished around the same time. All are part of the amazing legacy of a philanthropist with a vision equal to his wealth. Closed Monday. Admission. ~ 1151 Oxford Road, San Marino; 626-405-2100; www.huntington.org, e-mail publicinfo@huntington.org.

Eastern San Gabriel Valley

The Eastern San Gabriel Valley, once a bountiful agricultural area, is today a cluster of communities that sprung up as Los Angeles residents began to move out of the city center in the 1880s. The area's main attractions are composed of an arboretum, a historic mission, and a world-famous racetrack.

SIGHTS

Fourth in California's historic chain of missions, **Mission San Gabriel Archangel** is an oasis in an urban setting. Built in 1771, the church is fashioned from cut stone, brick, and mortar. Its buttressed walls and vaulted roof indicate Moorish influences and lend a fortress-like quality, but inside the sanctuary peace reigns: the grounds are covered in cactus gardens and grape arbors and flanked by a cemetery. The chapel features an 18th-century altar built in Mexico City as well as colorful statues from Spain. The winery next door was once the largest in California. Admission. ~ 428 South Mission Drive, San Gabriel; 626-457-3048, fax 626-282-5308; www.sangabrielmission.org, e-mail sgmission@aol.com.

Rarely does a racecourse represent a work of art, but **Santa Anita Park**, built in 1934, is one of the country's most beautiful tracks. Surrounded by landscaped gardens and ornamented with wrought-iron fixtures, the clubhouse is a local landmark. Added to the aesthetics is another unique attraction: the family-oriented park, featuring picnic areas and playgrounds and offering free admission to children accompanied by parents. During the morning from 7:30 to 9:30 the public is admitted free and, during race season, visitors can take a guided tour on weekends and watch the horses work out. Thoroughbred racing season is from October to mid-November and from Christmas through April. Admission. ~ 285 West Huntington Drive, Arcadia; 626-574-7223, fax 626-445-4202; www.santaanita.com.

The **Arboretum of Los Angeles County** located across the street may be the most photographed location in the world. Everything from Tarzan movies to Bing Crosby's *Road to Singapore* to television's "Fantasy Island" has been filmed in this 127-acre garden. With plants from every corner of the globe, the arboretum has portrayed Hawaii, Burma, Africa, Samoa, and Devil's Island. Wander past the duck pond, tropical greenhouse, fountain, and waterfall and you'll be retracing the steps of Humphrey Bogart, Cary Grant, Ingrid Bergman, and Dustin Hoffman.

The history of the surrounding region, captured in several historic structures still standing on the grounds, long precedes the movies. There are **wickiups** similar to those of the original Gabrieleño Indians, who used the local spring-fed pond as a watering hole. Representing the Spanish era is the **Hugo Reid Adobe**, an 1840 structure built with over 3000 mud bricks. Crudely furnished in 19th-century Mexican fashion, the adobe dates to the days when the area was part of a huge Mexican land grant. E. J. "Lucky" Baldwin, the silver-mining magnate who helped introduce horse racing to Southern California, bought the ranch in 1875, and built a **Queen Anne Cottage**. His castle-in-the-sky dream house, painted white with red stripes and topped by a bell tower, is a gingerbread Victorian. The interior, decorated in period style, is a masterwork of hardwoods and crystal, stained glass and marble. Admission. ~ 301 North Baldwin Avenue, Arcadia; 626-821-3222, fax 626-445-1217; www.arboretum.org, e-mail comments@arboretum.org.

The Rancho Santa Ana Botanic Garden boasts the largest collection of native California plants in the world.

Also part of this never-ending complex is the **Santa Anita Depot**. Built in 1890, it's a classic brick train station filled with equipment and memorabilia from the great age of railroads. Open Sunday, Tuesday, and Wednesday. Admission. ~ 301 North Baldwin Avenue, Arcadia; 626-821-3222, fax 626-445-1217.

In the trim little town of Claremont, near the foothills of the San Gabriel Mountains, you can tour another idyllic enclave. The **Claremont Colleges**, a collection of six independent colleges, including the famous Harvey Mudd engineering school, form a continuous campus studded with shade trees. There are walking tours of turn-of-the-20th-century buildings and strolls through pretty parks. ~ From Route 10 take the Indian Hill Boulevard North exit; go right on 1st Street; go left on College Avenue, Claremont; 909-621-8000.

HIDDEN ► Several hundred yards closer to the mountains lies the **Rancho Santa Ana Botanic Garden**. This enchanting 86-acre preserve is dedicated to native desert plants, coastal vegetation, wildflowers, and woodlands. Wandering its nature trails is like touring a miniature version of natural California. A particularly pretty time to visit is during spring when the California poppies are in bloom. Be sure to visit the garden shop. ~ 1500 North College Avenue, Claremont; 909-625-8767, fax 909-626-7670; www.rsabg.org.

DINING

HIDDEN ► On race days from 7:30 a.m. to 10 a.m., anyone can park for free and eat breakfast at **Clocker's Corners**, Santa Anita Racetrack's outdoor restaurant, without paying the park's entrance fee. What could be better on a beautiful Southern California winter day than lingering over eggs Benedict while watching jockeys exercising their steeds against the backdrop of the San Gabriel Mountains? ~ Santa Anita Park, 285 West Huntington Drive, Arcadia; 626-574-7223, fax 626-446-1456. BUDGET.

East conquers West at **Chez Sateau**, where a Japanese chef prepares French meals with special flair. The frosted-glass-and-private-booth dining room features a menu that changes seasonally, including specialties such as rack of lamb. Filling out the *carte* are outlandish desserts like soufflés and crêpes suzettes. No lunch on Saturday. Closed Monday. ~ 850 South Baldwin Avenue, Arcadia; 626-446-8806, fax 626-446-0402. MODERATE TO DELUXE.

SHOPPING **Santa Anita Fashion Park** is a colossal 150-store mall adjacent to Santa Anita Park. ~ Baldwin Avenue and West Huntington Drive, Arcadia.

NIGHTLIFE During the thoroughbred horse-racing season, beautiful Santa Anita Racetrack attracts huge crowds every day. At night the bawdy track crowd goes to sing along karaoke-style at the **100 to 1 Club.** ~ 100 West Huntington Drive, Arcadia; 626-445-3520.

FRANK G. BONELLI REGIONAL PARK 🏃 🚵 🐎 🛶 ⚓ ⛵ 🎣   **PARKS**
⛴ 🚤 ⚓ This 1799-acre facility combines tree-covered hills and theme-park attractions. For the outdoor-minded there are trails, stables, and a 250-acre lake with boating and fishing facilities; swimming is good at Swim Beach. Bicycles, boats, and horses can all be rented here. There are also picnic areas, restrooms, and a snack bar. The rest of the crowd beelines to **Raging Waters** (909-802-2200; www.ragingwaters.com, e-mail extreme@ragingwaters.com), an aquatic theme park with waterslides and simulated surfing waves. Open spring and summer. Visitors who can't decide between the natural and artificial head for the adjacent golf course and hot tubs. Day-use fee, $6 per car; free from November through February except on weekends and holidays. ~ 120 Via Verde, San Dimas; 909-599-8411, fax 909-599-6020.

> For a bike trip from the mountains to the sea, try the San Gabriel River Trail. It begins at the base of the San Gabriel Mountains and extends 38 miles to the Pacific.

▲ Permitted at **East Shore RV Park,** located within the park. There are 519 campsites (all with full hookups), $32 to $34 per night, and 14 tent sites, $24 per night. ~ 909-599-8355, 800-809-3778.

San Gabriel Mountains

The San Gabriel Mountains and adjoining Angeles National Forest encompass 700,000 acres of wilderness on the northern edge of the L.A. metropolis, a mere one-half-hour drive from Pasadena and Glendale. Hard to believe that here, in the environs of seemingly perpetually sunny Los Angeles, snow in the upper elevations can hang on until July.

Eaton Canyon, set in the foothills, is a 190-acre park laced with   **SIGHTS** hiking trails that traverse an arroyo and four different plant communities. Sufficiently close to the ocean and mountains to support flora from both regions, the park is a mix of coastal sage scrub, chaparral, oak woodland, and riparian vegetation. Trails meander through the park and lead deep into the adjacent Angeles National Forest. In 1993 about half of Eaton Canyon, including the interpretive center, burned in a fire. Since then, the park has built a new Nature Center, and a fire ecology trail shows the amazing regeneration of foothill flora. ~ 626-398-5420, fax 626-398-5422; www.ecnca.org.

HIDDEN ► Another of the region's botanic preserves, **Descanso Gardens** stretches across 160 acres at the foot of the San Gabriel Mountains. This former estate has one of the largest camellia gardens in the world, numbering over 60,000 plants, as well as a rose garden where droves of the species' strains are cultivated. There is also a Japanese teahouse and garden, a section devoted to native California plants, and iris and lilac gardens. An art gallery showcases a changing roster of local art. Unifying this restful hideaway is a tumbling stream that meanders through an oak forest past bird preserves and duck ponds. Admission. ~ 1418 Descanso Drive, La Cañada; 818-952-4401, fax 818-952-1238; www.descanso.com.

Stretching from San Bernardino County across the entire northern tier of Los Angeles County, the Angeles National Forest separates the Los Angeles Basin from the desert.

To fully explore the San Gabriel Mountains, follow the Angeles Crest Highway (Route 2) in its sinuous course upward from La Cañada. With their sharp-faced cliffs and granite outcroppings, the San Gabriels form a natural barrier between the Los Angeles Basin and the Mojave Desert. Embodied in the 693,000-acre **Angeles National Forest**, these dry, semi-barren mountains are a mix of high chaparral, pine forest, and rocky terrain. Hiking trails crisscross the heights and wildflowers bloom in spring.

A side road from Route 2 leads to 5710-foot **Mount Wilson**, from which you can gaze across the entire expanse of Los Angeles to the Pacific. **Mount Wilson Observatory**, the region's most famous landmark, supports a 100-inch reflecting telescope used by Edwin Hubble in his formulation of the Big Bang theory of the expanding universe. Today the telescope can be seen through an observation window. There's also a museum here. ~ 626-793-3100, fax 626-793-4570; www.mtwilson.edu.

For complete information on the mountains and the Angeles National Forest, stop by the **Chilao Visitors Center**. Located on Route 2 about 14 miles past the turnoff for Mount Wilson, this small facility has its own nature center and two miles of self-guided nature trails. Closed Tuesday; call for changing hours. ~ 626-796-5541.

DINING

HIDDEN ►

Way up in the San Gabriel Mountains, where Angeles National Forest creates an ideal retreat, you'll find **Newcomb's Ranch Inn**. This remote restaurant, set in a rustic wooden building, serves an array of American dishes, burgers, and sandwiches. Little more than a log diner, it's a welcome sight for anyone wandering the mountains. Open for breakfast, lunch, and dinner. ~ Route 2, Chilao; 626-440-1001; www.newcombsranch.com, e-mail mail@ newcombsranch.com. BUDGET.

ANGELES NATIONAL FOREST 🚶 🚴 🏇 🏕 🚣 🎣 ⛴ ⛴   **PARKS**
🚤 🛶 Nature is rarely reducible to statistics, but numbers are unavoidable in describing this 693,000-acre forest. There are four rivers, eight lakes, a 10,000-foot peak, and 189 miles of fishing streams. The 36,000-acre San Gabriel Wilderness is contained within the National Forest. Overall the forest attracts more than 30 million visitors annually. Most are daytrippers intent on sightseeing and picnicking, but campers and hikers, enjoying 60 campgrounds and 556 miles of trails, are also prevalent. Flora and fauna range from green-winged teal to black bear to horned toads and rattlesnakes. This is also a prime ski area, with five winter sports centers. Other facilities include picnic areas and restrooms. Parking fee, $5 per day. ~ Route 2 is the main highway through the southern sector of the forest; the northern region is located east of Route 5; 626-574-5200, fax 626-574-5233.

▲ There are 60 campgrounds for tents and RVs (no hook-ups); $3 to $12 per night.

▼▼▼▼▼▼▼▼▼▼▼▼▼▼▼
Glendale and Burbank

The land that became the cities of Glendale and Burbank was, in the latter part of the 19th century, covered in citrus orchards and vineyards. Burbank, despite a promising start in the early 1900s, didn't really establish itself until the 1920s, when movie studios and Lockheed Aircraft came to town. Neighboring Glendale experienced a real estate boom in the 1920s, and a setback in 1933 when a devastating storm killed 44 people and demolished or severely damaged at least 100 homes. Today, however, both towns are thriving. Glendale spans over 30 miles and is Los Angeles' third-largest city, while Burbank is home to a busy airport and several movie and television studios.

The portal to the land of the living, some say, is through the gates   **SIGHTS**
of death. In the San Fernando Valley that would be **Forest Lawn**, one of the most spectacular cemeteries in the world.

Within the courtyards of this hillside retreat are replicas of Michelangelo's "David," Ghiberti's "Baptism of Jesus," and a mosaic of John Trumbull's painting "The Signing of the Declaration of Independence." There are also re-creations of a 10th-century English church and another from 14th-century Scotland. The museum houses a collection consisting of every coin mentioned in the Bible. "The Crucifixion," the nation's largest religious painting, a tableau 195 feet long and 45 feet high, is also on display.

Death has never been prouder or had more for which to be prideful. On the one hand, Forest Lawn is quite beautiful, a parkland of the dead with grassy slopes and forested knolls, a garden planted with tombstones. On the other, it is tasteless, a theme park of the dead where the rich are buried amid all the pomp their heirs can muster. ~ 1712 South Glendale Avenue, Glendale; 818-241-4151, fax 323-551-5073.

HIDDEN ►

The **Casa Adobe de San Rafael** is a single-story, mud-brick home built in the 19th century. Once occupied by the Los Angeles County Sheriff, the hacienda's chief feature is the grounds, which are trimly landscaped and covered with shade trees. The house itself is furnished in Early California style. ~ 1330 Dorothy Drive, Glendale.

Situated in the foothills overlooking Glendale is the **Brand Library & Art Center**. Neither the library nor the galleries are exceptional, but both are located in **El Miradero**, a unique 1904 mansion modeled after the East Indian Pavilion of the 1893 Columbian World Exposition. With bulbous towers, crenelated archways, and minarets, the building is Saracenic in concept, combining Spanish, Moorish, and Indian motifs. The grounds also include a spacious park with nature trails and picnic areas as well as "The Doctor's House," a heavily ornamented 1890 Queen Anne Eastlake Victorian. Closed Sunday and Monday. ~ 1601 West Mountain Street, Glendale; 818-548-2051, fax 818-548-5079.

Blinded by the glitz and glamour of Tinsel Town, most visitors overlook the unassuming, Ozzie-and-Harriet suburb of **Burbank**, located in the San Fernando Valley about ten miles north of downtown Los Angeles. This is, however, where the majority of "Hollywood" films and television shows are shot—NBC, Warner Bros., and Walt Disney Productions all have studios

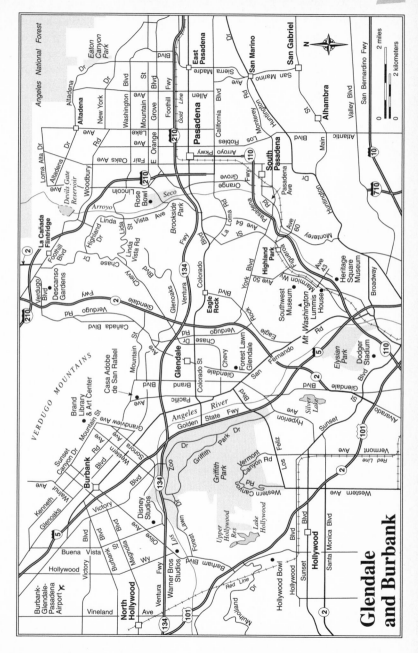

Glendale and Burbank

here (see "Hollywood in Action" in Chapter Four for information on studio tours). With this in mind, keep an eye open if you spend time here: having lunch at an eatery near the studios or browsing through a local bookstore might just lead to a chance spotting of a star from "ER" or "Will & Grace" taking a breather between tapings.

MT. WASHINGTON AREA   If an entire neighborhood could qualify as an outdoor museum, the Mt. Washington district would probably charge admission. Here within a few blocks are several picture-book expressions of desert culture.

The **Lummis House,** or El Alisal, is the work of one man, Charles Fletcher Lummis, whose life is inextricably bound to the history of the region. Though born in the Northeast, Lummis fell in love with the Southwest, devoting his life to defending the region's Indian tribes and promoting local arts and crafts. A writer and magazine editor, he built this stone house himself, carving the doors by hand and even embedding photographs from his South American travels in the windows where the sun still shines through them. Surrounded by a "waterwise" garden, the house is an excellent example of turn-of-the-20th-century Southwestern sensibilities. Closed Monday through Thursday. ~ 200 East Avenue 43; 323-222-0546, fax 323-222-0771; www.socialhistory.org, e-mail hssc@socialhistory.org.

> The Lummis House was contructed using stone from the nearby arroyo.

Perhaps Charles Lummis' most important role was as founder of the **Southwest Museum.** Set in a Mission-style structure overlooking downtown Los Angeles, this important facility contains exquisite jewelry, basketry, weaving, and other handicrafts from Pueblo Indian tribes. California's Indians are represented by their petroglyphs, pottery, weapons, and decorative beadwork. In fact, the museum has so expanded its collection since Lummis' day that the current theme focuses more on American Indians in general than on the Southwest. There are bead cradle boards, a tepee, and leather clothing hand-painted by Plains Indians; totem poles and artifacts from the Pacific Northwest tribes; and an excellent research library. Changing exhibits present the work of contemporary American Indian artists. Closed Monday. Admission. ~ 234 Museum Drive; 323-221-2164, fax 323-224-8223; www.southwestmuseum.org, e-mail info@southwestmuseum.org.

That antique neighborhood on the other side of the Pasadena Freeway is **Heritage Square Museum**, an open-air, living history museum with a collection of historic buildings. Several impressive Victorian buildings, a Methodist church, and the old Palms Railroad Depot are here. There's also an exhibition area, guided tours, and rotating exhibits. Open Friday (though access to buildings is restricted) through Sunday, and select holiday Mondays. Admission. ~ 3800 Homer Street; 626-449-0193, fax 626-304-9652; www.heritage.square.org, e-mail director@heritagesquare.org.

LODGING

The Safari Inn is that rarest of creatures, a motel with soul. In fact this 55-room facility also possesses a pool, restaurant, and lounge. The film location for several movies, it offers rooms and suites decorated in high '50s style. The amenities and accoutrements here are definitely a step above those of a roadside motel. ~ 1911 West Olive Avenue, Burbank; 818-845-8586, 800-633-1144, fax 818-845-0054; www.coasthotels.com. MODERATE.

The **Coast Anabelle Hotel** offers a fresh look reminiscent of a posh European-style hostelry. Designed to accommodate visitors to the nearby NBC and Warner Bros. studios, its 47 guest rooms and suites are traditionally furnished in warm color schemes. The staff, which seems to almost outnumber the guests, prides itself on friendliness. ~ 2011 West Olive Avenue, Burbank; 818-845-7800, 800-633-1144, fax 818-845-0054; www.coast hotels.com. DELUXE.

DINING

A small Japanese restaurant, **Aoba**, contains a sushi bar and fewer than a dozen tables. The menu offers a standard array of Japanese dishes, including teriyaki entrées, tempura specials, and, of course, sushi. ~ 239 North Brand Boulevard, Glendale; 818-247-9789, fax 818-247-9486. MODERATE.

SHOPPING

Glendale shopping centers around the **Glendale Galleria**, a mammoth 240-store complex anchored by such heavies as **Macy's** (818-240-8411) and **Nordstrom** (818-502-9922). A host of apparel stores, specialty shops, knickknack stores, and restaurants offer variety, if not imagination. ~ Central Avenue and Broadway, Glendale.

If it happens to be the first Sunday of the month, add the **Glendale Civic Auditorium** to your list of must-see addresses.

That's when more than 80 antique dealers gather to sell their wares. Admission. ~ 1401 North Verdugo Road, Glendale; 818-548-2147; www.ci.glendale.ca.us.

A promised land for browsers is **Glendale Costumes**, which rents over 60,000 costumes from the tights of Renaissance dandies to the tights of Batman. Closed Sunday and Monday. ~ 746 West Doran Street, Glendale; 818-244-1161.

Burbank is not really geared to shopping, with the exception of San Fernando Boulevard between San Jose and Tujunga avenues. Home to several used bookstores, the area includes **Movie World**, which adds volumes about movies to its inventory of books. ~ 212 North San Fernando Boulevard, Burbank; 818-846-0459.

For New Age titles consider stopping in at the **Psychic Eye Book Store**. Decorated with crystals and Asian statuary, it carries volumes on metaphysics, palmistry, numerology, and the occult. ~ 1011 West Olive Avenue, Burbank; 818-845-8831; www. pebooks.com.

HIDDEN ►   **It's a Wrap** sells used clothing with a Southland twist. The shop gets most of its merchandise from the studios, where the items were worn on TV shows by sitcom and soap opera stars. ~ 3315 West Magnolia Boulevard, Burbank; 818-567-7366.

NIGHTLIFE   **Jax Bar & Grill**, with its brass elephants and local clientele, is a supper club where notable jazz musicians headline nightly. ~ 339 North Brand Boulevard, Glendale; 818-500-1604.

For sophisticated entertainment there's the **Glendale Centre Theatre**, which presents musicals and comedies. ~ 324 North Orange Street, Glendale; 818-244-8481; www.glendalecentre theatre.com.

The **Third Stage** is a comedy and improv venue. Closed Monday. ~ 2811 West Magnolia Boulevard, Burbank; 818-842-4755; www.thirdstage.org.

Colony Theatre Company hosts classic dramas, musicals, comedies, and new plays. ~ 555 North 3rd Street, Burbank; 818-558-7000; www.colonytheatre.org.

Named after Shirley Temple, **Dimples** is a showcase for fledgling singers. Dance music alternates every half hour with musical auditions. Sing for your drinks while pursuing those dreams of stardom! ~ 3413 West Olive Avenue, Burbank; 818-842-2336.

TEN

San Fernando Valley

The San Fernando Valley, known locally as simply "The Valley," is Los Angeles' answer to Middle America. It sprawls across 220 square miles and contains a population of more than 1.3 million suburbanites who tend to be conventional, conservative, and less tolerant of ethnic and lifestyle differences than folks in some other parts of town. Nonetheless, this smog-shrouded gridwork of tract homes and shopping malls is a kind of stucco version of the American Dream.

Bounded by the Santa Monica Mountains to the south and the San Gabriels on the east, The Valley first entered the history books in 1796 when Spanish padres established the San Fernando Mission, an isolated outpost that became a cultural center for the ranchos that soon sprang up between the mountains. During the 1870s, when Spanish land grants were subdivided and railroads entered the area, the San Fernando region enjoyed its first boom. But the major escalation in population and real-estate prices came early the next century during one of the biggest scandals in Los Angeles history.

When L.A. voters passed a $1.5 million bond issue in 1905 to buy water-rich land in the distant Owens Valley, they believed they were bringing water to their own parched city. In fact, much of this liquid gold poured into the San Fernando Valley, filling the coffers of a cabal of civic leaders who bought up surrounding orange groves and transformed them into housing developments.

In 1914, when Universal turned a 230-acre chicken ranch into a world-acclaimed movie studio, The Valley found a home industry. With its stark mountains and open spaces, the place proved an ideal location for filming Westerns. By the post–World War II era, the aerospace industry had landed in The Valley, adding money to an area fast becoming a kind of promised land for the middle class.

Today rising executives raise their families in uninspired but tidy neighborhoods of cookie-cutter houses with manicured lawns. Many strive to eventually score a place on the Westside, but most will stay in The Valley, commuting every day to Los Angeles and spending weekends at local malls and family barbecues. Don't sell these suburbanites short, though; they've got plenty of backbone, having bounced back after a multitude of nature disasters, including two devastating earthquakes (1971 and 1994) and countless floods, mud slides, and fires.

Beyond all of this suburban sprawl, The Valley has plenty to attract visitors. Thrill seekers can be terrified on as many as 16 roller coasters at Six Flags Magic Mountain, fans of *E.T.* can bicycle alongside the famous extraterrestrial at Universal Studios, hikers can experience tranquility in the area's natural areas, and night owls can check out the hip clubs on Ventura Boulevard.

▼▼▼▼▼▼▼▼▼▼▼▼▼▼

Ventura Boulevard

Only in the San Fernando Valley could a single street define an entire geographic area. Running from east to west along the southern edge of The Valley, Ventura Boulevard parallels the Santa Monica Mountains as it passes through Studio City, Sherman Oaks, Encino, and Tarzana, then continues to the distant towns of Woodland Hills and Calabasas.

Originally part of El Camino Real, the road that linked California's first settlements and missions, Ventura Boulevard was the main road from the San Gabriel Valley to Ventura County before the 101 freeway was built. Today the Boulevard is lined with shops, restaurants, motels, and office buildings. While in Studio City and Sherman Oaks low-rise commercial establishments seldom top three stories, loftier chrome and glass structures have popped up in Encino and Tarzana. Historic and modern, Ventura Boulevard has been and continues to be the San Fernando Valley's most famous thoroughfare.

SIGHTS

Campo de Cahuenga is a 1923 re-creation of a building constructed in 1845. Of little architectural interest, the place is noteworthy because the treaty ending the Mexican War in California was signed here by Lt. Col. John C. Fremont and General Andrés Pico in 1847. Closed to the public. ~ 3919 Lankershim Boulevard, Universal City; 818-763-7651, fax 818-756-9963.

Several phases of San Fernando Valley life are preserved at **Los Encinos State Historic Park**. This five-acre facility is studded with orange trees, which covered the valley at the turn of the

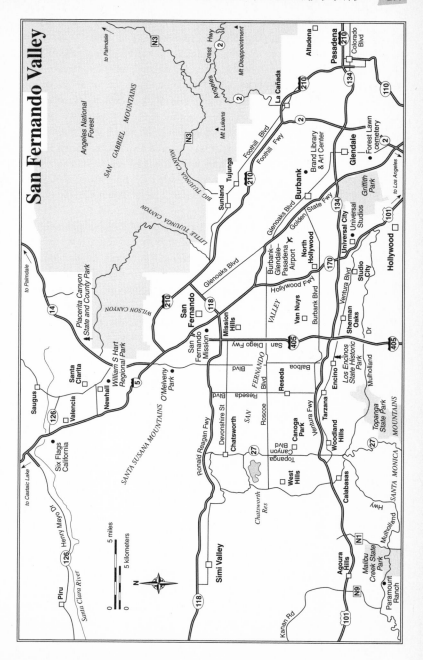

San Fernando Valley

20th century. The De La Osa Adobe, built in 1850 and utilized as a resting place along El Camino Real, is a squat eight-room ranch house. Nearby stands the Garnier Building, a two-story limestone residence constructed in 1872 after the fashion of a French farmhouse. However, the buildings that serve as a visitors center and museum remain closed. With its duck pond and shaded lawns, the park is a choice spot for a picnic. Closed Monday and Tuesday. ~ 16756 Moorpark Street, Encino; 818-784-4849.

Making these old houses seem like youngsters is the **Encino Oak Tree**. With branches spreading 150 feet and a trunk eight feet thick, this magnificent specimen dates back about 1000 years. ~ Ventura Boulevard and Louise Avenue, Encino.

Farther out in The Valley lies the town of Calabasas, which prides itself on a Wild West heritage but looks suspiciously like surrounding suburban towns. It does possess a few remnants from its romantic past, including the **Leonis Adobe**, an 1844 mud-brick house that was expanded around 1879 into a stately two-story home with porches on both levels. This Monterey-style beauty stands beside the **Plummer House**, an antique Victorian home. There's also an 1880s-era Victorian rose garden. Closed Monday and Tuesday. Admission. ~ 23537 Calabasas Road, Calabasas; 818-222-6511, fax 818-222-0862; www.leonis adobemuseum.org, e-mail leonisadobe@aol.com.

An ersatz but enchanting version of the Old West awaits at **Paramount Ranch**, a 750-acre park that once served as the film location for Westerns. Paramount owned the spread for two decades beginning in the 1920s, using it as a set for *Broken Lullaby* (1932) with Lionel Barrymore, *Thunder Below* (1932) with Tallulah Bankhead, and *Adventures of Marco Polo* (1937), the Samuel Goldwyn extravaganza that included a fortress, elephants, and 2000 horses. During the heyday of TV Westerns in the 1950s, the property was a location for "The Cisco Kid," "Bat Masterson," and "Have Gun, Will Travel."

Today you can hike around the ranch, past the rolling meadows, willow-lined streams, grassy hillsides, and rocky heights that made it such an ideal set. "Paramount Ranch" still stands, a collection of falsefront buildings that change their signs depending on what's being filmed. ~ In Santa Monica Mountains National Recreation Area; 805-370-2301, fax 805-370-1850; www.nps. gov/samo.

Universal City

Universal Citywalk is a two-block-long pedestrian mall that connects the Universal Studios Hollywood theme park (see "Hollywood in Action" in Chapter Four) and Amphitheater to the Cineplex Odeon movie theaters. Although the emphasis is on shops and restaurants, you can stroll down the middle of this "city street" and enjoy a collection of vintage neon signs and wacky, eclectic architecture. Street performers entertain visitors nightly, and in the central court, children enjoy darting in and out of jets of water shooting up from the sidewalk fountain. ~ 100 Universal Center Drive, Universal City; 818-622-4455, fax 818-622-0407; www.universalstudios.com.

With so many dining, shopping, and entertainment opportunities vying for your attention, you may want to stay overnight here just to pack it all in. There are many highrise hotels in the area. Among the most luxurious is the **Universal City Hilton and Towers**, a 24-story steel-and-glass structure overlooking the San Fernando Valley. Guest rooms are contemporary in decor and feature plate-glass views of the surrounding city. Among the amenities are one restaurant, two lounges, shops, a pool, a jacuzzi, and a exercise room. ~ 555 Universal Terrace Parkway, Universal City; 818-506-2500, 800-445-8667, fax 818-509-2058. DELUXE TO ULTRA-DELUXE.

The **Lobby Bar** at the Universal City Hilton and Towers represents a choice piano bar and a great way to unwind after all the glitter and bustle of Citywalk. ~ 555 Universal Terrace Parkway, Universal City; 818-506-2500.

Orcutt Ranch Horticultural Center, once a private estate, is now a 24-acre historical monument in full bloom. You'll see a ranch house (not open to the public), rose gardens, and citrus orchards. You can wander through the oak groves, enjoying a vision of the San Fernando Valley before the advent of suburbia. ~ 23600 Roscoe Boulevard, West Hills; 818-346-7449, fax 818-346-0376.

LODGING

A subtle charm pervades the atmosphere at **Sportsmen's Lodge Hotel**, a Ventura Boulevard fixture for well over 50 years. Back in the day, you could catch a trout in the hotel's stocked pond, and the dining room would cook it for you. Today, hidden within this English country–style establishment are gardens with waterfalls and foot-bridges, as well as a swan-filled lagoon. The interior courtyard contains an Olympic-sized swimming pool and the lobby features shops, restaurants, and a pub. Numbering about 200 rooms (each with private patio and room service), the hotel is worth its price. ~ 12825 Ventura Boulevard, Studio City; 818-769-4700, 800-821-8511; www.slhotel.com, e-mail information@slhotel.com. DELUXE TO ULTRA-DELUXE.

Ventura Boulevard, a major thoroughfare in The Valley, is chockablock with motels. Passing through Sherman Oaks, Encino, and Tarzana, you'll find a multitude of possibilities. Among the more upscale motels is **St. George Motor Inn**, a 57-unit, mock-Tudor facility. Microwaves and refrigerators are in every room, and a pool and spa are on the premises. ~ 19454 Ventura Boulevard, Tarzana; 818-345-6911, 800-845-8919, fax 818-996-2955; www.stgeorgemotorinn.com, e-mail stgeorge@aol.com. MODERATE.

Adding to the Valley's hospitality industry is the 15-story **Woodland Hills Hilton**. The updated art-deco look extends from the lobby to the 325 guest rooms and suites. Suites offer wet bars; other amenities include a restaurant and sports bar. ~ 6360 Canoga Avenue, Woodland Hills; 818-595-1000, 800-922-2400, fax 818-595-1003, www.woodlandhills.hilton.com. ULTRA-DELUXE.

DINING

One of Southern California's great restaurant strips, Ventura Boulevard stretches for miles along the southern rim of The Valley, offering fine kitchens all along the route.

The decor at **Teru Sushi** is as inviting as the cuisine. Hand-painted walls and carved figures combine with slat booths and a long dark wood sushi bar. The sushi menu includes several dozen varieties; they also serve a selection of traditional dishes. There is a beautiful garden dining area with a koi pond. No lunch on Saturday and Sunday. ~ 11940 Ventura Boulevard, Studio City; 818-763-6201, fax 818-763-5016; www.terusushi.com. DELUXE TO ULTRA-DELUXE.

For Belgian cuisine and charming intimacy try **Mon Grenier**. With a name that translates as "my attic," this whimsical dining room has a solid reputation for fine cuisine. Entrées include pepper steak, crispy duck, tenderloin of ostrich, and salmon in crust. Dinner only. Closed Sunday. ~ 18040 Ventura Boulevard, Encino; 818-344-8060, fax 818-993-9634; e-mail mongrenier18040@ aol.com. DELUXE TO ULTRA-DELUXE.

The **Sagebrush Cantina** is a sprawling restaurant and bar with ample patio space. In addition to an assortment of Mexican dishes they feature steak, salads, and seafood. ~ 23527 Calabasas Road, Calabasas; 818-222-6062, fax 818-222-6053. BUDGET TO DELUXE.

Way up in the Santa Monica Mountains, that rocky spine separating the San Fernando Valley from the ocean, you'll uncover a rare find at **Saddle Peak Lodge**. A true country lodge, this antique building is constructed of logs lashed together with leather straps. Flintlocks and trophy heads adorn the walls and leather upholstered chairs surround a stone fireplace. Open for dinner and Sunday brunch, the restaurant offers a varied assortment from roasted elk tenderloin to grilled duck. If you have the time, it merits the mountain drive. Closed Monday and Tuesday. ~ 419

AUTHOR FAVORITE

All the critics agree that the food at **Anajak Thai** is outstanding. The menu features more than four dozen noodle, curry, beef, and chicken dishes. Small and comfortable, the restaurant is painted mauve and decorated with white latticework and Asian art. No lunch on Saturday and Sunday. Closed Monday. ~ 14704 Ventura Boulevard, Sherman Oaks; 818-501-4201, fax 818-501-7623. BUDGET.

Cold Canyon Road, Calabasas; 818-222-3888, fax 818-222-1054; www.saddlepeaklodge.com, e-mail spl@saddlepeaklodge.com. ULTRA-DELUXE.

Over at **Delhi Palace** you can dine on affordable Indian cuisine. Cloth napkins and Asian decor are part of the bargain at this excellent restaurant. The dishes include lamb curry, chicken *tandoori*, and numerous vegetarian dishes. ~ 22323 Sherman Way, Canoga Park; 818-992-0913, fax 818-992-0944. BUDGET TO DELUXE.

If meat seems inappropriate just **Follow Your Heart** to a vegetarian restaurant and natural foods market popular with folks from miles around. Specialties at this gathering place include stir-fry, deep-dish pizza, nutburgers, black bean and tofu tacos, and steamed organic vegetables. Open for breakfast, lunch, and dinner. ~ 21825 Sherman Way, Canoga Park; 818-348-3240, fax 818-348-1509; www.followyourheart.com. BUDGET TO MODERATE.

HIDDEN ▶ Ask anyone in the Valley where to go for downhome cooking and they will tell you **Dr. Hogly Wogly's Tyler Texas Bar-B-Que**. It's just a regular old café that happens to serve delicious brisket of beef and stick-to-the-ribs ribs. Dinner comes with half a loaf of home-baked bread and your choice of baked beans, cole slaw, potato salad, or macaroni salad. Chow down! ~ 8136 Sepulveda Boulevard, Van Nuys; 818-780-6701. MODERATE TO DELUXE.

Another conversation piece is the **94th Aero Squadron**, a wildly imaginative establishment obliquely modeled after a World War I aviation headquarters in France. The building resembles a provincial French farmhouse, but it's surrounded by charred airplanes and other artifacts of war. The interior is a sandbagged warren with wings and propellers dangling from the ceiling. The cuisine, which somehow seems irrelevant, is American. Prime rib, Cajun shrimp, and "farmhouse" chicken are regulars on the menu. There's also Saturday and Sunday brunch. ~ 16320 Raymer Avenue, Van Nuys; 818-994-7437, fax 818-994-0442. MODERATE TO DELUXE.

SHOPPING   Out in "The Valley," shopping is such popular sport that the area has bred a new species—"mallies"—who inhabit the shopping malls from the moment the stores open until the second they close.

Cities blend into one another on Ventura Boulevard, the busy east–west corridor that stretches across the entire southern rim of the San Fernando Valley. Shops line every point along the thoroughfare, with only subtle distinctions marking changes in locale. Start in Studio City and you'll find your credit cards still working in Sherman Oaks, Encino, Tarzana, and points west.

Traders of Studio City may not look like a pawnshop, but a hock shop it is. You'll find everything from bangles to cameras at this secondhand store. Closed Sunday. ~ 12238 Ventura Boulevard, Studio City; 818-985-6136.

Strange as it may sound here in Shopperland, there are no department stores at **Encino Town Center** and **Plaza de Oro**. These multitiered plazas provide for more relaxed shopping. Within these open-air facilities are several novel stores offering everything from clothing to chocolate, as well as the Valley's only cinema offering foreign films. ~ 17200 and 17171 Ventura Boulevard, Encino.

Specializing in 19th-century works, **Charles Hecht Gallery** offers a museum-quality selection of impressionist paintings. This exemplary gallery also features work by other artistic schools. Closed Monday. ~ 18584 Ventura Boulevard, Tarzana; 818-881-3218; www.hechtgalleries.com.

Out in the Western-style town of Calabasas, a two-block shopping area offers a chance to browse. Wander **Calabasas Road** and you'll discover a variety of small, one-of-a-kind shops.

Representative of the gay scene in The Valley are a couple of Studio City clubs. **Oil Can Harry's** is a country-and-western club that offers dance lessons on Tuesday and Thursday, open dancing on Friday, and retro disco dancing on Saturday. ~ 11502 Ventura Boulevard, Studio City; 818-760-9749.

NIGHTLIFE

Apache Territory is the area's most popular gay disco. Occasional cover. ~ 11608 Ventura Boulevard, Studio City; 818-506-0404.

AUTHOR FAVORITE

The **L.A. Connection Comedy Theatre** developed a unique comedy concept several years back. They show camp film classics with house comedians ad-libbing the dialogue. Other shows include regular audience participation improvisation. Closed Monday through Wednesday. Cover. ~ 13442 Ventura Boulevard, Sherman Oaks; 818-784-1868; www.laconnectioncomedy.com.

Firefly is *in*—so in, in fact, that they don't even sport a sign: Look for an ivy-covered building with a valet out front. The bar scene takes place in a dark and cozy reproduction of a well-heeled Beverly Hills art patron's den. Sipping a martini and sitting on an overstuffed sofa surrounded by oil paintings here is more like visiting someone's home than drinking in a bar. But the place is far from stuffy, as is evidenced by the unisex bathroom, which can make for some interesting encounters over the soap dispenser. Closed Sunday. ~ 11720 Ventura Boulevard, Studio City; 818-762-1833.

Just as the name implies, **Clear** is big on transparent and uncluttered. Bar stools are Plexiglas, the front door is translucent, the patio favors sparse 1950s decor, benches and walls are covered in white leather, and even the business cards are see-through. This is an ultra-hip place to chill and listen to top deejays spin everything from cool jazz to the latest hip-hop. Closed Monday. ~ 11916 Ventura Boulevard, Studio City; 818-980-4811.

Forget about bowling being outdated—the PINZ **Bowling Alley**, a Studio City hotspot, is so busy on the weekends that you're likely to be looking at a two-hour wait to score one of the 32 lanes. On Friday, Saturday, and Monday nights, bowlers sling balls at glow-in-the-dark pins, while a light show, complete with mirror ball and fog machine, is accompanied by billboard hits by artists like Justin Timberlake (who's been rumored to have bowled here himself). ~ 12655 Ventura Boulevard, Studio City; 818-769-7600; www.sportscenterbowl.net.

The **Baked Potato** serves up contemporary jazz and blues every night. If you want to rub shoulders with L.A. music heavies, this is the place. It's also the place to sample one of 21 different kinds of baked spuds. Cover. ~ 3787 Cahuenga West Boulevard, Studio City; 818-980-1615; www.thebakedpotato.com.

The outdoor patio and country atmosphere at **Sagebrush Cantina** draw steady crowds. Here you can sip margaritas, linger after sunset and, on weekends, work out on the sawdust floors to the sound of rock bands. ~ 23527 Calabasas Road, Calabasas; 818-222-6062.

▼▼▼▼▼▼▼▼▼▼▼▼▼▼▼▼▼

North San Fernando Valley

North San Fernando Valley's attractions run the gamut from heart-stopping roller coaster rides to shaded parks with babbling brooks. Visit one of the area's wooded canyons and it's hard to believe that the giant urban sprawl called Los Angeles is only a short drive away.

The **Tujunga Wash Mural** is one of the Southland's local wonders. Extending for one-half mile along the wall of a flood control channel, it portrays the history of California from prehistoric times to the present. Bright-hued panels capture the era of American Indians and early Spanish explorers, the advent of movies, and the terrors of World War II. ~ On Coldwater Canyon Boulevard between Burbank Boulevard and Oxnard Street, North Hollywood.

SIGHTS

◄ *HIDDEN*

The Tujunga Wash Mural is reputedly the world's longest mural.

In Mission Hills stands Los Angeles' second oldest house. Built before 1834 by mission Indians, the **Andrés Pico Adobe** is a prime example of Spanish architecture. Possessing both beauty and strength, it's a simple rectangular structure with a luxurious courtyard. ~ 10940 Sepulveda Boulevard, Mission Hills.

Just in case you thought Los Angeles County was entirely urban, there are 350 acres of oak forest and native chaparral at **Placerita Canyon State and County Park**. A stream runs through the property and there are hiking trails and a nature center. ~ 19152 Placerita Canyon Road, Newhall; 661-259-7721, fax 661-254-1426; www.placerita.org.

Over at **William S. Hart Regional Park** there's another 260-acre spread once owned by a great star of silent Westerns. A Shakespearean actor who turned to cinema—starring in his last feature, *Tumbleweeds*, in 1925—William S. Hart left his mansion and estate to the movie-going public.

While much of the property is wild, open to hikers and explorers, the most alluring features are the buildings. The old ranch house, once Hart's office, contains photos of friends and mementos from his career. The central feature is Hart's home, a 22-room Spanish hacienda filled with guns, cowboy paintings, and collectibles from the early West. ~ 24151 North San Fernando Road, Newhall; 661-259-0855, fax 661-253-2170.

California's haunting history of earthquakes is evident at **Vasquez Rocks County Park**, where faulting action has compressed, folded, and twisted giant slabs of sandstone. Tilted to 50° angles and rising 150 feet, these angular blocks create a setting that has been used for countless Westerns as well as science fiction films such as *Star Trek* (1979) and *Star Wars* (1977).

◄ *HIDDEN*

Tataviam Indians first lived among these natural rock formations over 4000 years ago. During the 1870s the infamous bandito Tiburcio Vasquez hid amid the caves and outcroppings to elude sheriff's deputies. A kind of Mexican Robin Hood, Vasquez gave his name to the rocks when he shot it out with lawmen here and escaped, only to be captured and hanged later. ~ Escondido Road, northeast of Newhall off Route 14; 661-268-0840, fax 661-268-1343.

To explore this parched and rocky terrain further, head up into **Bouquet Canyon** (Bouquet Canyon Road), a curving, lightly wooded valley with hiking trails and picnic areas. **San Francisquito Canyon** (San Francisquito Canyon Road) is a river-carved valley that parallels Bouquet Canyon. Back in 1928 the Saint Francis Dam collapsed, inundating this quiet canyon and killing more than 400 people in one of the worst natural disasters in United States history. Today it's a placid mountain valley providing ample opportunities to wander. Like Bouquet Canyon it lies outside Saugus near a region appropriately tagged Canyon Country.

Six Flags California encompasses Six Flags Magic Mountain, a quintessential roller-coaster park, and Six Flags Hurricane Harbor, a family-oriented water park featuring water slides and a wave pool. Though adjacent to one another, Magic Mountain and Hurricane Harbor are separate parks with their own entrances and admission fees, not to mention distinct personalities.

At one point during the Superman the Escape ride, you'll experience 4.5 Gs before you go into weightlessness for six and a half seconds.

Spreading across 260 acres and featuring more than 100 rides, shows, and attractions, *Six Flags Magic Mountain* is an entertainment center featuring everything from picnic areas to danceclubs to super-thrill rides. Take for instance "Superman the Escape." It's an exceptional adventure-filled ride that accelerates from 0 to 100 miles per hour in seven seconds and rockets up a 41-story tower, then freefalls back down. "Viper," a 188-foot-high megacoaster, takes you on three vertical loops, plus a boomerang and corkscrew, all experienced at 70 miles per hour. The newest addition "Scream" offers seven 360-degree inversions while fearless riders are strapped into flying chairs or bottomless trains. At a speed of 65-miles-per-hour and a length of 4000 feet, it's a ride that's sure to thrill and chill the heartiest of coaster fans. There are also gentler rides for small children, such as the classic 1912 carousel.

Hurricane Harbor is a fantasy entertainment environment of lost lagoons and pirate coves that was designed with children in mind; one attraction doesn't even allow adults. Of the five themed areas there's "Castaway Cove," a large water play area with slides, waterfalls, and swings. On a raft, you can float along on the "River Cruise," a 1300-foot-long lazy river that surrounds Castaway Cove and Shipwreck Shores. A wave pool called "Forgotten Sea" generates two-foot waves and is up to six feet deep. "Taboo Tower," with a 325-foot enclosed spiraling slide, is one of the four water slides in Hurricane Harbor. Call ahead to check their schedule (Hurricane Harbor is open May through September). Admission. ~ 26101 Magic Mountain Parkway, Valencia; 661-255-4100, fax 661-255-4817.

NIGHTLIFE For live jazz nightly, try **The Money Tree**, located just outside of Burbank. ~ 10149 Riverside Drive, Toluca Lake; 818-752-8383.

Norah's Place is an altogether different experience. This lively Bolivian supper club serves up tango music. In between sets by the resident band the dancefloor fills with dancers moving to merengue, cumbia, and salsa tunes on Saturday nights. Closed Monday and Tuesday. Cover. ~ 5667 Lankershim Boulevard, North Hollywood; 818-980-6900.

PARKS **CASTAIC LAKE RECREATION AREA** Set at the foot of the Castaic Mountains, two manmade lakes are surrounded by rugged slopes. The countryside—covered with chemise, sage, and chaparral—is stark but beautiful. Along the upper lake, which carves a V in the hills, are facilities for picnicking, boating, and waterskiing; there are fishing boat and waverunner rentals. Swimming is good in the lagoon. Castaic is filled with bass, trout, and bluegill. Other facilities are restrooms, picnic areas, and playgrounds. Day-use fee, $6 per vehicle. ~ Access to Castaic Lake is at 32132 Castaic Drive, Castaic; 661-257-4050, fax 661-257-3759; www.castaiclake.com.

Index

Lodging Index

Dining Index

HIDDEN GUIDES

Adventure travel or a relaxing vacation?—"Hidden" guidebooks are the only travel books in the business to provide detailed information on both. Aimed at environmentally aware travelers, our motto is "Where Vacations Meet Adventures." These books combine details on unique hotels, restaurants and sightseeing with information on camping, sports and hiking for the outdoor enthusiast.

THE NEW KEY GUIDES

Based on the concept of ecotourism, The New Key Guides are dedicated to the preservation of Central America's rare and endangered species, architecture and archaeology. Filled with helpful tips, they give travelers everything they need to know about these exotic destinations.

PARADISE FAMILY GUIDES

Ideal for families traveling with kids of any age—toddlers to teenagers—Paradise Family Guides offer a blend of travel information unlike any other guides to the Hawaiian islands. With vacation ideas and tropical adventures that are sure to satisfy both action-hungry youngsters and relaxation-seeking parents, these guides meet the specific needs of each and every family member.

Ulysses Press books are available at bookstores everywhere. If any of the following titles are unavailable at your local bookstore, ask the bookseller to order them.

You can also order books directly from Ulysses Press
P.O. Box 3440, Berkeley, CA 94703
800-377-2542 or 510-601-8301
fax: 510-601-8307
www.ulyssespress.com
e-mail: ulysses@ulyssespress.com

HIDDEN GUIDEBOOKS

____ Hidden Arizona, $16.95
____ Hidden Bahamas, $14.95
____ Hidden Baja, $14.95
____ Hidden Belize, $15.95
____ Hidden Big Island of Hawaii, $13.95
____ Hidden Boston & Cape Cod, $14.95
____ Hidden British Columbia, $18.95
____ Hidden Cancún & the Yucatán, $16.95
____ Hidden Carolinas, $17.95
____ Hidden Coast of California, $18.95
____ Hidden Colorado, $15.95
____ Hidden Disneyland, $13.95
____ Hidden Florida, $18.95
____ Hidden Florida Keys & Everglades,
      $13.95
____ Hidden Georgia, $16.95
____ Hidden Guatemala, $16.95
____ Hidden Hawaii, $18.95
____ Hidden Idaho, $14.95
____ Hidden Kauai, $13.95

____ Hidden Los Angeles, $14.95
____ Hidden Maui, $13.95
____ Hidden Montana, $15.95
____ Hidden New England, $18.95
____ Hidden New Mexico, $15.95
____ Hidden Oahu, $13.95
____ Hidden Oregon, $15.95
____ Hidden Pacific Northwest, $18.95
____ Hidden Salt Lake City, $14.95
____ Hidden San Francisco & Northern
      California, $18.95
____ Hidden Seattle, $13.95
____ Hidden Southern California, $18.95
____ Hidden Southwest, $19.95
____ Hidden Tahiti, $17.95
____ Hidden Tennessee, $16.95
____ Hidden Utah, $16.95
____ Hidden Walt Disney World, $13.95
____ Hidden Washington, $15.95
____ Hidden Wine Country, $13.95
____ Hidden Wyoming, $15.95

THE NEW KEY GUIDEBOOKS

____ The New Key to Costa Rica, $18.95

____ The New Key to Ecuador and the
      Galápagos, $17.95

PARADISE FAMILY GUIDES

____ Paradise Family Guides: Kaua'i, $16.95
____ Paradise Family Guides: Maui, $16.95

____ Paradise Family Guides: Big Island of
      Hawai'i, $16.95

Mark the book(s) you're ordering and enter the total cost here ⇨ [_____]

California residents add 8.25% sales tax here ⇨ [_____]

Shipping, check box for your preferred method and enter cost here ⇨ [_____]

❑ BOOK RATE   FREE! FREE! FREE!

❑ PRIORITY MAIL/UPS GROUND   cost of postage

❑ UPS OVERNIGHT OR 2-DAY AIR   cost of postage   [_____]

Billing, enter total amount due here and check method of payment ⇨ [_____]

❑ CHECK   ❑ MONEY ORDER

❑ VISA/MASTERCARD _____EXP. DATE_____

NAME _____PHONE_____

ADDRESS _____

CITY_____ STATE _____ ZIP_____

MONEY-BACK GUARANTEE ON DIRECT ORDERS PLACED THROUGH ULYSSES PRESS.

ABOUT THE AUTHORS

ELLEN CLARK is an award-winning writer and photographer who specializes in travel. Her articles and photographs have appeared in numerous publications, including *The Los Angeles Times* and *Outside* magazine, and she is a contributor to *Best Places Southern California*. A second generation Southern Californian, she was born in Pasadena and has spent the last 35 years in Los Angeles, which she loves for its infinite variety and free-thinking attitude.

RAY RIEGERT is the author of nine travel books, including *Hidden Southern California* and *Hidden San Francisco & Northern California*. His most popular work, *Hidden Hawaii*, won the coveted Lowell Thomas Travel Journalism Award for Best Guidebook as well as a similar award from the Hawaii Visitors Bureau. In addition to his role as publisher of Ulysses Press, he has written for the *Chicago Tribune*, *San Francisco Chronicle* and *Travel & Leisure*. A member of the Society of American Travel Writers, he lives in the San Francisco Bay area with his wife, co-publisher Leslie Henriques, and their son Keith and daughter Alice.